The Public Metropolis

The Public

Canadian Scholars' Press Inc.
Toronto CSPI

FRANCES FRISKEN

Metropolis

*The Political Dynamics
of Urban Expansion in the
Toronto Region, 1924–2003*

The Public Metropolis:
The Political Dynamics of Urban Expansion in the Toronto Region, 1924–2003
Frances Frisken

First published in 2007 by
Canadian Scholars' Press Inc.
180 Bloor Street West, Suite 801
Toronto, Ontario M5S 2V6

www.cspi.org

The research, writing, and publication of this book has been
supported by the Neptis Foundation: www.neptis.org

Every reasonable effort has been made to identify copyright holders. CSPI would be pleased to
have any errors or omissions brought to its attention.

Canadian Scholars' Press Inc. gratefully acknowledges financial support for our publish-
ing activities from the Government of Canada through the Book Publishing Industry
Development Program (BPIDP) and the Government of Ontario through the Ontario Book
Publishing Tax Credit Program.

Library and Archives Canada Cataloguing in Publication

Frisken, Frances
    The public metropolis : the political dynamics of urban expansion in the Toronto region,
1924-2003 / Frances Frisken.

Includes bibliographical references and index.
ISBN 978-1-55130-330-7

    1. Metropolitan government—Ontario—Toronto—History.   2. Cities and towns—
Growth—Government policy—Ontario—History.   3. Regional planning—Ontario—
Toronto Region—History.   4. Urbanization—Ontario—Toronto Region—History.
5. Toronto (Ont.)—Politics and government—20th century.   6. Urban policy—Ontario—
History.   I. Title.

JS1789.25.F75 2007   320.8'509713541   C2007-905451-X

Cover design, interior design and layout: Zack Taylor, mail@zacktaylor.com

07 08 09 10 11   5 4 3 2 1

Printed and bound in Canada by Marquis Book Printing Inc.

Canadä

Contents

List of Figures

List of Tables

Foreword

Toronto has a well-deserved reputation for innovation in urban governance and policy. Frances Frisken understands the reasons for this reputation and she understands why in recent years it has been under considerable threat. In this important and accessible book, she shares her vast knowledge of urban governance in Toronto, not just with fellow specialists, but with anyone who has an interest in how governments at all levels shape the quality of urban life.

The great strength of Frisken's work is that she knows the full context of events she is studying. Not one to be caught up in the latest academic or political fad, she describes events as she sees them, knowing that jargon and rhetoric often obscure more than enlighten. Instead of an elaborate theoretical framework, Frisken wants her readers to know how governance in Toronto has been influenced by what has been happening elsewhere in North America and internationally. She is particularly concerned that we also understand the full historical context that continues to influence even the most recent headlines about shaping urban growth and enhancing the capacity of municipalities to ameliorate urban problems. She has seen such headlines before.

Some of the ground that Frisken covers here has been covered earlier by other scholars, the creation of the Municipality of Metropolitan Toronto being one such example. But she always provides a fresh perspective, usually on the basis of documentation or interview material not readily available elsewhere. Her account of the decision by the provincial government of Ontario in 1996 to amalgamate the municipalities in Metro Toronto is especially insightful.

But Frisken also goes where very few Canadian urban scholars have gone before. She knows what has happened in the regions beyond Metro and is able to incorporate such knowledge into the careful account she presents of a growing metropolis whose developers are constantly pushing urban areas into the surrounding rural hinterland. She also knows about the kinds of services the new inhabitants of such areas receive—or do not receive—from their suburban municipalities, especially if they are new immigrants or if they require social housing. Perhaps her most significant contribution is the analysis of the politics of Toronto's schools, a subject that has been woefully understudied by all of us involved in trying to understand the role of government in Canadian cities.

This book will naturally appeal to Torontonians and students of Toronto. All the familiar characters make their appearances: Fred Gardiner, Carl Goldenberg, John Robarts, Darcy McKeough, Bill Davis, David Crombie, John Sewell, Anne Golden, Hazel McCallion, Mike Harris, and Al Leach, to name a few. Frisken obviously believes that individuals matter in politics. Their actions might be influenced by broad social and economic forces, but they are not predetermined. Individuals in high positions in government have the freedom to make real choices, and the choices they make affect the quality of our everyday life. Readers should not expect to find hitherto unrevealed details about the decisions of Toronto notables, but they will learn how these disparate individuals and their careers have connected with each other in shaping the city that Torontonians know today.

But the issues Frisken addresses in their Toronto context merit study by all scholars of North American cities. As Frisken herself has argued in other publications, Toronto has been a North American pioneer with respect to metropolitan governmental institutions, the connection between public transit and land-use planning, and in the distribution of social housing across a wide swath of differing urban residential environments. Many North American urban scholars know about these original accomplishments but, apart from Frisken's own earlier writings, they have only limited resources for knowing about more recent, and often less happy, developments. This book eliminates their excuses for not knowing about the full complexity of later developments.

One of the book's particularly important features is that it treats all levels of government—especially the government of Ontario—as part of a network of public institutions that are collectively crucial to the well-being of the entire city-region. Frisken is concerned about what is good for Toronto and its residents, not just what is good for its municipal governments. Rather than take it on faith that local governments always serve city interests better than the federal or provincial governments do, she explains why a system of collaborative multilevel governance might be what Toronto really needs if it is to regain its reputation for urban innovation and success.

This book has been a long time in the making because Frances Frisken is a demanding scholar who will not take shortcuts. During her long and active career in the Urban Studies Programme at York University there were always many distractions, not the least of which was the active mentoring of her best students, with several of whom she co-published important articles and studies. But we are fortunate indeed that she has persevered to finish the manuscript about which she has been thinking for so long.

Some of her references to newspaper articles go back to about the time when Frances and I first met, about 30 years ago. My suspicion is that these clippings—like many of mine—had been waiting in a dusty file for decades precisely so that they could be resurrected as part of an argument about how these past events help us to understand what is happening today. This argument is the great strength of Frances Frisken's fine book.

Andrew Sancton, December 2005

On the Study of
Regional Governance

In 1971 I returned to Canada after seven years in the United States, five of which I had spent as a post-graduate student at Case Western Reserve University in Cleveland, Ohio. My newly minted academic credentials rested in part on a detailed study of a fractious regional organization—the Northeast Ohio Areawide Coordinating Agency (NOACA)—created to produce a plan for the Cleveland city-region (a geographical abstraction known at the time as a metropolitan area), and to use that plan as a basis for reviewing and coordinating local government applications for federal government grants. NOACA was responsible for seven counties, the largest of which, Cuyahoga, included the City of Cleveland and 56 other municipalities.

My study of NOACA grew out of a personal interest in a county government plan to build a limited access, multi-lane highway through parkland and residential neighbourhoods not far from my home, and the intense local opposition that this plan aroused. The political battle ended early in 1970, when Ohio's Governor Rhodes promised that he would not approve any freeway location against the wishes of affected communities. I had a strong sense of déjà vu, therefore, when I learned on arriving in Toronto one year later that Ontario Premier William Davis had just withdrawn provincial government support for the last phase of a multi-lane, limited access highway (the Spadina Expressway), designed to slice through middle-class suburban and city neighbourhoods and a ravine park on its way to downtown Toronto. Like Governor Rhodes, Davis had responded to a well-organized, intensely fought campaign mounted by local residents and the local politicians and planners who supported them. Both the similarities in these two events and the differences between the settings in which they occurred was the impetus for much of the research that is summarized in this volume.

At the time I began this study, I was impressed by what I saw as significant differences between the city-region I had recently joined and the one I had left behind. Most obvious was the thriving state of the City of Toronto. To someone who had been exposed both at first hand and in the literature to the severe problems of U.S. cities, Toronto seemed little short of miraculous. Its downtown office and commercial sectors were thriving—in fact, the city would soon witness the opening of the massive Eaton Centre, a five-storey indoor shopping mall covering nearly half a city block of prime real estate in the downtown core.[1] Inner-city neighbourhoods were not only valued and well tended but several were being substantially upgraded. Streets anywhere in the city seemed safe. For all these reasons and more, James Lemon would later characterize Toronto in the 1970s as "the alternative future" that urban reformers in the United States could only dream of.[2]

On the basis of what I already knew about metropolitan problems and politics in the United States, I quickly concluded that Toronto was different from Cleveland because Toronto had a metropolitan government whereas Cleveland did not. In fact, an attempt to give the Cleveland area such a government in 1959 had failed to win support in a county-wide referendum. Since that time the City of Cleveland, like many other U.S. cities, had experienced a serious race riot and an accelerated decline in its population, which dropped from 915,000 to 751,000 between 1950 and 1970, with most of the loss occurring between 1960 and 1970.[3] Whether the City of Cleveland would ever again play a significant role in the life of its region or the economy of its nation was still in doubt at the end of the 20th century.

Because Cleveland's experience was similar to that of many other U.S. cities, my initial explanation for Toronto's vitality concurred with the opinion of American writers who had pointed to Metropolitan Toronto's federated system of local government as the way to a better urban future.[4] As I soon discovered, however, political activists in Toronto who fought urban freeways and inner-city redevelopment sometimes viewed Metro as a contributor to core city problems rather than as a way to resolve them.[5] Moreover, it was already clear that the Metro government no longer had either the jurisdictional scope or the necessary powers to oversee the physical and social development of a city-region that was spreading well beyond its boundaries. The provincial government had taken over those responsibilities.

---

1. The first time I walked into the Eaton Centre in downtown Toronto I was struck by its similarities to the Cleveland Arcade, a five-storey office and commercial complex built in downtown Cleveland during the City Beautiful period of the late 1800s. Although the Eaton Centre was much larger than the Arcade, both structures were modelled on the Galleria Vittorio Emmanuele II in Milan, Italy. The Arcade still displayed signs of its architectural elegance in the 1960s, but it was a fading beauty, with many of its offices and stores unoccupied and neglected. It has since been bought by the Hyatt Corporation, which converted its top three floors into a hotel. (Online at: www.clevelandskyscrapers.com/clevelandarcade.html.)

2. Lemon 1996, 242.

3. It would go on dropping. By 2000, Cleveland's population of 478,400 was just over half the size it had been in 1950.

4. Committee for Economic Development, Research and Policy Committee 1970, 41.

5. See for example, Michael Goldrick, "The anatomy of urban reform in Toronto," *City Magazine*, 3 (May–June 1978), 29–38.

In short, I began this study by asking a relatively straightforward question: How had metropolitan government helped to make the Toronto area, and particularly its urban core, different from the sprawling metropolitan areas and their declining central cities that were preoccupying students of metropolitan and city governance in the United States? No sooner had I begun to look at Metropolitan Toronto and its history more closely, however, than I was asking a different question: To what extent did the activities and interactions of different units and levels of government account for the differences that I observed between Toronto and Cleveland? And how significant were those differences? Were they just different and superficial glosses on a common reality, or did they signify more substantial differences in the way city-region issues were perceived and addressed in the United States and Canada?

Having posed my research question in this way, I quickly realized that the study of city-region governance is neither a simple nor a straightforward undertaking. City-regions are societies in miniature, where challenges to government effectiveness and social coherence can take intense and concentrated forms. At various times, therefore, my interest in city-region governance led me to examine and write about the evolution and administration of public transportation both in Metropolitan Toronto and in the much larger Greater Toronto Area (the name applied to this city-region from the 1980s onward), local government finance, land-use planning (both local and regional), local economic development, provincial–local and provincial–federal relations, government-assisted housing, the role of values in shaping U.S. and Canadian public policies, and, most recently, local government responses to immigrant settlement. This study draws on much of that work, some of which I have referred to in the text and included in the list of references.

To make this book as useful as possible to a general readership, I have not included a detailed discussion of the theories advanced or conclusions reached by the large number of writers who have analyzed city-region politics and governance and their effects on regional character. Nonetheless, theoretical ideas and empirical findings were important influences on the way I conducted my research and organized my results. In fact, the study occurred during a time of keen academic and professional interest in the way metropolitan areas or city-regions were governed, so there was no shortage of material on which to draw. The challenge was to select from this material those insights and ideas that best helped me to decide what to study and how to study it, and then to interpret the information I had assembled. The following summary of my intellectual odyssey is meant only to provide an overview of the way my thinking evolved.[6] It certainly does not do justice to the rich lode of ideas and arguments that the study of regional governance has produced.

My early inclination to attribute differences between Toronto and Cleveland to differences in the way their metropolitan areas were governed was consistent with the "structural-functional" assumptions underlying most efforts to restructure governmental systems in city regions. Broadly speaking, these assumptions link the types of policies emerging from any governmental system to the characteristics of the decision-making institutions (provincial/ state or national legislatures, city or regional councils, leadership structures, public bureaucracies, political parties); the way those institutions are chosen or sustained (including the way elections are organized and leaders chosen, voting patterns, hiring and appointment procedures); the powers assigned to or exercised by government institutions; and the way government institutions use their powers. Looked at from this perspective, a city-region without a city-regional government is a structural aberration both because it lacks unified direction and because its many and disconnected political units fail to give its residents a democratic say in regional management.

By the time I began my study, however, the institutional perspective on metropolitan governance had already been undermined in the United States by the pronounced tendency of local electorates to vote down proposals for any change in the way their regions were governed. Whatever structural reformers might say, a majority of those who cared enough to vote on their proposals did not agree that the creation of a regional government was the best way to protect their democratic rights. They were more interested in asserting or protecting the identity of their own communities within the larger urban complex, and with maintaining the autonomy of their local governments in the face of outside threats. In a majority of U.S. states, in fact, state governments had already responded to local protectionism by passing "home rule" laws or constitutional amendments that included legal protections of local boundaries and local powers. In these circumstances, the best hope for achieving some kind of agreement on matters of region-wide importance seemed to lie in persuading local officials to join councils of government of the type I studied in the Cleveland area, and then to work out approaches to regional problems that all could agree on.

---

6. It is impossible to credit all the works that influenced my thinking. In addition to those cited in the chapters that follow, the following also come to mind: Adams, Lewis and McCroskey 1974 [1929], Chapter 6; Danielson and Doig 1982; Dupré 1972; Greer 1962; Gulick 1962; Gurr and King 1987; Jones 1942; Kantor 1995; Long 1958, 1962, 1972; Sharpe 1995, pp. 11–31; Studenski 1930; Teaford 1979; Williams, Herman, Liebman and Dye 1965; and Wood, 1959 and 1964 [1961].

While U.S. governments and public administrators promoted inter-local co-operation as the best or most feasible way to address metropolitan problems, urban political scientists and political economists were trying to explain the persistence of metropolitan political fragmentation. Some writers focused on the intergovernmental nature of metropolitan politics and governance; that is, on the way different governments in metropolitan areas interacted with each other as they tried to protect or promote the interests of their communities within the larger urban complex. Others tried to identify the types of professional and political interests in both cities and suburbs that either supported or opposed local government restructuring, and to find reasons for the positions they took. Still others studied the characteristics of suburbia and the political attitudes and preferences of suburban residents. These latter works not only confirmed what referenda had already shown—that most metropolitan area residents tended to favour the status quo over alternative modes of metropolitan area governance—but also identified a variety of reasons for their doing so.[7] Among those reasons were a fear of higher taxes; an attachment to an idealized version of the small-town, agrarian lifestyle that they hoped to achieve in the suburbs; a desire to distance themselves from the growing African-American populations of the inner cities, or a less specific desire to escape the social problems they associated with population change in city neighbourhoods.

The most influential but also the most controversial challenge to proponents of regional government came from a group of "public choice" political economists, who not only explained but also defended political fragmentation as the best guarantor of both local government efficiency and local democracy.[8] It was their contention that metropolitan areas containing a large number of local governments allowed individuals, households, and businesses to shop around for the location that provided the combination of local services and local taxes that best suited their preferences. As a result, local taxpayers paid only for the services they wanted, thus helping to keep down the costs of services. Moreover, such areas offered a larger variety of locations in which people could choose to live and do business, as well as a larger variety of public services, than did a more centralized system. They also allowed residents or firms that did not like the tax and service mix in one community to "vote with their feet" by moving to a community that offered a mix that was more to their liking.

Critics were quick to point out that the system favoured by public choice writers was not an effective way to provide seamless services to a large urban

---

7. See for example Hawley and Zimmer 1970.
8. For a detailed summary of this school of thought, see Keating 1995.

settlement segmented by many municipal boundaries. They also challenged the implicit assumption that people in city-regions were equally free both to choose and to change their place of residence, when in fact income and racial differences meant that some people were much freer to move around than others. These and other criticisms have been part of a debate, discussed more fully in Chapter 1, that has continued to this day. It is part of a larger debate about the appropriate role for government in market economies dominated by private investors; that is, about whether and how governments should intervene in the lives of individuals and communities to counter market outcomes that are inconsistent with other social objectives. In the city-region context, the outcomes that most concerned U.S. critics of "public choice" ideas were large disparities in the wealth of different metropolitan area communities, in the services they were able to offer, and in the well-being of their residents.

At the time I first came across them, however, public choice and other social choice theories of city-region development and politics seemed to work better as explanations or justifications for metropolitan political fragmentation in the United States than as aids to understanding what had happened and was still happening in the Toronto region. For one thing, many such works implied that central city decline was an inevitable and irreversible consequence of suburbanization. As long as choices were available, they suggested, urban residents would gravitate to suburbs that taxed them only for those services that they expected to use, or that allowed them to live in non-threatening environments among socially compatible neighbours. As this happened, the neighbourhoods they left behind would be taken over by the urban poor and become increasingly obsolete and run down. Yet the City if Toronto in the 1970s, while surrounded by fast-growing suburbs, was not a city in decline. In fact the regeneration of some of its oldest neighbourhoods had begun to force lower income tenants out of the core and into more peripheral districts.

Explanations of suburbanization in the United States were also inconsistent with the 1966 findings of a study conducted by Toronto sociologist S.D. Clark, who concluded that people in the Toronto area had gone to the suburbs primarily to find "a house they could afford. All other considerations seemed to be secondary."[9] Only after they were settled in their new homes did these residents become aware that local services were minimal, and complain about not having access to services they had used in the city. They also began to make distinctions between life in the suburbs and life in the city, sometimes but not always casting the city in an unfavourable light. At least in the Toronto region, in other words, a stated preference for a suburban lifestyle was an outcome and not a cause of locational choice.

---

9. Clark 1966, 47–81.

American writers of that time also attached much more importance to the federal government's role in metropolitan area governance than did those who wrote about urban and metropolitan affairs in Canada. In doing so, they not only recognized the U.S. government's growing involvement in urban affairs, but also implicitly relegated state governments to a minor, almost insignificant role in the governance of cities and city-regions, even though state governments were legally responsible for the way cities and other local subdivisions were governed. In Canada, on the other hand, provincial governments not only jealously guarded their constitutional responsibility for municipal institutions but several of them had exercised it only recently by making large changes in their systems of local government.[10]

Differences between state and provincial governments became much less pronounced, however, when I began to look at the historical record. What emerged was that the American political system had not always opted for municipal fragmentation over unification as the best way to deal with metropolitan area growth and expansion. (I discuss these findings more fully in Chapter 1.) At some point in the development of most city-regions, however, state governments had not only ceased to restructure their governmental systems but had also made it difficult for locally based restructuring efforts to succeed. By doing so, the states lost importance in the eyes of urban analysts, especially those who considered metropolitan area problems and the way they were dealt with as fundamental to an understanding of the characteristics and the fate of urban America. Even Daniel Elazar, a writer who continued to emphasize the importance of state governments in local affairs, warned in 1966 that "whatever their successes in the past—the future role of the states will be determined by their ability to come to grips with those [metropolitan] problems."[11] State governments did not regain prominence in U.S. urban policy-making, however, until after the federal government began to reduce its support for and direct involvement in urban programs in the late 1970s. By that time state governments could do little more than implement spending cuts made necessary by reductions in federal funding.

Taken together, contemporary and historical studies of city-region politics and governance in the United States raised the possibility that differences between the Toronto region and its U.S. counterparts might simply mean that suburban development in the Toronto region had lagged behind suburban development in the U.S., and so had government attempts to deal with it. This possibility became more plausible after a comprehensive review of Metropolitan Toronto's government concluded in 1977 with recommendations

---

10. Tindal 1977.
11. Elazar 1966, 199–200.

that, had they been adopted, would have made local government systems in the two countries more alike.[12] The Ontario government did not act on those recommendations, however, but neither did it show any interest in extending Metropolitan Toronto's boundaries or subjecting the region to management by a higher authority, either its own or that of a new regional government.

Ontario's limited responses to regional growth issues in the 1970s (see Chapter 4) raised further questions about how to relate a study of Toronto region governance to the U.S. experience. Why was the Ontario government unwilling to make even small changes to a system of regional governance that it had modified extensively in the 1950s and again in the 1960s? One answer was that the region had simply become larger, and so had the number of municipal governments. Political opposition to change, therefore, was likely to be stronger and more politically costly for the province.

A different answer was implicit in a growing body of works by political economists who drew their inspiration from the writings of Karl Marx. In general, these works depicted local governments as components of an extensive state apparatus made up of different levels and branches of government, all of which worked in different ways to serve and preserve a capitalist economy. For a time such works implied that the only reason to study different forms of metropolitan area governance was to show how each of them served the interests of those who presided over capitalist modes of production.[13] The results of this type of analysis could sometimes be confusing. For example, according to Ann Markusen, metropolitan political fragmentation in the United States, and the laws and policies that supported or encouraged it, contributed to the accumulation of private wealth by enabling industry, commerce, and affluent homeowners to escape the high policing and social service costs of the central city.[14] For Canadian writer Michael Goldrick, on the other hand, the creation of Metropolitan Toronto in 1953 was a way to raise the "enormous sums of money" needed to support the massive urban growth generated by industrial expansion in both the city of Toronto and its suburbs.[15]

It was possible to reconcile these contradictory viewpoints by noting that Markusen was writing about regions where central cities were declining, suburban development was well advanced, and suburban governments were able to fund many of their own services (either by themselves or with financial

---

12. I examined this possibility in "Stages in Metropolitan Reform: from Community of Interest to Communities on their Own," in Peter Homenuck and Harvey K. Newman, eds., *Selected Papers from the 1979 Annual Meeting of the Council of University Institutes for Urban Affairs* (Atlanta: The College of Urban Life, 1979), 209–240.

13. For a summary see Pickvance 1995.

14. Markusen 1978.

15. See for example Goldrick, "The Anatomy of Urban Reform," op. cit., 31.

help from state and federal governments); Goldrick was writing about a much younger metropolitan area where the central city was still financially strong, industrial and residential expansion were occurring faster than suburban governments could keep up with, and there was little help available from senior governments. It was harder, however, to explain why campaigns for regional government with strong backing from downtown business interests almost invariably failed, even in regions (like Toronto) where those interests were playing a dominant role in the regional economy.

Marxian ideas were important for strengthening historical and comparative perspectives in the study of urban and city-region governance and for highlighting the importance of economic trends and pressures to public policy-making. Nonetheless, urban policy analysts soon rejected the idea that governments in democratic societies were merely the servants of dominant economic interests. Economic interests, they conceded, were likely to be important to policy-makers both because jobs and the income they generated helped to ensure social stability and because a strong economy yielded the tax revenues that governments required in order to do what economic interests and voters asked of them. Voter demands could be many and various, however, and policies that won or kept voter support were not always the policies that were best for business. Moreover, those who controlled governments and staffed government agencies had interests of their own, including an interest in protecting their authority from outside threats and an interest in securing their jobs and gaining status. Consequently, government decisions affecting city-region governance (including decisions to change local institutions or create new ones) were elements of a process in which different levels and units of government tried to achieve a balance between three types of objective: doing what was necessary to strengthen the regional economy, maintaining electoral support, and protecting government prerogatives. The task of understanding decisions affecting city-region governance, therefore, meant considering both the economic circumstances in which city-regions found themselves at different stages of their development and the political calculations that entered into the decisions that governments made.

What these ideas implied, and what I adopted, was a multi-dimensional approach to Toronto region government. It conforms most closely to "regulation theory," which argues the need to examine and explain "the connections and interrelations between social, political, economic and cultural change."[16] Such an approach not only rests on the idea that "economic change depends upon, and is partly the product of, changes in politics, culture and social life," but also assumes that changes in political institutions are likely to be responses

---

16. Painter 1995.

to changes in economic and social circumstances. With these ideas in mind, I broke the study period into five stages, each of them characterized by distinctive economic, political, and social pressures on governments and each giving rise to a different set of government responses to regional issues.

It became increasingly clear as the study progressed that governance in the Toronto city-region, at least from an institutional standpoint, was heading in a similar direction to that taken by U.S. city-regions at various times in the past (Chapter 1). Nonetheless, it was still possible that similarities between the physical development and governance characteristics of the Toronto region and U.S. city-regions hid more fundamental and lasting differences in the way growth problems had been and were still being addressed. There were two possible reasons why such differences might exist. One was that observable differences between Toronto and U.S. city-regions attested to fundamental differences between the political cultures or political values of the two countries.[17] Another was that differences in political institutions simply made it easier for central governments in Canada to override narrowly based local preferences in order to enlist cities or city-regions in the pursuit of economic and social objectives.

The cultural explanation was an attractive possibility, for it implied that Toronto region governance had diverged from regional governance in the United States in ways that were likely to persist. It was a slippery and unreliable concept on which to base a case study of a single region, however. For every writer who related differences in the character of U.S. and Canadian urbanism to differences in national values, there was another who argued that such differences could just as easily be explained by differences in the circumstances with which governments had to deal.[18] Moreover, explanations that linked the political behaviour of U.S. urban residents to fundamental national values (such as individualism, anti-urban sentiments, or an idealization of small communities) had to be weighed against explanations that emphasized the influence of racial attitudes and racial tensions on American city life and urban politics.

Differences in political institutions seemed to be a more promising basis for policy differences. As already mentioned, the prominence of the Ontario government in Toronto region governance, as well as that government's unfettered ability to adapt local boundaries and local institutions to regional growth and change, set it apart from most of the state governments responsible for large U.S. cities. At the very least, it meant that the Ontario government

---

17. For an early version of this argument, see Clark 1962. Goldberg and Mercer (1986) have made it more recently.

18. See, for example, Ewing 1992.

could take steps to counteract some of the negative consequences of local politics and policies for the distribution of wealth and poverty among a region's municipalities and their residents. This potential was important because, as I discuss in Chapter 1, there was a growing body of research linking growing inequalities in U.S. city-regions to the ways in which municipal governments used powers ceded to them by state governments. Moreover, the Toronto region's long history of experimentation with ways to deal with regional problems made it a particularly interesting case study of the many ways in which regional issues might be addressed.

But how to determine if this experimentation had made any difference? Although this would seem to be the most important question for any work of this type, it had not received as much attention in city-region analysis as had efforts to make a case for institutional change or efforts to explain why changes did not occur. Yet arguments for reform variously imply that a change in regional governance may have at least five consequences: a stronger regional economy, lower servicing costs, less urban sprawl and environmental degradation, more social equity, and enhanced local democracy. (These objectives are discussed in more detail in Chapter 1.) Because each of these objectives is likely to be important to sizable sectors of the urban community, any attempt to achieve a balanced assessment of the consequences of city-region governance needs to take all of them into account.

The analytical framework I finally adopted, therefore, focused more on results than on process, while still highlighting the economic, political, and social factors that had been most important in shaping regional governance as the Toronto region evolved. My findings, which are summarized in Chapter 7, did suggest that there were still important differences at the end of the study period between the characteristics of the Toronto region and the characteristics of the U.S. city-regions with which it is often compared. Most of those differences could be traced to the way government policies, particularly Ontario government policies, had addressed disparities in both the ability and the willingness of the region's local governments to deal with problems associated with demographic change and suburban expansion. It was for this reason that I decided to name this book *The Public Metropolis*, as a way of distinguishing the Toronto experience from that described by Sam Bass Warner in *The Private City*, a work that emphasized the importance of the private sector in shaping the character of Philadelphia and, by implication, other U.S. cities.[19]

The Toronto story did not end with the end of this book, however. As Benjamin and Nathan observe in their recent study of the New York metropolitan region, "[r]egionalism is a process, not a result.... When it comes to

---

19. Warner 1968.

changes, one generation's answers can produce the next generation's problems."[20] As the 21st century began, those responsible for governance in the Toronto region were just beginning to face some of the more difficult challenges that had preoccupied U.S. analysts of city-region governance for more than 50 years. It appeared, therefore, that the real tests for governance in the Toronto region were still to come.

---

20. Benjamin and Nathan 2001, 267.

Acknowledgements

This work owes a great deal to the many organizations and individuals who supported and encouraged my research over the past 35 years. First, I thank Martha Shuttleworth and Tony Coombes of the Neptis Foundation for persuading me to compress my research findings into one volume, and for supporting the work financially. Particular thanks go to Richard White for patiently seeing this project through to completion, to Marcy Burchfield of Neptis and the staff of the University of Toronto Cartography Office for their excellent work on the maps and figures, to Philippa Campsie, who read the manuscript several times and made many well considered and always useful suggestions, to Zack Taylor, who arranged for the work's publication, and to Jack Wayne, Rebecca Conolly, Martha Keenan, and Kim Ukrainec of Canadian Scholars' Press for making the manuscript into a book. Thanks also to Andrew Sancton and Don Stevenson for perceptive and helpful comments on an earlier draught.

In addition to the Neptis Foundation, I thank several other organizations whose financial support for various projects helped me to accumulate knowledge of the Toronto region and its governance: the Canada Council; the Canada Mortgage and Housing Corporation; Citizenship and Immigration Canada; the City of York; the Metropolitan Toronto Planning Department; the Ontario Advisory Task Force on Housing Policy; the Ontario Ministry of Municipal Affairs; the Ontario Planning Act Review Committee; the Ontario Ministry of Transportation; the Social Sciences and Humanities Research Council; UMA Engineering; the University of Toronto–York University Joint Program in Transportation; and the York University Small Grants Program.

I have also benefited from the wisdom and encouragement of colleagues both inside and outside academic settings. Special thanks go to Larry Bourne, Nino Campitelli, Gunter Gad, Engin Isin, James Lemon, Wayne McEachern, Robert Murdie, Donald Norris, Mario Polèse, Donald Rothblatt, Ed Sajecki, Richard Stren, Timothy Thomas, Marie-Odile Trépanier, and Marcia Wallace. Our collaborations and conversations were not only enriching but also enjoyable.

I also thank former students who assisted with various stages of the research: Judith Bates, Beate Bowron, Joan Brown, Dale Hauser, Alison MacGregor, Marc McAree, Gwynneth McLachlan, Christina White, and Joanne Wolfson.

Thanks also to the many individuals in a large number of agencies who agreed to be interviewed for this study. Although there is not space here to name them all, I make special mention of Gardner Church, Eli Comay, Donald Stevenson, and Katharine Bladen, to whom I went back again and again with new questions, and to Anne Golden, John Matheson, Lynn Morrow, and Alan Tonks for their thoughtful discussions of events leading up to the amalgamation of Metropolitan Toronto and the dissolution of the Greater Toronto Services Board. The project owes a great deal to the generosity with which they gave their time and their insights. I take full responsibility for any errors in the way I have presented or interpreted the information they gave me.

I acknowledge a great personal debt to four former teachers—John Glasson, Eugene Uyeki, the late Benjamin Nelson, and the late Malcolm Ross—who not only showed me that a scholarly life was a rich and rewarding one, but who also helped me to achieve it.

I am also deeply grateful to my family—my husband, William, and my daughters, Barbara, Sarah, and Amanda—for their unfailing support, love, and friendship.

ONE
Introduction

This study covers the evolution of institutional and financial arrangements for providing selected local services in the Toronto city-region between 1924, the year that some form of metropolitan government was first contemplated, and 2003, when a change of government in Ontario brought an end to a tumultuous period of local government reorganization that had left many regional issues unresolved. It pays particular attention to arrangements for providing three types of services with considerable potential for shaping a city-region's physical and social character: (1) basic infrastructure to support population and economic growth, including water supply, sewage and waste disposal, and major transportation facilities; (2) strategies to plan or manage spatial organization and outward expansion; and (3) services that affect the ability of a city-region's less affluent residents to participate in economic and community life, such as social housing, public education, transit, social assistance, and community services.

In this study, the general term "governance" is used to encompass not only service-providing arrangements and the processes that brought them into being, but also the way those arrangements distributed services and service costs among different sectors of the region. Thus the study is about more than just "government," a term that usually refers to a set of institutions with a precise constitutional or legal definition (e.g., a national government) and what it is empowered to do. Governance in the Toronto region during the study period involved four levels of government, although the nature and importance of their involvement varied from one time to another. It was also influenced by groups and individuals who were not part of government in a formal sense, but who nonetheless affected the content of public policies and the ways in which they were delivered and distributed.

Although governance in the Toronto region was multi-layered, diffuse, and constantly changing, the government of the Province of Ontario was always pre-eminent in determining its form and content. Thus its role dominates the study. The emphasis on a central government's importance to city-region governance sets this study apart from most North American studies of its type, which have tended to treat changes in—or efforts to change—the way a city-region is governed as local political events in which other levels of government are only peripherally involved.[1] For reasons that will become increasingly apparent as the account unfolds, however, a focus on the local dimensions of city-region governance would not adequately explain the many changes that occurred in the governance of the Toronto region in the second half of the 20th century. Only a detailed look at the province's role in the region can do that.

The objectives of this work are threefold:

- to describe the different approaches taken to governing the Toronto region since 1945 and explain why they took the form they did;
- to assess how each of the different approaches worked in terms of achieving several objectives for regional governance reform;
- to provide a basis for assessing the political viability and likely effectiveness of options for addressing challenges facing the region at the beginning of the 21st century.

The historical narrative relates changes in Toronto-region governance not only to events and changes in Canadian society since the end of the Second World War, but also to past and recent trends in regional governance in the United States. A comparative focus is justified because Toronto, both as a city and as a region, was often compared to cities and city-regions south of the border. For most of the study period, such comparisons tended to cast Toronto in a favourable light, depicting it as a region that had managed to sustain rapid population growth and outward expansion while avoiding the physical and social decline that had become the defining characteristics of older U.S. cities during the second half of the 20th century.[2] At least some of the credit for Toronto's achievements went to its mode of governance, particularly the 1953 creation of the Municipality of Metropolitan Toronto, a federation of 13 municipalities (reduced to 6 in 1967) created by the Ontario government to harness the resources of the region to the tasks of providing new infrastructure and addressing some social needs.

Comparisons were becoming more equivocal, however, by the time the study period ended. Some writers argued that Canada's governments had fallen behind governments in the United States in their failure to renew public infrastructure fast enough to keep up with the region's growth, thereby endangering Toronto's ability to compete successfully with other city-regions

---

1. The focus has begun to change, however. Several recent writers have emphasized the importance of state governments to the governance of the U.S. city-regions they have studied (Benjamin and Nathan 2001; Gainsborough 2001(a); Orfield 1997, 104–155; Rusk 2003, 93–98).

2. See Lemon 1996, 241–294.

in a globalizing economy.[3] Others pointed to growing income disparities between the City of Toronto and its suburbs, together with increasing levels of individual and neighbourhood poverty in Toronto and a few nearby suburbs, as threats to the quality of life and financial stability of the region's urban core.[4] These critics implied that the Greater Toronto Area (GTA) was facing some of the same problems that had preoccupied U.S. writers on city-regional issues for several decades, and that its future depended on the way they were addressed.

The provincial government responded to these concerns in 1995 by creating a Greater Toronto Area Task Force to recommend changes in the region's mode of governance that would set "a new course for a new century."[5] The Greater Toronto Area that the task force looked at contained not only Metro Toronto but four other municipal federations, called regional municipalities, created between 1969 and 1974 (Durham, Halton, Peel, and York) (see Chapter 3). Thus the task force was just the latest in a series of attempts by the Government of Ontario to find ways to adapt governance in the Toronto region to the pressures of rapid population growth, outward expansion, and social change. To find out whether those attempts had helped the region to avoid problems associated with the development of U.S. city-regions, or whether in fact they were making those problems more likely, it was necessary to look for similarities and differences in the way regional governance had evolved in the two countries over an extended period of time.

The following section takes a brief look at the place occupied by Toronto in the annals of regional governance in North America. It is followed by a discussion of five sets of issues commonly identified with city-region growth and expansion, both in the United States and in Canada. Together, these issues constitute a regional agenda, all or parts of which can give rise to efforts to change the way a region is governed. This agenda provides a framework for assessing the nature and consequences of changes made to Toronto region governance during successive stages in the region's development—changes that involved virtually all of the institutional arrangements that can be brought to bear on city-region problems.

These institutional alternatives are the subject of the next-to-last section of this chapter, which leads into a brief discussion of the approaches most commonly used to finance regional services in North America and the way issues of finance enter into debates about institutional and policy alternatives.

---

3. Berridge Lewinberg Greenberg 1992; Berridge 1999; David Crombie, "Grow smart or grow worse," *Globe and Mail*, April 4, 2001.

4. Bourne 2003; United Way of Greater Toronto and Canadian Council on Social Development, 2004.

5. GTA Task Force 1996, 229.

The chapter ends with a brief overview of the way governance in North American city-regions has tended to evolve as such regions have increased in size and social complexity, noting broad similarities between the Toronto region's experience and the experience considered typical of U.S. city-regions, but also noting important differences. These are explored in more detail in the concluding chapter.

Toronto in the North American Context

Although few major changes were made to the governmental systems of large North American city-regions during the second half of the 20th century, such changes were more common in Canada than in the United States.[6] One explanation for this difference is the fact that provincial governments in Canada retained full authority under both the *British North America Act* (1867), and the Canadian Constitution that replaced it in 1982, to modify municipal institutions or create new ones without the consent of municipal governments or local voters.[7] Many American states, on the other hand, changed their laws or amended their constitutions to make it difficult or impossible for state governments to alter municipal boundaries or municipal institutions without the consent of municipal electorates.[8]

Among Canadian city-regions, the Toronto region stands out for the number and variety of changes made to its mode of governance. It is best known, however, for the 1953 creation of Metropolitan Toronto, the most sweeping change in city-region governance in North America since the New York State legislature consolidated 25 municipal units into (Greater) New York City in 1898. Of the two, New York's was the more radical form of local government restructuring, not only because it embraced a larger number of municipal units, but also because it resulted in a city of 3.4 million people (as compared to Metropolitan Toronto's initial population of 1.2 million), in which most local powers were vested in one city government, with relatively few assigned to the five borough councils. In Metropolitan Toronto, by contrast, local powers were divided more equally between new metropolitan and existing municipal units.

New York State's interest in city-region governance was short-lived. In 1924 it did what some other state governments had already done and others would do later: it passed a Home Rule Law that gave its cities powers and protections that prevented the state from making unilateral changes in the way

---

6. Sancton 2001.
7. Birkhead 1974, 6–7.
8. Grad 1970, 42–48.

municipal governments were organized. By that time, New York City, with its population of 5.6 million people, was being defined by the U.S. Census as the central city of a "metropolitan district" of 8.5. million people.[9]

By contrast, as this study documents, Ontario continued to alter arrangements for local governance in the Toronto region to deal with growth-related issues for half a century, though with varying degrees of commitment and enthusiasm. Meanwhile, Metropolitan Toronto's population doubled and the region's population increased to between 4.9 and 7.2 million people—its size depending on the boundaries used to define it (see Figure 7.1, Chapter 7, p. 295).

To provide a basis for explaining provincial interventions and the forms they took, the next section identifies the regional challenges that confront all governments with legal or constitutional responsibilities for municipal institutions, especially when city-regions are under stress.

The Agenda for Regional Governance Reform: Competing Objectives

From an institutional standpoint, the basic problem posed by the expansion of city-regions is local government fragmentation and complexity. In its simplest form, it is a problem of "too many governments" resulting from the internal division of the city-region into many political entities, even though the region may function "as one integrated social entity" within which people move freely for purposes of work, play, and social interaction.[10]

To say that a local government system is inadequate, however, is immediately to raise the question: Inadequate in what sense? Members of any urban community have different expectations about what their governments should do, both locally and regionally, depending on their own priorities and the role they want governments to play in their communities and their lives. These expectations translate into five recurring objectives for governance reform.[11]

    1. To increase the region's ability to provide the basic infrastructure (e.g., water supply, sewage and waste disposal, roads, highways and public transit, hospitals and schools) needed to support population and economic growth (an economic development objective). This objective has been assigned particular urgency by those recent writers who emphasize

---

9. U.S. Department of Commerce, Bureau of the Census 1948.

10. Bourne, Starkweather, and Basu 2000, 1.2, p. 3; Goodall 1968, 14–15.

11. Other objectives tend to be dictated by the circumstances of a particular time or place. For example, a central government may reorganize local governments in order to reduce or weaken the political importance of a city or regional government controlled by a different political party.

the critical role that city-regions play both in building and sustaining national economies and in helping nations to compete successfully on a global scale.[12]

2. To minimize or better control the costs of providing services to all or parts of a region (an efficiency or cost-effectiveness objective). City-regions may be important engines of economic growth, but they also make voracious claims on public resources. Thus they often challenge public policy-makers to look for ways to balance the need to spend public money on new or improved public services against the need (or voter pressure) to conserve public funds.

3. To control the pattern of regional growth and development in order to avoid or minimize the negative consequences of low-density urban sprawl (a regional planning or growth management objective). Rising public service costs, however, constitute only one negative consequence associated with sprawl. Also frequently cited are the loss of agricultural land, historical sites, and natural heritage to urban development; the damage to the environment associated with low-density, automobile-dependent forms of settlement; and (especially in the United States) a decline in the financial health and social well-being of the urban core as economic activities and middle-class homeowners shift to the outer parts of the region.

   The most commonly recommended device for combatting sprawl is comprehensive regional planning. Others include the strategic use of infrastructure to channel growth to some areas and discourage it in others; laws to protect some types of land from urban development; or policies to make inner-city areas or poor municipalities more attractive to business investors and middle-class residents.

4. To achieve a more equal distribution of the benefits and costs of urban growth among a region's municipalities (an equity or redistributive objective). Municipalities within a city-region differ, sometimes greatly, in population size and social characteristics; in the amount and type of economic activities they contain; in the age, quality, and value of their housing stock; in the size and strength of their tax base; and in the type and quality of public services they offer their residents. If nothing is done to reduce these differences, say their critics, the disparities tend to increase over time, making it steadily more difficult for a region's poorer

12. Barnes and Ledebur 1998; Voith 1992.

municipalities and those who live in them to contribute effectively to the regional economy or share in a region's achievements.[13]

Moreover, growing poverty in some parts of a region can have negative consequences that spill over into the rest of the region or even the entire society—such as increased rates of crime, communicable diseases, and dependency on social assistance; low productivity among persons educated in poorly funded schools; and accelerated urban sprawl driven by the outward movement of middle-class households in search of safe and congenial living environments well removed from blighted neighbourhoods.

Initially, these negative consequences were linked primarily to living conditions in the core cities of older U.S. city-regions. More recently, they have been associated with a growing number of older suburbs located just outside those cities, particularly suburbs built immediately after the Second World War and former industrial suburbs. Some argue, in fact, that the plight of declining suburbs can be worse than the plight of declining core cities because the former lack the variety of attractions and economic activities that still give core cities a unique role in their regions.

The first four objectives in the regional agenda rest on the assumption that all municipalities in a city-region stand to gain from its successes and suffer from its failures. The fifth objective addresses the political impediments to regional change.

5. To unite the region's local decision-makers in devising and administering policies and programs that will benefit the region as a whole, and perhaps give the region a stronger, more effective political voice in national and even international arenas (a political efficacy objective).

All five elements of the regional agenda may be present in any campaign to persuade governments of the need for changes in the way a region is governed. Different participants in such campaigns, however, are unlikely to support all of the objectives with equal fervour. In fact, debates about regional issues often highlight contradictions or incompatibilities among the objectives being sought.

---

13. This discussion about the nature of intermunicipal inequalities and ways to address them draws mainly on Dreier, Mollenkopf, and Swanstrom 2001, a work that summarizes a large amount of research on this topic.

For example, an emphasis on the need to invest in physical infrastructure to support development at the edge of a region may conflict with an emphasis on the need to manage or contain growth or on the need to spend public money on programs to improve impoverished districts or the lives of the urban poor. An emphasis on giving the entire region a strong voice in regional policy-making conflicts with the desire of local governments and local residents to give priority to the immediate needs of their own communities, and to control what happens there. Strong regions also threaten the authority of the national or sub-national governments that are legally responsible for municipal institutions and for the functions they assign to them.

Some observers insist that regional problems are not problems of governance, but problems of growth, and argue for government measures (such as ending immigration or withholding services from developing districts) that will slow growth down or stop it altogether. Among those who want to encourage growth, on the other hand, there are vastly different opinions about how much or what kinds of government intervention are needed to help a city-region realize its potential.

For example, defenders of the governmental status quo in U.S. city-regions insist that political fragmentation is not a barrier but an aid to a region's economic and social success. The existence of many municipalities in a city-region, they say, means that business investors will be better able to find locations that meet their requirements and people looking for a place to live can choose from a large number of communities offering the tax and service arrangements that best meet their preferences.

To succeed in this competitive environment, the argument goes on, municipal governments in a city-region have to make themselves as attractive as possible to potential investors and homeowners, and their efforts to do so can only benefit the region. Some even argue that old cities and suburbs that fall behind can be safely ignored because the types of activities in which they once specialized have simply relocated to newer activity centres ("edge cities") in the suburbs. Others acknowledge a need for government aid to poor individuals or families living in depressed communities, but insist that such help has to come from central governments with access to broadly based, progressive forms of taxation. If municipal governments try to alleviate local poverty using revenues from local taxes, they say, poor municipalities with high poverty rates will become even poorer, while rich municipalities will continue to thrive.

Critics find many flaws in such arguments. For one thing, they reject suggestions that distressed cities can safely be written off as unimportant to regional well-being, maintaining that what happens in any one part of a city-region has consequences (good or bad) for the economic and social well-being of all other parts. They also point out that municipal governments, for reasons beyond their control, are inherently unequal in their ability to change their economic and residential characteristics and circumstances. Geographical location and historical patterns of residential and employment location have been largely responsible for the financial and social characteristics of individual municipalities. Moreover, some municipalities are more fully developed than others, and the amount of land still available for development helps to determine what municipal governments can do to improve their situations. In addition, individuals are unequal in their ability to take advantage of what a city-region has to offer, not only because of differences in education, ability, and motivation, but also because of the way the economy distributes income and wealth. Two people who work equally hard at what they do can end up with very different amounts of money to spend on housing, transportation, and other requirements for a productive urban life.

Some of the sharpest criticisms, however, are directed at the claim that the physical and social characteristics of city-regions result solely from corporate and individual choices made in a politically neutral market for land and housing. Especially in the United States, such criticisms have linked the physical and social decline of the inner parts of city-regions to policies adopted by federal, state, and municipal governments. These policies, they charge, have had the cumulative effect of confining the poorest urban residents in a few municipalities with declining tax bases while giving financial and legal supports to low-density suburban development.[14] In particular, they point to federal and state government support for new home and highway construction; tax benefits to homeowners; and state- and court-sanctioned municipal land-use practices (zoning, building codes, and the like) that exclude lower priced housing from most suburban municipalities.

Disagreements about the role that governments should play or have played in structuring city-regions have been the subject of both political and academic debates for a long time, and all participants can muster evidence to support their points of view. It is unlikely, however, that weighing the evidence will resolve the issues, because different positions emerge out of different values about what constitutes a satisfactory or desirable urban environment. The question that is really at issue is: What kinds of cities and city regions do we want? And because cities are often the harbingers of social and cultural change, this question is part of a larger question: What kind of society do people want to live in? For some, socially segmented city-regions are the justifiable outcomes of the exercise of individual rights in a free society, and signify a healthy democracy. For others they violate the principle of equal

---

14. Dreier, Mollenkopf, and Swanstrom 2001. See also Danielson 1976.

opportunity and the rights of citizenship, and imply a weakening of social bonds.

The suggestion that values play an important role in shaping city-region governance links this study to broader questions about whether national differences in culture and political institutions have different consequences for urban development and urban life.[15] And in addressing such questions in a North American context, we cannot overlook the influence that has long been ascribed to racial factors—particularly the attitudes and behaviour of white Americans toward African-Americans—on urban development and urban policy-making in the United States.[16] That critical element of the American urban experience became increasingly relevant to this study as the Toronto region gained a growing number of immigrants classified by Statistics Canada as "visible minorities."[17] Also relevant is the fact that the urban development pattern associated with racial and income sorting in U.S. cities is not the only way of segregating the poor from the rest of society. In South America, sprawling slums have grown up at the very edge of large cities; in France, suburban public housing estates house large numbers of the urban poor, including many immigrants from North Africa.[18]

Value preferences, socio-cultural differences, and long-term goals are seldom addressed explicitly, however, in debates about regional governance issues. Instead those debates tend to focus on more pragmatic questions: What kinds of institutional arrangements and public policies are needed to alleviate the service deficiencies and social problems associated with city-region growth? And how should those arrangements be paid for? These questions may arise quite early in the outward development of any city-region and then recur from time to time during its history, challenging the government responsible for municipal institutions, together with those institutions themselves, to find new ways to improve basic services and address social needs.

Alternative Approaches to Governing City-regions: The North American Experience

There are several ways in which a central government can reorganize or support local governments in the interest of achieving regional objectives. This

---

15. Clark 1962; Goldberg and Mercer 1986.

16. Bollens and Schmandt 1982, 247–253; Harrigan 1985, 417–420.

17. The 1996 Census of Canada defined visible minorities as "persons, other than Aboriginal peoples, who are non-Caucasian in race, or non-white in colour." Using this definition, the Census placed the following groups in the visible minority category: Chinese, South Asians, Blacks, Arabs and West Asians, Filipinos, Southeast Asians, Latin Americans, Japanese, Koreans, and Pacific Islanders.

18. Dreir, Mollenkopf, and Swanstrom 2001, 53–54.

section reviews these alternatives, using both Canadian and U.S. examples, and notes some of the advantages and disadvantages of each one. It provides a basis both for categorizing the different modes of governance used in the Toronto region at different stages in its development and for trying to determine reasons for their adoption.

The main institutional alternatives are:

- allowing or compelling the core city to expand to take in territory where new growth is occurring;
- metropolitan or regional federation;
- delegation of one or a few functions to specialized agencies;
- reliance on the private sector to provide regional services;
- direct action by the central government responsible for municipal institutions or, in federal states, by both central governments (federal and state/provincial); and
- intergovernmental or government–community consultation.

Allowing or compelling the core city to expand

A city may decide (or a central government may force it) to *annex* outer districts, thereby moving its boundary further out. Alternatively, a central government may *consolidate* or *amalgamate* several local units (usually a core city and some or all of its suburbs) into a single city that takes in outer territory that is undergoing development. This approach gives a region a single government that can draw on a common tax base to provide services to all of an urbanizing territory while reducing service differences among its varied sectors.

Annexation and consolidation were the most common ways of dealing with growth in North America's older city-regions in the 19th and early 20th centuries, with the creation of Greater New York City being the most radical example.[19] Toronto was no exception: the city grew from 22.7 to 58.8 square kilometres between 1883 and 1921.[20] Amalgamation and annexation were still being used to integrate city-regions at the end of the 20th century, both in Canada and the United States.[21] Nonetheless this approach has become politi-

---

19. Jackson 1972.

20. Toronto City Council Minutes 1919, Appendix C, 191.

21. A recent Canadian example of the use of consolidation to provide a city-region with a single government was the 1994 creation of the Halifax Regional Municipality, which consolidated the former cities of Halifax and Dartmouth and a large expanse of suburban territory containing many small towns and villages. The Ontario government's consolidation of the regional municipalities of Hamilton-Wentworth, Ottawa, and Sudbury made all or most of these city-regions into single cities. The 1997 consolidation of Metropolitan Toronto into a new, greatly enlarged City of Toronto affected only the

cally more difficult to assert as city-regions expand to take in more territory and local jurisdictions.

Opposition may come either from the city or from the suburbs. City officials may resist taking on new districts because of the anticipated costs of expanding city services, as happened in Toronto after the First World War and again in the late 1920s (see Chapter 2).[22] Suburban officials and voters may object to the loss of local identity, to the disappearance of local political jobs and/or influence, or to the added costs that joining a large city implies, particularly if that city is beginning to experience financial or social decline. In fact, such opposition had become effective enough in the United States by the early 1900s to push advocates of local governance reform to look for less controversial alternatives. Most of these alternatives have also been tried in the Toronto region and many of them were still in use when this study ended.

Metropolitan or regional federation

Under a federated arrangement, local government in a city-region is divided into two tiers. The upper tier consists of one or more governmental units that provide selected services to the region as a whole; the lower tier consists of individual municipal governments that provide services within their own boundaries.

The principal advantage ascribed to metropolitan or regional federation is that it leaves existing municipal governments in place, though with fewer responsibilities. Thus it is less disruptive of the status quo, and therefore (at least in theory) less likely to meet with strong opposition from affected municipalities. It also preserves some of the political benefits associated with local democracy by retaining local governments that are more accessible to local residents.

Despite these perceived advantages, proposals to establish federated arrangements in U.S. city-regions were no more likely to win popular approval than were amalgamation or consolidation.[23] Consequently, the Ontario government's creation of the federated municipality of Metropolitan Toronto in 1953 was hailed as a significant event in the political development of city-regions in North America. Although a few state governments (notably Indiana, Michigan, and Oregon)[24] did establish second-tier metropolitan authorities in

---

core of the Toronto city-region, however (see Chapter 6). In the United States, cities in Texas retained the right to annex suburban territory, although political resistance seemed to be making annexations more difficult by the 1990s. Gainsborough 2001(a), 503.

22. Lemon 1985, 33–35.

23. Harrigan 1985, 332–338.

24. Indianapolis "Unigov," the Minneapolis–St. Paul Metropolitan Council, and the Portland Metro Council.

the years that followed, at the time of Metro's creation, most state governments were either ignoring city-region problems altogether or were addressing them in ways that entailed little or no interference with existing local governments. The most common approach was to delegate certain functions to one or several specialized agencies.

Delegation of selected functions to specialized agencies

Specialized agencies—which are variously known as special-purpose authorities, special districts, boards, commissions, or public corporations—may be authorized to deliver one or a few services to all or part of a city-region, or to an even larger territory. The functions typically assigned to such agencies are those considered necessary to support economic activity or protect elements of the environment, such as transportation, parks, airports, air quality, water and sewer systems, regional planning, and economic development. Members of the agencies are usually appointed, and may or may not hold elected office within the region.

Special-purpose agencies have been operating in the Toronto region since the early 20th century. Probably the best-known and one of the oldest is the Toronto Transit Commission, a successor to the Toronto Transportation Commission created by Toronto City Council in 1920 to operate the street railway system that the city had bought from a private company. Many others were added in the years that followed, with members appointed either by the province or by local governments, or sometimes by both. A few have also been created by the federal government.[25] Governments formed by all three of Ontario's political parties (Liberal, New Democratic, and Progressive Conservative) made increasing use of this means of providing services on a regional scale in the 1980s and 1990s (see Chapter 5).

The special-purpose authority tends to be favoured by those who want to ensure the "businesslike" operation of specific services (in other words, to make a service more financially independent of government, or to distance it from direct interference by elected politicians) while retaining some political control through the appointment and budget review processes. Because the authority's members are usually appointed rather than elected, however, this approach is often criticized as an undemocratic way of providing city and regional services.

If special-purpose authorities are able to finance their operations by selling services to consumers, they can reduce costs to local governments and

25. Canadian Urban Institute, *Inventory of Existing Governance Structures in the Greater Toronto Area*. A Report Prepared for the Greater Toronto Area Task Force, 1995.

their taxpayers. Another way to achieve the same advantage is to rely on or contract with the private sector to provide selected services.

Reliance on the private sector

Reliance on the private provision of municipal services (either by individual households or by private companies) was the preferred means of securing most city services before the expansion of city government activity in the 20th century. Like service provision by special-purpose authorities, service provision by private companies (either alone or in partnership with government agencies) implies a weakening of a government's ability to plan and coordinate public services in the interest of objectives that are not directly related to that service. It also reduces the ability of local residents to participate in or influence decisions of importance to the character of their communities and their own lives. Nonetheless, this approach is favoured by those who believe that the private sector can perform some tasks more cost-effectively than unionized public agencies or large public bureaucracies, and by governments that view it as a way to reduce their own costs.

Direct action by the central government responsible for municipal institutions

Rather than modifying local service-providing arrangements, the central government responsible for municipal institutions (the provincial government in Canada, the state government in the U.S.) may decide to deal with city-region problems on its own. It can take back responsibilities previously delegated to local governments, special-purpose agencies, or private suppliers, and assign them to its own departments. The Ontario government's 1997 takeover of responsibility for most aspects of public education was a dramatic example of this approach, although it was a step that several other provincial governments had already taken.[26] Alternatively, the central government can use laws, regulations, financial incentives, or financial penalties to compel or influence local governments to participate in or contribute to regional programs.

Central government intervention has the advantage of having regional issues addressed by a government with full constitutional or legal authority to act. From a local government standpoint, however, it diminishes local democracy either by taking important responsibilities away from elected local officials or by restricting the ability of local governments to set their own priorities. It also means that regional problems and ways of addressing them are likely to be defined or evaluated in terms of the demands and priorities of the

---

26. Woolstencroft 1990, 150–151.

central jurisdiction (province, state, or nation) and not necessarily in terms of what is best for the region.

From the perspective of the central government, becoming involved in providing local and regional services may embroil it in divisive local political issues, thereby antagonizing voters both inside and outside the region. This approach is also likely to raise expectations that the central government will pay a large share of the costs of the services for which it has assumed responsibility.

Some of these disadvantages dissuaded the Government of Ontario from intervening in Toronto region governance at various times after 1945. Nonetheless, direct provincial government involvement in regional service provision was as much a distinguishing feature of Toronto region governance during the study period as were the structural changes that the province made in local institutions. Direct intervention was particularly evident during the 1960s and early 1970s, after which it subsided but did not end (see Chapters 3 to 6).

A U.S. variation: Direct action by the federal government

Federal government policies can have important, if often unanticipated, consequences for the physical and social character of city-regions. For that reason alone, the role of the federal government has to be considered, even where it lacks responsibility for municipal affairs. In addition, a federal government may decide to intervene directly in city or regional affairs, as began to occur in the United States even before the Depression of the 1930s. Federal interventions (usually in the form of grants-in-aid for specific, local government functions) initially occurred in response to pleas for financial help coming from big-city mayors, pleas that state governments had begun to ignore because of a lack of money, or because they saw no political advantage in helping cities.[27]

Federal grants did not always ease big-city problems, however. In fact, some were later blamed for making those problems worse. Critics charged, for example, that federal government housing, highway, and taxation policies contributed to rapid suburbanization and urban sprawl, central city abandonment, and core city deterioration.[28] Only after serious rioting broke out in major U.S. cities in the mid-1960s did federal programs become more focused on core cities and their social needs. Spending on such programs began to decline in the 1970s, however, as the federal government withdrew support from social programs in order to reduce taxes and increase military spending.

---

27. Gelfand 1980.
28. Dreier, Mollenkopf, and Swanstrom 2001, 92–112.

The problems of large U.S. cities helped to stimulate a brief period of Canadian government interest in urban affairs in the late 1960s and early 1970s (see Chapter 3). Otherwise, the Canadian government showed little interest in the development and problems of Canadian cities and city-regions for most of the study period. Nonetheless, its policies, particularly those relating to housing, immigration, and transportation, affected both the way the Toronto region evolved and the way it was governed. In addition, federal cost-sharing programs were a source of money for provincially administered social programs and a stimulus to or constraint on provincial activity.

A revival of federal government interest in urban affairs in the late 1990s, accompanied by modest financial support for some programs (particularly the development of new urban infrastructure and affordable housing) suggested that the federal government was preparing to play a more active role in Toronto region governance once again. It also gave added significance to its earlier contributions to the region and its governance.

Intergovernmental or government–community consultation

If political or financial obstacles to central government involvement become too great, or if central governments decide that city-region problems are not important enough to justify the political or financial costs of dealing with them, they may ask a region's municipal governments to work out co-operative agreements among themselves.

Before the 1960s, intermunicipal co-operation typically took the form of voluntary agreements among two or more municipalities for the joint provision of specific services (such as public education, public transit, or water supply), or arrangements whereby one municipality bought services from another. For example, in the Toronto region, the Regional Municipality of York has long bought some of its water from the City of Toronto (formerly Metro Toronto).

This approach has also been used on a larger scale. For example, local governments in the Vancouver city-region are part of a Greater Vancouver Regional District that is mandated by the province to provide certain services to the entire region, but that can also provide additional services to municipalities that wish to buy them. A few county governments in the United States also operate in this way.

Intermunicipal consultation or co-operation gained greater importance in the United States in the 1960s, however, when municipalities in several regions decided to organize voluntarily to plan or make policies for their regions. The type of organization that embodied this idea was the council of governments, or COG, the first of which appeared in the Detroit region in 1954.[29] Although the earliest COGs were voluntary associations, most were created after 1963 to comply with requirements and incentives built into federal grant programs.

Councils of governments had the advantage of causing minimal disruption to existing political arrangements, and thus posed little threat to local autonomy. Local governments usually had the right to choose whether to participate in them or to help pay their costs. These advantages, however, made them weak instruments for resolving regional issues. In the absence of strong incentives from either the federal or state governments, they often made little effort to fulfill the functions expected of them, such as producing regional plans or promoting coordinated regional policies that took both central city and suburban needs into account.[30] They were particularly unlikely to undertake programs that involved redistributing costs and benefits among municipalities within a region, or that threatened the lifestyles of a region's more affluent residents (by introducing lower priced housing into middle-class neighbourhoods, for example, or by changing the social composition of local school populations).

Despite their disadvantages, COGs are still the preferred way to address city-region problems in the United States. They can take a variety of forms, some of which include the participation of or even leadership from the business and non-profit community sectors as well as representatives of local governments. When constituted in this way, they tend to be called regional councils rather than councils of governments.

The Ontario government asked municipal officials in the Toronto region on several occasions to try to resolve regional issues co-operatively, although it often sent its own representatives to these meetings. It used this approach to regional governance more formally in 1997 when it created a consultative forum, the Greater Toronto Services Board (GTSB), with authority to act on regional issues (see Chapter 6).

The GTSB resembled COGs in being made up entirely of local politicians. It lasted only until 2001, however, when the province disbanded it and created a Central Ontario Smart Growth Panel with a mandate to prepare a plan and coordinate infrastructure investments for a much larger region than the one over which the GTSB had presided. The inclusion of representatives of the business and community sectors made this second body similar to the regional councils operating in some U.S. city-regions at that time.

---

29. Harrigan 1985, 353–356.
30. Ibid., 356–358.

Service Delivery and Service Financing Go Hand in Hand

Debates about how to organize or administer regional services are usually intertwined with debates about how to pay for them. Deciding how to fund region-wide programs and services can be a highly contentious process, because funding decisions are ultimately decisions about how to distribute the costs and benefits of regional growth, not only among a region's taxpaying residents and businesses but also between taxpayers in the region and taxpayers in other parts of the province/state or nation.

In a broad sense, there are only five ways to pay for regional services:

- out of locally raised taxes;
- out of income or other taxes collected by a central government;
- by borrowing;
- from fees charged to users (individuals, businesses, or entire municipalities) of specific services; and
- by shifting the costs to the private sector.

Each of these alternatives raises different issues for central and local governments and their constituents.

Issues related to the use of local taxes

Municipal governments in North America depend heavily on property taxes to fund the services they provide. For that reason alone, property taxes are important to regional development and governance because of their influence on municipal decision making. In general, municipal governments want to maximize their tax bases while minimizing service costs. Thus they tend to favour types of development that pay more in taxes than they require in services. Commercial development and non-polluting industries fall into this category. So do dwellings intended for small and relatively affluent households, which are expected to make fewer demands on municipal services.

Because municipal governments need to maintain or enhance their tax bases, there is ongoing intermunicipal competition for preferred types of development. The more municipal governments depend on property taxes to fund their services, the more intense this competition is likely to be. The result is a process of social and financial sorting (intentional or otherwise) within a city-region. Some municipalities (usually the newer suburbs) absorb a larger share of a region's more affluent residents and new or relocating businesses, while others (usually older municipalities at or near the core of the region) retain or attract a disproportionate share of a region's poorer households, often losing industrial and commercial firms at the same time. This sorting process is one reason why municipalities within a city-region can diverge considerably in the size, strength, and characteristics of their tax bases and in the types of services their residents demand or consume.

If municipal taxes are used for regional services, therefore, the tasks of collecting money to pay for them and deciding how services will be distributed across a region become increasingly challenging as a region becomes more fragmented and its population more diverse. The simplest way to accomplish these tasks, as suggested earlier, is for big cities to annex their suburbs or for a central government to bring municipalities together in an organization that can spread the costs of local services over a wider and more varied tax base. Alternatively, a central government may require municipalities within the region to contribute to the costs of regional services, or municipalities may decide to do so themselves.

Municipal contributions (either imposed or voluntary) to regional services may be based on one of several criteria, including population size, amount of the service consumed, or ability to pay as determined by the size of the local tax base or some part thereof. Where property taxes are the main source of local revenue, as they are in all of North America, an important measure of a municipality's ability to pay for regional services is the total assessed value of the properties it contains. To ensure fairness, therefore, this measure requires that properties in a region be assessed and taxed in a uniform way. Because changes in Toronto-region governance usually involved some degree of local revenue sharing, recurring efforts to achieve uniformity in property assessment and taxation were important aspects of governance in the region during the period covered by this study.

Issues related to central government funding

As an alternative to requiring municipal governments to pay for regional services out of local taxes, central governments may decide to pay all or part of their costs themselves. They can do so either by making grants to municipal governments or regional agencies, or by providing and paying for some regional services directly.

Grants from central governments were an important source of funds for regional services throughout the study period, although in the Toronto region, as in the rest of North America, such grants increased as a proportion of total funding in the early part of the period and declined in its later years. Their use from the 1950s onward generated much discussion about how responsibility for regional services should be divided among different levels of government to best satisfy the principles of economy, efficiency, distributional fairness, accountability to taxpayers, and equal treatment of citizens.

Different writers took different positions on this issue, depending on the amount of importance they attached to the different principles.[31] Attempts to build all the principles into a single framework imply, however, that regional governance requires a three-tier arrangement consisting of agencies of central government, one or more regional authorities, and individual municipal governments.[32] In such a three-tiered system, the cost of services can be divided among the different levels of government according to the revenues that each of them raises and the geographical scale of the services they provide. The breakdown might be as follows:

- Services such as social welfare and social housing that entail a substantial degree of income redistribution would be paid for and perhaps administered by the national or sub-national government that collects taxes (such as income taxes) that are based on ability to pay.
- Services that have impacts (wanted or unwanted) that are likely to spill over municipal boundaries within a region would be delivered and paid for by a level of government that has been authorized to make policies for the whole region, using funds collected regionally. This category might include water supply, sewage and solid waste disposal, cross-boundary transportation, policing, fire protection, land-use planning, economic development, and environmental protection.
- Services "that do not generate spillovers, and where local preferences are important in determining ... quality and quantity,"[33] would be assigned to (or remain with) local municipalities. They could include the maintenance of local roads, local transit, public health, garbage collection, parks and recreation services, libraries, and some local planning.

Decisions about how to fund services of importance to a region, however, do not necessarily adhere to abstract principles of what constitutes "good" or "fair" or "effective" governance. They are as likely to be dictated by political, historical, and ideological considerations as by administrative

---

31. See, for example, Richard R. Barnett, "Subsidiarity, Enabling Government and Local Governance"; Harry Kitchen, "Pricing of Local Government Services"; and Enid Slack, "Finance and Governance: The Case of the Greater Toronto Area," in Hobson and St-Hilaire 1997, 59–78; 135–168; 81–111.

32. The breakdown suggested here is based primarily on Slack, "Finance and Governance: The Case of the Greater Toronto Area," 102–107.

33. Ibid, 103.

values. Moreover, services used by a region's population do not always fall neatly into a particular category, thereby making it difficult to decide which level of government should pay for them.

Take the example of public education, which is often at the heart of debates about the merits and drawbacks of local fiscal and administrative autonomy. In the United States, public education has remained largely in the hands of local school boards, which fund it mainly out of local taxes supplemented by state grants. In many states, this means that the quality of the public schools is determined mainly by the size of the local tax base. Critics have argued (and some state courts have agreed) that this system has resulted in large disparities in the quality of education offered in poor and rich municipalities, not only in different states, but also in city-regions within a single state. As a result, children who attend poorly funded schools in high-poverty school districts do not get the education they need to escape the situations in which they grow up.[34]

Public health is also difficult to confine to a single category. Although many of the responsibilities assigned to public health units (such as monitoring water supply or inspecting restaurants) can safely be circumscribed by local boundaries, others (such as controlling the spread of infectious diseases) are critical to the well-being of an entire region, province/state, or nation.

Local public transit is another service that has both local and regional importance. To the extent that it draws most of its users from the municipality in which it operates, it qualifies as a "local service." If, however, local transit services in a city-region stop at local boundaries and make no or few connections with other transit systems, travel across municipal boundaries becomes difficult or impossible for those without a car. This problem is likely to increase as a city-region expands and a growing proportion of its jobs occur in outer districts with little or no transit service.

Land-use planning is a fourth service that is difficult to assign to a single level of government. As discussed earlier, local governments fiercely defend their right to control the use of land in their communities from encroachments by other levels of government, not only in the interest of protecting local autonomy, but also because it is their principal means of furthering or protecting the financial and social well-being of their communities. In exercising this right, however, local governments can have a large impact on the way jobs and housing opportunities are distributed throughout a region, and on the transportation links between them.

Finally, decisions about how to fund and where to build major infrastructure, while important to a region's ability to expand, can imply major and often unwanted consequences for municipalities in which the new facilities are

---

34. Kozol 1991.

located, and thus become matters of intense interest to local governments and residents.

The difficulty of deciding how the costs of services will be allocated among different levels of government, as well as the political controversies that such decisions often entail, mean that the contributions of central and local authorities to regional governance may vary substantially among different city-regions, even within the same country.[35] As this study shows, they can also undergo substantial changes in the same city-region over time as a result of changes in external circumstances and in the pragmatic or ideological preoccupations of the governments involved.

Issues related to borrowing

Municipal governments in Canada may borrow only to pay the capital costs of new infrastructure, not to pay the costs of operating facilities after they are built. And because those governments have to pay debt charges out of local revenues, borrowing does not eliminate the political difficulties of persuading taxpaying voters to pay for regional services, although it may lighten the apparent costs of doing so by spreading them over a longer period. Moreover, borrowing to fund regional services can be done only by a government that has the authority to incur debt and collect taxes to pay it off. In the absence of regional institutions with this kind of authority, the central government has to be willing to pay such costs itself. In order to do so, it will have to raise taxes or reduce the amount of money it spends on services that are valued more highly by taxpayers and voters outside the region. The alternative is to look for ways to have new services paid for by private producers or consumers.

Issues related to private financing

Privatizing the costs of municipal and regional services can take a number of forms, such as:

- making residents pay fees to cover all or part of the costs of the services they use;
- creating public agencies that can finance themselves in this way;
- requiring those who develop urban land for profit to install necessary services themselves or to reimburse local governments for the costs of installing them; and

---

35. Melville L. McMillan, "Taxation and Expenditure Patterns in Major City-Regions: An International Perspective and Lessons for Canada," in Hobson and St-Hilaire 1997, 1–56.

- contracting with private companies to provide those services from which they can expect to make a profit.

There are many arguments both for and against shifting costs to consumers and private-sector providers. Those in favour argue, for example, that imposing the costs of services on those who actually use them is fairer than imposing them on all taxpayers, only some of whom are users. They also claim that user fees, development charges, and privatization mean that services and resources will be used more efficiently. Whether these advantages are actually realized depends, of course, on how user fees and development charges are structured and administered.[36]

An argument against user fees, at least for some services, is that they may have negative impacts on other public-sector agencies or on municipal well-being. Fees that make public transit or child care unaffordable to low-wage earners, for example, may deter some residents from seeking employment and thus result in lower income-tax returns and higher demands for social assistance. Fees for using public parks or recreation programs may cause young people to find less socially acceptable ways to amuse themselves, thereby adding to local law enforcement costs. Impacts like these are more likely to occur in a region's low-income communities or neighbourhoods than in its wealthy ones, thereby increasing socio-economic disparities within a region.

Shifting the costs of public services to private-sector providers is likely to mean that governments and local residents give up some of their ability to control or influence the way a region evolves or the way services are provided. Nonetheless, this approach gained a good deal of support from urban analysts and public policy-makers in the last decades of the 20th century.

Historical Trends in the Governance of North American City-Regions

For more than 150 years, North Americans have tried to unify local governments in city-regions to achieve one or more of the objectives contained in the regional agenda. These efforts show five similar tendencies.

First, the interest of central governments in creating larger or more authoritative city-region governments declined as city-regions grew in size and complexity. Instead, central governments chose institutional alternatives (such as creating special-purpose authorities) that increased rather than reduced institutional fragmentation and complexity.[37] State governments in the United

---

36. Kitchen, in Hobson and St-Hilaire 1997, 144–165.

37. Jackson 1972; Fox 1977, 138–160; Owen and Wilburn 1985, 192–193; Wakstein 1972.

States also responded to regional growth by giving municipal governments and their residents more powers to resist changes in municipal boundaries or in the way municipal services were delivered.

Second, the locus of financial hardship within city-regions shifted over time, as did the perception of the nature and causes of intermunicipal inequities. In the early years of regional expansion, decision-makers looked for ways to use city tax dollars to help fund suburban infrastructure. As regions matured, they looked for ways to enlist suburban governments and suburban tax bases in efforts to solve social problems in the core city.

Third, regional organizations, where they existed, tended to be more successful at improving regional infrastructure than at redistributing service costs and benefits among the municipalities that make up a region.[38] They succeeded as infrastructure providers, however, only to the extent that they remained responsible for all the territory undergoing development and had enough funds to pay for their activities.

Fourth, the interest of central governments in the financial and social condition of core cities tended to decline as those cities lost population and economic activity relative to the rest of their regions. In other words, the amount of central government concern seemed to depend on a city's perceived economic and political importance to the region, state/province, or nation.[39]

Finally, in the 1950s and 1960s the costs of servicing cities and city-regions tended to shift away from local governments and local property taxes toward senior levels of government. They began to shift back to local governments in the 1970s, however, as senior governments looked for ways to cut spending and pursue other priorities. In the final decades of the 20th century, there were increased efforts to involve the private sector in the funding and administration of urban and regional services, as well as greater reliance on organizations of municipal officials or community representatives to work out mutually acceptable ways of tackling regional problems.

These trends have been documented more fully in the United States than in Canada. Nonetheless, some of them were evident in the evolution of governance in the Toronto region during the period covered by the study. The major difference between the two settings was the much larger role played by the Ontario government than by most U.S. state governments in regional administration. This study considers what provincial involvement meant for regional character, for the challenges the region faced at the end of the 20th century, and for the region's ability to meet those challenges. The next five chapters examine five successive periods in the region's development, each

---

38. Hawley 1976.
39. Gainsborough 2001(b).

one characterized by a different approach to regional governance. The findings and conclusions are summarized in the final chapter, which ends with a discussion of the challenges facing the region at the beginning of the 21st century and the options available for dealing with them.

TWO

1924–1966
Debating and Creating
Metropolitan Institutions

The 1953 creation of Metropolitan Toronto was the first major change in Ontario's system of local government since the system was put in place by a *Municipal Corporations Act* in 1849. It was a noteworthy event, therefore, but it was not a sudden or impulsive one. In fact, the 1953 legislation was the culmination of more than two decades of serious efforts to find workable ways to tackle the infrastructure deficiencies and social needs that accumulated in the Toronto region during the Great Depression of the 1930s and the six war years that followed it. The provincial government usually initiated and took an active role in these efforts, thereby declaring a direct interest in the region and the way it was governed. It did not take decisive action, however, until it had engaged municipal governments in discussions about what should be done.

Background and Context

Until the early part of the 20th century, Toronto grew by annexation in the same way as many other North American cities, taking in small municipalities or suburban districts that are still well known by their original names (for example, Yorkville, the Annex, Parkdale, North Toronto, Moore Park). In 1912, however, City Council ruled out further annexations, having decided that the costs of providing services to annexed districts exceeded any benefits they might bring to the city.[1] Council held firmly to that position in the face of later requests for annexation from the suburbs of York and East York, which viewed annexation as a way to secure better services, particularly those offered by the city-owned Toronto Transportation Commission.

The first proposal for a two-tier form of government for the region appeared in the early 1900s, at about the time that annexation was losing its political appeal.[2] Nothing came of it. In 1924, however, George S. Henry, a cabinet minister in Ontario's Conservative government, asked his cabinet

---

1. Plumptre 1935.
2. Weaver 1979, 56.

colleagues to consider draft legislation containing a similar proposal. (Henry was a former member of the government of York County, home to all the suburban municipalities that had asked at one time or another to be annexed to the city.[3]) His proposal called for the creation of a Toronto "metropolitan district" in which a council composed of city and suburban members would provide several major services to the whole area, leaving existing municipalities in place and in charge of all other services. It failed to win support from Toronto members of the Conservative caucus, however, and the proposal quickly died. Henry became leader of his party and then premier in 1930, but by that time the provincial government was having to deal with a much broader range of issues in its municipal sector.

A crisis in municipal finance

The onset of the Depression in 1929 plunged Ontario municipalities into severe financial difficulties because of the rising costs of unemployment relief (for which municipal governments were fully responsible) and falling local tax revenues. Within a short time, many Ontario municipalities, including 10 of Toronto's 12 suburbs, were insolvent, and the provincial government had taken charge of their financial affairs. The two survivors were the small residential suburbs of Forest Hill and Swansea. The City of Toronto, while financially stressed, also remained solvent and in full control of its finances during this period.

The government responded to the plight of its municipalities both by assuming the largest share of the costs of unemployment relief[4] and by seeking ways to keep municipal spending under control. The agency the Conservative government turned to for this purpose was the Ontario Railway and Municipal Board, an appointed, quasi-judicial agency established in 1906 to regulate relations between municipalities and the private companies that operated their street railways. The government renamed this body the Ontario Municipal Board (OMB) in 1932, and asked it to establish a Committee of Supervisors to help municipal governments straighten out their financial affairs.

The Liberal government that replaced the Conservatives in 1934 soon announced that it had inherited a large deficit. The new premier, Mitchell Hepburn, called this "a pitiful showing," and pledged "a return to the old-

---

3. Colton 1980, 55. Except where otherwise noted, the discussion of events leading up to Metropolitan Toronto's creation is based on this work.

4. It paid 45.5 per cent of those costs between 1930 and 1937, with the rest being paid by the federal government (just under 31 per cent) and municipalities (23.5 per cent). Ontario Government 1938, 71.

fashioned methods of living within our income."[5] His government passed legislation that made municipal governments legally responsible for unemployment relief for the first time in the province's history.[6] It also took away their right to borrow money to pay relief costs—a right that the Conservatives had given them just two years earlier—although it continued to give them yearly grants to assist with this function. It cut its grants to education and empowered the OMB to approve all municipal borrowing for capital works. It also created a Department of Municipal Affairs (DMA) primarily to advise municipal governments on how to manage their financial affairs and reduce their debts.[7]

Premier Hepburn would later describe the DMA as the department "performing the most important function of the Government and [the one] which reflects more than any other department the considered policy of this administration."[8] But the powers given to the OMB then and later would make that body at least as important as the DMA to policy-making for Ontario municipalities in general and the Toronto metropolitan area in particular. It was an agency with few counterparts in Canada and none in the United States.

In 1935 the Liberal government took away the right of municipal governments to tax local incomes, something that provincial law had required them to do to supplement the local property tax. Only a few municipalities had used this power, however, even after a committee of the legislature had affirmed that the tax was mandatory, not optional. As a result, according to a later review of provincial–municipal finance, some municipalities were serving as "tax havens for the well-to-do."[9]

After taking the income tax away from municipalities, the government initiated one of its own. It also instituted a special subsidy to the few local governments, including Toronto's, that had been collecting one. One year later, it replaced this subsidy with grants to all municipalities based directly on the size of their assessments.[10] (The larger the assessment, the larger the grant.) As the costs of unemployment relief fell in the latter part of the 1930s, the province also introduced grants to help municipalities pay some of their social service and road-building costs. It also increased its support to local school boards.

---

5. Ontario Budget Address, delivered by the Honourable Mitchell F. Hepburn, Premier and Treasurer of Ontario, April 2, 1935, 12.

6. Toronto Bureau of Municipal Research, "The Relation of the Province to the Municipality," White Paper #221, March 1, 1937.

7. Ontario Government 1938, 71–73.

8. Ontario Budget Address, delivered by the Honourable Mitchell F. Hepburn, Premier and Treasurer of Ontario, March 30, 1939, 25.

9. Ontario Committee on Taxation 1967, 46.

10. Toronto Bureau of Municipal Research, "The Relation of the Province to the Municipality," White Paper #221, March 1, 1937; Ontario Committee on Taxation 1967, 47.

Revisiting the metropolitan problem

The financial problems experienced by Toronto's suburbs in the 1930s resulted not only from the Depression, but also from the nature of Ontario's local
government system, which made a distinction between city and rural forms of
government. In rural areas, responsibility for providing local services was divided among upper-tier county councils and lower-tier municipalities (towns,
villages, and townships). County governments performed relatively few functions, road and bridge building being the most important, using local taxes
collected for county purposes. Cities were stand-alone units that performed
all municipal functions for themselves and did not contribute to the county
levy (although the Ontario government required Toronto to pay 25 per cent
of the cost of York County roads classified as "suburban"). Moreover, as
suburbanizing districts broke away from rural townships to form separate municipalities, they took on new responsibilities and reduced their contributions
to the county.[11] Rural taxpayers then had to pay higher taxes to fund services
demanded by urban migrants to unincorporated districts.

The financial difficulties experienced by most suburban municipalities in the Toronto area during the Depression stimulated a renewed search
for ways to tap Toronto's healthy tax base for suburban purposes. Between
1933 and 1937, a Metropolitan Area Committee set up by the County of
York, a Metropolitan Area Commission appointed by the Conservative
government, and a committee appointed by the Liberal government "for the
Study of Municipal and Related Problems in Toronto and Its Neighbouring
Municipalities" considered ways to restructure the area's system of governance.[12] The Liberal government also asked A.W.F. Plumptre, an academic
consultant, to prepare a detailed study of the issue.

In his report, Plumptre observed that a few local and provincial agencies
(the Toronto Transportation Commission, the Ontario Hydro Commission,
the provincial Department of Health) were already providing important services to all or parts of the Toronto metropolitan area.[13] Nonetheless, he said,
the area needed a metropolitan form of government to overcome "financial
and social injustice," which he related to the boundary-imposed separation
of taxable resources from service needs in Toronto and its 12 suburbs.[14] The
situation was such, he noted, that the poorest suburban municipalities were
burdened by the highest tax rates. Moreover,

---

11. Lemon 1985, 35.
12. Colton 1980, 56; Rose 1972, 11.
13. Plumptre 1935, 52–60.
14. Ibid., 86–89.

[t]he fact that it is legally permissible for the city of Toronto to throw heavy relief and educational burdens back upon the poorer suburbs, and the fact that it is legally permissible for the residents of … richer suburbs to avoid their share of taxation and their share of responsibility for the administration of the whole area—these legal facts do not justify the existing situation but only suggest that the law should be changed.[15]

He later criticized the city's opposition to annexation as "short-sighted." If the province did not act, he said, the city would begin to experience the same process of decline that was already apparent in some large American cities.[16]

Plumptre's arguments for reform based on equity criteria was consistent with what others were saying about intermunicipal disparities in the Toronto area at the time. It was an argument that meant different things to different local politicians, however.

Like all discussions invoking justice, this one was exceedingly divisive and was difficult to carry to the point of resolution without some mechanism for coercing the losers. Everyone, it seemed, had a grievance. The rural districts of the county felt hard done by at having to shore up the suburbs. Many in the suburbs saw it as equally intolerable that at a time when "all must bear their share of the responsibility, the poorer districts being unable to maintain themselves," they should be denied the benefit of the city's accumulated wealth. To all of this City of Toronto politicians reacted with an outraged defensiveness, saying they could not ask their constituents to pay for the tribulations of other areas.[17]

Any local politician who tried to argue differently soon backed down.

The government did not act on any of the recommendations it received, and the outbreak of the Second World War in 1939 brought a temporary halt to the discussion. Before that happened, however, the government had empowered the OMB to authorize annexations and amalgamations after holding a public hearing, thereby ending Toronto's right to make or refuse to make boundary changes on its own.[18]

---

15. Ibid., 89.
16. Ibid., 145.
17. Colton 1980, 57.
18. The OMB lost its responsibility for hearing municipal boundary disputes in 1981, when the government decided that municipalities should resolve these disputes themselves

Ontario versus Canada

Arguments for reducing intermunicipal inequities also appeared in a background study of municipal finance prepared by Montreal lawyer Carl Goldenberg for the federally established Royal Commission on Dominion–Provincial Relations (the Rowell-Sirois Commission), which studied dominion [federal]–provincial financial relations between 1937 and 1940. In his report, Goldenberg documented large variations in the financial capacities of municipalities and school districts, and then went on to argue that

> the interests of the province as a whole are injured by the sheer inability of some municipalities to raise the same revenue as others in proportion to population and the amount of expenditure required, not to mention the obstacles to provincial uniformity arising from the deliberate adoption by a municipality of a lower standard than that desired by provincial policy.[19]

Such problems, he suggested, could be addressed in single metropolitan areas by merging municipalities or by adopting other means to achieve a high degree of service coordination and cost equalization. He pointed out, however, that intermunicipal inequalities existed on a province-wide scale, and called for remedies that only the provincial or federal governments could implement. For example, these governments could assume some municipal functions (unemployment relief being the one that posed the greatest problems to cities, and education being the source of greatest difficulty for rural municipalities), make larger grants to municipalities based on some criteria of need, or improve the administration of the property tax system.[20]

Goldenberg's study had little immediate impact, but it did anticipate most of the issues that would dominate debates about provincial–municipal finance from that time on. The Royal Commission was careful to note that municipalities were areas of provincial responsibility, and therefore outside its mandate. It advised the federal government, however, to attack inequalities among provinces by establishing a system of national adjustment grants, to be paid to any province that "established that it could not supply Canadian average standards of service and balance its budget without taxation (provincial and municipal) appreciably exceeding the national average in relation to income."[21]

---

through direct negotiations. At time of writing, the OMB mainly hears appeals of municipal planning decisions and land expropriations.

19. Goldenberg 1939, 31.
20. Ibid., 102–104.
21. The Royal Commission on Dominion-Provincial Relations, 1940, Vol. II, 83.

The appointment of the Rowell-Sirois Commission was the federal government's response to several years of infighting between itself and the provinces about the way the Canadian federation was financed. Some disputes centred on the federal government's refusal to give up the right to tax incomes, which it had secured from the provinces to help finance the First World War.[22] Others focused on the need for provincial governments to negotiate every year for federal government help with unemployment relief. The Ontario and Quebec governments delayed the adoption of a more permanent arrangement by insisting that the federal government should not use money collected from their taxpayers to help out poorer provinces.[23] The dispute ended in 1937 with the federal government agreeing to pay 40 per cent of the costs of relief.

With more federal aid available, the Ontario government relieved municipalities of their 25 per cent share of old age pensions, reduced the municipal share of relief from 33.3 to 25 per cent, and assumed full responsibility for mothers' allowances. The next year it increased the size of its education grants to their pre-1935 level. Its goal, it said, was to reduce the burden on property taxes, which the government blamed not only for the financial problems of municipalities, but also for stagnation in the building industry.[24]

The government also said that it would distribute the costs of education more equitably by increasing grants to districts with small assessments—a policy that resulted in the bulk of education grants going to rural schools.[25] Nonetheless, it was firmly against the idea of equalizing resources among provinces, depicting it as a threat to Ontario's financial position and a way to get Ontario to subsidize the rest of Canada.[26] Taking a position very like the one Toronto had taken toward the rest of its region, Ontario told the Rowell-Sirois Commission that inter-regional inequalities was not a problem that should concern provincial governments.

> It is of the essence of self-government that a people shall be permitted to establish and enforce its own considered standards of fiscal justice. Different regions of Canada have varying conceptions of the usefulness of particular types of taxes in achieving their own standards of public morality. In part these differences of opinion with regard to public morality arise out of different economic

22. The *British North America Act* assigned the right to "direct taxation" to the provinces.

23. Neatby 1972, 136.

24. The Ontario Committee on Taxation 1967, 74.

25. Ontario Budget Address, delivered by the Honourable A. St. Clair Gordon, Treasurer of Ontario, March 19, 1943, 11.

26. Alway 1965, 270, 244.

conditions, but also, in part, they arise out of varying conceptions of the ends of the State, the objectives of government, and the foundation of political ethics.[27]

In fact, Premier Hepburn told the Commission that Ontario and its municipalities would look after their own relief needs if the national government would give the provinces full powers to collect income and corporation taxes.

Spotlight on housing

Ontario's Liberal government also showed little interest in participating in federally initiated programs to address the deteriorating condition of housing in downtown Toronto and other cities Its lieutenant-governor, Dr. Herbert A. Bruce, drew attention to this problem in 1934 by politely chastising the city for allowing the emergence of "slum districts" in what was otherwise "a great and beautiful city."[28] Although not recognized as such at the time, Bruce had identified one of the main issues that would eventually lead the city to reverse its stand against amalgamation with the suburbs. At this time, however, the city addressed the housing problem by pressuring the federal government for help.

The first federal housing legislation (the *Dominion Housing Act* of 1935) did little more than commit the federal government to providing mortgage assistance as a way to stimulate the construction industry and generate employment. Advocates for low-rental housing kept up the pressure in the face of widespread opposition from defenders of free enterprise, even after city voters voted overwhelming against a slum clearance and low-income housing scheme in 1937.[29]

In 1938 a new *National Housing Act* made low-interest loans available to any local authority that undertook to provide low-cost housing, provided that the provincial government passed enabling legislation containing guarantees on principal and interest. The Ontario government did not pass such legislation, however, nor did it want to become involved. While there was a serious housing problem, Premier Hepburn told the Rowell-Sirois Commission, and perhaps some need for slum clearance and government-supervised housing programs, the main requirements for solving it were low real estate taxes, low interest rates, and sound city and town planning.[30] Toronto City Council

---

27. Government of Ontario, "Statement to the Royal Commission on Dominion-Provincial Relations. Book II. General Statement," 1938, 60–61.

28. Toronto Committee to Enquire into Housing Conditions, 1934, 5.

29. Lemon 1985, 68.

30. Government of Ontario, "Statement to the Royal Commission on Dominion-Provincial Relations," 1938, op. cit., 34.

also decided not to participate, having been advised by its Board of Control that the program would assist the construction of new, low-cost housing on vacant land, but not the clearance and reconstruction of existing slum areas. Circumstances would have to change and the housing situation become worse before the city tackled the housing issue again.

Changing circumstances, changing politics

The changes that would help to persuade Toronto's government to alter its views on both metropolitan area governance and housing issues were a rapid expansion of industry during the war, which brought improvements in local finances but also increased pressures on the city's housing stock, and a surge of population growth in municipalities outside Toronto. There was also an election in 1943 that the Liberals lost by a wide margin, with the largest number (but not a majority) of seats going to the Conservatives. The Conservative party's situation was precarious, in fact, because it had only a four-seat advantage over a new social democratic party, the Cooperative Commonwealth Federation (CCF), which had been advocating a broad range of social programs since its formation in 1932.

The election result was a repudiation of the fiscal conservatism of the Hepburn government and a triumph for Conservative party leader George Drew, who had worked hard since becoming leader in 1938 to revive a party badly hurt by internal disagreements about what to do about the Depression. At his urging, and following the lead of their federal counterparts, the Conservatives renamed their party the Progressive Conservatives and fought the 1943 election on a 22-point program promising "economic and social security from the cradle to the grave."[31] Of particular interest to municipalities was a government pledge to assume 50 per cent of the cost of public education, but without affecting "the authority of the local school boards."[32] The party platform also included promises to increase government contributions to housing and other social services, and to undertake "a sweeping revision of our whole system of real estate taxation so that owning and improvement of homes and farm land ... will not be discouraged by excessive taxation."[33]

By the early 1940s, therefore, the context for debating issues of regional governance was very different from the one that had existed in 1930. There had been much discussion and several studies of intergovernmental problems (both regional and national) that had emphasized large differences in the

31. Dyck 1986, 283; Penner 1978, 213.
32. Quoted in Graham 1990, 90.
33. Ontario Budget Address, delivered by the Honourable Leslie M. Frost, Premier and Treasurer of Ontario, March 16, 1944, 30.

ability of different municipalities and different provinces to finance public services, and the need to do something about those differences. The provincial government had given two of its agencies (the Ontario Municipal Board and the Department of Municipal Affairs) considerable authority to oversee municipal affairs. It had also relieved municipal governments in Ontario of a potential but seldom-used source of revenue (the income tax), while adding another one (provincial grants). Provincial grants would become increasingly important to the funding of municipal and regional services in the years that followed. Finally, Ontario had a new government that seemed ready to tackle municipal and social problems more vigorously than had its predecessor, if only to avoid losing office to an upstart social democratic party (the CCF) that had made a radical commitment to social change.

The Post-war Situation: Defining the Regional Agenda

With the end of the Second World War in 1945, the Toronto region entered a period of reconstruction complicated by a lack of agreement between the federal and provincial governments about where the national economy was headed. The federal government expected a return of depression, as had happened after the First World War, and favoured job-creating programs to cushion its impacts; the Ontario government looked for ways to sustain the high rate of private investment and employment growth that had accompanied wartime industrialization. No sooner had the war ended, therefore, than provincial officials began to urge municipal politicians in the Toronto area to address deficiencies in municipal services without relying on the Ontario government to do so.[34]

As would continue to be the case, those participating in intergovernmental discussions disagreed about what needed to be done to secure the Toronto area's future. Provincial officials wanted municipalities to speed up the rate of housing production to accommodate industrial workers.[35] Suburban politicians and business interests insisted that new infrastructure (roads, public transit, sewers, water supply) and new schools should be in place before housing was built. Those concerned about the City of Toronto emphasized the need to address physical deterioration and overcrowding in older downtown neighbourhoods and increasing traffic congestion on city streets.[36]

34. Metropolitan Toronto Council Minutes, April 15, 1953, 14.
35. The Honourable L.M. Frost, Premier of Ontario, "Address re First Reading of 'An Act to Provide for the Federation of Municipalities in the Toronto Metropolitan Area for Certain Financial and other Purposes,' to the Third Session of the Twenty-Fourth Legislature of the Province of Ontario," February 25, 1953.
36. Toronto Bureau of Municipal Research, "Where are Toronto and its Metropolitan Area Heading?" White Paper #305, December 20, 1945; Toronto Civic Advisory Council, The Committee on Metropolitan Problems 1949.

Despite these concerns, the City of Toronto was not showing the same signs of physical and financial decline that had begun to appear in some older U.S. cities in the 1930s or even earlier.[37] The city emerged from the Second World War with a strong economy, its Depression debts repaid, able to undertake neglected repairs to its public works.[38] With the approval of city voters in a 1945 referendum, Toronto City Council agreed to allow the city-owned Toronto Transportation Commission (TTC) to replace a heavily used streetcar line with an underground subway. The TTC was ready to pay most of the costs out of surplus funds accumulated during the Depression and war years, but the city would have to replace or improve underground services as needed and secure (but not pay) the project's capital debt.[39] TTC management insisted that subways would do more than ease severe overcrowding on downtown streets; they would also encourage industry and business to remain in the core, thereby preventing its gradual deterioration.[40]

Leading the way in public housing

In 1947 the City Council also obtained voter support for Canada's first public low- to moderate-rental housing project in the downtown neighbourhood of Regent Park.[41] Although the plan promised some relief to those suffering because of a severe shortage of rental housing, its proponents wooed voter support by emphasizing the economic benefits it would bring to the city. The housing scheme, they said, would (a) increase the attractiveness of the city to potential investors, (b) remove physical barriers to the redevelopment of downtown property for more profitable uses, (c) increase the city's tax base, and (d) reduce the cost of city services.[42]

Economic arguments for a public housing program were aimed not only at those who objected to any government intervention in the private housing market, but also at those who claimed that government-subsidized housing, like any other form of social assistance, should be funded by senior governments, not by local property owners. The Bureau of Municipal Research disagreed.

---

37. Gelfand 1980, 31; McKenzie 1933, 314–315.

38. City of Toronto Treasury Department, "Report of the Commissioner of Finance," 1949, 36; City of Toronto Annual Report 1953, 30; Robert H. Saunders [Mayor of Toronto], "Inaugural Address," Toronto City Council Minutes 1945, Appendix C, 2.

39. W.E.P. Duncan, "Rapid Transit in Toronto," address to a meeting of the Citizens' Committee of Montreal, November 24, 1949, *Canadian Railway and Marine World*, 52 (1949), 673; Toronto City Council Minutes 1949, Appendix A, 269–70. For an account of the debates that preceded the subway decision, see Frisken 1984, 262–264.

40. *Canadian Railway and Marine World*, 45 (1942), 151–152.

41. At the time, provincial law required municipalities to hold referenda on proposals to incur new capital debt.

42. Rose 1958, 53.

"If a man is drowning in river or lake," it wrote in support of the project, "he does not refuse to save himself because [other] persons are not interested in his fate."[43] The electors approved the housing plan by a larger majority than they gave to a new civic square,[44] and the city immediately set up a Housing Authority to oversee the project's development and management.

Concern about the Toronto area's long-run economic prospects was therefore prominent in arguments for service improvements and governance changes in the Toronto region immediately after the Second World War. Whereas suburban officials focused on infrastructure deficiencies that deterred residential and industrial investment, Toronto officials stressed the need to remove roadblocks to the city's continued prosperity. For redevelopment to occur in aging inner neighbourhoods, they said, there had to be housing elsewhere for people displaced from the centre. For downtown congestion to ease, there had to be a reduction in traffic on the city's narrow streets.

There were also concerns about the distribution of social costs and social spending among the area's 13 municipalities. Toronto participants expressed fears that the city would become the area's principal provider of low-cost housing and social services, and said the suburbs should do their part. Suburban governments did not want low-rental housing, however, or the higher social service costs they expected it to bring.[45] The social issue that most concerned them was large and growing disparities in the funding of public schools. Because the City of Toronto's healthy commercial and industrial tax base allowed it to spend more per pupil than most other municipalities in the area, some of the most disadvantaged schools were in the suburbs.[46]

Excursions into city and regional planning

Conflicting ideas about the region's most pressing needs emerged not only in critical assessments of its local government system, but also in early ventures into local and regional planning. Toronto's first comprehensive plan was produced in 1943 by an advisory planning board appointed by the City Council in 1942 at the instigation of the Board of Trade and other civic organizations. Billed as a "metropolitan plan," this document took in a semi-circular, 259-

---

43. Toronto Bureau of Municipal Research, "Letter to Electors Regarding the Civic Election on January 1, 1947."

44. City of Toronto Minutes, 1947, Appendix C, 91.

45. Lemon 1985, 90; Toronto Reconstruction Council, *Report of Housing Committee*, December 1948, 4.

46. Mimico Research Committee, "Metropolitan Area of Toronto and Suburbs, Report to the Members of the Council of the Corporation of the Town of Mimico," August 1949.

square kilometre territory nearly three times the size of the city itself, radiating outward from downtown Toronto to a distance of 16.7 kilometres.[47]

The 1943 plan touched on many of the themes that would continue to dominate discussions about the future of the region: the interdependence of core city and suburbs; the importance of maintaining the physical and functional well-being of the core to counter trends toward physical decline and residential decentralization; the need for better services (particularly transportation) to relieve downtown congestion and accommodate the area's rapid growth; and the need for measures (such as an agricultural belt around the city) to control sprawl. It also endorsed a Toronto Parks Department proposal for a system of regional parks based on the area's many ravines.

In developing these ideas, the plan sowed the seeds of planning conflicts that would characterize city and metropolitan politics for decades to come. It called for highways (or parkways) to be built in the same ravines that it wanted reserved for recreational use; it placed equal emphasis on public transit and road improvements as ways to relieve downtown congestion; and it called for the replacement of older residential neighbourhoods near the downtown with multiple-unit buildings (apartments and office towers). The City Council did not act on the plan, however, finding it "not entirely satisfactory."[48] It could do little in any case, because the province had not given municipal governments the authority to plan for their own communities, let alone for territory outside their boundaries. After the province provided a framework for municipal planning in a *Planning Act* passed in 1946, the Council dissolved the advisory planning board and appointed a City of Toronto Planning Board with a mandate to produce an Official Plan for the city alone.[49]

The plan produced by the City of Toronto Planning Board and adopted by City Council in 1949 was a more prosaic, less visionary document than the plan of 1943. Although it emphasized that new highways, measures to improve the city's appearance, and the redevelopment of downtown residential districts were important to the city's economy and living conditions, it advised against further spending of city tax dollars on new housing developments. These costs, it said, should be paid by the federal and provincial governments. The plan also advised the city not to spend heavily on new parks.

While Toronto was working on its first Official Plan, the Ontario government was trying to engage Toronto area municipalities in efforts to address regional problems collectively. In 1946 the cabinet used its new planning legislation to appoint a Toronto and Suburban Planning Board to prepare an

47. Moore 1979, 326; City Planning Board of Toronto 1943.

48. City of Toronto Planning Board 1959, 9.

49. A plan became "official" only after it had been adopted by a municipal council and had been approved by the Ontario Minister of Municipal Affairs.

area-wide plan to which the plans of the city and its 12 suburbs would have to conform. When the suburbs refused to help pay for this work, the government placed the Board under the jurisdiction of the County of York (which contained all of Toronto's 12 suburbs), renamed it the Toronto and York Planning Board (TYPB), and made the county responsible for paying the suburban share of its costs.[50]

These two planning boards focused mainly on the need to improve the area's transportation, sewage disposal, and water supply systems. The TYPB also endorsed the idea of incorporating river valleys and other open space into a "green belt" that would pass through five of the twelve suburban municipalities. In doing so, it noted that a few municipalities had already acquired land within this green belt for parks. Others, however, were unwilling to contribute to parklands located in municipalities other than their own.[51]

The TYPB concluded that only a unified metropolitan government could solve the area's problems, and in late 1949, it recommended that the city be amalgamated with its suburbs. The City of Toronto Council reached the same conclusion, endorsed the TYPB report by a vote of 19–2, and asked the OMB to authorize the change.[52]

Suburban governments had other ideas. Some suburban officials defended the status quo, saying that the problems would recede as the suburbs matured, or that the province should do what needed to be done. The only suburban council to propose an alternative to amalgamation was the small Town of Mimico, one of the area's older suburban municipalities, which asked the OMB to approve a special services board to provide seven major public works on a regional basis.[53]

With a population of just over 11,000 and a land area of less than 500 acres, Mimico had little ability to take advantage of the development opportunities that came with post-war expansion. Furthermore, its high ratio of residential to industrial/commercial assessment (75:25) made its government highly dependent on taxes paid by a predominantly working-class population. It was a good example, therefore, of the type of municipality that is ill-equipped to take advantage of opportunities that come with urban expansion.

Other inner suburbs had even higher ratios of residential to commercial assessment than Mimico, but they also had higher proportions of middle-class and well-to-do homeowners. Particularly noteworthy was the wealthy suburban village of Forest Hill, which had 90 per cent of its assessable property

50. Colton 1980, 61.
51. Toronto and York Planning Board 1949, 36.
52. Colton 1980, 64.
53. Ibid., 67; Rose 1972, 19–20.

in residential use but still had the area's highest per capita assessment.[54] As a result, its government not only managed to spend more per capita than all other municipalities in the area, but its taxes were lower than those of all but three of them.

With Mimico's and Toronto's very different applications before the OMB, Ontario Premier Leslie Frost tried again to get municipal representatives in the Toronto area to work out their differences themselves. The attempt only helped to make those differences more apparent.[55] In June 1950, therefore, Frost allowed the OMB to begin hearings on the two applications.

Architects of change

Applications to the OMB were customarily heard by only one Board member, and in this case the task fell to Lorne Cumming, whom the government had asked to chair the Board only a few months before the hearings began. Cumming was a former Solicitor for the City of Windsor and an active member of the Community Planning Association of Canada, which in 1946 had asked the provincial government to enact legislation "'to enable the planning of housing on a metropolitan basis in the Toronto area.'"[56] He was already familiar, therefore, with some of the issues that were fuelling the regional debate.

Although the government would adhere closely to Cumming's recommendations when it set up Metropolitan Toronto in 1953, he was only one of three individuals who played important roles in getting Metropolitan Toronto launched. The second was Premier Frost, who had replaced George Drew as Conservative party leader and provincial premier in 1948, and who would lead the party into an election for the first time in 1951. Frost had supported Drew and other members of the "progressive" wing of the Conservative party when it developed the 22-point program on which it fought the 1943 election. In fact, Frost's own suggestions for party reform were similar to those later outlined in the Conservative platform.[57]

As an ex-officio member of York County Council, Frost had become disillusioned with that council's unwillingness to act on problems in the county's fast-growing southern municipalities. He was also a shrewd politician, however, and well aware of the dangers posed to his party and his own position within it by the wide differences of opinion about how the Toronto area should be governed. His instinct, therefore, was to look for a safe path through the

---

54. Milner 1957, 572.
55. Colton 1980, 65.
56. Quoted in McMahon 1990, 14.
57. Graham 1990, 80–81.

political minefield that Toronto's metropolitan problem had become. He kept closely in touch with the OMB hearings, therefore, consulting with Cumming frequently as they progressed.[58]

The third and most colourful figure in the story of Metro's formation was Frederick Gardiner, a long-time and active member of the Progressive Conservative party, and one who had also supported the party's adoption of a "progressive" platform in 1942. Although he was a family friend and close adviser of Premier Frost, he argued strongly for the amalgamation option before the OMB, having come to accept the City of Toronto's view that full unification of city and suburbs was a "sine qua non" of the area's economic prosperity, which he very much wanted to see.[59]

Like the City Council itself, Gardiner was a convert to the cause of amalgamation. Only a few years earlier, while serving as Reeve of the Village of Forest Hill, he had been an ardent defender of local autonomy, including the right of Forest Hill to refuse to share its assets with any of its poorer neighbours. He had also opposed the idea of transferring any local services to York County. What changed his mind was his service on the York County Roads Commission, the Toronto and Suburban Planning Board, and its successor, the Toronto and York Planning Board, where he discovered that it was virtually impossible to persuade suburban governments to contribute money to regional projects, even after they had agreed to them in principle. By February 1949, therefore, he was telling Premier Frost that "'nothing short of a unified municipality' could measure up to the problems facing the metropolis."[60]

The institutional compromise: A metropolitan federation

Frost's more accommodating approach would prevail in the arrangement for the Toronto area that Cumming recommended and the province largely adopted in 1953. What the government put in place was a federation of the City of Toronto and 12 suburban municipalities (Figure 2.1) in which new metropolitan organizations became responsible for providing area-wide services, and existing municipalities remained in charge of more local matters. Although Gardiner never wavered in his support for amalgamation while the hearings were going on, he accepted the decision with good grace. Frost immediately asked him to serve as Metropolitan Toronto Council's first chair, which he agreed to do for only one year. He held the job until 1961, however, serving as the elected choice of Metro Council after his first term was over.

---

58. Colton 1980, 69.
59. Ibid., 65.
60. Quoted in Colton 1980, 63.

Figure 2.1 Metro Toronto administrative boundaries, 1953

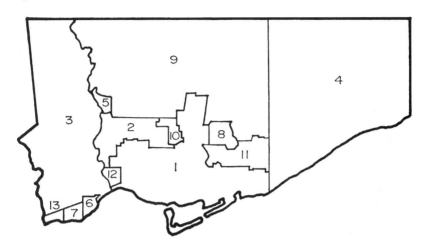

1 City of Toronto	8 Town of Leaside
2 Township of York	9 Township of North York (1922)
3 Township of Etobicoke	10 Village of Forest Hill (1923)
4 Township of Scarborough	11 Township of East York (1924)
5 Town of Weston	12 Village of Swansea (1925)
6 Town of Mimico	13 Village of Long Branch (1930)
7 Town of New Toronto	

Rose (1972), 93 [scanned reproduction].

The Council over which Gardiner presided was made up of 12 representatives from the city and one representative from each of the 12 suburban councils. The province also created a Metropolitan Toronto School Board (MTSB), its members selected by the area's 11 local public school boards.[61] A Metropolitan Separate School Board would operate all Roman Catholic schools in the area.

The new system was a compromise between the extremes of general purpose, authoritative, metropolitan-area government on the one hand and a consultative forum of local officials on the other. While giving metropolitan and local units clear mandates to perform some functions, the province left it up to municipal officials to decide what to do about several of the concerns that had fuelled the case for change. It also assigned a few important functions (notably public transit, public housing, and metropolitan planning) to special-purpose agencies headed by appointed boards or commissions, thereby placing them beyond the direct control of local or metropolitan councils (see Figure 2.2).

---

61. The Lakeshore municipalities of Mimico, New Toronto, and Long Branch had consolidated their school boards in 1951.

Figure 2.2 Toronto region governance, 1958[a]

Function	Ontario government	Toronto Region	Metropolitan Toronto	Area Municipalities	Intergovernmental
Education	Department of Education		**Metropolitan Toronto School Board**[b] **Metropolitan Toronto Separate School Board**	**11 municipal boards of education**	
Finance			Assessment Dept. Treasury Department	Municipal finance departments	
Housing			Welfare and Housing Department **Metropolitan Toronto Housing Company Limited** (housing for elderly persons)	**Housing Authority of Toronto** (public housing in the city) **City of Toronto Limited Dividend Housing Corp.** **York Township Housing Company Limited** (housing for elderly persons)	**Metropolitan Toronto Housing Authority** (federal–provincial: public housing in Metro Toronto.)
Infrastructure (*water, sewers, waste disposal*)		**Metropolitan Toronto and Region Conservation Authority**	Works Department	Works or Works and Transportation departments	
Libraries				**Municipal Public Library Boards**	
Parks			Parks Department	Parks or Parks and Recreation departments	

Function	Ontario government	Toronto Region	Metropolitan Toronto	Area Municipalities	Intergovernmental
Planning/ Land Use	Department of Municipal Affairs **Ontario Municipal Board**	**Metropolitan Toronto Planning Board**		**Municipal planning boards**	
Protection	**Ontario Provincial Police**			Municipal fire departments	**Metropolitan Board of Commissioners of Police** (provincial–municipal)
Public Health				Local departments or **Boards of Health**	
Social and Community			Welfare and Housing Department	Municipal Social Services departments	**Children's Aid Societies** (provincial/ metropolitan or county)
Transportation	Department of Highways	**Toronto and York Roads Commission**	Roads Department Traffic Engineering Dept. **Toronto Transit Commission**	Transportation or Works and Transportation departments **Toronto and other municipal Parking Authorities**	**Toronto Harbour Commission**

a. This Figure includes only those departments and agencies engaged in activities of particular importance to regional development and well-being. As interpreters and administrators of provincial laws, provincial departments influenced the content and delivery of all services provided to municipal populations. Also, there was a large number of special-purpose bodies providing services in both Metropolitan Toronto and municipalities in the region. See, for example, DelGuidice and Zacks 1972.

b. All units in bold type were special-purpose bodies. Municipal school boards differed from other special-purpose bodies in being directly elected by local voters. Some locally elected members of the local school boards represented those boards on the Metropolitan Toronto School Board. Members of other special-purpose bodies were appointed by the Metropolitan Toronto or municipal councils, and/or the provincial or federal governments.

Sources: Kaplan 1967, 51; Rose 1972, 23–44; Royal Commission on Metropolitan Toronto 1965, 38–77.

Thus it was a more institutionally fragmented and complex arrangement than is usually intended by those who argue for regional unification.

Because it was created after repeated failures to achieve similar federations in the United States, the new system was heralded as an innovative and politically courageous initiative, and as evidence that the Canadian and American systems of government addressed urban issues in fundamentally different ways.[62] Nonetheless, as Cumming was careful to point out, it was an incremental rather than a radical change in Ontario's local government system.[63] Not only had Ontario had a two-tier system of local government for more than 100 years, but Canada itself was a political federation based on the idea "that the establishment of a strong central authority is the best method of dealing with vital problems affecting the entire area, and a conviction that the retention of local governments for local purposes is not only desirable but necessary."[64]

The most radical element of Metro's creation was the incorporation of the City of Toronto into a two-tier arrangement in which it had to contribute to the costs of services provided by upper-tier agencies. A smaller York County with a considerably reduced population and property tax base continued to exist in the rural area north of Metro.

Who did what, and why

Under the two-tier arrangement, Metro Council became responsible for property assessment, major physical infrastructure (sewers, water mains, and roads), metropolitan parks, and the administration of justice. The 13 municipal councils remained responsible for financing and administering local infrastructure (water supply and sewage disposal, local streets), local parks, social welfare, public health, fire protection, libraries, and property tax collection. They were also responsible for policing and licensing until 1957, when these functions were transferred to Metropolitan Toronto, to be administered by special-purpose agencies.

In making his case for restructuring, Cumming stated that

> [t]he basic problem to be solved in the Toronto metropolitan area is
> indicated in the significant contrast between the underlying social
> and economic unity of the area on the one hand, and the illogical

---

62. Birkhead 1974; Committee for Economic Development, Research and Policy Committee 1970.

63. Ontario Municipal Board 1953, 90.

64. Ibid., 44–45.

and inequitable but extremely rigid divisions of political jurisdiction and available taxable resources on the other.[65]

He returned to this point at the end of his report, emphasizing that his recommendations adhered to a principle already operating at the county level: that the costs of important common services should be distributed among their recipients according to their ability to pay, not according to the level of services they received. He applied the principle mainly to the funding of physical services, however, thereby indicating that the most compelling reason for giving the Toronto region a metropolitan government was to hasten the construction of new infrastructure to sustain suburban growth; other functions were secondary. Even so, the system that he recommended and that the province adopted meant a substantial redistribution of local tax dollars to raise money for Metro. Cumming also implied that it was just a first step toward "a more general acceptance of [the cost-sharing principle] … in the field of local government," which he saw as necessary "to the success of any plan of metropolitan government for the Toronto region."[66]

Financing the New Arrangements

Property taxes and revenue sharing

Of the various sources of revenue used to fund services in Metropolitan Toronto, property taxes were by far the most important. In 1954, Metro's first year of operation, they paid for 70 per cent of Metro's costs, including its contributions to public education.[67] Metro collected this money from member municipalities according to the size of their assessments. Some of it went to the Metropolitan Toronto School Board, which combined it with provincial grants and reallocated it to area boards in the form of "maintenance assistance payments" (MAPs) to enable poorer boards to improve the quality of education they offered.

Reactions from suburban politicians were mixed, and seemed to depend on what their municipalities might expect from the new arrangements. For example, the Mayor of Leaside, a village with a large industrial tax base, foresaw "a frightening and fantastic increase in taxes."[68] The Reeve of York Township, on the other hand, called it "a major step forward in the develop-

---

65. Ibid., 43.
66. Ibid., 90.
67. Royal Commission on Metropolitan Toronto 1965, 98.
68. Sam Crystal, "Hot fight likely over federation," *Toronto Telegram*, January 22, 1953.

Table 2.1: Changes in per capita assessment,
Metropolitan Toronto and area municipalities, 1954–1964

	Per Capita Assessment		Rank		% Increase
	1954	1964	1954	1964	1954–1964
Metro Toronto	2,073	2,613			26.0
East York	1,413	1,794	12	12	27.0
Etobicoke	2,174	2,998	5	4	37.9
Forest Hill	2,803	3,432	3	3	22.4
Leaside	3,093	4,178	1	1	35.1
Long Branch	1,287	1,873	13	10	45.5
Mimico	1,541	1,947	11	9	26.3
New Toronto	2,927	3,435	2	2	17.4
North York	1,830	2,519	8	7	37.7
Scarborough	1,586	1,969	9	8	24.1
Swansea	2,075	2,519	6	7	21.4
Toronto	2,265	2,990	4	5	32.0
Weston	1,960	2,618	7	6	33.6
York	1,581	1,802	10	11	14.0

Source: Royal Commission on Metropolitan Toronto 1965, 81. Based on data prepared by the Metropolitan Toronto Assessment Department.

ment of sane municipal government." He spoke for a municipality that was all that had remained of a much larger township after various parts had been annexed to Toronto or had broken away to form separate municipalities (including Leaside). In 1954 Leaside ranked first and York tenth among Metro's 13 municipalities in total assessment per capita (Table 2.1).

City of Toronto politicians, on the other hand, were almost unanimous in their opposition to federation. With 56.7 per cent of Metropolitan Toronto's population (1953) but 62 per cent of its tax base (1954),[69] Toronto would pay a disproportionately large share of Metro's costs. Moreover, it was required to turn over to Metro its major capital assets—sewage disposal plants, waterworks, major roads, a public transit system, and a large park on Toronto Island, just off the city's southern shore. "We seem to be requested to give everything, and in return we get nothing but possibly higher taxes," said one alderman.[70] "It's like taking a page from Karl Marx," said another.[71]

City department heads also expressed "alarm," insisting that amalgamation would have been the better option for the city. The Mayor of Toronto,

69. Royal Commission on Metropolitan Toronto 1965, 11, 78.
70. "City taken for a ride while suburbs gain—Aldermen's views." *Toronto Telegram*, January 22, 1953.
71. "Federation plan hits Council." *Toronto Telegram*, February 2, 1953.

on the other hand, called it "the greatest opportunity possible."[72] He cast the only vote in favour of Metro when the Council expressed its opinion in a non-binding vote.[73]

In the years that followed, city politicians would continue to complain that Toronto had got the worst of a bad financial bargain. Whether or not they were justified must remain an open question. As Frank Smallwood observed 10 years after Metro's formation, it is impossible to compare the Metro Toronto that existed in 1963 with the Toronto that would have existed if Metro had never been created.[74] What can be said, however, is that over the next 40 years, the City of Toronto fared better than most other North American central cities in the sense of retaining economic investment, a socially balanced population, and a healthy tax base as the city-region continued to expand outward.

Centralized borrowing

Important to the workings of the Metro system was the sole right given to Metro Council to borrow or to approve borrowing for all metropolitan and local purposes, including the construction of new schools. Like other Ontario municipalities, Metro could borrow to cover only capital costs, not operating expenses, and had to have its borrowing approved by the OMB. At the same time, the provincial government made borrowing easier by repealing a law requiring municipal governments to ask for voter approval before they spent money on new capital projects.

Metro inherited the high credit rating formerly enjoyed by the City of Toronto, which meant that it and its member municipalities could finance new infrastructure at lower interest rates than the rates available to many of the former suburbs. Metro also became responsible for all existing school board debt and for part of the cost of new school construction; local school boards were required to pay off the rest.

Other local revenue sources

In addition to borrowing money, Metro's local governments raised money from two other sources: fees charged to users of metropolitan and local services, and "lot levies" on developers to pay for roads, sewers, and water facilities. Cash-strapped municipal governments had begun to impose these levies on developers in the 1950s as a condition of subdivision approval. OMB

72. Ibid.
73. Oliver 1985, 54–55.
74. Smallwood 1963, 4.

Commissioner Cumming criticized the practice in his 1953 report, saying that it added to the costs of housing, "especially for the workers required by the industries so eagerly sought by the municipalities themselves.[75] Nonetheless, Metro Chairman Frederick Gardiner persuaded the government to let Metro municipalities continue to tap this source of funds for physical services (sewers, water mains, and roads). In 1959 the government revised the *Planning Act* to make the practice legal for all municipalities in Ontario.[76]

Increased provincial grants

The creation of Metro coincided with the introduction of a new provincial grant structure that increased provincial aid to municipalities. The government also replaced assessment-based grants with grants that took population size and other factors into account. Their purpose, it said, was to help defray the costs of welfare, social services, and the administration of justice.[77]

The changes in provincial grants followed recommendations made by a Provincial–Municipal Relations Committee established in 1951, the first of a succession of committees that would examine and recommend changes in the provincial–municipal financial relationship in Ontario.[78] Because the introduction of new grants coincided with the legislation that created Metropolitan Toronto, they helped reduce local political opposition to restructuring. The province also made small grants to assist Metro with some of its capital projects and continued to subsidize road construction both by Metro and by the local municipalities. In 1958 it reduced the municipal contribution to general welfare assistance from 40 to 20 per cent, and the municipal share of the cost of clearing land for housing from 50 to 25 per cent.

After allowing its education grants to decline as a proportion of school costs in the early 1950s, the government began to work on a new grant system in 1957. Complicating this effort was the divisive issue of the Separate (Roman Catholic) School Boards, which administered a system of denominational public education that had been guaranteed by the *British North America Act* in 1867.[79] These boards had access only to those property taxes that local tax-

---

75. Ontario Municipal Board 1953, 24.

76. Colton 1980, 24; Ontario Municipal Board 1953, 126; Slack and Bird 1991. For a more detailed discussion of the role of development charges in financing Metro's development, see White 2003, 22–24.

77. Budget Statement of the Honourable Leslie M. Frost, Premier and Treasurer of the Province of Ontario, in the Legislative Assembly of Ontario, Thursday, March 11, 1954 (Toronto: Baptist Johnson).

78. Ontario Provincial–Municipal Relations Committee 1953.

79. This Act of the Bristish parliament had united Upper and Lower Canada—later Ontario and Quebec—with the British provinces of New Brunswick and Nova Scotia, and

payers (both residential and commercial) specifically assigned to them. They were also eligible for provincial grants, but only up to the end of elemntary school. Any move to increase these grants met with strong resistance from the provincial electorate.

The issue was of particular interest to the City of Toronto, where a growing number of Roman Catholic immigrant children were crowding into the separate schools. Many of the parents of these children were not home-owners and so did not pay school taxes, and the Separate School Board was threatening to turn these children away, a move that would add to pressures on the city's public schools.[80] Those schools were already handicapped by a provincial grant structure that awarded grants in inverse ratio to assessment (as a way to help assessment-poor school districts), without taking account of the high costs of building new schools or upgrading old ones in fast-growing areas.

The new grant system adopted in 1958 aimed to overcome these prob-lems without making major concessions to separate schools. The government not only increased the size of its grants, but also began to base them on school attendance rather than total municipal population. It added a "growth-needs factor" that made additional funds available to schools in rapidly growing municipalities. It also began to apply an equalization factor to local assess-ments to achieve a fairer basis for calculating assessment-based grants.

In general, therefore, after 1958 the province based its grants to municipal institutions on the principle that population size and rate of population growth usually meant higher costs for providing local services, a bias that worked in Metropolitan Toronto's favour.

An ill-defined but important federal presence

The search for ways to improve public services in the Toronto area began when the federal government seemed about to play a much larger role in urban affairs than it had done in the past. It had set aside funds for post-war reconstruction that included money for new urban infrastructure. A federal government agency, Wartime Housing Limited, was already negotiating with municipal governments about the development of housing for war workers and veterans. The federal government also gave money to the City of Toronto to help cover the costs of emergency housing, some of which was in federal buildings that had been converted for that purpose.[81] Federal government

---

specified its form of government.

80. Graham 1990, 384.

81. Toronto City Council Minutes 1947, Appendix A, 57.

requirements attached to its housing assistance had helped to stimulate the City of Toronto to take an interest in planning in the early 1940s, and later to persuade the provincial government to give municipal governments authority to plan.[82] The TTC had also used the prospect of a federal government grant in its campaign to sell the idea of a subway to the city's electors in the 1945 referendum.[83]

The promise of direct federal aid to city governments was short-lived, however. The amended *National Housing Act* adopted by the federal government in 1949 required the Central (later Canada) Mortgage and Housing Corporation to enter into housing partnerships with provincial governments before it could allocate federal money to low-rental housing projects. Provincial governments were responsible for initiating and administering such projects, although they could delegate that responsibility to municipal governments. Costs were split between the two senior levels of government on a 75/25 (federal/provincial) basis, but provincial governments could pass some of these costs on to municipal governments. The Ontario government required municipalities to pay 7.5 per cent of both the capital and operating costs of public housing.

Federal support for subway construction did not materialize, because the project did not meet federal funding criteria. One of these—that federally funded public works projects had to generate jobs—became redundant as the economy continued to improve. Although Metro was able to borrow some money from the federal government for capital purposes, its efforts to secure federal grants for its public works program were largely unsuccessful.[84]

Despite its lack of financial involvement in Metro programs, the federal government was a silent player in Metro finance. The provincial government often cited the growing financial needs of municipalities to justify its frequent demands for more federal money. The federal government responded to these demands by gradually granting Ontario and other provinces an increasing portion of the income tax and by agreeing to share the costs of a number of provincially supported services, such as general welfare assistance, technical and vocational training (although this ended in 1963), hospital insurance, old age pensions, and family allowances.

During this period the federal and provincial governments also worked out an agreement for a federally administered equalization program, as had been recommended by the Rowell-Sirois Commission in 1940. Derived from the federal government's share of the income tax, equalization payments would

---

82. Toronto City Council Minutes 1941, Appendix A, 1512.
83. Toronto City Council Minutes 1946, Appendix A, 481.
84. Colton 1980, 132–136.

go to provinces whose total revenues from a variety of sources fell below a specified minimum. In reversing his government's long-standing opposition to such payments, Premier Frost agreed to a policy that would make Ontario, Canada's wealthiest province, a net contributor to the coffers of all other provinces.[85] Although Ontario attached some conditions to its agreement, the policy embodied a principle of intergovernmental sharing that the government would find hard to ignore in deciding how to exercise its responsibilities for municipalities and manage intermunicipal relations.

As cost-sharing programs made new federal funds available, the province expanded its own programs, some of which it administered jointly with municipal governments. At times it also reduced the shares it required municipal governments to contribute, as in the case of general welfare assistance. Therefore, while federal contributions to municipal services were virtually invisible to local residents, they were still important to Metro's physical and social development.

Assessing Metro's Performance

Because it was unique at the time it was created, Metropolitan Toronto attracted a good deal of scrutiny from urban professionals and students of urbanism. They were virtually unanimous in concluding that Metro had accomplished its principal objective: to speed up the provision of infrastructure to support suburban population growth and industrial expansion.[86]

There were also criticisms, however, both from disgruntled politicians who felt that their municipalities were ill-served by the Metro system and from sections of the community and the media. The government began to act on these in 1957 when it asked Lorne Cumming, author of the 1953 OMB report, to head up a Commission of Inquiry into all aspects of Metropolitan Toronto's affairs. The Commission found little wrong with Metro as it was, however, and nothing came of its work.[87] Further studies and reports followed, culminating in a comprehensive examination of the entire Metro system conducted by labour lawyer Carl Goldenberg, appointed by the provincial government in 1963 as a one-person Royal Commission on Metropolitan Toronto. Goldenberg's report, published in 1965, would provide the rationale for several important changes in the structure and responsibilities of Metro institutions legislated in 1966. His and other studies and their background

---

85. Budget Statement of the Honourable James N. Allan, Treasurer of Ontario, in the Legislative Assembly of Ontario, February 12, 1964; Martin 1974, 10–11.

86. See, for example, Kaplan 1967, 246–263; Rose 1972, 155–156; Royal Commission on Metropolitan Toronto 1965, 172–175.

87. Rose 1980, 40–44.

reports provided a large amount of information about what Metro institutions had accomplished or failed to accomplish in their first decade of operation.

Rapid provision of new infrastructure

The first task carried out on a metropolitan-wide basis in the early 1950s was a reassessment of all properties in the area, using a provincial manual based on 1940 property values. OMB Commissioner Lorne Cumming described this work as "essential to the operation of any type of metropolitan government," and the province appointed a Greater Toronto Assessment Board to carry it out even before it received Cumming's report. The work of this Board enabled Metro to implement tax-sharing arrangements that allowed it to move ahead quickly with infrastructure construction.

Metro's rapid production of new infrastructure was credited with a rapid surge in the region's economy. Metro's total non-residential (industrial and commercial) assessment rose by nearly 80 per cent between 1954 and 1964, while the area's population grew by only 41 per cent.[88] "A magnificent development machine," was how one American writer would later describe Toronto's metropolitan system in its early years.[89]

Public transit on the sidelines

Of the metropolitan agencies devoted to improving metropolitan infrastructure, the one that gave least satisfaction was the Toronto Transit Commission, which became responsible for integrating city and suburban transit companies into a metropolitan system in 1953. Criticisms of this agency's performance came mainly from suburban politicians, who claimed that the TTC did not move fast enough to bring services to their municipalities or wards. They also objected to a zone-fare system, instituted when the TTC became a metropolitan agency, that required suburban riders to pay more than city riders to travel to downtown Toronto. In other words, the suburban politicians wanted the TTC to do more than help sustain or promote development in the downtown core; they also wanted it to promote intermunicipal equity in transit access and mobility.

Suburban dissatisfaction with TTC performance made transit a source of city–suburban disputes in which the city sided with the TTC on the zone-fare question, insisting that city tax dollars and city transit riders should not subsidize suburban transit users. They also pitted the TTC, a venerable

88. Royal Commission on Metropolitan Toronto 1965, 78, 11.
89. Mogulof 1972, 56.

institution with a reputation for efficient management and a strong desire to guard its autonomy, against a recently created political body that was still trying to define itself. At one point they became a personal quarrel between two colourful and outspoken individuals, Metro Chairman Fred Gardiner and TTC Chair Allan Lamport. At the root of all these disputes was the provincially imposed requirement that the TTC be self-supporting. With Metro's creation, the size of the TTC's service area had immediately increased from 91 to 622 square kilometres (much of it still sparsely populated). The TTC also had to unite the city system with eight suburban bus lines, four of which it was already operating under contract to municipal governments, and four of which were owned and operated by independent bus companies.

The TTC, therefore, began life as a metropolitan agency with a debt to the metropolitan corporation of $66.6 million ($13 million for the purchase of bus lines and $53.6 million to complete the subway begun in 1949).[90] At the same time, its ridership had begun to drop because of an increase in automobile use after the war. To try to keep its costs under control, the TTC not only introduced the zone-fare policy but also refused to provide service to new districts until residential densities were high enough to generate enough riders to make those services cost-effective. This operating philosophy not only led to conflicts between the TTC and disgruntled members of Metro Council, but also created dissension between TTC staff and its politically appointed governing board.[91]

Adding to the TTC's difficulties was the fact that those involved with Metro's creation did not view transit as being as important to the area's development and economic success as sewer, water, and road facilities. Thus they did not feel the same need to ensure that development of the transit system kept pace with the development of the built-up area. As Metro got underway, therefore, transit operated in relative isolation from the rest of the Metro bureaucracy. Although this arrangement suited TTC management, because it wanted to keep transit decisions free from political interference, it meant that those responsible for operating the transit system were less involved than other Metro officials in making decisions about the way the area would develop.

Transit did win an early ally in Chairman Gardiner, however, despite his fervent belief in the area's need for new roads and highways.[92] Under his leadership, Metro had acted quickly to acquire and then improve arterial roads and to plan a system of limited-access highways serving all parts of Metro. After only two years as Metro Chair, though, Gardiner concluded that high-

90. Toronto Transit Commission, *Annual Report*, 1955, 6.
91. Kaplan 1967, 137–140.
92. Colton 1980, 61.

ways alone would not meet the area's growing transportation needs. He then set out to persuade Metro Council and the federal and provincial governments to support the construction of new rapid transit lines. In 1958 Metro Council agreed to pay 55 per cent of the construction costs of an east–west subway along Bloor Street, with the TTC to pay the rest.

Gardiner got nowhere with the federal government, however, and the provincial government refused help for several years. Premier Frost was "particularly unreceptive," his "general preference for the automobile ... [being] reinforced by the province's financial stake in road transportation"—meaning the provincial tax on gasoline.[93] The government gave Metro short-term help to cover transit costs, but did not make a long-term commitment to transit until 1963.

Despite the fractious nature of transit politics, the TTC still operated in a political environment that was more favourable to public transit than that found in most North American cities. Not only was there less senior government money available for highway building than there was in the United States,[94] but Metro planners promoted the merits of a transportation plan that provided a "balance" between highways and transit, with transit presented as the best way to move people into or around more densely populated districts.[95]

Within this context, the TTC performed well when compared to other North American transit systems. By 1963 Metro had two north–south subways (the Yonge Street and University Avenue lines), both paid for by the TTC, and Metro Council had approved and said it would help to pay for an east–west line (the Bloor subway). As these lines opened, the TTC added new bus services to feed passengers to subway stations. Between 1953 and 1963, the number of surface routes in Metro increased from 53 to 80 and the number of route miles increased from 244 to 428. Because of this activity, together with a reduction in the number of fare zones from five to two, transit ridership in Metro declined by only 30 per cent between 1953 and 1963, compared to 48 per cent in other Canadian cities and 57 per cent in the United States.[96]

---

93. Ibid., 167.
94. Beginning in 1956, the U.S. government paid 90 per cent of the cost of interstate highways, some of which penetrated or traversed large cities. State governments usually paid some of the remaining costs. Urban transportation planners worked hard, therefore, to integrate their highway plans with the interstate system. The Ontario government paid only 50 per cent of Metro's highway costs, leaving Metro to pay the rest.
95. Dakin 1969, 18–22.
96. Royal Commission on Metropolitan Toronto, 1965, 44.

Paying for and managing the costs of regional services

One argument for regional government reform that was not emphasized by proponents of local government restructuring in the Toronto metropolitan area was the idea that a larger, more unified form of governance would reduce service costs. A comprehensive study of the area's problems concluded, in fact, that

> any system of metropolitan government would be likely to cost the taxpayers more, in total, than the sum of present municipal expenditures. The advantage of a metropolitan system will lie in spreading costs more equally throughout the area and not—unless present services are skimped or future development improperly delayed—in reducing overall costs. At the same time, an improved structure of government should make it possible to secure a fuller return in municipal services and improvements for each tax dollar.[97]

Frederick Gardiner argued similarly that costs were likely to rise, not fall, under a metropolitan government, mainly because labour costs would go up.[98] He insisted nonetheless that the change would enable the area to realize its potential for growth.

As Gardiner had predicted, spending on almost all local services increased relative to assessment after Metropolitan Toronto's restructuring, and debt costs rose by nearly 71 per cent. (The only area in which spending declined was health, undoubtedly because the federal and provincial governments substantially increased their support for hospital construction.) Commissioner Goldenberg argued, however, that "costs would have risen whatever system of local government prevailed" because of "the growth of the area and the consequent expansion of municipal services."[99] He also concluded that Metro's monopoly over borrowing would save area taxpayers "millions of dollars" by the time the debts were repaid.[100] Gail Cook, who documented a substantial rise in education costs in Metro as compared to other Ontario cities, came to a slightly different conclusion. "Metropolitan government," she wrote, "may ... more appropriately be viewed as a means of equalizing standards of service,

97. Toronto Civic Advisory Council, The Committee on Metropolitan Problems 1951, 14.
98. Colton 1980, 64.
99. Royal Commission on Metropolitan Toronto 1965, 177.
100. Ibid., 110.

coordinating existing services; and, in general, raising service standards," than as a way of achieving economies of scale.[101]

The advantages of metropolitan government for the public purse went mainly to the province because Metro's creation meant that most of the costs of Metro services were paid out of local taxes rather than the provincial budget. The province did not avoid such costs entirely, because it made grants to help Metro avoid large tax increases for capital projects.[102] Nonetheless Metro did help to save the province money. Provincial grants to Metro increased by the same percentage (2.6 per cent) as provincial grants to non-Metro municipalities, even though Metro's share of the provincial population grew from 25.2 per cent in 1953 to 26.7 per cent in 1963.[103] This meant that the province's per capita share of Metro costs was lower by 1963 than it had been 10 years earlier.

It is not possible to say how much of the growth in the Toronto area was due to Metro's activities and how much to the growth then taking place in the Canadian economy as a whole. Nonetheless Goldenberg concluded that Metro's creation had been "a bold experiment which has been justified by the accomplishments of more than a decade of operations."[104]

There were limits, however, on how far Metro and the province were willing to go in funding new infrastructure. At the beginning, Metro Council imposed an annual ceiling on capital borrowing, which rose from $60 million in 1955 to $100 million in 1958 and then stayed at that level. In 1957, it imposed a small additional levy on member municipalities for special projects, and in 1958 dedicated income from this source to subway construction. In 1959 it added a half mill levy to education assessments to reduce the need to borrow money for new schools.[105] In general, however, Gardiner was able to keep Metro spending under the prescribed annual ceiling, but only with the help of grants and forgivable loans from both the provincial and federal governments.[106]

Temporary successes in managing regional growth

The creation of Metropolitan Toronto seemed to be a clear victory for those who had argued for a comprehensive metropolitan plan to guide the growth

101. Cook 1973, 590.
102. Royal Commission on Metropolitan Toronto 1965, 110–111.
103. Ontario Department of Municipal Affairs, *Annual Report of Municipal Statistics,* 1953.
104. Royal Commission on Metropolitan Toronto 1965, 199.
105. Ibid., 97.
106. Ibid., 111.

radiating outward from Toronto. Legislation governing the new system not only made Metro responsible for approving such a plan, but also gave it planning jurisdiction over three times as much land outside its boundaries as was contained within them (Figure 2.3). This extraterritorial responsibility was in keeping with Cumming's opinion that "the Metropolitan Council should be given a reasonable degree of planning control over the so-called 'fringe areas' otherwise beyond its jurisdiction" because of the rapid outward spread of urban settlement.[107] All other planning jurisdictions within this "metropolitan planning area" became "subsidiary planning areas," which would have to make their own official plans and public works proposals conform to the Metro plan as soon as it was approved by the province.

Metro quickly assembled a well-qualified professional planning staff to work with an appointed Metropolitan Toronto Planning Board (MTPB) to produce an official plan. The MTPB brought its first "draft official plan" to Metro Council in 1959, and a second version in 1965. Council rejected the first one out of hand and decided not to send the second one to the province for approval. Instead Metro treated it as an "unofficial official plan," to be used for advisory purposes only. It made this decision because municipal councils both inside and outside Metro were unwilling to give legal status to a document that would take precedence over municipal plans.

Another impediment to metropolitan planning was the provincial government's failure to clarify Metro's planning role vis-à-vis that of local municipalities or the province. Although provincial authorities tended to support Metro recommendations in the early years, later they treated them as having no greater weight than the more narrowly focused arguments of persons who lobbied for specialized functional agencies or local municipalities.[108]

The draft plan brought by the MTPB to Metro Council in 1965 acknowledged provincial ambivalence by claiming to deal with "those development principles, policies and regulations which are considered to be directly of Provincial concern." These included the highway system, the general pattern of development in the surrounding region, and provincial financial obligations to Metropolitan Toronto and surrounding municipalities.

> While the Province exercises a measure of direct control over municipal financial affairs through various statutory and procedural arrangements, it is evident that the basic development policies of the municipality are important in determining the ultimate financial obligations of both the municipalities and the Province.[109]

107. Ontario Municipal Board 1953, 72.
108. E. Comay, "A Brief to the Royal Commission on Metropolitan Toronto," 1964, 19–20.
109. Metropolitan Toronto Planning Board 1965, 1.

Figure 2.3 Metropolitan Toronto Planning Board planning area, 1953–71

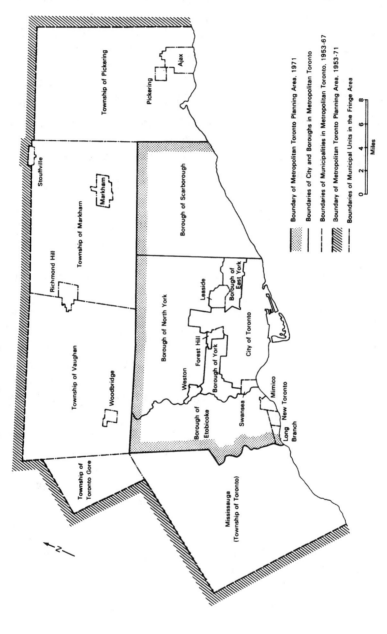

Boundary of Metropolitan Toronto Planning Area, 1971

Boundaries of City and Boroughs in Metropolitan Toronto

Boundaries of Municipalities in Metropolitan Toronto, 1953-67

Boundary of Metropolitan Toronto Planning Area, 1953-71

Boundaries of Municipal Units in the Fringe Area

Miles

Township of Pickering

Ajax

Pickering

Stouffville

Township of Markham

Markham

Borough of Scarborough

Richmond Hill

Borough of North York

Leaside

Borough of East York

Township of Vaughan

Weston

Forest Hill

Borough of York

City of Toronto

Woodbridge

Township of Toronto Gore

Borough of Etobicoke

Swansea

Mimico

New Toronto

Long Branch

Mississauga (Township of Toronto)

N

Rose (1972), 94 [scanned reproduction].

The planners' appeal to the province's interests went unheeded. The province not only accepted Metro's decision not to seek "official" status for the plan, but engaged in activities that would sharply curtail Metro's planning responsibilities. These are described in Chapter 3.

CONTRIBUTIONS OF METROPOLITAN TORONTO
PLANNERS TO A REGIONAL PLANNING CULTURE

Despite an absence of strong political support for metropolitan planning among both local and provincial officials, metropolitan planners were important participants in the governance of the Toronto region during Metro's early years. Metro used important parts of the Draft Official Plan when it adopted plans prepared by the Planning Board (or by agencies that had worked closely with the Planning Board) for sewage disposal and water supply systems, parks, conservation, roads, transit, and a public housing program.[110] Furthermore, metropolitan planners acted as unpaid advisers to local planners who were preparing local official plans. Because large parts of Metro's outer districts and even larger parts of the fringe were undeveloped when Metro was created, and because many municipalities were just beginning to prepare plans of their own, Metro planners could comment on and sometimes influence the way local municipalities allocated land among different uses. Their influence seemed to decline, however, as suburban municipalities acquired permanent planning staffs of their own.

Metro planners based their own work and the advice they gave to local planners on a set of principles that would be restated in planning documents for the rest of Metro's history, even though they were not always observed in practice.[111] They favoured a relatively compact regional urban structure with a well-defined urban boundary. Within this built-up region, the core was to remain the primary site of commercial, cultural, and institutional activities and would also contain substantial amounts of housing in the form of apartment buildings in redeveloped downtown neighbourhoods. Commercial activities situated away from the central core would be concentrated in sub-centres developed around shopping centres or major transportation nodes, with high-density housing nearby.

According to these principles, providing opportunities for new industries to locate in all parts of Metro and providing an extensive system of public and private transportation would minimize residents' need to commute while maximizing their opportunity to do so. This transportation system would provide

---

110. E. Comay, "A Brief to the Royal Commission on Metropolitan Toronto," 1964, op. cit., 23.

111. Metropolitan Toronto Planning Board 1959, S3.

good access to the centre from all parts of the area, as well as making suburban employment districts easily accessible to suburban residents. All parts of the region would have "a wide-range of housing types suitable for families of different sizes and of different income levels," but situated "in identifiable communities; without ... being isolated from the larger, metropolitan community." New areas opened up for development would be supplied with a full range of services, and all residential districts would have easy access to green belts and open areas.

Although these Metro planning principles anticipated some features of Metro's subsequent evolution, it is not clear how much influence they actually had on municipal land-use decisions. Such decisions tended to conform to the principles only when the principles fitted in with local development aspirations or won acceptance from local residents. When projects that conformed to metropolitan plans or planning principles ran into strong local resistance (as in the case of the highway elements of the Metropolitan Toronto Transportation Plan, the redevelopment of core city residential neighbourhoods at higher densities, or proposals to locate lower priced rental housing within or near middle-class neighbourhoods), the principles tended to be ignored or rejected.

TEMPORARY CONSTRAINTS ON SPRAWL

Policies that probably had more to do with promoting a higher density development pattern in Metropolitan Toronto than in most North American cities were those that constrained new urban settlement outside Metro's boundaries. These included Metro's policy of extending sewer and water services outward from the centre only as population growth and the pace of development warranted, and provincial restrictions on peripheral development based on wells and septic tanks.[112] Because of these restrictions, Metro's 63 per cent share of the 1.5 million people who settled in the Greater Toronto Area between 1951 and 1971 was probably larger than it would have been in an environment that was more conducive to suburban expansion. Metro's planning commissioner concluded, in fact, that "[t]he provision of unified services under some form of central authority would appear to be a far more effective method of regulating the size of the ultimate urban area than 'official plans' as such."[113]

Given the constraints on peripheral development, the fringe accommodated only 14 per cent of the nearly 600,000 people who swelled the population of the Metropolitan Toronto planning area between 1951 and 1961.[114] By

---

112. Bower, 1979, 21.

113. E. Comay, "A Brief to the Royal Commission on Metropolitan Toronto," 1964, op. cit., 36–37.

114. Based on figures in Metropolitan Toronto Planning Board, Research and Transportation Divisions 1974, Table 1.

the early 1960s, however, there was growing pressure on the province to allow more development outside Metropolitan Toronto. The province was also more willing to allow it to happen, even in contravention of Metropolitan Toronto planning objectives.[115] Thus any constraints Metro planners were able to impose on outward development were short-lived.

A more lasting Metro contribution to the regional land-use pattern was a comprehensive system of metropolitan parks in the ravine lands and river valleys that City of Toronto planners had earlier said should be used for that purpose. Metro owed much of that achievement to Hurricane Hazel, which caused severe damage and several deaths in river valleys in 1954. This natural disaster prompted the provincial government to appoint a Metropolitan Toronto and Region Conservation Authority (MTRCA) to protect such lands, with the provincial government to pay between 50 and 75 per cent of the costs of land acquisition, flood control, and recreational facilities.[116] The MTRCA turned some of these areas over to Metro to develop and maintain as metropolitan parks.[117] Given the reluctance of lower-tier municipal councils (including Toronto) to sacrifice potential tax revenues by allowing land to be used for parks,[118] it is likely that the Toronto area is more generously endowed with regional parks than it would have been if Metropolitan Toronto had not existed.

Intermunicipal equity remains elusive

In his detailed report on the workings of the Metro system, Commissioner Goldenberg focused much of his attention on Metro's failure to reduce inequalities in the size of local tax bases, and the amount spent on local services. Some of these differences, according to Goldenberg, were the result of the "planning for assessment" or "fiscal zoning" used by municipalities to "secure commercial and industrial assessment and the construction of expensive homes and high-rise apartments," and to keep out less expensive housing.[119] The result, as Goldenberg saw it, was that

> some of the problems described in the Cumming Report of 1953 persist and have grown. They flow from continuing "illogical and inequitable but extremely rigid divisions of political jurisdiction and available taxable resources." ... While the equalizing influence

---

115. E. Comay, "A Brief to the Royal Commission on Metropolitan Toronto," 1964, op. cit., 35.

116. Don Stevenson, private communication. January 9, 2005.

117. Royal Commission on Metropolitan Toronto 1965, 59.

118. Kaplan 1982, 724.

119. Royal Commission on Metropolitan Toronto 1965, 82.

of Metro has prevented far greater inequalities from developing, the spread between the lowest and highest taxed municipalities has tended to widen.[120]

PARITY, NOT EQUITY, IS THE MUNICIPAL GOAL

Unlike Cumming and Goldenberg, however, municipal politicians did not consider intermunicipal equity to be an important goal of metropolitan government. Instead, according to Harold Kaplan, Metro councillors (all of whom were elected to serve on local councils, and then served on Metro either *ex officio* or as appointees of local councils) judged Metro institutions according to whether or not they maintained regional balance or "parity" in the distribution of Metro funds. The "parity" objective required that the benefits that a member municipality derived from Metro spending would "bear some relation to the tax revenues Metro collected within that municipality's boundaries," and "that the city and suburbs would each receive roughly half of Metro's benefits."[121] It had nothing to do, therefore, with trying to put the area's municipal governments on a more equal financial footing or ensuring that Metro residents had access to local services of similar quality.

Metro partly satisfied the parity standard, at least in its early years, in its role as provider of basic infrastructure. Initially there were complaints from the City of Toronto that Metro spending on new roads, sewers, and water mains benefited the suburbs much more than the city, even though the city was contributing a disproportionately large share of their costs. These complaints diminished, however, after Metro Council decided to help finance the east–west subway line, a service seen to benefit the city primarily.[122] More persistent, however, were criticisms of Metro institutions for failing to deal adequately with inequalities in spending on local services, particularly welfare and education.

PERSISTENT INEQUALITIES IN SPENDING ON WELFARE AND EDUCATION

In the case of welfare, local spending in 1963 ranged from $0.91 per capita in Leaside to $19.34 per capita in Toronto.[123] The differences could be attributed to a number of factors: the City's larger per capita share of welfare recipients; the fact that the city provided a wider range of optional services (services, that is, that the province did not require municipalities to provide but that it would help to pay for); and variations in the amounts that the different municipalities spent on mandatory assistance.[124] Local politics were also important in

---

120. Ibid., 172.
121. Kaplan 1982, 687.
122. Kaplan 1967, 108–109.
123. Royal Commission on Metropolitan Toronto 1965, 93.
124. Ibid., 56–57.

determining how much a municipal government spent on this service, with the result that there were large differences in welfare spending relative to local assessment. Suburban officials insisted, however, that the level of service they provided was adequate for the populations they served, and blamed the city's high costs on an inflated welfare bureaucracy.[125] They did not want to help solve the city's problems or provide incentives for welfare recipients to move to the suburbs.[126] The Toronto Social Planning Council argued, on the other hand, that variations in services available in different parts of Metro meant hardships for some Metro residents, particularly those living in the lower priced, high-density rental housing being built in the suburbs.[127] They were also straining the capacity of voluntary agencies serving rapidly growing suburban communities.

Metro's 11 school boards also remained far apart in the amount they spent per pupil in both elementary and secondary schools, although the Metro system had benefited from the 1958 changes in the provincial grant structure.[128] Four factors, in addition to differences in assessment, contributed to the differences. First, enrolments rose more rapidly in the faster growing communities and so did school costs, including the capital costs paid by local taxpayers. Second, the province required the Metropolitan Toronto School Board to make its maintenance assistance payments (MAPs) to local school boards on a per pupil basis, which meant that the payments did nothing to reduce assessment-related differences. Third, the MAPs did not increase as fast as school capital and operating costs, forcing local boards to pay a growing share of these costs out of local taxes. Boards in high-assessment communities could do so at less cost to their taxpayers than boards in low-assessment communities. Finally, there was no limit on the amount that boards could raise on their own to supplement money received from Metro. Boards that raised considerably more than others were able to provide better facilities and attract better qualified teachers.

As a result of all these factors, per pupil spending in Metropolitan Toronto in 1963 ranged from $378 in Scarborough to $633 in Leaside for public elementary schools, and from $562 in Weston to $768 in Toronto for public secondary schools. The spending gap was considerably lower than those reported for some U.S. urban areas during the 1960s. Moreover, the gap did not imply that core city schools were in trouble. The City of Toronto was not only one of the highest spending school districts in Metro, but also had the assessment to support it. Through its contributions to Metro it also accounted for the largest per capita share of Metro's maintenance assistance payments.

---

125. McGilly 1972, 323.
126. Kaplan 1967, 114.
127. Social Planning Council of Metropolitan Toronto, 1963, 82.
128. Royal Commission on Metropolitan Toronto 1965, 134–135.

Nonetheless, Goldenberg concluded that Metro's maintenance assistance payments had "not succeeded in achieving the degree of equalization which should exist."[129]

AFFORDABLE HOUSING: ACHIEVEMENTS AND DISAPPOINTMENTS

Proponents of local government reorganization had looked to Metro to pursue three distinct housing objectives. Provincial and some suburban officials emphasized the need for moderately priced family housing for workers. Those most concerned with conditions in the City of Toronto wanted an increase in the supply of low-cost rental housing (either to ease residential overcrowding in older districts or to accommodate residents displaced by downtown redevelopment). They also argued for a more equitable distribution of low-cost rental housing throughout the metropolitan area.[130]

Metro realized the first objective relatively quickly. Between 1954 and 1961 the yearly rate of new home production was more than double the rate that had prevailed between 1948 and 1953.[131] Because the rate of production outstripped the rate of population growth, the average number of persons per dwelling declined. Metro's infrastructure program helped make this achievement possible. The federal government also helped after 1954 by insuring mortgage loans made by private lending institutions, thereby virtually freeing them from risk.

Criticisms of Metro's performance in the housing field were directed mainly at its limited progress toward meeting the second objective, that of increasing the supply of low-rental public housing, especially for families. Such criticisms dwelt mainly on Metro's failure to meet a target it had set for itself in 1958, when it had adopted a housing program that called for the construction of 5,000 units of family public housing and 2,500 units of senior citizen housing during the next five years. When it set that target, Metro had 3,170 units of family public housing either completed or near completion, 2,130 of them built or initiated by the Toronto Housing Authority before Metro got underway, the other 1,040 built by the federal–provincial partnership.[132] The partnership had appointed the Metropolitan Toronto Housing Authority (MTHA) to administer Metro's supply of family public housing after it was built, and the

---

129. Ibid., 143.

130. Toronto Civic Advisory Council, The Committee on Metropolitan Problems 1949, 20–24; Rose 1972, 28–29.

131. Colton 1980, 160.

132. Figures are based on various reports of the Metropolitan Toronto Welfare and Housing Committee. They have been rounded because of slight discrepancies in the figures used in different reports.

MTHA asked the staff of the Metropolitan Toronto Planning Board to help it to identify suitable sites throughout Metro.

By September 1964, Metro had 3,700 completed units, which meant that the federal–provincial partnership had added slightly more than 500 units, or one-tenth of Metro's five-year target, to those that were already available or becoming available in 1958. Although he was not impressed with this record, Goldenberg observed that it was consistent with what had happened in the rest of the country. "It is apparent," he wrote, "that public housing has not yet attained wide political acceptance in Canada."[133] Senior citizens had done better. By 1964 the Metropolitan Toronto Housing Company (MTHC), which Metro Council had created 10 years earlier to build low-rental housing for people in this category, had built nearly 1,900 new units—just 600 short of the Metro target. "[T]he provision of low rental units for elderly persons," Goldenberg commented, was "Metro's major [housing] accomplishment."[134]

While Goldenberg was writing his report, however, Metro also had another 5,000 units of family public housing under construction or in the proposal stage. And as Goldenberg himself acknowledged, Metro was not entirely to blame for its lack of progress. Several local agencies shared Metro's authority to build public housing in Metro, and some of them were competing for the same government funds.[135] Moreover, the means of securing those funds involved working through an application and approval process at both the federal and provincial levels of government that was Byzantine in its complexity.[136]

Metro's municipalities also helped to slow down the process. Metro planners and the MTHA found it difficult to reach agreements with different local governments about where public housing should go and how much should be built. Metro staff favoured building public housing in the suburbs, where land was cheaper and where it was easier to build family units, a view that Chairman Gardiner shared.[137] Toronto Council, on the other hand, had begun to look on public housing as an aid to the renewal of aging inner-city districts and did not want government housing funds spent in the suburbs. Suburban

---

133. Royal Commission on Metropolitan Toronto 1965, 52.
134. Ibid.
135. In addition to the MTHA and the MTHC, there was the Housing Authority of Toronto (disbanded in 1968), a City of Toronto Limited Dividend Housing Corporation created in 1956 to qualify for federally backed limited-dividend mortgage loans for moderately priced rental housing; and a Housing Company set up by York Township to build and administer housing for the elderly. Moreover, each local council was a housing authority in its own right, because each could ask the federal–provincial partnership for assistance in implementing a low-cost housing plan.
136. Feldman 1963; Royal Commission on Metropolitan Toronto 1965, 33.
137. Colton 1980, 162; E. Comay, "A Brief to the Royal Commission on Metropolitan Toronto," 1964, op. cit., 47.

governments had little or no interest in public housing, and made little use of their right to propose public housing projects themselves or to identify sites for that purpose. Instead they typically used their site approval authority to prevent or delay new projects, or to reduce the number of units that could be built.[138]

Despite these many constraints, public housing enjoyed greater success in Metropolitan Toronto than in other parts of Canada during this period. In 1964 Metro accounted for only 9 per cent of Canada's population but 30 per cent of Canada's total supply of family public housing. Similarly, with just over a quarter of Ontario's population, it had half of all family public housing built in the province by 1964.[139]

All of the new public housing built after 1959 (and some units built before that date), as well as all projects still being built or considered, were in the suburbs. The suburbs also accounted for most assisted housing for the elderly and for a substantial share of private rental housing built with the help of a limited-dividend program initiated by the federal government in 1946.[140] By the end of its first decade, therefore, Metro was well on the way toward achieving the third housing objective (Metro-wide distribution) sought by proponents of metropolitan restructuring.

Regional objectives contend with local preferences

Much of the credit for Metro's early accomplishments went to Chairman Gardiner, whose determination to get Metro to fulfill its mandate—to "get the shovels in the ground" as he put it—matched his earlier determination to convince local and provincial leaders that only a metropolitan government could do the job. Despite a sometimes abrasive or bullying manner, Gardiner showed a talent for working out agreements among Metro council members whose determination to defend local interests had been strengthened by several years of divisive debates. At the same time, he was able to build support for Metro within the community at large. Without his forceful leadership, Metro would have got off to a much shakier start, and might not have survived at all.

It would be a mistake to conclude, however, that Metro owed its successes entirely to the determination and persuasive powers of one individual. The Metropolitan Toronto School Board, which never acquired leadership of

---

138. Colton 1980, 161.

139. The total number of units included those built by the Toronto Housing Authority before Metro's creation.

140. The limited dividend program provided low-interest loans to private-sector apartment builders and municipal housing corporations that agreed to charge modest, government-set rents for their units in exchange for a guaranteed 5 per cent annual profit.

Gardiner's prominence, nonetheless moved quickly to meet the area's urgent need for new schools. According to its Executive Secretary, however, the "fine spirit of cooperation" that characterized the Board's early years gradually gave way "to one of growing self-interest and mutual rivalry."[141] The change occurred as Board members became accustomed to the new political arrangements and began to put the interests of their municipalities ahead of those of the federation. This tendency also became increasingly apparent in Metro Council debates as Metro got its more pressing infrastructural needs under control. Even Gardiner had to take a more accommodating approach in dealing with Metro Council about contentious issues. As already discussed, these tended to be ones that could only be resolved by shifting advantages (financial or otherwise) among Metro municipalities. For local politicians, therefore, experience with a metropolitan system did not seem to result in "a more general acceptance of [the cost-sharing principle] ... in the field of local government" that Cumming had described as necessary to the success of his plan.

Metro not only survived, however, but managed to win widespread acceptance within the Toronto community. Although Commissioner Goldenberg heard many arguments for changing the system, he observed in his report that none of the briefs he had received "suggested a return to the pre-Metro forms of municipal organization in the area."[142] In the eyes of those most involved in or affected by its activities, Metro had clearly been doing some things right.

There was nothing to prevent Metro Council and the Metropolitan School Board from trying to deal on their own with those matters for which they were most often criticized, such as their failure to develop comprehensive programs to address Metro's social needs or the failure of their representative structures to fulfill the requirements of local democracy. They could ask the provincial government to give them new powers, modify their representational structures, or change the ways they financed the services for which they were responsible.

Metro Council did ask the government in 1956 to make policing a metropolitan function, even though nine of the thirteen municipalities disagreed with the idea.[143] It also took over business licensing from the area municipalities and initiated an air pollution control program. Although the province put policing and licensing under the control of independent commissions and

141. McCordic 1964, 465.
142. Royal Commission on Metropolitan Toronto 1965, 173. See also Smallwood 1963, 5.
143. Gail C.A. Cook, "Reorganization in Greater Toronto: Autonomy, Federation and Consolidation," Chapter 4 of *Public Economic Organization in Metropolitan Areas* (unpublished draft prepared for the C.D. Howe Institute, 1973), 17–19.

appointed a majority of their members, the new bodies derived most of their funding from Metro. Thus they signified that Metro's importance in the area was likely to increase, at least financially. Local politicians, however, made it clear that they would not support any further enlargement of Metro powers.

Metro Council and the MTSB did not ignore contentious issues altogether. In fact, they often debated them at considerable length, sometimes at the urging of the province. Where they fell short in the eyes of their critics was in not going far enough in trying to resolve them. The failure to act, or to act forcefully or comprehensively enough, paved the way for provincial government decisions both to become involved in the provision of key services in the mid-1960s and to restructure Metro government itself. Nonetheless, Metro-sponsored studies and debates about public transit, social welfare, public education, housing, and political inequities helped to clarify the issues at stake and identify possible ways to address them.

OVERCOMING POLITICAL BARRIERS TO A METROPOLITAN TRANSIT SYSTEM

Public transit was the controversial issue that Metro council went furthest toward resolving. Not only did a majority of Metro councillors agree to help finance construction of the east–west Bloor Street subway in 1957, but in 1959 a council majority also decided to dedicate most of a special two-mill capital levy to subway building.[144] The decision helped to settle a lingering dispute between Metro Council and the City of Toronto, which stopped insisting that Metro supply water to the city at a lower rate than it charged other municipalities. (The differential rate structure was to compensate the city for the water purification and supply systems it had turned over to Metro when Metro was formed.) The tradeoff was an example of the type of quid pro quo that helped Chairman Gardiner achieve the balance or parity in Metro spending that local politicians wanted.[145]

Transit disputes did not end, however, after Metro began to contribute to subway construction. There remained the matter of operating subsidies, and also the question of what roles the TTC and Metro, particularly the Metro chair and Metro's planning staff, should have in planning new subway routes. At first, the planners seemed to gain the upper hand, thereby reducing the TTC to an advisory role on transportation planning matters. Ultimately, however, Metro Council would decide where it wanted subway lines to go. In doing so, it would often allow the political priorities of the Council's locally elected members to outweigh either land-use or transportation considerations (see Chapter 5).

---

144. McGilly 1972, 188–192.
145. Colton 1980, 113.

Metro planners played an early role in politicizing Metro's rapid transit system when they proposed in the early 1960s that subway lines be extended into Etobicoke, Scarborough, and later into North York as a way to get suburban support for a transit operating subsidy. "We took the position," said Eli Comay, Metro's planning director at the time, "that subways served a political purpose."[146] The ploy worked, for in 1964 Council accepted responsibility for 70 per cent of both the cost of subway construction and of the TTC's accumulated capital debt. It was then able to persuade the province to reimburse it for 33.3 per cent of the cost of subway roadbeds.

TTC management initially opposed the suburban extensions, arguing that the outer suburban population was not large enough to support high-capacity transit. They wanted to build a new subway line to replace a heavily used streetcar line on Queen Street in downtown Toronto. Nonetheless the subway extensions helped make the rapid transit system a metropolitan resource and paved the way for future attempts to link high-density suburban development within Metro to the development of the rapid transit system. They also made downtown Toronto more accessible by transit to Metro's growing suburban population. Thus they helped to keep the urban core attractive to private land developers and new business investors after political opposition ended the construction of downtown highways in the 1970s.

ADDRESSING DISPARITIES IN SPENDING ON WELFARE AND EDUCATION

Other issues, however, were difficult or impossible to resolve by working out a financial or administrative quid pro quo that satisfied all affected municipalities. Differences in welfare spending was a particularly contentious issue, even after an increase in provincial support lowered the municipal share from 40 to 20 per cent of mandatory costs in 1958. After many bitter debates, Metro Council voted narrowly in favour of asking the government to let it provide mandatory welfare services and pay the 20 per cent local share of their costs. Only the Mayor of Scarborough, a relatively poor suburb, voted with the city for the motion.[147] The decision left it up to individual municipalities to cover the full costs of whatever optional services they chose to provide. The City of Toronto continued to provide and fund optional services; most of the suburbs did not, and intermunicipal differences declined only slightly.

Whereas disparities in welfare spending were more a function of local political preferences than of local wealth, disparities in spending on public education were more closely linked to disparities in local assessments. In this case, it was a matter for the Metropolitan Toronto School Board to try to

146. Interview with Eli Comay, January 24, 1982.
147. McGilly 1972, 317.

resolve, and in 1961 it appointed the first of two special committees to study and report on the issue.[148] These committees debated several alternatives, such as increasing the size of Metro's maintenance assistance payments to poorer boards, changing the way these payments were allocated, changing the way taxes were collected for education, and changing the structure of the metropolitan federation itself (by reducing the number of local boards from 11 to 4, for example).[149] After three prolonged debates, the MTSB decided not to choose any of them, but to leave the decision up to the province. At the same time it "went on record as recognizing the necessity for change in the existing administrative and financial arrangements in education in Metropolitan Toronto."[150]

A problem for both Metro Council and the MTSB was rising school debt and its uneven distribution among the 13 municipalities. When it was formed, Metro had assumed responsibility for all local school debt incurred before January 1, 1954, but for only a portion of the debt incurred after that date. As school board debt increased, the province amended the *Metropolitan Toronto Act* to allow Metro to pay more or all of it. After debating the matter, however, Metro Council and the Metro School Board decided that Metro would pay only the costs of new debt incurred after January 1, 1964, up to a prescribed mill rate ceiling.[151] Local boards would still be responsible for repaying debt accumulated during the previous 10 years.

DEBATING METRO'S ROLE IN PUBLIC HOUSING

Metro Council partially accepted responsibility for low-rental housing in 1954, its first year of operation, by creating the Metropolitan Toronto Housing Company to build low-rental housing for senior citizens anywhere in Metro. The decision served two purposes. It gave Metro an incorporated agency (a public corporation) that could qualify for federal government funds for limited dividend housing.[152] It also related directly to a Metro responsibility—to develop and staff Homes for the Aged—by providing a housing alternative for low-income seniors who could live independently.[153] It promised a financial advantage as well, because Metro would pay only 10 per cent of the

---

148. The committee reports were: The Metropolitan School Board, *The Case for a Single Mill Rate or Uniform Tax for Education in Metropolitan Toronto*, December 12, 1961; and The Metropolitan School Board, *The Case for Equalization of Educational Opportunity in Metro Toronto*, 1962.

149. For the substance of these debates, see McCordic 1964.

150. McCordic 1964, 472.

151. The mill rate is the rate applied to the assessed value of local properties to determine the amount of taxes they will pay each year.

152. McMahon 1990, 18.

153. Ibid., 23.

capital costs of limited dividend units, as compared to 50 per cent of the costs of Homes for the Aged.

Housing low-income senior citizens was one thing, however; housing low-income families was a different and much more controversial matter. Nonetheless, in 1958 Metro Council established an Interim Housing Committee (IHC) with powers to select and, where possible, acquire sites suitable for public housing, to negotiate with federal and provincial officials about the number and type of units to be built on those sites, and to recommend a permanent metropolitan organization to administer an assisted housing program.[154]

The IHC, working with Metro planning staff, identified seven large sites in peripheral districts, well removed from existing neighbourhoods.[155] Metro Council asked the federal–provincial partnership to build housing on these sites, but made no further moves toward setting up its own agency. It lost the opportunity to do so in 1964 when the provincial government created the Ontario Housing Corporation (OHC) to draw on federal funds to build public housing throughout Ontario.

Trying to Reduce Political Inequities

For many local politicians, the most serious inequities associated with the metropolitan system of government had to do with the way Metro was organized and the way different municipalities were represented on Metro Council and the MTSB. City officials continued to push for amalgamation, undoubtedly hoping that it would give them full control over the area's development and tax base. Suburban officials opposed such a change, which would have obliterated both their municipalities and their official status. What the larger suburbs wanted, and the city opposed, was a representational structure that better reflected the growth of the suburban population, particularly in the outer suburbs.

In 1961, at the urging of Chairman Gardiner, Metro Council constituted itself as a Special Committee on Metropolitan Affairs (a committee of the whole) to consider ways to restructure Metro's representational form and system of finance. The Special Committee commissioned two studies of the metropolitan system. One, carried out by the provincial Department of Economics, looked at the financial implications of consolidating Metro's thirteen municipalities into fewer units of more equal size as a way to reduce persistent inter-local inequalities in revenues and services. The second, done by a Committee of Heads of Metro Departments, looked at how Metro and

---

154. Metropolitan Toronto Council Minutes 1958, Appendix A, 127, 340.

155. Comay Planning Consultants, "Memorandum Re: Metropolitan/Local Planning Relationships," prepared for the Royal Commission on Metropolitan Toronto, October 1975, 6.

local government departments carried out their responsibilities. It also considered the administrative and financial implications of amalgamating the 13 municipalities into 1.[156] After receiving their reports Metro vigorously debated a variety of restructuring schemes. It could not agree on a plan, however, and the province turned the matter over to Commissioner Goldenberg.

Commissioner Goldenberg possessed several credentials that blended well with the types of concerns that dominated discussions of Metropolitan Toronto at the time. He had prepared studies of local government in Saint John, New Brunswick, and Winnipeg, Manitoba, so was well versed in the workings of local government.[157] He specialized in labour law and labour relations, which undoubtedly sharpened his skills in negotiation and conflict management. Perhaps most important to the task at hand, he was also the man who had made a case for reducing intermunicipal financial inequalities to the Royal Commission on Dominion–Provincial Relations in 1939, and thus was very familiar with the equity issues that fuelled many Metro disputes.

PAVING THE WAY FOR METRO'S RENEWAL

Although Metro institutions had been unable to resolve those disputes, Metro-sponsored studies and debates about public transit, social welfare, public education, housing, and political inequities helped to clarify the issues at stake and identify possible ways to address them. They provided much of the background material that Goldenberg used in his report, and so contributed to the findings on which he based recommendations. These recommendations would pave the way for a number of important changes in the structure and responsibilities of Metro institutions (Chapter 3). The changes did not occur in a vacuum, however. Rather they were elements of a large-scale restructuring of Ontario's system of local government and local finance that would reshape governance for a city-region that extended well beyond the boundaries of Metropolitan Toronto.

---

156. Rose 1972, 85.
157. Ibid., 103.

THREE

1966–1975
Three-Tier Regional Governance under Provincial Stewardship

Introduction: Growth-related Challenges Redefined

The provincial policies that shaped Toronto region governance in the 1960s reflected several interconnected concerns. Economic development, always a provincial concern, garnered particular attention after the provincial economy lapsed into recession in the late 1950s.[1] The government's approach to economic development gradually changed, however, from helping provide the public infrastructure needed to create "the appropriate climate for private investment" to using public policy to guide investment to parts of the province that had lagged behind others in the post-war industrial buildup.[2]

Economic growth affected the province's urban sector primarily, making the capacity of that sector to deal with new demands a second major preoccupation of the Ontario government by the end of the 1950s. Like its economic development policy, Ontario's municipal policy evolved from a search for ways to help municipalities help themselves to direct intervention in virtually all aspects of municipal administration and service provision.

A third preoccupation was the province's relationship with the federal government. After a period of relative harmony in the early 1950s, federal–provincial relations deteriorated as Ontario's leaders insisted that the federal government should help to defray the costs of rapid urban growth. The federal response typically took the form of social and economic programs funded on a cost-shared basis with the provinces. While Ontario often seized on the opportunities presented by these programs, it was quick to defend its interests in the face of real or perceived threats to its constitutional right to manage municipal affairs. It clung to the position that "[a] supportive role for the

1. McDougall 1986, 86.
2. Richmond 1974, 20.

federal government is the only one that is constitutionally acceptable."[3] The federal government acquiesced by giving provincial governments increasing freedom to decide how they would deliver federally assisted services. Thus, Ontario's municipal policy developed in the midst of an ongoing federal–provincial struggle for ascendancy.

One consequence of the Ontario government's efforts both to adapt to an urbanizing and industrializing society and to manage its relationship with the federal government was a greatly enlarged, more professional provincial bureaucracy. Another was the entanglement of the provincial government and its agencies more closely with the affairs of municipalities in all parts of the province. As a result, by the end of the period, the provincial government had acquired (but not acknowledged) the role of de facto government of the Toronto region. Because it had also grouped municipalities in the region into two-tier regional municipalities structured similarly to Metropolitan Toronto, Toronto region governance was essentially a three-tier arrangement in which legal authority to make and implement policy clearly rested with the province.

The Origins and Evolution of Policies for a City-Centred Region

Because they arose from disparate concerns and priorities, provincial policies and programs affecting the Toronto region after 1960 resulted in a system of regional governance that was considerably less focused on the specific needs of the Toronto region than the federated system instituted in 1953. Understanding the system, therefore, means understanding the various strands of provincial government policy-making and how they were loosely woven into a set of programs and policies of regional importance.

Regional economic development

Ontario's regional economic development program originated in federal–provincial agreements in 1953 to establish economic regions throughout the country.[4] Initially, provincial staff divided Ontario into 10 economic regions, primarily for data-collection purposes. Regional development activities intensified in the early 1960s, however, after the federal government adopted programs to assist agricultural communities and underdeveloped parts

---

3. W. Darcy McKeough, "Municipal Fiscal Reform," *Municipal World*, 87 (July 1977), 171, 174.
4. Toronto Bureau of Municipal Research 1972, 19.

of the country. Ontario and several other provinces saw these programs as unwelcome intrusions into areas of provincial jurisdiction and decided to counter them with programs of their own.[5] A recession between 1958 and 1962 was an added incentive to diversify and strengthen the provincial economy.

In 1962 the government merged its Department of Commerce and Development and its Department of Economics into a new Department of Economics and Development, which began to work on an economic development program that would "harness underutilized resources for growth where it was needed while relieving pressure on already-committed resources in high-growth areas."[6] The aim, in other words, was to reduce large and growing disparities between the province's economically successful urban centres (Metropolitan Toronto being the most prominent) and other parts of the province that were lagging behind.

The economic development program gained momentum in 1965, when the government established the office of Chief Economist of Ontario within the Department of Economics and Development. According to Ian Macdonald, Chief Economist from 1962 to 1974, the office had a wide-ranging mandate: to coordinate intergovernmental affairs, to conduct the research needed to support economic policy and policy planning, and to prepare development plans for the 10 economic development regions. One of these regions took in Metropolitan Toronto and a large swath of surrounding territory.[7]

Increased support for municipal infrastructure

Sewer and water

The Ontario government had begun to address infrastructure deficiencies in the municipal sector even before it began to enhance the economic development program. Among the matters calling for attention were inadequate or obsolete methods of municipal sewage disposal and water treatment. These were seen not only as deterrents to industrial investment, but also as sources of pollution in provincial rivers and streams, some of which flowed into the Great Lakes that separated Canada from the United States. Citing an international agreement, the federal government began to pressure the province in the early 1950s to do something about them.[8]

---

5. Richardson 1981, 565; Don Stevenson, "Federalism and the Provision of Public Services" (paper presented at a North American–Yugoslavian seminar on federalism, University of Indiana, June 1967).

6. McDougall 1986, 211.

7. H. Ian Macdonald, "The Toronto-Centred Region in Retrospect," in Frisken 1982, 62.

8. Graham 1990, 206–210.

The province urged municipal governments to act, insisting that they were responsible for these services. Municipal governments insisted, however, that they could not afford to build new sewage and water treatment facilities. The outcome of this intergovernmental wrangling was a provincial government decision in 1955 to create a special-purpose body, the Ontario Water Resources Commission (OWRC), to study the province's sewage disposal and water supply systems and work with municipal governments to improve them.

The creation of the OWRC coincided with the creation of the Metropolitan Toronto and Region Conservation Authority (MTRCA) (see Chapter 2). The two agencies worked together on the flood-control program that contributed to the development of Metropolitan Toronto's extensive park system. After the federal government agreed in the mid-1960s to share the costs of trunk sewers and sewage treatment plants with the provinces, the Ontario government authorized the OWRC to construct 340 water and sewage facilities throughout the province.[9] The agency also began to plan two major servicing schemes for areas surrounding Metropolitan Toronto.[10]

ADDRESSING TRANSPORTATION CONGESTION

Regional transportation problems, especially increasing traffic congestion on highways leading into and out of Metro Toronto, began to attract the province's attention in the early 1960s. In 1962 the government established a Metropolitan Toronto and Region Transportation Study (MTARTS) to examine ways to meet the needs of the growing number of commuters in the larger Metropolitan Toronto region.

The area encompassed by MTARTS was four and a half times the size of the Metropolitan Toronto planning area (Figure 3.1). Although it contained 85 rural and urban municipalities, 57 per cent of its population of 2.8 million lived in Metropolitan Toronto. Described at the time "as the most forward step ever taken in provincial-municipal relations in Ontario,"[11] the study involved representatives of four provincial departments (Highways, Municipal Affairs, Economics, and Transportation); the Ontario Water Resources Commission; Metropolitan Toronto's Council, Planning Board, and Department of Roads; the Toronto Transit Commission; two national railways; and several private consultants.

---

9. Ontario Budget Address, delivered by the Honourable J.N. Allan [Treasurer of Ontario], February 9, 1966.

10. For more on the OWRC and its role in servicing Metro's suburban surroundings, see White 2003, 35–48.

11. "Ontario Transportation Study," *Municipal World*, 73 (May 1963), 170.

Figure 3.1 Metropolitan Toronto and Region Transportation Study
(MTARTS), 1967

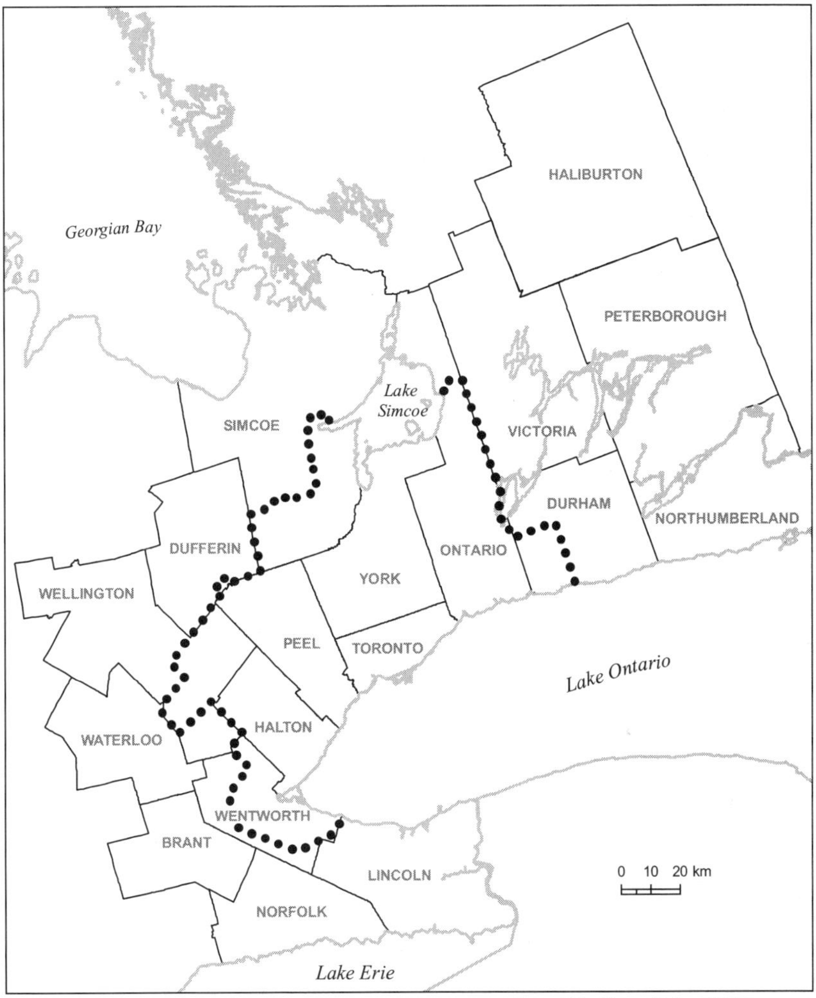

Upper-Tier Municipal Boundary

●●● Metropolitan Toronto and Region Transportation Study 1967

Sources: National Topographic Survey; 2001 Census
Statistics Canada; Central Ontario Lakeshore Urban
Complex Task Force, Advisory Committee on Urban and
Regional Planning, *Report* (December 1974).
© 2007 Neptis Foundation

TAKING THE LEAD IN PUBLIC HOUSING

In 1964 the Ontario government created a crown agency, the Ontario Housing
Corporation (OHC), to build public housing in all parts of Ontario. It did so
in response to an amendment to the *National Housing Act* that authorized the
Central Mortgage and Housing Corporation, a federal agency, to lend money
to cover up to 90 per cent of the costs of public housing projects created and

owned by provinces, municipalities, or public housing agencies, and to pay 50 per cent of their annual operating costs.[12] The amendment ended the federal–provincial housing partnership and helped to speed up the provision of a service that had become bogged down in intergovernmental red tape and local resistance, but for which there was growing local demand. The Ontario government also saw the new arrangement as a source of capital for its construction industry, and thus as an aid to its economic development program.[13]

The OHC took over the assets of the Metropolitan Toronto Housing Authority and other local housing authorities to become the only agency entitled to build public housing anywhere in Ontario.

Local government restructuring

By the middle of the 1960s, therefore, the Ontario government had begun to tackle infrastructural and bureaucratic barriers to economic and community development in the Toronto region and other parts of the province. In the latter half of the decade it turned its attention to making municipal governments more effective in dealing with urban growth.

The Ontario government's efforts to restructure public education and local governments in the 1960s grew out of its attempts to engage municipal governments in planning and helping to pay for new services to support economic development. It also recognized that large disparities in local assessments were resulting in large differences in the types and quality of the local services that Ontario residents were receiving.

Restructuring had two main objectives: (1) to shift some services (particularly education, social welfare, and public health) from smaller to larger units of local government in the interest of making their administration more professional, uniform, and equitable across the province; and (2) to improve the capacity of municipal governments to finance services out of local property taxes, thereby taking pressure off the provincial budget.

The initiative began with provincial attempts to persuade municipal governments to make adjustments within the existing two-tier county system. When few of them did so, the government created a Select Committee of the Legislature to Investigate the Municipal Act and Related Acts, with Toronto backbencher Hollis Beckett as chair. The Beckett Committee recommended the creation of two-tier regional governments throughout Ontario, to be based on existing county boundaries, but also to include cities and large towns

---

12. The name of the federal housing agency was changed to Canada Mortgage and Housing Corporation in 1979.

13. McDougall 1986, 143–144; Ontario Ministry of Municipal Affairs and Housing 1984.

that had not been part of the county system. The government then invited local governments to study ways to implement the recommendation, saying it would pay half the cost of the studies itself. When municipal governments dragged their feet, the province began to commission local government reviews, giving priority to high-growth areas.[14] Four of them adjoined or were close to Metropolitan Toronto.

Local government restructuring was also a prominent concern in a comprehensive study of the provincial and municipal tax systems conducted between 1963 and 1967 by the Ontario Committee on Taxation (OCT), commonly known as the Smith Committee after its chairman Lancelot Smith. The Committee was asked to recommend "means by which … [the tax system] can be made to exert the least possible drag on the people's willingness to work, save and contribute to development." It concluded that a restructuring of government along regional lines was a necessary step toward reforming the provincial–municipal financial relationship.[15]

Throughout the 1960s, therefore, discussions of local government restructuring in Ontario pointed toward the creation of a province-wide system of municipal federations (dubbed "mini-Metros" by some commentators). The question at issue was whether these units would conform to existing county boundaries or whether they would be given new and different boundaries, thereby causing counties to disappear. The Beckett Committee favoured building the new system on the existing county structure, a model that was consistent with the province's efforts to get county governments to take on more responsibilities. The Smith Committee, on the other hand, argued for dividing territory outside Metropolitan Toronto and other large cities into "urbanizing regions and "county regions," according to whether or not they were being strongly affected by the pressures of urban development.[16] The three regions it recommended for suburban districts around Toronto took in parts of more than one county but left out others.

The Smith Committee based its recommendations on five criteria that, it said, would help the restructured system to "achieve the twin objectives of access [meaning widespread opportunities for citizen participation] and service [meaning a combination of economic efficiency and 'technical adequacy']." Briefly, it argued for regional governments that would (1) promote or sustain a sense of community; (2) balance diverse interests; (3) have tax bases that were

14. For accounts of the process that led to the creation of regional governments, see Ron Farrow, "Lessons Learned from the Establishment of Ontario's Regional Governments" (paper presented at the University of Western Ontario, May 22, 1990); Jacek 1985, 108–110.

15. DelGuidice and Zacks 1969, 265–267.

16. Ontario Committee on Taxation II, 1967, 510.

adequate to the tasks that had to be performed; (4) had the capacity to perform those tasks; and (5) could form co-operative relationships with neighbouring regions.[17]

Although they sometimes referred to the Metro model, discussions of local government restructuring gave little attention to a third governance option for the Toronto region: enlarging Metropolitan Toronto to take in peripheral territory that was then experiencing rapid urban growth. The Smith Committee decided that this option was incompatible with the goals of promoting a community of interest and preserving regional "balance." If Metro were combined with outer districts, it suggested, the more densely populated core would be able to dominate the rest of the region. Goldenberg conceded that the urban growth occurring outside Metro "would justify extensions of Metro's limits," but said that "prior consideration should be given to municipal reorganization on the fringe area."[18] As both studies had been commissioned by the province, the lack of attention they gave to enlarging Metro undoubtedly meant that the government did not want them to recommend this option.

Reorganizing Metropolitan Toronto

The provincial government legislated a complete restructuring of Metropolitan Toronto in 1966 before deciding what it would do about local government in the rest of the Toronto region. It reduced the number of Metro municipalities from 13 to 6 (the City of Toronto and the suburban municipalities of East York, Etobicoke, North York, Scarborough, and York, Figure 3.2). It also made Metro Council fully responsible for two important local services: welfare (both mandatory and optional services) and solid waste disposal.

These changes were even more disruptive of the municipal status quo than the changes the government had made in 1953. They occurred, however, only after the government had circulated Goldenberg's report among "members of the Legislature, municipal councils, boards, commissions, rate-payers' associations and others."[19] These consultations took a year, and resulted in departures from Goldenberg's recommendations that made Metro less able to overcome some of the problems that he had identified, particularly problems related to inequities in financial resources and voting structure.

What Goldenberg had recommended was a Metropolitan Toronto containing only four more equally sized municipalities, which he saw as a way to overcome two problems: (1) the large inter-suburban differences in population and taxable assessment, and (2) the growing disparity between the size of the

---

17. Ontario Committee on Taxation II, 1967, 515–516.
18. Royal Commission on Metropolitan Toronto 1965, 171.
19. Robarts 1966, 22.

Figure 3.2 Metropolitan Toronto after the 1966 reorganization

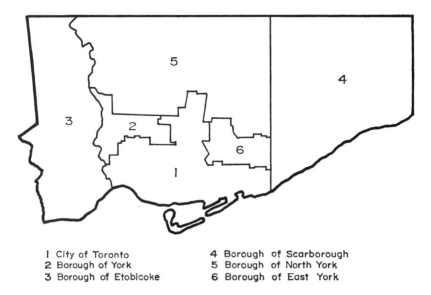

1 City of Toronto	4 Borough of Scarborough
2 Borough of York	5 Borough of North York
3 Borough of Etobicoke	6 Borough of East York

Rose (1972), 93 [scanned reproduction].

city and suburban populations, and thus in the voting strength of the two blocs on Metro Council. His proposed scheme would have left the city with slightly more than half of Metro's population, and thus would have given the city and the suburbs the same number of representatives (11) on Metro Council.[20] The system the province put in place resulted in five suburbs ranging in size from 91,000 (East York) to 342,000 (North York). The suburbs had a total population of 1.07 million compared to Toronto's 682,000.[21] With only 40 per cent of Metro's population, Toronto had only 12 members on the new Metro Council, compared to 20 for the suburbs, although the government allowed the city to provide half the members of Metro's Executive Committee for the next eight years.

The government also reduced Metro's 11 local school boards to 6, 1 in each of the consolidated municipalities, instead of following Goldenberg's recommendation to replace the 11 existing boards with 11 restructured school districts of more equal size and taxable resources. His recommendations were closely linked to one that the province did accept: to make the Metropolitan

20. Royal Commission on Metropolitan Toronto 1965, 184.
21. Rose 1972, 115.

Toronto School Board (MTSB) fully responsible for financing education out of a uniform education tax collected by Metro Council. Under his scheme, the MTSB would distribute all money received from this source and from provincial grants to the district school boards according to standard criteria, making some provision for funding special needs. This would mean, Goldenberg argued, that "there will be no need for continuing the existing relationship between local school boards and municipal councils and for coterminous school districts and municipal boundaries."[22] The aim, in other words, was to end a system that had allowed wealthier school boards to raise extra money in local taxes and spend more than other boards on teachers and equipment.

The province did transfer responsibility for school finance to the Metropolitan Toronto School Board. It also made the MTSB retroactively responsible for all school debt. By consolidating local school boards into six municipal boards, however, it preserved the close linkage between local education and local councils (the local taxing authorities). In fact, it explicitly gave local boards the right to supplement both their operating and their capital budgets with money raised by a local tax levy, although only up to specified limits. "A successful solution to the educational problems of Metropolitan Toronto," said Premier Robarts, "can be achieved only through a continued application of the principles which have guided education in this Province from the beginning." And one of those principles was "local control of education as far as practicable,"[23] even if it meant allowing inequalities in education spending to persist or to widen.

COUNTY/REGIONAL SCHOOL BOARDS AND REGIONAL MUNICIPALITIES

It soon became evident that the principle of "local control of public education" did not guarantee the survival of all or even most of the province's local school boards. Local government reorganization outside Metro Toronto began in 1967 with the consolidation of 1,400 municipal school boards into 182 much larger (usually county) boards.[24] Some of these boards became regional boards after the government created two-tier regional municipalities between 1969 and 1974. Of the 11 regional municipalities created during this period, 4 (Durham, York, Peel, and Halton) would later be considered part of the Greater Toronto Area (GTA). A fifth, Hamilton-Wentworth to the west of Halton, was included in most regional transportation planning studies and transportation proposals for the Toronto region.[25]

---

22. Royal Commission on Metropolitan Toronto 1965, 146.
23. Robarts 1966, 22.
24. Ontario Ministry of Treasury, Economics and Intergovernmental Affairs 1976, 10.
25. The Regional Municipality of Hamilton-Wentworth was consolidated into the new City of Hamilton in 2000.

Local government restructuring also meant the consolidation of small municipalities into larger ones. As a result, the number of municipalities in Metropolitan Toronto and the four suburban regional municipalities decreased from 66 to 30 (or from 77 to 36 when Hamilton-Wentworth was included).

Within the regional municipalities, the division of responsibilities between upper and lower tiers was similar but not identical to the division of responsibilities within Metro Toronto. Regional councils were responsible for major capital infrastructure (trunk water mains, trunk sewers and sewage treatment facilities, arterial roads, waste disposal, regional parks), while local councils provided similar services (water distribution, local sewage collection, local streets, garbage collection, local parks) to their own constituents. Planning was a shared responsibility, a characteristic of the two-tier system that gave rise to more confusion and dissension than any other feature. Regional governments administered most social services and paid the municipal share of their costs (usually 20 per cent). Provincial grants (which included money received from the federal government) paid the rest. Policing was nominally a responsibility of the regional municipalities, but was in fact administered by boards of Police Commissioners, which consisted of three members appointed by the provincial government and two members appointed by regional councils. Fire protection remained a local responsibility.

The structural changes made to local institutions in the Toronto region created the system of local governance that characterized the Toronto region until the end of the century. The one major change in its character was the consolidation of Metropolitan Toronto and its six municipalities into a single, greatly enlarged core city in 1997 (see Chapter 6).

Developing a provincial–municipal planning system

The Ontario government not only departed from Commissioner Goldenberg's recommendations in deciding Metro's internal boundaries and responsibilities, but it also ignored his two recommendations that acknowledged that Toronto-related growth was rapidly spreading beyond Metro's boundaries. These had called on the province to make the Metropolitan Toronto planning area larger and to strengthen Metro's authority to produce and implement a plan that would "delineate the limits of urban development and project a desirable rate of growth."[26] The government instead divided those parts of the suburban fringe that had been included in the Metropolitan Toronto planning area among the regional municipalities, which were authorized to produce official plans to which the plans of lower-tier municipalities would have to conform.

---

26. Royal Commission on Metropolitan Toronto 1965, 167.

Henceforth Metro could plan for land and infrastructure only within its own boundaries. In these circumstances, the Metropolitan Toronto Planning Board embarked in 1972 on a review of the "unofficial" 1965 plan.

As Metro and the regional governments began to work on official plans, the provincial government completed preliminary work on a land-use concept for the Toronto region, thereby implying that it intended to subsume both regional and local plans to a unified and coherent regional vision. Four trends in provincial development and provincial policies contributed to this venture into regional planning.

OVERSIGHT OF MUNICIPAL PLANNING

The first trend was increasing provincial oversight of municipal planning. This began with a revision of the provincial *Planning Act* in 1953 that gave the provincial government the explicit right to

> look at the following specific features of any subdivision plan: whether it is premature or in the public interest; whether it conforms to the official plan and adjacent plans of subdivision; the suitability of the land for the purposes proposed; the dimensions and shape of the lots; proposed restrictions on the land, buildings and structures proposed to be erected; conservation of natural resources and flood control; the adequacy of highways, utilities, municipal services, and school sites; the land to be conveyed for public purposes.[27]

It then gave the Department of Municipal Affairs authority to approve all municipal official plans after they had been circulated within the provincial bureaucracy.[28] These changes meant that a growing number of provincial staff could ask for changes in municipal plans before approving them. Typically they did so without reference to any consistent planning philosophy. They might even disagree among themselves about what to allow or disallow in the documents they saw.

The haphazard and inconsistent nature of the plan approval process brought pressure on the government to provide a policy framework (such as a provincial plan or regional plans) to guide the decisions of provincial and local planners.[29] Municipal governments, especially those in small towns and rural areas, added to these pressures by approving scattered residential developments without giving much thought to how they would be serviced and how services would be paid for.

---

27. Miron 1988, 258–259.
28. Gomme 1984, 104.
29. Comay Planning Consultants Ltd.; P.S. Ross & Partners; Proctor, Redfern, Bousfield and Bacon 1973, 16.

GROWTH OF THE PROVINCIAL PLANNING BUREAUCRACY

A second important influence on the province's move toward regional planning was the provincial Department of Economics and Development, where staff members who had been assembled to formulate regional development plans were soon arguing the need for regional land-use planning as well. Their arguments gained ground when they began to interact with the staff of the Department of Municipal Affairs. The Minister of Municipal Affairs, Darcy McKeough, was tireless in his efforts to promote regional planning and regional government both within the provincial cabinet and in public forums.[30]

THE INFLUENCE OF MTARTS

The third and most visible influence on the province's venture into regional planning was a final report of the Metropolitan Toronto and Region Transportation Study (MTARTS). It argued that it was not possible to plan a regional transportation system without some knowledge of how the province wanted the region to develop.

The report's discussion of land-use options for the Toronto region began with a "Trends Plan" scenario based on a consolidation of the projections contained in municipal plans and policies.[31] These projections, it pointed out, implied the continuing loss of agricultural land, the obliteration of significant natural landmarks because of urban expansion, the merging of existing towns, and the steady outward spread of low-density residential development that would become increasingly costly to serve. After outlining 12 goals for the region's future development, the report presented four alternative plans that would meet these goals better than the land-use pattern implied by the "Trends Plan" scenario.

A GROWING AWARENESS OF INTERREGIONAL DISPARITIES

A fourth influence on the regional planning program was the growing imbalance between the south-central part of the province and other areas. By 1966, Metropolitan Toronto and the outer suburban fringe contained more than one-third of Ontario's population, living on less than 1 per cent of its land. Areas in northern and eastern Ontario were experiencing an absolute loss of population. These disparities gave rise to complaints from communities that felt left out of the booming provincial economy. Local politicians from municipalities to the east of Metro were also complaining that most new investment was going into Metro and its neighbours to the west, not to areas to the east.[32]

---

30. Ian Macdonald, "The Toronto-Centred Region in Retrospect," in Frisken 1982, 62.

31. Ontario. Community Planning Branch, Department of Municipal Affairs 1967.

32. D.G. Newman [Mayor of the Town of Whitby], "Ontario Provincial-Municipal Conference—a Presentation on Regional Government," *Municipal World*, 80 (June 1970), 150–155.

Within Metro, on the other hand, there was growing political opposition to the impacts of regional economic growth on already built-up districts. This opposition gave rise to a strong anti-development and anti-growth movement, particularly among City of Toronto politicians and residents' associations, directed at highway and urban renewal projects that earlier generations of City of Toronto politicians had enthusiastically promoted, but that their opponents had come to identify with Metropolitan Toronto plans and policies.[33] The movement provided a base of urban support for efforts to direct growth away from the city, or from Metro as a whole, to other parts of the region or the province.

Countering the threat of federal intervention

Although the provincial government was prominent as a regional policy-maker during this period, federal government activities also affected regional governance. As discussed more fully in the next section, federal contributions to provincial finances, which allowed the provincial government to contribute more to municipal services, were an important source of federal influence. Another was the federal government's role in housing, both as a guarantor of low-interest mortgages for private home buyers and apartment developers and as a contributor to the construction of assisted rental housing.

Criticisms of the way assisted housing programs were administered led the federal government to create a Task Force on Housing and Urban Development (the Hellyer Task Force) in 1968. This task force marked a turning point in Canadian urban policy-making for at least three reasons. First, it bypassed the existing "housing fraternity" (federal civil servants, pressure groups, volunteer organizations, and some provincial and local government officials) and housing "experts" to consult directly with local communities, a form of public policy-making that would become increasingly common in the years that followed.[34] Community consultations demonstrated that citizens' opinions on policy issues were often at odds with those expressed by public officials and housing experts.

Second, the Hellyer Task Force led the federal government to phase out its support for public housing, a program that funded housing only for the very poor, and replace it with grants and loans for non-profit housing providers and housing co-operatives.

---

33. Colton 1980, 156; Goldrick, "The Anatomy of Urban Reform," op. cit., 29–38; Kaplan 1982, 609. Both types of Toronto politician were known as "reformers" at the times they were most active and influential.

34. Axworthy 1971, 137–138, 146–148.

Finally, the task force emphasized that Canada had become a predominantly urban nation and urged the federal government to create a department to conduct research on ways to improve urban development and city life.[35] Instead of doing so, the federal government commissioned Harvey Lithwick, an economist, to conduct Canada's first major study of urban development with a view to helping it "determine what, if any, role it should play in urban affairs and the likely consequences of such a role."[36] Only after Lithwick released his study in 1970 did the government create a Ministry of State for Urban Affairs (MSUA) to conduct urban research and coordinate provincial and federal government activities that impinged on Canadian cities.

While the MSUA lacked the broad policy-making mandate that Hellyer, Lithwick, and others had recommended, its creation suggested that the federal government would acquire the expertise and influence needed to take the lead in managing the nation's urban affairs. Thus most provincial governments, Ontario's included, resented its creation because of the threat it posed to provincial authority, and because its very existence implied that the provinces had failed to deal effectively with urbanization. The MSUA also had difficulty securing co-operation from other branches of the federal bureaucracy. Even municipal governments, which had long been pressuring the federal government for help, were disappointed by the MSUA. What they wanted was money, and the MSUA had no money to give out.[37] Instead, federal government officials told municipal petitioners to take their funding requests to the provinces.[38]

The Ontario government insisted that it could give municipalities more money only if Ottawa altered its revenue-sharing agreements in the provinces' favour. After much urging from municipalities, however, it agreed to take part in unprecedented meetings of all three levels of government to discuss financial and other issues. One of these meetings focused on Metropolitan Toronto, and it ended with an agreement that provincial governments were still in charge of cities.[39]

Lacking support from any of the governmental sectors with which it had to deal, MSUA fell victim to federal government cost-cutting in the late 1970s. Although its demise signalled the end of the federal government's attempt to carve out a distinctive role in urban affairs, several federal policies adopted during this period were nonetheless influencing the character of the

35. Federal Task Force on Housing and Urban Development 1969, 72–75.

36. Lithwick 1970, letter of transmittal.

37. Anthony Westell, "Ottawa, provinces wrangle over cities," *Globe and Mail*, November 10, 1971.

38. "Ask provinces, municipalities told," *Globe and Mail*, March 20, 1972.

39. Jonathan Manthorpe, "Ontario cautiously agrees to tri-level forum," *Globe and Mail*, September 16, 1972; Jonathan Manthorpe, "Governments to tackle city problems together," *Globe and Mail*, November 22, 1972.

Toronto region. Among the most important were amendments to the federal *Immigration Act* adopted in the 1960s, which ended the preference given to immigrants from the British Isles, northern Europe, and the United States. Immigration to Canada became an option for anyone in the world who could satisfy certain criteria. Because a substantial percentage of each year's immigrants gravitated to the Toronto region, these changes in immigration policy produced a gradual but steady change in the composition and character of the region's population.

Finance: The Driving Concern

The need to find more effective ways to finance urban services was a recurring theme in the reasons given by provincial officials for the changes they made to systems of local government and local finance that had been in place (except in Metropolitan Toronto) since 1849. It prompted the government to look for ways to reform local property taxation, improve the provincial grant structure, and maximize federal government contributions to provincial and municipal services while minimizing federal intrusion in provincial and municipal affairs.

The Ontario Committee on Taxation (the Smith Committee) was an important contributor to these efforts. Having been asked to recommend "means by which ... [the tax system] can be made to exert the least possible drag on the people's willingness to work, save and contribute to development,"[40] it carried out the most detailed study of provincial–municipal finance ever conducted in Ontario. Not only did it outline a comprehensive plan for restructuring local governments in southern Ontario into 22 regions (metropolitan, urbanizing, or county), but it also emphasized the need for substantial reforms in the province's property tax and municipal grant systems. Although the government did not always follow its recommendations, provincial politicians and public officials frequently referred to the work of the OCT in justifying the decisions that were made.

Regional governments as instruments of financial reform

In announcing its plan to create regional municipalities in 1968, the Ontario government acted in accordance with the Smith Committee's contention that "the fiscal soundness of the Province hinges upon far-reaching reform in the structure of local government."[41] It did not act, however, on that commit-

---

40. Ontario Budget Statement, delivered by The Honourable J.N. Allan, Treasurer of Ontario, February 7, 1963, 7.
41. Ontario Committee on Taxation 1967, 445.

tee's recommendation that it should create regional municipalities composed of communities of similar characteristics (predominantly urban or predominantly rural) in the interest of preserving a sense of community and of making it easier to harmonize services across regional boundaries.[42] Instead, it established two-tier systems based on existing county boundaries, which meant combining rural municipalities with cities or towns and urbanizing districts.

To justify the approach chosen by the government, the Ministry of Municipal Affairs supplemented the five criteria used by the Smith Committee with three of its own: (1) community participation in the design of regions and, where possible, community acceptability—all existing governments, said McKeough, should be involved in discussions about restructuring; (2) the boundaries should be useable by other institutions providing services in the region (provincial departments, for example); and (3) in two-tier regions, it should be possible to use the same criteria in designing both tiers of government.[43] These criteria implicitly acknowledged the objections of local politicians and local and provincial officials to the prospect of radical changes in the existing municipal system. Moreover, the government had already restructured local school boards along county lines; to create different boundaries for regional governments would only cause administrative confusion.

By consolidating small municipalities into larger ones, however, the government showed less respect for municipal than it had shown for county boundaries. Provincial officials insisted, however, that the changes were necessary. Distinctions between rural and urban were breaking down, said Municipal Affairs Minister Darcy McKeough in 1968, and many municipalities were too small to be viable. Moreover, there was a need to control "scattered and isolated development ... as the cost of providing urban services [has] become a burden on a municipal system which is not equipped to provide [them]."[44] Putting the case more bluntly, he told the annual convention of the Ontario Association of Rural Municipalities that "[a] municipal structure created for a horse-and-buggy society is hopelessly inadequate for this age of space travel."[45]

McKeough and other provincial officials also claimed that the reforms would strengthen local government by increasing the size of local tax bases,

---

42. Ibid., 515–518.

43. The Honourable Charles MacNaughton [Treasurer of Ontario], "Why Regional Government?" *Municipal World*, 77 (December 1967), 381–383; W. Darcy McKeough, "Regional Government in Ontario," *Municipal World*, 78 (December 1968), 323–324.

44. W. Darcy McKeough, "Restructuring Local Government along Regional Lines," *Municipal World*, 78 (November 1968), 300–302.

45. W. Darcy McKeough, "Regional Government: The Overall Picture," *Municipal World*, 79 (March 1969), 65.

reducing costly competition and service duplication among municipalities, lessening reliance on special-purpose bodies, and enabling provincial officials to better coordinate their activities at the municipal level.[46]

As with Metropolitan Toronto, however, the government's primary purpose in restructuring local governments was to consolidate local taxes to fund infrastructure in areas undergoing or likely to undergo urban development. The government also decreed that taxes in the regional municipalities would be pooled to cover the costs of public education and social services, as they had been in Metro Toronto.

Tackling an outdated and inequitable property tax system

An obstacle to the government's efforts to make property taxes more useful was a property assessment and taxation system that had developed many inequities since its overhaul in the 1950s, including differences in the way municipalities assessed properties and in the tax rates they applied to different types of property. Similar types of property could have very different assessed values in different municipalities, and occupiers of similar properties could pay very different amounts in property taxes. Metropolitan Toronto accounted for some of the largest inequities in the province, some of them dating back to the days before Metro was formed.

Property tax inequities not only violated the principle of "equal treatment of equals" in taxation, but they also made it difficult to determine how much individual municipalities should contribute to metropolitan or regional councils and school boards. Moreover, the absence of a uniform basis for deciding what municipalities were worth made it difficult for provincial agencies to allocate municipal grants fairly. To deal with the latter problem, the Department of Education applied "equalizing" formulae to local assessments to smooth out differences among them, but regarded this approach as a temporary measure.

Citing the need to correct such problems, the provincial government announced in 1969 that it was taking over property assessment from municipalities. According to the provincial Treasurer, it would reassess all properties in the province at "market value" as a first step toward a complete reform of Ontario's system of local finance.[47] In addition, the government intended to rationalize and simplify the provincial grant structure.

---

46. *Municipal World*, 80 (June 1970), 143, 165–167; Arthur K. Meen [Parliamentary Assistant to the Treasurer of Ontario], "The New Structure of Government," *Municipal World*, 82 (September 1972), 227–228.

47. The Honourable Charles MacNaughton, [Treasurer of Ontario], "The Reform of Taxation and Government Structure in Ontario," Budget Paper B, *Ontario Budget, 1969* (Toronto: Department of Treasury and Economics, 1969), 63.

Restructuring provincial grants

Awarding grants to municipal governments for a growing number of specified purposes was the principal way in which provincial government involvement in the municipal sector increased after 1950. Because most grants came with conditions attached, there were long-standing concerns about what this trend implied for local autonomy. Moreover, according to the Smith Committee, the provincial–municipal grant structure had become "chaotic," with "grant payments [bearing] little relation to anything."[48] The Committee recommended replacing conditional with unconditional grants to simplify the system and give municipal governments more decision-making autonomy.

The Ontario government began to act on this recommendation in the late 1960s by enriching some of its unconditional grants and adding new ones, including grants to help the new regional municipalities to organize and develop their services, and grants to allow tax shifts (mainly from urban to rural taxpayers) associated with the creation of regional school boards and regional governments to be phased in over a period of years. It also began to look for ways to consolidate 90 conditional grant programs into a smaller number to reduce administrative costs.

Even as it was adding to unconditional grants, however, the province was increasing the size of its contributions to municipal services. In 1969 it promised to increase provincial support for elementary and secondary education from 45 to 60 per cent of provincially recognized costs (averaged across the province) by 1975. It also assumed full financial and administrative responsibility for three services that municipalities had previously operated and helped to pay for: administration of justice, assessment of property, and a "family benefits" program that provided long-term financial assistance to families in need. In 1972 it increased its contributions to Metro's subway construction costs from 50 to 75 per cent (Metro Council had to pay the other 25 per cent) and promised the same level of support for capital costs (primarily the purchase of new buses) for all municipal transit systems. It also agreed to refund municipal governments half the cost of any transit operating deficits.

Maximizing federal contributions while minimizing federal involvement

Ongoing federal–provincial discussions about cost-sharing programs and the distribution of the federal income tax were critical elements of provincial–municipal policy-making during this period. The rising cost of municipal services was prominent among the province's arguments for more federal

---

48. Ontario Committee on Taxation 1967, 410.

dollars. The often rancorous federal–provincial disputes led to a number of new cost-sharing programs, most of them welcomed by the Ontario government. The exception was the national health insurance plan, or Medicare, which the federal government instituted in 1968 over Ontario's insistence that it would be too expensive. Ontario fought for an alternative that would involve both government and private-sector insurers. It gave in to intense political pressure, however, and signed the agreement in 1969.[49]

The federal–provincial programs of most immediate importance to cities were the 1964 *National Housing Act*, which freed up money for public housing, and the Canada Assistance Plan, adopted in 1966, which committed the federal government to reimbursing the provinces for 50 per cent of their expenditures on virtually all forms of social assistance.[50] These and other programs, said the provincial Treasurer, would make possible "significant improvements and an extensive broadening of our health, housing and welfare activities."[51] The Ontario government remained adamant, however, that federal aid should always be channelled through the provinces, which would distribute it to municipalities as they saw fit. This stand by Ontario and other provinces set Canada apart from the United States, where city governments already received some types of aid directly from Washington.[52]

Consequences of Three-Tier Governance for the Regional Agenda

Most of the institutional and financial changes made during this period to Ontario's arrangements for providing local services were elements of overlapping provincial government strategies to promote economic development and strengthen local government throughout the province. Nonetheless, they had lasting effects on the character of governance in the Toronto region and the services provided to its residents.

New infrastructure to support growth

Trunk water and sewer facilities

New or restructured institutions proved to be effective devices for pursuing the objective that typically heads the regional agenda—providing infrastructure to support economic investment and outward expansion—but not without

---

49. McDougall 1986, 226.
50. Cameron and Dupré 1983, 367.
51. The Honourable Charles MacNaughton [Treasurer of Ontario], "Ontario Budget Address," February 14, 1967, 481.
52. Elazar 1966, 76–77.

a large amount of financial support from senior governments. The Ontario Water Resources Commission, using federal and provincial funds, built water mains and sewage treatment facilities to the west of Metro (in the southern part of Peel County) before the creation of the Regional Municipality of Peel in 1974. It began work on sewage treatment facilities for York and Durham regions after York acquired a regional government in 1971. From then on, regional governments were expected to pay the capital and operating costs of these facilities, as well as expand them when needed, out of property tax dollars collected from local municipalities. When politicians in York region complained that the costs were too high, however, the province forgave the region "many millions in capital" to help keep down charges to local municipalities.[53]

Regional governments in fast-growing regions found their jobs more difficult than expected because local governments, on learning of the province's plan to restructure, postponed spending on services that they expected would be regionalized.[54] On the other hand, regional governments were able to limit their spending on new roads because both the province and municipalities had done extensive upgrading to their road systems before reorganization occurred.[55] Moreover, the provincial government decided to relieve pressures on Toronto region roads and highways by diverting some of its transportation dollars to regional and local public transit.

AN EMPHASIS ON PUBLIC TRANSIT

The one tangible outcome of the work of the Metropolitan Toronto and Region Transportation Study (MTARTS) was a commuter rail system linking downtown Toronto with lakeshore communities to the east and west of Metro. First announced in 1965 and instituted on an experimental basis in 1967, the system's trains ran on tracks leased from the two national railways (Canadian National and Canadian Pacific) and were operated by railway company personnel. The provincial government named the new service GO (Government of Ontario) Transit and paid all its equipment costs and operating deficits.

Ridership on the GO rail system grew from 4.7 million passengers in 1968 to 21 million in 1973.[56] By 1973 GO was also running buses on other routes and was planning to add services on three additional rail lines. It was no longer an experiment, but a fixture in the region.

---

53. White 2003, 52–53.
54. Ontario Ministry of Treasury, Economics and Intergovernmental Affairs 1976, 35–36.
55. Ibid., 22.
56. Thomas Coleman, "Commuters complain, but GO's real problem is its success," *Globe and Mail*, August 14, 1973, 5.

Another important transportation decision was the 1971 cancellation of provincial funding for a north–south expressway (the Spadina Expressway) in Metro Toronto. Premier William Davis made this decision without consulting his Department of Roads and Transportation, and after the Ontario Municipal Board (OMB) had ruled that the project should go ahead. Having just been chosen to head the long-governing Progressive Conservative Party, Davis saw the hotly debated expressway as an opportunity to establish himself as a strong leader committed to addressing environmental concerns and supporting public transit.[57] "If we are building a transportation system to serve the automobile," he told the provincial legislature, "the Spadina Expressway would be a good place to start. But if we are building a transportation system to serve people, the Spadina Expressway is a good place to stop."[58] Legislation adopted one month later authorized the government to cover 50 per cent of the transit operating deficits paid by local municipalities, as well as a portion of the capital costs of local transit systems.

GO's success in attracting riders, together with the development of suburban transit systems, may have slowed the trend toward automobile dominance in the Toronto region but it did not reverse it. While GO ridership grew by 4 per cent a year between 1968 and 1973, automobile traffic on parallel highways grew by 12 per cent a year during the same period.[59] Demand for new roads and highways persisted, therefore, particularly in the suburban regions.

A LEADER IN PUBLIC HOUSING

By 1975 the Ontario Housing Corporation had added more than 15,000 units of assisted rental family housing to the 3,700 units that existed in 1964.[60] Some of these units were already being planned when OHC was formed; others were built on sites identified by Metro planners and agreed to by local councils. Nonetheless, the number of units produced was more than double the number Metro had asked the OHC to provide in 1965 and substantially more than the 3,700 units built between 1947 and 1964. By 1975, when the public housing program was almost at an end, Metro had 60 per cent of the family housing stock in Ontario, but only 26 per cent of Ontario's population.

Paying for regional services: The province bears most of the costs

The need to relieve municipal governments and municipal taxpayers of the high costs associated with rapid urban growth was a frequent theme in provincial–

---

57. Hoy 1985, 89.

58. Quoted in Pill 1979, 43.

59. Coleman, "Commuters complain," op. cit.

60. Based on figures contained in Rose 1980, 175; and Royal Commission on Metropolitan Toronto 1965, 52.

municipal discussions during this period. Provincial interventions helped to achieve this objective. Despite the rapid growth of the urban population, the early 1970s were good years for municipal revenues. Provincial grants as a percentage of municipal expenditures, excluding grants to education, rose from 24.4 per cent of revenues for general municipal purposes in 1960–61 to 36 per cent in 1975.[61] Grants to local school boards rose from 33.9 per cent to 61 per cent of total education costs during the same period. As a result, some Ontario municipalities were able to reduce their property taxes.[62]

Metro Toronto shared in this trend. Provincial grants as a percentage of Metro revenues rose from 19.1 per cent in 1968 to 27.9 per cent in 1974.[63] Metro and its municipalities, however, still derived a smaller proportion of their combined budgets from provincial grants and a larger proportion from taxation than the Ontario average.[64] There were two ways of explaining the difference. One was that Metro's higher assessments (especially commercial/ industrial assessments) made its governments better able to look after their own needs. The other (advanced by some Metro officials) was that the province was treating Metro unfairly, especially in view of the large contributions Metro residents made to income and provincial sales tax revenues.[65]

Whatever the reason, taxes in Metro continued to rise despite increased provincial grants, leading some to suggest that Metro was heading down the same road to financial disaster as large U.S. cities. When New York City declared bankruptcy in 1974, Metro staff compared Metro's general financial situation with that of the beleaguered American city. Their study looked at spending commitments in the two jurisdictions, their ability to borrow, the purposes for which they used borrowed funds, the relative health of their assessment bases, their relative success in collecting property taxes owed to them, and the contributions of federal and state/provincial funds to their budgets.[66] It concluded that

---

61. W. Darcy McKeough, Treasurer of Ontario and Minister of Economics, *Provincial-Municipal Reform: A Progress Report*, Budget Paper B, Ontario Budget, presented in the Legislative Chamber of Ontario, April 26, 1971 (Toronto: Department of Treasury and Economics, Government of Ontario, 1971), 73; Ontario Ministry of Treasury, Economics and Intergovernmental Affairs, *Local Government Finance in Ontario 1975 and 1976* (Toronto: Municipal Finance Branch, The Ministry), 118.

62. Royal Commission on Metropolitan Toronto 1965, 52.

63. Kitchen 1977, 88.

64. Zamparo 1984, 24.

65. Alden Baker, "Metro seeks new revenue sources to take heat off property owners," *Globe and Mail*, December 28, 1973.

66. Metropolitan Toronto Clerk's Department, "Financial Statement on Metro Toronto and New York City," November 1975.

[t]he claim that Metro is going "the way of New York" is unnecessary verbal overkill. The attitude of the Government of Ontario; the [oversight of municipal borrowing exercised by the] Ontario Municipal Board; the requirements of the Metro Act which states we must levy taxes to cover deficits, and which places a code of financial behaviour on the Metro Treasury function; are checks in our system of Municipal government which would balance against any New York situation occurring in Metro.

Providing relief to municipal taxpayers was only one of the province's financial objectives during this period, however. Another was to control the costs that urbanization imposed on the provincial treasury. That goal proved to be more elusive. According to a study of provincial finances conducted in 1975, provincial payments to municipal governments increased nearly 300 per cent between 1966 and 1974.[67] These increases could be partially explained by happenings over which governments had little control, like high rates of population growth in some parts of the province and high inflation in the early 1970s. There were other explanations, however, that pointed to decisions taken by regional and local governments in response to restructuring, and increases in the number and size of provincial grants. These highlighted large increases in the salaries paid to regional and municipal staff, and increases in both the volumes and standards of many local services, especially in the regional municipalities.[68]

Costs in several other provincial spending categories (health care, post-secondary education, debt service, and institutional care) rose even more than municipal costs during this period). Nonetheless, finding ways to limit provincial contributions to municipal services would dominate the province's municipal policies from the mid-1970s onward.

Toward a strategy for regional growth management

In announcing plans for the creation of the regional Municipality of York, north of Toronto, in 1969, Municipal Affairs Minister McKeough outlined the comprehensive planning vision evolving within the provincial government at the time.[69] It depicted a hierarchical planning system in which plans prepared

67. Ontario Ministry of Treasury, Economics and Intergovernmental Affairs 1975, 23.

68. Ontario Ministry of Treasury, Economics and Intergovernmental Affairs, 1976, 14–24.

69. W. Darcy McKeough, "Structure and Political Organization of Local Government North of Metropolitan Toronto," *Municipal World*, 79 (May 1969), 120–121.

by the regional municipalities would be consistent with provincial guidelines for the physical and economic development of provincially defined economic regions. These regional plans would also guide the more detailed plans prepared by local municipalities. The government would be responsible for coordinating provincial policies and regional plans with each other.

The task of providing a provincial framework for the overall development of the Toronto region fell to staff members of the Ontario Department of Economics and Development. In defining the Toronto region, they ignored not only the boundary of the Metropolitan Toronto planning area, but also the boundaries used by other provincial agencies (such as MTARTS and the Smith Committee). Instead they identified a Toronto-Centred Region (TCR) of 22,274 square kilometres, almost 12 times larger than the Metropolitan Toronto planning area and nearly 3 times as large as the territory looked at by MTARTS. Nonetheless, they drew on material contained in briefs submitted to MTARTS and on two of the MTARTS "goals plans" to prepare a regional policy.[70] (Figure 3.3) The legislature adopted this statement in 1971 as a guide to the future planning and development of the Toronto region.

The TCR statement, which provincial officials always referred to as a "concept" and not a "plan," had four objectives:

- to slow down rapid growth in southern Ontario, particularly in Metropolitan Toronto and districts to the west, and direct more economic investment (particularly manufacturing) to other parts of the province;
- to shift growth in the Toronto region from the west to the east of Metro;
- to encourage more compact or nodal forms of development in the interest of making transportation systems more efficient;
- to stem the loss of agricultural land and natural open space by directing development in the southern part of the region into two tiers of well-defined communities, one close to the lake and the other separated from the lakeshore "by a parkway belt of open space with mainly non-urban uses, but containing high performance interurban transportation and other trunk services."[71] Land outside designated urbanized zones was to be reserved for agriculture or as recreational open space.

---

70. Ontario Intergovernmental Advisory Committee on Regional Development 1970.
71. Ibid., 3.

Figure 3.3 Toronto-Centred Region (TCR), 1970

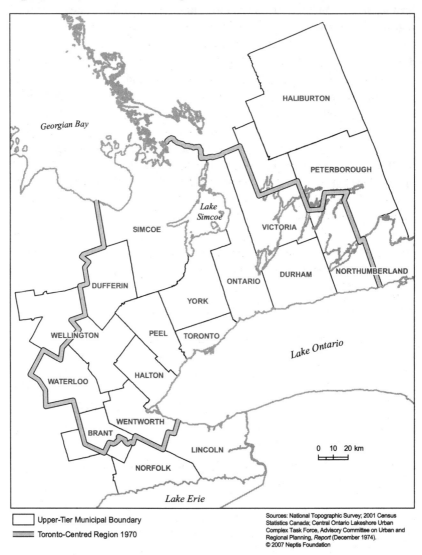

Upper-Tier Municipal Boundary

Toronto-Centred Region 1970

Sources: National Topographic Survey; 2001 Census
Statistics Canada; Central Ontario Lakeshore Urban
Complex Task Force, Advisory Committee on Urban and
Regional Planning, *Report* (December 1974).
© 2007 Neptis Foundation

NOT ONE TORONTO REGION, BUT THREE

At the beginning of the 1970s, therefore, three spatial definitions of the Toronto region coexisted for planning purposes. They ranged from 1,865 square kilometres (the Metropolitan Toronto planning area), to 8,288 square kilometres (the MTARTS study area), to 22,274 square kilometres (the Toronto-Centred Region). Conceptualizations of these three spatial entities proceeded from three different assumptions about how the region should develop.

First, Metro planners continued to argue for a gradual expansion of the region from the centre outward, with controls to prevent development in outer districts that had not yet received basic services.[72]

But Metro planners also participated in MTARTS, and its work rested on a second, different assumption: that the outer suburban population would continue to grow and its transportation needs had to be accommodated. Metro planners were also early proponents of that study's principal outcome—the GO Transit commuter system—which some would later accuse of encouraging urban expansion.

Finally, the Toronto-Centred Region concept shifted the focus of regional planning away from Metro Toronto toward redistributing some of southern Ontario's growth to other parts of the province.

An *Ontario Planning and Development Act* adopted in 1973 outlined a step-by-step planning process for the province's five economic regions.[73] One of these, the Central Ontario Region, included but was considerably larger than the TCR.[74] The government approved two other pieces of land-use legislation at the same time, however, that supported TCR principles. The first established a system of parkway belts and multiple-use corridors to the north and west of Metropolitan Toronto. These would eventually be referred to collectively as a "utility corridor," and were to contain highways, hydro lines, and some green space. The stated purpose of this space was to separate existing communities and halt urban sprawl.

The other piece of legislation created a commission to protect and administer lands on and bordering the Niagara Escarpment, a ridge of land extending north–south over 725 kilometres in the west-central part of the province. A large part of it traversed the regional municipalities of Peel, Halton, and Hamilton-Wentworth. It had been the subject of government study at least since 1967, when Premier John Robarts had declared an interest in "preserving its entire length."[75] The 1973 legislation required the Niagara Escarpment Commission to produce a plan for 5,180 square kilometres of land within and beside this land mass with a view to preserving it as a continuous natural environment. As it did with the parkway belts and multiple-use corridors, the government intended to use planning controls rather than outright purchase to protect the Escarpment lands from urban development.

---

72. E. Comay, "A Brief to the Royal Commission on Metropolitan Toronto, 1964, op. cit., 33–37.

73. John Perry, "Inventory of Regional Planning Administration in Canada," Staff Paper No. 1 (Toronto: Intergovernmental Committee on Urban and Regional Research, 1974), 39. The number of economic regions was reduced from 10 to 5 at this time.

74. Central Ontario Lakeshore Urban Complex Task Force 1974, 4.

75. Thoman 1971, 47.

No provincial land-use plan for the southern Ontario region, nor indeed for any other part of Ontario, would appear, however. Even before passing the *Planning and Development Act*, the government was showing ambivalence about the TCR "concept." On the one hand, it had persuaded the federal government to choose a site east of Metro for a proposed new airport, and it had purchased land immediately to the south of that site for a planned self-contained community (North Pickering, later referred to as Seaton) containing a balance of industrial, residential, commercial, recreational, and agricultural uses. On the other hand, it had agreed to land-use proposals to the north and west of Metro that violated TCR principles. These violations were noted in the 1974 report of a task force of provincial and local officials that studied the implications of TCR ideas for the southern part of the region (Metropolitan Toronto and the regional municipalities of Durham, York, Peel, Halton and Hamilton-Wentworth). The task force concluded that "[t]he Government of Ontario is in fact now faced with a major decision: To reaffirm the TCR policy, or to abandon it."[76]

The government did neither, and the TCR concept remained part of the context in which Metro and the regional governments carried out their own planning studies and prepared official plans for the rest of the 1970s.

A partial redistribution of service costs and benefits

METROPOLITAN TORONTO

Although the new City of Toronto that emerged from Metro's 1966 restructuring would send a minority of members to Metro Council, its consolidation with the wealthy residential enclave of Forest Hill had moved it from third to first place in per capita assessment within Metropolitan Toronto, a position it would hold for the next three decades. Its strengthened finances meant an increase in its relative shares of Metro costs, but it also meant that Toronto had a larger local tax base on which to draw for funding its own services (Table 3.1). Its larger commercial/industrial tax base also made it less reliant than the suburbs on residential taxpayers.

SOCIAL HOUSING: DISPERSED CONCENTRATIONS

By reorganizing Metro the way it did, the provincial government made Metro institutions rather than restructured municipalities responsible for dealing with some of the area's more pressing social needs. The exception was the provision of rent-geared-to-income housing for families, which the province made the exclusive responsibility of the Ontario Housing Corporation

---

76. Central Ontario Lakeshore Urban Complex Task Force 1974, 48.

Table 3.1 Distribution of property assessment in Metropolitan Toronto after 1966 reorganization

	Assessed population 1967 as per cent of Metro's	Total assessment as per cent of Metro's total assessment	Residential assessment as per cent of Metro total	Commercial/ industrial assessment as per cent of Metro total
East York	5.0	4.8	5.6	3.6
Etobicoke	13.6	15.9	16.2	14.3
North York	25.1	20.4	24.9	14.2
Scarborough	17.2	11.2	13.2	8.4
Toronto	32.2	42.8	33.8	55.3
York	6.8	5.5	6.4	4.2

Source: Based on figures contained in Jarrett, Gould, and Elliott 1975, 1, 13.

(OHC) after 1964. By pursuing an aggressive policy of land acquisition, new construction, and the purchase of existing housing, OHC was able to locate most of its housing in Metro's suburban municipalities, thereby achieving a more balanced distribution of Metro's poorest households (those eligible for rent subsidies) among central and suburban locations.

OHC was not, however, able to achieve another objective expressed by the provincial premier at the time of its creation: that of distributing public housing into all parts of Metro as a way to integrate tenants into many different communities, rather than concentrating them in large projects, as had been happening up to that time.[77] Government-imposed limits on what OHC could spend, neighbourhood opposition to public housing, and a shortage of suitably zoned sites meant that public housing units tended to go into high-rise, high-density apartment buildings in a small number of locations. Some buildings were even more isolated from the rest of their communities than those that had been built in the past. Public objections to such projects and to the demands they made on local services added to criticisms of public housing in the late 1960s.

Part of the problem was that OHC was never able to build or acquire enough housing to meet demand, despite giving Metro the largest stock of public housing of any city-region in Canada. It therefore allocated units according to a points system designed to identify applicants in greatest need. This practice resulted in the concentration of Metro's poorest families in relatively few districts. As these districts became associated with various social problems, public opposition hardened not just toward social housing,

---

77. John Robarts [Premier of Ontario], "Ontario Housing Corporation Formed," *Municipal World*, 74 (September 1964), 293–294.

Table 3.2 Increases in Toronto Transit Commission route miles, 1966–1976

	Metro Toronto population	Per cent increase	Total route miles	Per cent increase	Bus route miles	Trolley miles	Streetcar miles	Subway miles
1966	1,884,842		535.9		441.9	26.7	52.7	14.6
1971	2,089,729	10.9	597.9	11.8	500.2	28.7	48.3	20.7
1976	2,124,291	1.7	698.1	16.8	595.9	32.1	44.4	25.7

Source: Statistics Canada.

but toward all forms of low-rental, multiple-unit housing in most parts of the region.

WELFARE SERVICES MORE UNIFORM, THOUGH NOT NECESSARILY MORE ACCESSIBLE

Metro's assumption of responsibility for welfare implied an end to the large disparities in welfare services available to residents of different municipalities. It also reduced the likelihood that the area's poorest households would gravitate to the city in search of better services, making conversion of single-family neighbourhoods in the urban core less disruptive. The change in welfare administration also meant that suburban residents became eligible for optional services that had previously been available only to people living in the city. Accessing these services could be difficult, however, for people living in remote outer districts.

BETTER SUBURBAN TRANSIT

The dispersal of assisted rental housing to suburban locations within Metro gave suburban politicians one more reason to press the TTC for better public transit service and an end to the zone-fare system. The province's 1970 decision to reimburse municipal governments for half of any transit operating deficits helped the suburbs to realize these goals. By 1973 Metro Council had persuaded the TTC to do away with the zone-fare system. From that time forward, Metro residents could travel anywhere within Metro boundaries for a single fare.

The TTC continued to add new transit routes, most of them in the suburbs, after 1966. It added more after than before 1971, when subsidies came into effect, even though Metro's population growth was slowing down (Table 3.2). By 1973 the TTC operated the third-largest transit system in North America in terms of passengers carried, at a time when there were eight North American cities larger than Toronto. It had also brought transit service to within about 1,000 feet (300 metres) of more than 80 per cent of the Metropolitan Toronto population (although subdivision layouts sometimes meant longer walking distances).[78]

INEQUALITIES IN PUBLIC EDUCATION PERSIST

The consolidation of local school boards into larger units was one of a succession of government efforts, begun in the 1950s, to reduce province-wide inequalities in local school board spending resulting from inequalities in local taxable assessments. The pursuit of equality remained an elusive goal in Metropolitan Toronto, however. Shifting financial responsibilities to the MTSB meant redistributing more of Metro's education taxes among Metro's wealthier and poorer school districts, as well as levelling out the amounts that its local boards were able to spend per pupil. Foreseeing that these outcomes would cause administrative difficulties for local boards and political difficulties for the province, the government allowed Metro's local boards to supplement the money they received from Metro with an additional education tax on local ratepayers (a "discretionary levy") up to a specified mill rate.

For its first few years, the newly empowered MTSB proceeded cautiously, generally approving the budgets of local boards so that they made little use of the discretionary levy.[79] It also tried to accommodate differences among school populations by developing a weighting system that based the amounts given to individual boards on such criteria as pupil–teacher ratios, provision of junior kindergartens, the special requirements of "inner-city" schools, and special education classes (classes for pupils who were developmentally handicapped).

The most difficult issue to resolve was teachers' salaries. Some boards argued for a uniform salary scale across Metro to end inter-board competition for qualified teachers. Others opposed this idea. After two years of compli-cated and sometimes acrimonious salary negotiations, the teachers themselves asked for area-wide negotiations under the auspices of the Metro Board. With the help of a mediator, a Metro-wide agreement was reached for 1969–70. Although not formalized as standard practice, this agreement amounted to an informal understanding that future negotiations would be Metro-wide.

Despite tensions and disagreements associated with school board restructuring, the Metro Board's Executive Secretary concluded in 1969 that three years of operation under the new arrangements had demonstrated "that it is possible to maintain a high degree of local autonomy and at the same time achieve cooperatively an overall plan for the entire area."[80] This was so, he said, because "the Metropolitan Toronto School Board is not an agency apart

---

78. Metropolitan Toronto Transportation Plan Review 1973, 27, 29.
79. McCordic 1969, 92–94.
80. Ibid., 94.

from the local boards but is in fact the local boards meeting together to share their problems and to reach decisions on matters relating to budget."

The willingness to compromise waned rapidly after 1969, however, when the province revised its scheme for distributing education grants. Under the new scheme, grants were based on school operating costs instead of school enrolments, with amounts to vary inversely with local assessments. The purpose of the grants was to enable school boards throughout the province to spend and tax at the same rates, regardless of the taxable wealth of their communities, although the grants did take into account the higher costs of educating students in northern areas and large urban centres.[81] The government also extended financial support to separate (Roman Catholic) schools from the end of elementary school to the end of Grade 10.

As part of the change in the grant system, the government began to deliver aid to public education in the form of block grants, thereby giving elected school boards more freedom to spend money according to their own priorities.[82] The Ministry of Education agreed to confine itself to passing laws; planning, research, and development; providing technical assistance to school boards that asked for it; and pursuing equality of educational opportunity for students in all parts of the province. It would leave the operation of schools to local school boards, which could decide what material would be taught within broad, centrally determined guidelines, and hire and evaluate teachers.[83] Thus educational restructuring meant that elected school boards could operate schools with less provincial supervision than at any previous time in their history.

After 1969, the government had gradually increased the size of its grants for education, and by 1975, it was paying 61 per cent of Ontario's total public education costs. In keeping with its stated intention to put school boards across the province on an equal financial footing, the percentage of grant income varied among school districts according to the size of their assessments. The government weakened the equalizing potential of the new grant formula, however, by placing ceilings on the size of its total contributions to school spending. For the first two years, it allowed local boards to raise additional taxes, both to increase spending on activities recognized in grant calculations and to cover "extraordinary" expenditures, up to a prescribed mill rate limit.

When school board restructuring and the new grant program turned out to be more costly than expected, however, the government withdrew the

81. Rideout 1974, 172–174.

82. Ontario Commission on the Financing of Elementary and Secondary Education in Ontario 1985, 17.

83. Fisher 1972; E. Rideout, "Alternatives for Educational Finance within the Established Parameters" (paper prepared for the Commission on Declining School Enrolments, 1978), 2–3.

right of school boards to supplement their budgets out of local taxes, and in 1971, it imposed an absolute ceiling on what all school boards could spend. Boards that were already spending above the ceiling had three years to bring their spending into line. "It is difficult to visualize a more effective method of achieving equality of [education] provision than that adopted by Ontario," wrote one school board official about the ceiling, "short of the complete takeover of school administration and finance by the central authority. But as more and more districts reach the ceilings, local autonomy in terms of revenue raising power will have ceased to exist."[84] Nowhere was this more apparent than in Metropolitan Toronto, where all six boards were spending above the ceiling when it was imposed. Conflict soon broke out within the MTSB, where staff sought both to reduce the budget and to shift funds from richer to poorer boards to keep per pupil spending relatively uniform across Metro.[85] Dissension would persist until well into the 1980s.

ENTRENCHING DIFFERENCES WITHIN THE TORONTO REGION

Spreading the costs and benefits of local services more equally among local municipalities was one of the objectives that provincial officials ascribed to local government restructuring in the late 1960s.[86] The government applied it to regional governments separately, however, and not to the Toronto region as a whole. For example, each of the regional governments outside Metro became responsible for social welfare, which meant that each could decide which, if any, services it would provide over and above those mandated by the provincial government. Moreover, there were four important differences between Metro and the suburban regions in the way services important to social well-being were organized.

First, lower-tier municipalities in the regional municipalities retained the right to negotiate separately with the Ontario Housing Corporation for public housing, whereas in Metro that right belonged exclusively to Metro Council. In 1976 the four regional municipalities had 31 per cent of the Toronto region's population but only 6 per cent of its public housing (661 units for families; 1,883 units for senior citizens).[87] Metro, with 69 per cent of the region's population, had 94 per cent of its public housing, three-quarters of it for families. These differences seemed likely to persist.

Second, public transit was a local responsibility in the regional municipalities, but remained in the hands of a single agency (the TTC) in Metro.

---

84. Rideout 1974, 178.
85. Williams 1976.
86. The Honourable Charles S. MacNaughton [Treasurer of Ontario], "The Need for a Better System of Local Government," *Municipal World*, 83 (February 1973), 33–34.
87. Klein and Sears 1975, 59.

TTC passengers were able to transfer among subway lines, streetcars, and buses for a single fare. The four suburban regional municipalities, on the other hand, were not made responsible for transit. They had 14 local transit systems, most of them serving single municipalities, and only some of them linked to the GO system. Both the TTC and suburban transit systems operated independently of each other and of GO. Consequently, transfers between transit systems meant paying additional fares.

Third, public health was assigned to regional boards of health outside Metro, but remained a lower-tier responsibility in Metro.

Finally, in reorganizing Metro, the province retained the two-tier system of public education. In the regional municipalities, on the other hand, public education was administered by two elected regional boards, one responsible for public schools, the other for separate (Roman Catholic) schools. There were no second-tier school boards.

These differences implied variations in the costs, type, quality, and quantity of services available to people living in different parts of the region, a situation likely to reinforce a sense of difference rather than connection among them.

METROPOLITAN TORONTO: NEW TENSIONS ADDED TO OLD ONES

According to Albert Rose, the most remarkable feature of Metro's 1966 reorganization was "the virtual absence of public dissent."[88] Evidently the lengthy debates that had taken place on Metro Council and the MTSB, the airing of alternatives before the Goldenberg Commission, and the compromises made by the province had made restructuring seem, if not completely acceptable, at least inevitable.

It was not long, however, before both Metro Council and the MTSB were engaged in new disputes arising from fundamentally different viewpoints about how contentious issues should be addressed. Most disputes at the MTSB were about the allocation of the education budget among the area's six local school boards. Disputes on Metro Council were more wide-ranging. Some observers attributed them to the dominance of anti-development politicians on Toronto City Council and their persistent opposition to what they saw as a Metro bias in favour of new highways and high-density, high-rise redevelopment. Others ascribed them to weak leadership, an unwieldy and poorly managed administrative structure, and the unwillingness on the part of Metro members to put Metro-wide issues ahead of local concerns.[89] Both city and

---

88. Rose 1972, 123.

89. Alden Baker, "Metro Toronto's prestige, efficiency, morale on decline," *Globe and Mail*, May 9, 1973; Alden Baker, "Metro moves to strengthen authority of Council, chair-

suburban members complained that Metro Council did not serve their interests, the city because it now had a minority of Metro Council members, the suburbs because the city and two inner suburbs made up a council majority, and because city representatives still made up five of the eleven members on Metro's influential Executive Committee.[90]

The election of Paul Godfrey as Chair of Metro Council in 1973 gave city politicians more cause for concern. Godfrey, a former member of the North York Board of Control (a directly elected executive committee), had supported the Spadina Expressway and openly criticized some of the city's representatives to Metro Council. At his urging, the provincial government changed the *Metropolitan Toronto Act* in 1974 to give the three outer municipalities five more members on Council. These municipalities then had twenty members, while Toronto had twelve and the two inner suburbs only five. The province also increased the number of Executive Committee members from eleven to fourteen, while reducing Toronto's members from five to four.[91]

Elected officials in other parts of Metro were also chafing at having to work within the two-tier system. They asked the province to return some of Metro's powers (particularly for planning and housing) to the local municipalities. They also insisted that the representatives they sent to Metro Council should not act as free agents, but should vote according to the instructions of their local councils.[92] Chairman Godfrey countered by urging the province to consider giving Metro overriding powers in planning and housing.[93] He also began a full-scale reorganization of Metro's administrative structure that implied an overall strengthening of Metro relative to the local municipalities and more powers for the chairman's office.[94]

In this atmosphere of city–suburban disaffection, the provincial government appointed a second Royal Commission in September 1974 to carry out a comprehensive review of the Metro system and "make appropriate recom-

---

man in administration," *Globe and Mail*, December 1, 1971; Alden Baker, "After 20 years of civic federation, is Metro's end now in sight?" *Globe and Mail*, March 1, 1973.

90. Alden Baker, "North York, Scarborough to ask for redistribution of representation on Metro Council," *Globe and Mail*, January 8, 1973.

91. Peter Mosher, "Growing suburbs to gain 5 more seats on council," *Globe and Mail*, June 14, 1974.

92. Alden Baker, "Dance to local tunes, councilors told," *Globe and Mail*, May 13, 1974; "A local voice is necessary at Metro level," *Globe and Mail*, May 16, 1974; Alden Baker, "Borough mayors criticize bureaucracy and growing role of Metro," *Globe and Mail*, August 5, 1974.

93. Alden Baker, "Boroughs express amalgamation fears," *Globe and Mail*, June 17, 1974.

94. Alden Baker, "Godfrey papers show early quest for chief officer," *Globe and Mail*, August 1, 1974; Alden Baker, "Borough mayors criticize bureaucracy and growing role of Metro"; Alden Baker, "Metro strongman," *Globe and Mail*, December 23, 1974.

mendations on the structure, organization and operations" of all aspects of local government, taking account of present conditions and future needs.[95] The head of the Commission was John Robarts, who as provincial premier (1961–71) had presided over the reorganization of Metro Toronto and the development of the province's regional government and Toronto-Centred Region initiatives.

THE TORONTO REGION: THE ADVANTAGES
OF DISUNITY OUTWEIGH ITS DISADVANTAGES

Despite the infighting that characterized Metro politics when he began his inquiry, Robarts later observed that

> there was no specific crisis in any single aspect of the local government system in Metropolitan Toronto which required immediate action. In fact, the system appeared to be working quite well, certainly in comparison with many other urban governments.[96]

Coming as it did from the man who had overseen the province's excursions into regionalism, and who had once described Metro as "one of the most successful forms of local government operating anywhere,"[97] his observation leads one to ask why the Ontario government created regional municipalities in the Toronto region at all. Why not simply enlarge Metropolitan Toronto and empower its government to address some of the region's more pressing infrastructural needs? That approach would have been a more straightforward and probably less costly way to tackle regional issues than the complex and fragmented arrangements the government had put in place. It also had a number of reputable advocates, including the Metropolitan Toronto planning director, the TTC, and such private-sector interests as the Urban Development Institute (an organization of private developers), the Automotive Transport Association of Ontario, and the Metropolitan Toronto Board of Trade.[98]

95. Royal Commission on Metropolitan Toronto 1977(a), xiii. At the time of Metro's formation in 1953, Premier Frost had promised that the government would review the Metro system every 10 years. The Robarts Commission was the second such review. It would also be the last.

96. Royal Commission on Metropolitan Toronto 1977(a), xv.

97. Ontario Legislature 1968, "Statement by John P. Robarts, Premier of Ontario," November 28, 7.

98. E. Comay, "A Brief...," op cit. 1964; The Board of Trade of Metropolitan Toronto, "Position Paper on Regional Planning, Growth and Government" (response to statements by the Honourable John Robarts, November 28, 1968, and the Honourable W. Darcy McKeough, December 2, 1968); Metropolitan Toronto Planning Board, "Report on Metropolitan Toronto and Region Transportation Study, Part II," November 14, 1968;

The government never looked at this option seriously, however. Instead it used staff research, special committees, a national conference, and local government reviews to build support for the more fragmented approach. There were at least two reasons why it acted in this way.

First, it simply did not want a bigger, stronger Metropolitan Toronto. The government recognized, said a close observer of events at the time, that "once Toronto's federation reached two million and was clearly headed for about eight million in the next century, if it ever did begin to plan, then Ontario would either be run by metropolitan Toronto or by the province, but not both."[99]

Second, there was little or no political support for enlarging Metro's role in the region. Few Metro politicians showed much interest in pursuing this possibility, although Metro Council did allow Metro staff to take part in regional policy-making. It was Metro planners, for example, who proposed a rail commuter service for the Toronto area based on existing rail lines, an idea that led to the GO Transit commuter system. When the province initiated the service, however, Metro Council refused to pay any of its costs, thereby giving up an opportunity to have a say in its development.[100] Metro councillors also greeted the regional government announcement in contradictory ways. Whereas some of them said that Metro should have annexed large sections of territory to the north and east while it was still possible to do so, others criticized the province for not creating regional governments fast enough to take growth pressures off Metro.[101]

The threat of annexation to Metro had been all that was needed to persuade some outer suburban officials that local government restructuring was a good idea. For example, the outspoken Mayor Desmond Newman of Whitby, to the east of Metro, told a provincial–municipal conference that allowing Metro to expand would destroy the economic base of surrounding counties; remove the opportunity to create a healthy environment of regional competition and co-operation; permit the creation of private, low-cost dormitory development in the fringe; result in sprawl that would increase the cost of urban transit to an impossible level; and create a situation "where a single municipal government is uniquely able to distort Provincial policy by virtue of its control over half of the Province's population."[102] Those who were demanding the expansion

Toronto Transit Commission, "A Submission from the Toronto Transit Commission to the Government of the Province of Ontario re the MTARTS Proposal," January 1969.

99. Pearson 1975, 179.

100. Metropolitan Toronto Council Minutes, September 20 and October 18, 1966.

101. Alden Baker, "Fear of urban strangulation haunts Metro," *Globe and Mail,* October 22, 1971.

102. D.G. Newman [Mayor of the Town of Whitby], "Ontario Provincial–Municipal Conference: A Presentation on Regional Government," *Municipal World,* 80 (June 1970), 153.

of Metro, he went on, should turn their attention "to the improvement in that which they have so successfully created, by a reduction in the human misery of the forgotten, and in the amelioration of those conditions which demean the social environment rather than to expansion which will inevitably lead to a stock-piling of the explosive called 'social unrest.'"

Missing from Mayor Newman's vision was any concept of the inner and outer parts of the region as having common interests or facing common challenges. Newman was ready to support the creation of regional municipalities, on the other hand, as long as they brought municipal governments new sources of taxation and more provincial aid in the form of unconditional grants.

The most formal gesture of local support for regional government came from the County of York, to the north of Metro, which was one of the few counties to undertake a full local government review on its own. It did so both because it did not want to lose any more territory to Metro and because the Smith Committee had advised the government to create a "Metropolitan Highlands District by amalgamating York County with sections of five other counties to its east and west.[103] York pointed out that it could dominate such a district because of its much larger population and assessment. Consequently, it argued, York County should be "the initial unit of regional government" in order to minimize disruption (and presumably costs to York County taxpayers). Expansion beyond York County boundaries could occur later. The province not only followed this advice when it created the Regional Municipality of York in 1971, but Municipal Affairs Minister Darcy McKeough later remarked, "The entire program for regional government throughout the Province of Ontario was given a strong positive impetus by the well-informed presentation of the York proposals."[104]

To the west of Metro, on the other hand, there was fierce opposition to the way restructuring occurred (though not necessarily to restructuring per se) from the small towns of Port Credit and Streetsville in Peel County, and from the Town of Burlington in neighbouring Halton County. Under the leadership of outspoken mayor Hazel McCallion, Streetsville fought a particularly bitter battle against consolidation with the larger municipality of Mississauga. It proposed instead to annex part of Mississauga to make room for new development in Streetsville, something it had been resisting up to that time.[105]

---

103. Interview with W.S. Addison, York Region, Summer 1981; Regional Municipality of York n.d., 19.

104. W. Darcy McKeough, "Structure and Political Organization of Local Government North of Metropolitan Toronto," *Municipal World*, 79 (May, 1969), 119.

105. John Beaufoy, "2 towns don't want to be part of Mississauga's growth," *Globe and Mail*, November 30, 1972.

Burlington officials were just as passionate in opposing a plan to unite their town with its nearest neighbour, the industrial city of Hamilton, and urged the province to leave it in a regional municipality based on the existing boundaries of Halton County, to which it then belonged. Burlington won, but Streetsville lost, first in the restructuring plan adopted by the government, and then on appeal to the OMB. The plans finally adopted by the government left existing county boundaries virtually unchanged. [106]

The municipal politicians and staff members who opposed provincial plans to change the existing system of local government tended to depict restructuring either as a violation of local autonomy or as likely to mean higher taxes. Undoubtedly they also saw it as a threat to their jobs. Just like those who supported change, these officials were more concerned with the immediate effects of restructuring on their communities and their own positions than they were on upholding abstract principles of regional unity.

Faced with qualified support from some local governments and outright resistance from others, the provincial government went ahead with local government reorganization but softened its impacts with compromises, just as it had done in reorganizing Metro a few years earlier. It created regional municipalities, but retained county boundaries; it consolidated local municipalities, but gave local councils authority to prepare official plans, to operate their own public transit systems, and to decide whether or not to accommodate social housing—all activities of importance to the physical and social character of the Toronto region. It instituted special grants to help regional governments get started and to ease the burden of restructuring on local taxpayers. It also legislated that all municipal employees were to be guaranteed a job (though not necessarily the same job) with no loss of pay for a year after the new arrangements took effect. [107]

THE RESULT: PERSISTENT FRAGMENTATION AND COMPLEXITY

The result of the government's attempts to protect its own authority, balance diverse interests, and allay the anxieties of municipal officials was a hybrid and potentially costly system of Toronto region governance that lacked both direction and a mandate to address region-wide issues in a coordinated way. It consisted of several provincial agencies with responsibility for specific regional services, five upper-tier regional municipalities, and thirty second-tier municipal units. There were also one elected public and one elected

---

106. One exception was the Regional Municipality of Durham, where local politicians could not agree on what they wanted. Durham was formed from parts of two former counties, while other parts remained in their old county structures.

107. Ron Farrow, "Lessons Learned from the Establishment of Ontario's Regional Governments" (paper presented at the University of Western Ontario, May 22, 1990), 20.

separate (Roman Catholic) school board in each of the regional municipalities and a two-tier system of public education in Metro Toronto, not to mention various special-purpose authorities serving different segments of the region and reporting to different governments.

What this system still lacked by the early 1970s was a capacity for leadership and coordination. The government seemed ready to provide this capacity in 1972, when it created a new Ministry of Treasury, Economics and Intergovernmental Affairs (TEIGA) as part of a major overhaul of the provincial bureaucracy. This new ministry combined the economic development and regional planning activities of the Department of Treasury and Economics with many of the responsibilities previously exercised by the Department of Municipal Affairs. The man appointed to head it, Darcy McKeough, was the member of the provincial government who best understood and had most strongly supported the province's regional initiatives. Thus the Ontario government seemed to be poised to assume control of governance in the Toronto region in fact as well as in law.

TEIGA never realized its potential, however. By the mid-1970s the province was losing interest in the system it had put in place, and was ignoring its own TCR initiative. For the next 10 years, the concept of an extended Toronto region virtually disappeared from political and professional discourse. Regional objectives would surface on various occasions and in various forms, but they never coalesced into a coherent agenda.

FOUR

1975–1985
Provincial Retrenchment
and Local Inaction

After creating eleven two-tier regional municipalities in southern Ontario between 1969 and 1974, the Ontario government backed away from regional initiatives. It was soon insisting that problems arising in cities or city-regions could be dealt with by municipal and regional governments in consultation with the province; such problems did not require the creation of new institutions with a focus on the entire Toronto region. Thus the period gave municipal officials in the region several opportunities to decide for themselves how they wanted to deal with matters that crossed municipal boundaries.

Why the Ontario Government
Backed Away from Regionalism

Explanations for the government's retreat from regionalism included changes in the province's economic circumstances, in the government's political fortunes, in the rate of regional growth, in policy-making practices and procedures, and in the federal government's interest in urban and regional affairs. Of the five, changes in the province's economic circumstances tended to dominate government policy statements from the mid-1970s onward.

A slowing and changing economy

Even while it was implementing several regional initiatives in the early 1970s, the Ontario government was becoming concerned with "a worldwide weakening of economic growth" and its effects on the provincial economy.[1] The trend was most apparent in the manufacturing sector, since by 1972 capital and labour were beginning to shift into the service and resource sectors,

---

1. W. Darcy McKeough [Treasurer of Ontario], "1975 Budget Statement," *Ontario Budget 1975* (Toronto: Ministry of Treasury, Economics and Intergovernmental Affairs, 1975), 2.

particularly energy production. "Fierce competition from other countries"[2] was also affecting the economy. The government's concern intensified after 1973 because of high inflation caused by a sharp rise in world oil prices resulting from export restraints imposed by Middle Eastern oil-producing nations.[3] The economic slowdown drew attention to the steady growth in government spending over the previous two decades and a spiralling government deficit.[4] By the end of the 1970s, therefore, all levels of government were focusing almost exclusively on economic concerns.[5]

The political costs of regional intervention

Political as well as economic volatility influenced the Ontario government's responses to regional issues after 1975. Although the Progressive Conservative Party won the 1971 election with a comfortable majority, its popularity began to decline soon afterward. The implementation of the government's regional initiatives contributed to its loss of support, as municipal politicians and local voters began to worry about what local government restructuring, property tax reform, and a province-wide planning framework implied for local autonomy and the size of local tax bills. Moreover, the 1971 accession of William Davis as party leader and premier meant a loss of leadership support for regionalism. Whereas Premier Robarts had been closely involved with and supportive of the regional economic development and regional government programs, Davis, as Minister of Education, had been responsible only for consolidating local school boards. Otherwise he had devoted his energy to reforming education administration and restructuring education grants.

As a representative of a riding in the suburban City of Brampton, to the west of Metro Toronto, Davis was more directly aware than Robarts (who came from the City of London, in southwestern Ontario) of the type of growth pressures the suburbs were under. He also counted land developers among his friends. Within a year of becoming premier, in fact, he and other members of his government were fighting media accusations that they had been involved too closely with land developers in several land deals. McKeough, the Minister of Treasury, Economics and Intergovernmental Affairs, the most vigorous government proponent of the regional initiatives, had to leave the cabinet

---

2. D.W. Stevenson, "Notes for Speech to the Ontario Association of Land Economists," September 23, 1972.

3. Simeon 1985, 155.

4. Between 1945 and 1973, Ontario's net expenditures increased more than 32 times in absolute dollars or 8.6 times in constant dollar terms, while the provincial population increased by only 2.5 times (Richmond 1974, 37, 39).

5. Dyck 1986, 296–298; Ron Hosking in "Roundtable," in Goldrick and Holmes 1981, 21–24.

for 18 months while he dealt with one such accusation. He did not become Treasurer again until 1975, by which time the ministry was preoccupied with finding ways to fight the deficit.

Disaffection with local government restructuring and media accusations of government corruption were among reasons cited for the failure of the Progressive Conservative Party to win an absolute majority in a 1975 election (the party's first electoral setback in 32 years), and a second such failure in 1977.[6] By the time the Conservatives regained their majority in 1981, the government had completely dismantled the bureaucracy that had fuelled its regional initiatives.

A slowing down and outward shift of population growth

After growing by more than 80,000 persons per year between 1961 and 1971, the Toronto region grew by fewer than 50,000 persons per year over the next decade. There was also an important change in the way new growth was distributed. Whereas Metro Toronto had absorbed 58 per cent of the area's population increase in the 1960s, or 47,000 persons per year on average, its growth fell below 4,800 persons per year between 1971 and 1981 (for a 9.6 per cent increase). Population growth outside Metro increased, on the other hand, from an average of 19,000 persons per year between 1961 and 1971 to an average of 45,000 in the next decade. Over the 10-year period, therefore, Metro's share of the Toronto region's population dropped from 71 to 63 per cent.[7] The largest share of new growth went to the Regional Municipality of Peel, continuing a growth pattern that the province's TCR concept had been designed to counteract. Nonetheless, the construction of new infrastructure in the three surrounding regional municipalities was relieving pressures on the province to deal with development-related issues.

Demands for municipal and public involvement

Changes in the way provincial and municipal governments made and implemented policy during this period occurred in response to complaints by municipal officials and provincial legislators that they had been largely excluded from the development of political institutions and financial policies that affected their communities.[8] At the same time, municipal residents were

---

6. Morton 1985, 14.

7. Based on figures contained in Metropolitan Toronto Planning Department, Research and Special Studies Division, 1995, Table 1.4

8. "Provincial financial supervision of local government criticized," *Globe and Mail*, October 10, 1972.

also demanding the right to participate in public policy-making at both the provincial and municipal levels. Many of these demands emerged out of community campaigns to stop major development and redevelopment programs (highways, urban renewal) in heavily built-up urban districts, especially the City of Toronto.[9] Others came from rural and small-town interests seeking to protect a vanishing way of life from urban invaders. Community involvement implied a rejection of policies and procedures that critics blamed on an impersonal bureaucracy with little understanding of the impacts of its decisions on established neighbourhoods or towns.

The provincial government responded to attacks on past practices by using more consultative modes of policy analysis (task forces, committees, and the like) to secure advice both from municipal officials and from the general public. It incorporated requirements for public participation into legislation and regulations that defined municipal responsibilities. Provincial officials also talked of rationalizing the *Municipal Act* in the interest of making "local governments more meaningful and more responsible for their own actions."[10]

The declining threat of federal intervention

After failing to overcome resistance to its activities within the federal bureaucracy and from the larger provinces, the Ministry of State for Urban Affairs was stripped of most of its responsibilities in 1976. Three years later, it was eliminated altogether as part of a government cost-cutting exercise.[11] Thus from the mid-1970s onward, federal government activities affecting the region were limited to matters directly related to its constitutional responsibilities, including immigration, the management of the national economy (the principal motivator of federal housing and housing-related programs), and international and interprovincial transportation. This last responsibility included the management of federally owned lands surrounding Toronto harbour. Although these activities were important to the physical and social character of the Toronto region, they did not directly challenge the province's authority to manage municipal affairs.

---

9. Much has been written about this eventful period in Toronto politics. See, for example, Fish 1976; Magnusson 1983; and Sewell 1993, 135–198.

10. W. Darcy McKeough, *Ontario Budget 1975*, Appendix C (Toronto: Ministry of Treasury, Economics and Intergovernmental Affairs, 1975), 32–33: Donald Stevenson, "The Ministry of Intergovernmental Affairs as we enter the 80's" (remarks to the Twenty-seventh annual conference of the Organization of Small Urban Municipalities of the Association of Municipalities of Ontario, Parry Sound, Ontario, May 3, 1980).

11. Higgins 1986, 112.

Growing social complexity

Even as federal, provincial, and municipal officials began to adopt a more decentralized approach to urban policy-making, new issues were finding their way into urban policy discussions. Among them were issues related to changes in the Toronto region's social composition and socio-spatial structure. These changes were the result of several forces, most notably federally sponsored immigration. Approximately one-third of all immigrants to Canada settled in the Toronto region every year, most of them in Metropolitan Toronto. Because of changes in federal immigration policy in the 1960s (see Chapter 3), a growing proportion of these immigrants belonged to ethnic groups that Statistics Canada would later categorize as "visible minorities."[12]

Social change in the Toronto region was also affected by a provincial government decision in the 1960s to reduce the number of people in custodial (mental health and correctional) institutions by releasing them into the community. Although the policy grew out of the province's desire to reduce demand for expensive services, advocates for persons with special needs also argued that their clients could function better and lead more normal lives outside institutional settings, preferably in their own communities. The availability of more effective drugs for treating mental illness and behavioural disorders added strength to this argument. As it turned out, however, many such persons came to live in the City of Toronto, either because they could not return to their own communities or because Toronto offered a wider range of services and opportunities than smaller communities.

Institutional Adaptations to Regional Change

After 1974 the government not only ended studies of regional (or county) and local government restructuring, but also left the newly created regional governments to work out problems largely on their own. The exception to this hands-off approach was Metropolitan Toronto, which the government subjected to the scrutiny of a second Royal Commission (the Robarts Commission) appointed in 1974 to "[e]xamine, evaluate and make appropriate recommendations" on all aspects of its "structure, organization and operations" and those of its member municipalities.[13] The Commission's study would be the last such study ever done of Metropolitan Toronto.

---

12. See note 17, Chapter 1.
13. Royal Commission on Metropolitan Toronto 1977(a), xiii.

Metropolitan Toronto stays as it is

The Robarts Commission began its work at a time when relations between Metro and the City of Toronto were being sorely tested by anti-development members of Toronto City Council, who associated Metro with the projects they opposed (such as expressway construction and urban renewal). The Commission acknowledged these tensions by considering two radical options for changing the Metro system: (1) amalgamating the six cities within Metro into one large city, and (2) abolishing the Metro tier of government. It rejected both. Amalgamation, said its report, "would decrease the sensitivity of the system" to local concerns. Moreover, there was no evidence that it would decrease local government costs. As for the second option, the Commission concluded that the advantages of maintaining the two-tier system far outweighed its shortcomings: "[N]o one has brought forward (nor has the Commission found) sufficient arguments to support the abolition of that level."[14]

As an alternative, the Commission recommended ways the government could make the two-tier system work more smoothly and equitably while giving municipal politicians more responsibility and authority. It favoured doing away with special-purpose bodies like the TTC, the Board of Police Commissioners, and the metropolitan and local planning boards, and making Metro Council directly responsible for the services they provided. It also recommended adjustments to Metro's internal boundaries to give the two smallest and poorest municipalities, York and East York, larger shares of the Metro population and the Metro tax base.

Provincial responses to the Robarts Commission's 127 recommendations showed how far the province had moved from using local government restructuring as an instrument of municipal policy. After hearing strong opposition to internal boundary changes from Toronto, Scarborough, and North York, the three municipalities that would lose population and territory, the government said that it would make only minor changes, and only if municipalities agreed to them.[15] None did so, and Metro's internal boundaries remained unchanged until 1997, when the provincial government consolidated its seven governments into one.

The government also did not act on a recommendation for the direct election of municipal representatives to Metro Council. Instead, it permitted the area's municipal governments to devise their own forms of direct election. Apart from making a few changes in administrative procedures, the province

---

14. Ibid., 42.

15. Alden Baker, "Remapping not popular, mayor says," *Globe and Mail*, October 26, 1977; Ontario Ministry of Treasury, Economics and Intergovernmental Affairs 1978, 1.

took the position that municipal governments in Metro and elsewhere should decide on structural or procedural changes for themselves. Among the few changes that did occur was the elimination of appointed planning boards. Most other special-purpose bodies remained in place.

Toronto region government not an option

By 1976, Metro Toronto and the four surrounding regional municipalities (Durham, York, Peel, and Halton) contained 38 per cent of the Ontario population. Various writers were beginning to define the Toronto region in terms of these five units, although some included Hamilton-Wentworth as well. This second definition was the one used by the task force of provincial and regional staff members that reviewed and tried to refine the Toronto-Centred Region concept in 1974, an exercise that had little or no impact on government policy.[16] It was also the definition used by the Robarts Commission in its 1977 report when it discussed "the interregional context" in which Metro operated.[17]

The government had told Commissioner Robarts when he began his work that the Royal Commission could recommend changes to virtually any aspect of the Metro system—except Metro's external boundaries.[18] Those were to remain as they were. The Commission did not ignore the region entirely, however. "In some ways," it observed, "the relationship of Metropolitan Toronto to the larger Toronto region resembles the relationship between the City of Toronto and the suburbs twenty-five years ago when the Metro system was created."[19] There were two important differences, however: (1) the recent emergence of several suburban municipalities as important centres of employment, and (2) the scale of the urban network.

Noting that the region lacked "established processes for coordinating public responsibilities on a larger interregional scale," the Commission recommended the creation of a Toronto Region Coordinating Agency made up of representatives of municipal and regional councils and a provincial minister "with responsibility for the Toronto region."[20] This Agency, it said, should

---

16. Central Ontario Lakeshore Urban Complex Task Force 1974.

17. Royal Commission on Metropolitan Toronto 1977(b), 128.

18. Don Richmond, "Remarks in a session on Comparative Canadian–U.S. Federal Responses to Urban Issues," Urban Affairs Annual Meeting, Toronto, April 1997.

19. Royal Commission on Metropolitan Toronto 1977(b), 131–132. The head of that Commission, John Robarts, had been provincial premier from 1961 to 1971, the period when regional issues were being discussed and regional policies formulated.

20. The other options it considered were: (1) provincial government assumption of a coordinating role, (2) expanding Metro Toronto; and (3) doing nothing, an option it described as having "ominous and disconcerting" implications. Nonetheless, it was essentially the option that the government chose.

have legal authority to facilitate "the planning and development of the Toronto region," advise governments, provide services that participating governments asked it to provide, and examine and comment on the budgets and plans of existing operating bodies from a regional perspective.

The Ministry of Treasury, Economics and Intergovernmental Affairs (TEIGA) rejected this recommendation. It was a "deficient" remedy for the problems of regional expansion, it said, because

> [p]roblems which transcend municipal or regional boundaries, are by definition, the responsibility of the province. Assigning a role to an agency which is not entirely responsible to the Province would confuse attempts at a clearer definition of responsibilities between the provincial and local levels of government.[21]

Delegates to such an agency, the statement continued, "could act independently and their views would not necessarily reflect the views of the majority of their Councils." Furthermore, according to this document, Metro, Durham, and Peel regions also opposed the suggestion, saying that "the task of coordinating inter-regional problems is (and should be) a provincial responsibility."

Ad hoc regionalism

Although the government implicitly accepted responsibility for dealing with issues that crossed the boundaries of Metropolitan Toronto and the regional municipalities, its failure to implement most of the Roberts Commission's recommendations was evidence of its loss of interest in addressing cross-boundary issues in an effective and coordinated way. Moreover, its own actions had added to the fragmentation and complexity of the Toronto region's governmental system. By 1978 the region encompassed five upper-tier municipalities (Metropolitan Toronto and the regional municipalities of Durham, York, Peel, and Halton)—or six, if Hamilton-Wentworth was included (see Figure 4.1). There were 30 or 36 lower-tier municipalities, depending on the definition used, as well as various boards and commissions, the members of which were appointed by one or more levels of government. Several provincial departments also carried out important responsibilities in the region (see Figure 4.2).

The federal government added to this institutional mix in 1976 by creating the Harbourfront [Crown] Corporation to manage and develop 35

---

21. Ontario Ministry of Treasury, Economics and Intergovernmental Affairs 1978, 37–38.

Figure 4.1 Greater Toronto Area plus Hamilton-Wentworth, 1974–2001

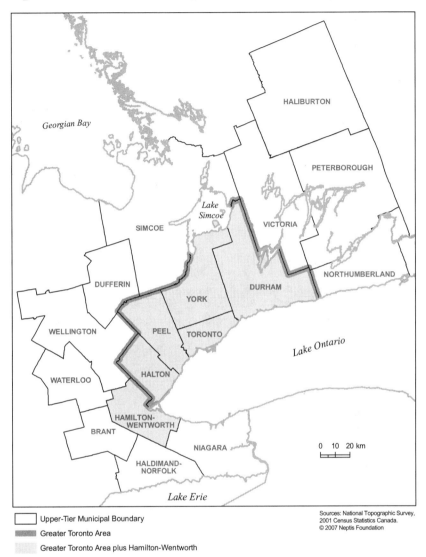

Upper-Tier Municipal Boundary

Greater Toronto Area

Greater Toronto Area plus Hamilton-Wentworth

Sources: National Topographic Survey,
2001 Census Statistics Canada.
© 2007 Neptis Foundation

hectares of land on the Toronto waterfront. It had assigned (but not given) the land to the City of Toronto in 1972, saying that it wanted to save the entire waterfront from additional high-rise development. It soon decided it did not want to pay all the associated costs, however, and neither did the city. Thus the Corporation's job was to develop the site in ways that would help it to finance the cultural, recreational, and educational programs that were already

Figure 4.2 Toronto-region governance, 1978[a]

Function	Ontario government	Toronto region	Metropolitan Toronto and regional governments	Local Municipalities	Intergovernmental
Education	Ministry of Education		**Metropolitan Toronto**[b] **and regional public and separate school boards**	**6 public school boards** (Metropolitan Toronto only)	
Finance	Ministry of Revenue		Metropolitan Toronto and regional Treasury and/or Finance departments	Finance departments	
Housing	Ministry of Housing **Ontario Housing Corporation (OHC)**		**Metropolitan Toronto Housing Company Limited** (housing for elderly persons) **Peel Living** (non-profit housing corporation)	Toronto Housing Department **Cityhome** (non-profit housing corporation)	**Metropolitan Toronto and Municipality Housing Authorities** (built and operated OHC housing)
Infrastructure (water, sewers, solid waste)	Ministry of the Environment		Metropolitan Toronto and regional Works or Works and Transportation departments.	Works or Works and Transportation departments	
Libraries			**Metropolitan Toronto Library Board**	**Public library boards**	
Parks	Ministry of Natural Resources (provincial parks) **Niagara Escarpment Commission**		Metropolitan Toronto Parks Department	Parks or Parks and Recreation departments	**Metropolitan Toronto and Region Conservation Authority and four other Conservation Authorities**[c] **Harbourfront Corporation**

Service	Provincial	Metropolitan/Regional	Municipal	Special-purpose bodies
Planning/ Land Use	Ministry of Housing; **Ontario Municipal Board**; Ministry of Treasury, Economics and Intergovernmental Affairs (Parkway Belt)	Metropolitan Toronto and regional planning departments	Planning departments	**Toronto Harbour Commission** **Harbourfront Corporation**
Protection	**Ontario Provincial Police**		Fire departments	Province/Metropolitan Toronto or Province/ regional municipality
Public Health		Regional departments or **Boards of Health.**	**Municipal Boards of Health** (Only in Metropolitan Toronto)	
Social and Community	Ministry of Community and Social Services	Metropolitan and regional Social Services departments		**Children's Aid Societies** (provincial–municipal)
Transportation	Ministry of Transportation and Communications	Metropolitan Toronto and regional Transportation or Works and Transportation Departments; **Toronto Transit Commission**	Transportation or Works and Transportation departments.	**Toronto Area Transit Operating Authority** (provincial/regional)

a. This figure includes only those departments and agencies engaged in activities of particular importance to regional development and well-being. As interpreters and administrators of provincial laws, provincial departments influenced the content and delivery of all services provided to municipal populations, but a comparison of this figure with Figure 2.2 suggests that more provincial agencies had become directly involved in [sub]regional and municipal administration than in 1958.

b. All units in bold type were special-purpose bodies. Municipal school boards differed from other special-purpose bodies in being directly elected by local voters, with some locally elected board members representing their boards on the Metropolitan Toronto School Board. Members of other special-purpose bodies were appointed by [sub]regional or municipal councils, and sometimes by the provincial government.

c. Boundaries of Conservation Areas did not coincide with boundaries of regional governments.

Sources: Bell and Pascoe 1988; Mary Collins Consultants 1975; Smith, Auld & Associates 1975.

operating there, as well as maintain some of the land as an urban park.[22] It coexisted with the federally appointed Toronto Harbour Commission, which had been managing and developing lands around the Toronto Harbour since 1911.

Financing Regional Services: An Emphasis on Restraint and Financial Restructuring

Municipal finance was one of the first policy areas to feel the effects of a changing economic and political climate. In 1975 Darcy McKeough, the provincial Treasurer who had promoted regional initiatives, chaired a Special Program Review charged with finding ways to reduce provincial spending. Noting that spending, taxes, and provincial grants had increased more in the regional municipalities than in Metro or in the rest of the province, the Review recommended postponing further restructuring. According to its report, restructuring should occur only if local governments asked for it, and even then its primary purpose should be "the achievement of cost savings rather than the expansion of services."[23] The report also pointed out that provincial grants had allowed municipal governments to increase spending without raising property taxes, thereby sparing them the need to account to local taxpayers for their decisions.

Incremental changes to provincial grants and subsidies

Soon after receiving the report of the Special Program Review, the government established a committee of senior provincial and municipal civil servants to investigate the provincial grant structure. This Provincial–Municipal Grant Reform Committee recommended eliminating some conditional grants and increasing the size of others, consolidating small grant programs into larger ones, and shifting some municipal responsibilities either to regional governments or to the province.[24]

The report of the Committee won approval from the Association of Municipalities of Ontario and the Provincial–Municipal Liaison Committee, a committee established in 1973 to allow municipal officials "to consider

---

22. Paul Monahan, "Report prepared for the Minister of Public Works, the Honourable Diane Marleau, P.C.M.P., in Connection with Harbourfront Centre," Submitted May 28, 1996, 2.

23. Ontario Ministry of Treasury, Economics and Intergovernmental Affairs 1975, 206–207.

24. Ontario Provincial–Municipal Grants Reform Committee 1977, 239.

Provincial Government policy proposals at the development stage."[25] It ran into immediate opposition, however, from virtually all parties that would feel the impacts of its recommendations, including some municipal governments, community organizations, and even provincial ministries that stood to lose parts of their budgets. According to the Chair of the Committee, opponents implied "that they do not trust local councils to put enough priority, in the absence of special financial incentives, on their areas of special concern such as libraries, community centres, museums, or in some cases, local roads."[26] Moreover, implementation of many of the Committee's recommendations depended on prior implementation of property tax reform, and that too fell victim to municipal and taxpayer resistance. The government backed away from comprehensive grant reform, therefore, and chose instead to modify its grant programs by placing upper limits on the size of its grants or annual grant increases.

Retreat from property tax reform

The government backed away from comprehensive property tax reform in the 1970s after it had modified its original proposals several times in response to concerns voiced by municipal officials and members of the public.[27] In a final attempt to save the project, Treasurer McKeough asked a working group of provincial and municipal officials to devise an alternative system, taking these concerns into account. He told the group to pay special attention to Metropolitan Toronto, where residential property owners were likely to experience the largest tax changes of any taxpayers in Ontario. When the working group members could not agree on a plan that would not cost the province more money, McKeough abandoned the effort. The government would not proceed with reform, he told the legislature, because

> [f]or [local politicians], tax equity may be something devoutly to be wished for, but perhaps not worthwhile if the cost is decreased grants, or an increased portion of shared costs, or incurring the wrath of those taxpayers who are presently paying less than their fair share in taxes.[28]

25. Michael J. Smither, "Provincial-Municipal Liaison Committee—What is it?" *Municipal World*, 83 (1973), 171.

26. Donald Stevenson, "Address to the Rural Ontario Municipal Association," February 7, 1978.

27. For a more detailed discussion of how the Ontario government tried to reform the property tax system in the 1970s, see Frisken 1991.

28. Legislature of Ontario, *Debates*, Second Session, 31st Parliament, June 8, 1978, 3236.

The government turned back responsibility for reassessment to municipalities, which could either do it for themselves or ask their regional governments to do it.

Changes in federal government transfer programs

The mid-1970s brought promises of federal financial assistance for urban demonstration projects in areas such as housing, sewage treatment, recycling, public transportation, and the creation of new communities. This money went to provincial governments and not to municipalities, however, and was used for relatively few projects before it dried up.

Of more importance to the character of urban places was a shift in federal housing policies away from programs to assist those in greatest need and toward programs to stimulate the private rental and home ownership markets during a period of economic slowdown.[29] The federal government replaced public housing with forgivable loans to aid the construction of mixed-income housing by public or private non-profit corporations and housing co-operatives. It also introduced incentives to persuade private builders to include rent-geared-to-income units in their buildings. The Ontario government put similar programs in place.

Consequences for the Regional Agenda

Servicing suburban expansion

Despite the provincial government's loss of interest in regionalism after 1975, various provincial agencies continued to influence the physical character of the Toronto region through their contributions to infrastructure and residential development patterns.

The Ministry of the Environment, which absorbed the Ontario Water Resources Commission in 1972, helped to build the York–Durham Servicing Scheme to the north and east of Metro.

The Ministry of Transportation and Communications financed highway construction and extended commuter rail and bus services outside Metro Toronto. In 1981 there were four multi-lane, limited-access highways under construction or planned in the regional municipalities of Peel and York.[30] By

---

29. Fallis 1985, 178.
30. Jim Foster, "Tough road ahead to keep Metro moving," *Toronto Star*, December 14, 1981.

1984 the GO system provided 14,570 kilometres of rail and bus service, nearly seven times the 2,126 kilometres of service it had provided in 1976.[31]

The Ministry of Housing, created in 1973, made loans to help municipalities increase their supply of serviced land, provided mortgage assistance to encourage the construction of new housing (mostly in the suburbs), and offered grants to first-time homebuyers. The government used tax cuts, grants, and other incentives "to encourage homeownership and to stimulate the automobile industry."[32] It pressed municipal governments to speed up subdivision approvals and to encourage the private sector to build more housing.

All these activities supported or encouraged development in the suburbs surrounding Metro and other large cities, where most new growth was taking place. A few programs, however, helped build or maintain physical and social infrastructure in the province's cities and larger towns. Among them were capital and operating support for municipal transit, programs to assist the construction of housing for low-to-moderate-income tenants, and a federal Neighbourhood Improvement Program (NIP) that replaced urban renewal in the late 1960s and ended 10 years later. NIP was intended to stem the deterioration of older urban neighbourhoods by assisting with home renovations, the construction of non-profit and co-operative housing, and the improvement of community services.

The Ontario Housing Corporation, which became part of the Ministry of Housing in 1973, continued to construct public housing until the late 1970s, though at a much reduced level. Most federal and provincial housing assistance was now going to non-profit and co-operative housing agencies (the third sector), which built housing for tenants with a range of incomes, only some of whom were eligible for rent supplements. In the early 1980s the provincial government also began to make interest-free loans to builders who agreed to set aside a certain percentage of new housing as rent-geared-to-income units, to homeowners who added accessory units to their homes, and to developers willing to convert non-residential buildings to rental use.

Cuts to control costs

Although provincial government agencies continued to invest in programs that contributed to the physical expansion of the Toronto region, much of the government's rhetoric and some of its policies focused on the need to control government costs throughout the province. The services most affected by

---

31. GO Transit Annual Reports, 1976, 1984.

32. Ontario Budget Address by the Honourable W. Darcy McKeough, Treasurer of Ontario, 1976, 2.

cost-cutting measures were the two that had benefited most from provincial initiatives a few years earlier—public transit and education.

In the case of public transit, the government replaced open-ended grants that covered half the operating losses of municipal systems with subsidies that tied provincial contributions to the population size of the service area. Under this formula, the largest per capita subsidies went to the smallest municipalities, some of which were in the Toronto region. Metro received the smallest per capita operating grant in the province, although it received the largest share of provincial operating subsidies because of the large population in the TTC's service area. It was also the only provincial municipality with a subway system, additions to which were eligible for 75 per cent provincial funding.

In the case of education, the provincial share of the education budget increased gradually until 1976, when it accounted for 61 per cent of province-wide costs. It then began to decline, even though provincial spending on education continued to rise by 10 per cent a year, except in Metro Toronto, where it dropped from 34 per cent of total costs in 1975 to 10 per cent in 1984 because of Metro's growing assessment and declining school enrolments.[33]

Decisions not to spend

Another cost-control device used by the province was the complete withdrawal of financial support from some projects. Twice the Ministry of Transportation and Communications developed plans for light rail rapid transit systems that would have greatly improved mobility through the northern parts of Metro Toronto. The more ambitious plan, announced in 1972, envisioned a technologically advanced elevated light rail transit system to supplement Metro's existing subway and bus system. Two of its five routes would have provided east–west service in central and northern Metro, with possible extensions to the outer suburbs. The government abandoned this plan in 1974, however, after a German partner withdrew its financial support from the development program. The government then created an Urban Transportation Development Corporation (UTDC) to develop new transit technologies for the Canadian market. It said it would support the construction of a light rapid transit link between the eastern end of the east–west subway and the Scarborough Town Centre, but only if the TTC used UTDC technology.[34]

The second proposal, announced in 1981, was billed as part of a $1.5-billion, five-year plan to electrify transit throughout Ontario. This GO-ALRT

---

33. Robert Matas, "School board fears squeeze on taxes," *Globe and Mail*, February 4, 1984.
34. The government wanted to showcase the light rail technology that UTDC was then working on.

system, said the government, would improve the economy by creating jobs, curbing oil consumption, and beefing up research and industrial development.[35] Although it would have done less to improve transit within Metro than the earlier plan, it would nonetheless have linked Metro's northern municipalities with each other, with municipalities to the east and west, and with the airport. The province decided instead to support a TTC-backed plan to build subways under Sheppard and Eglinton Avenues, saying that this was the cheaper option.[36]

A third scheme that went nowhere was for a planned community (Seaton) in the northern part of the Town of Pickering, northeast of Metro. The province had acquired land for this community just south of a site chosen by the federal government for a new international airport. The project stalled in 1980, however, after the federal government decided not to go ahead with the airport and the province decided not to provide services to the area.

Retreat from regional planning

THE QUIET DEMISE OF THE TCR CONCEPT

In withdrawing its support for the Pickering airport and the new community, the Ontario government essentially abandoned the TCR principle of encouraging more development to the east of Metro to counter that occurring in the west. The TCR strategy was largely irrelevant by then, anyway. Although it never formally repudiated the strategy, the government backed away from it after 1974 in the face of pressures from landowners wanting to develop lands in districts that the strategy had targeted for agriculture or open space; from suburban governments (particularly York region) that wanted to exceed their population and employment limits; from housing advocates (including a government-sponsored Advisory Task Force on Housing Policy) pushing for the construction of moderately priced housing near Metropolitan Toronto; and from government agencies with mandates to build or help build new sewer and water lines and new transportation facilities in areas undergoing expansion. Communities and residents to the east of Metro were also telling the government that they wanted no part of the additional development implied by the "go east" policy.

By the end of the 1970s, therefore, provincial planning in Ontario had "ceased to have any real substance," and the machinery to undertake it had

---

35. Joe O'Donnell, "Millions pledged to electrify Ontario transit," *Toronto Star*, January 27, 1981.

36. Geoffrey York, "Electric railway network plan in doubt," *Globe and Mail*, June 19, 1984.

"largely ceased to exist."[37] The government dismantled TEIGA in 1978 and assigned its functions to other ministries. It told its regional development planners to stop collecting data on a regional basis and to destroy what they already had.[38] The urban planning staff went to a newly created Ministry of Housing, where they focused once again on "the ongoing give and take between developers and municipal councils.[39]

PLANNING IN THE REGIONAL MUNICIPALITIES

With the decline of provincial interest in managing or containing regional growth, planning in the regional municipalities veered away from the hierarchical planning model proclaimed by provincial officials in the late 1960s. Of the four suburban regions closest to Metro Toronto (Durham, Halton, Peel, and York), only two (Durham and Halton) produced official plans within the three-year limit specified in provincial legislation.[40] These plans won regional council approval because they evolved out of consultations among regional and local planners, and because they were based on the planning preferences of the local municipalities. In Peel and York, regional planning quickly bogged down in political conflict. The provincial government would allow these regional municipalities to function without official plans until the early 1990s.

The planning decisions that shaped the development patterns of the suburban regional municipalities, therefore, were principally those of their local municipalities. These tended to be influenced by the preferences of local residents, the applications brought to municipal councils by private land developers, and the willingness of those councils to provide local access to trunk sewer and water lines (the cost of which they were able to pass on to developers in the form of "development charges," or even to the province, as happened in the case of the York–Durham Servicing Scheme[41]). Local residents tended to favour single-family neighbourhoods built at even lower densities than those found in Metro's outer districts, as well as the segregation of residential neighbourhoods from other types of land use. They also wanted ample provision for automobile movement combined with neighbourhood street patterns that would discourage through traffic (including buses).

PLANNING IN METROPOLITAN TORONTO

Metropolitan Toronto planners proceeded in a different direction. They began a review of Metro's "unofficial Official Plan" by reviewing the 1966

---

37. Richardson 1981, 571–576.
38. Interview with Gardner Church, April 6, 1993.
39. Don Stevenson, private communication. January 9, 2005.
40. For a more detailed discussion, see Frisken 1993, 187–190.
41. White 2003, 52–53

Transportation Plan, which by the early 1970s bore little relation to the way Metro's transportation system had actually evolved.[42] Because of strong political opposition to highways, Metro planners faced the difficult task of persuading governments to invest in public transit instead of roads at a time when automobile ownership and use were increasing faster than transit ridership. Their strategy was to argue that new rapid transit would help reduce urban sprawl and benefit the local economy by fostering the development of high-density nodes of commercial and office activity within Metro.[43] As expressed in the Official Plan that Metro Council adopted in 1980, the aim was to achieve "a multi-centred urban structure ... through the development of Metropolitan Centres along rapid transit facilities."[44]

Preparation of the Metro plan coincided with and complemented a major revision of the City of Toronto's official plan, which was aimed at slowing down redevelopment in the central area, preserving older single-family neighbourhoods, and encouraging residential investment in the downtown core. Metro's idea of a multi-centred urban structure also appealed to suburban officials who wanted to develop their own "city centres" to attract commercial and office activity that had traditionally gravitated to the core.

Metro Council approved its first Official Plan in 1980, but only because the province insisted that it do so. The province intervened, not because it wanted to show support for a multi-centred urban structure, but because it wanted to give legal status to a Metro planning policy that would allow residential group homes to be established in all parts of Metro Toronto. This politically divisive issue is discussed later in this chapter.

A REVISED PLANNING ACT: TOWARD A POLICY-DRIVEN PLANNING SYSTEM

Although the Ontario government took little interest in regional plans and regional growth management after 1974, it enhanced its potential to play a leading role in Toronto region governance when it substantially amended the provincial *Planning Act* in 1983. Although the revised act reduced some forms of provincial control over municipal planning, it asserted that the government had a right to intervene in municipal land-use decisions by issuing policy statements on "matters of provincial interest." Both provincial and local agencies would be required to "have regard to" such statements in making land-use decisions. Under the act, such statements could address:

---

42. Pill 1979, 46.
43. Municipality of Metropolitan Toronto 1976, 4.
44. Municipality of Metropolitan Toronto 1980, 15.

(a) the protection of the natural environment, including the agricultural resource base of the Province, and the management of natural resources;

(b) the protection of features of significant natural, architectural, historical or archaeological interest;

(c) the supply, efficient use and conservation of energy;

(d) the provision of major communication, servicing and transportation facilities;

(e) the equitable distribution of educational, health and other social facilities;

(f) the co-ordination of planning activities of municipalities and other public bodies;

(g) the resolution of planning conflicts involving municipalities and other public bodies;

(h) the health and safety of the population;

(i) the protection of the financial and economic well-being of the Province and its municipalities.[45]

The list gave the government broad scope to intervene in many types of municipal decisions affecting the physical, economic, and social structure of municipalities. It thus made municipal planning a potentially powerful tool for delivering provincial policy at the municipal level—if the provincial government chose to use it that way.

The growing challenge of maintaining intermunicipal equity

Pooling local taxes for metropolitan and regional government services, basing municipal contributions to regional services on the size of local assessments, and transferring responsibility for public education and social services to metropolitan/regional governments contributed to a more equitable distribution of the costs and benefits of urban expansion in the Toronto region than was typical of many city-regions in the United States. As the Toronto region expanded, however, and its population both grew and became more diverse, maintaining intermunicipal equity was an increasingly challenging and politically divisive objective.

Most controversies surrounding equity issues occurred in Metropolitan Toronto, where municipalities were diverging in their taxable resources but becoming more alike in their population characteristics. Because regional

---

45. Legislative Assembly of Ontario, *Bill 159: An Act to Revise the Planning Act*, 2nd Session, 32nd Legislature, Ontario, 31 Elizabeth II, 1982, 2.

Table 4.1a Change in non-residential assessment per capita,
Metro municipalities, 1971–1987

	Non-residential assessment per capita ($)			Non-residential assessment per capita as per cent of municipality's total assessment per capita		
	1971[a]	1976[a]	1987[b]	1971	1976	1987
East York	803	741	779	32	28	27.6
Etobicoke	1,377	1,583	2,000	43	45	47.4
North York	937	1,064	1,464	34	37	39.8
Scarborough	714	790	1,041	34	34	37.1
Toronto	1,812	2,283	3,142	56	57	57.0
York	685	654	628	34	31	26.7
Metro	1,235	1,407	1,830	44	45	46.3

a. Based on data in Dale E. Richmond and Edward Zamparo, *Assessment in Metropolitan Toronto: Trends and Selected Issues, A Report Prepared for the Sub-Committee on Economic Development*, December 1982, 74–80, and on Statistics Canada Census data for 1971, 1976.

b. Based on data in Metropolitan Toronto Planning Department, *Metropolitan Toronto Key Facts, 1988*, July 1988, 7.13, and on Statistics Canada Census data for 1986.

municipalities operated independently of Metropolitan Toronto and of each other, there were also inequalities in service provision both among the suburban regions and between them and Metropolitan Toronto.

METROPOLITAN TORONTO

GROWING ASSESSMENT AND PROPERTY TAX INEQUITIES

Changes in Metro's economy and residential patterns during the 1970s and 1980s made Metro municipalities more unequal in their ability to raise money from non-residential properties, and thus in the extent to which they relied on residential taxpayers to fund local services. Toronto had a large and growing downtown office sector that gradually compensated for its loss of industrial assessment. The three outer suburbs (Etobicoke, North York, and Scarborough) also gained assessment in this category relative to the Metro average, whereas industrial losses brought a decline in non-residential assessment in Metro's two smallest municipalities, East York and York (Tables 4.1a and 4.1b). Meanwhile, inequities in Metro's property assessment and tax systems were increasing because the values of different properties were changing at different rates.

Unlike the Ontario Municipal Board (OMB) in 1953 and the Goldenberg Commission in 1965, the Robarts Commission paid little attention either to inequalities in the tax bases and service structures of Metro's member municipalities or to their underlying causes. Its discussion of Metro finances

Table 4.1b Change in total assessment per capita, Metro municipalities, 1971–1987

	Total assessment per capita ($)			Total assessment per capita as per cent of Metro's total assessment per capita		
	1971[a]	1976[a]	1987[b]	1971	1976	1987
East York	2,536	2,601	2,821	91	83	71
Etobicoke	3,196	3,516	4,223	114	112	107
North York	2,720	2,896	3,678	97	92	93
Scarborough	2,092	2,302	2,809	75	73	71
Toronto	3,232	4,025	5,513	115	128	139
York	2,021	2,128	2,347	72	68	59
Metro	2,799	3,145	3,952			

a. Based on data in Dale E. Richmond and Edward Zamparo, *Assessment in Metropolitan Toronto: Trends and Selected Issues, A Report Prepared for the Sub-Committee on Economic Development*, December 1982, 74–80, and on Statistics Canada Census data for 1971, 1976.

b. Based on data in Metropolitan Toronto Planning Department, *Metropolitan Toronto Key Facts, 1988*, July 1988, 7.13, and on Statistics Canada Census data for 1986.

dealt principally with the federation's financial performance after 1971, which it termed "excellent"; with its ability to sustain that performance into the future; with alternative sources of local revenue; and with ways to improve Metro's financial dealings with the province.[46] The Commission did conclude, however, that Metro's two smaller boroughs, East York and York, were "too small in population and financial resources to provide services of similar range and quality to those of the other area municipalities, particularly in fields such as education and public health."[47] It was for this reason that it recommended changes in Metro's internal boundaries—changes that the province did not make.

The substantial rise in Toronto's total assessment per capita relative to the Metro total meant that Toronto was paying more to finance Metro services, a benefit to Metro's poorer municipalities. On the other hand, the provincial government's 1978 decision not to go ahead with property tax reform left in place the property assessment and taxation inequities that favoured home-owners in single-family housing in the City of Toronto.

Toronto was the only Metro municipality to come up with its own reassessment plan after the government turned this responsibility back to municipal and regional governments in 1978. The plan it adopted in 1982, however, maintained the bias in favour of homeowners in single-family

---

46. Royal Commission on Metropolitan Toronto 1977(b), 163–206.
47. Royal Commission on Metropolitan Toronto 1977(a), 50.

housing. Even so, Toronto City Council said it would implement the plan only if the province increased property tax credits to cushion the impact of reform on lower income households, and phased in tax changes over five years.[48] The government said it could not afford to meet these conditions. What it wanted was regional reassessment; that is, reassessment of all municipal properties within each of the province's two-tier regional municipalities, including Metropolitan Toronto, based on a common standard. Metro staff members began to work on such a plan even before the city plan came to a vote, leading city politicians to accuse Metro of trying to impose a heavier tax burden on hapless Toronto homeowners and small businesses. Metro Council remained hopelessly divided on the issue, therefore, and all three provincial parties showed little desire to become involved.

CONVERGING MUNICIPALITIES, DIVERGING NEIGHBOURHOODS

While Metropolitan Toronto's municipalities were growing apart in taxable wealth, they were becoming more like each other in their social characteristics, both because of the gentrification of downtown neighbourhoods and because of the dispersal of low-rental housing to suburban locations. As early as 1971, in fact, a Toronto newspaper had observed that changes in the social composition of central Toronto belied the image of inner-city decay associated with American central cities. "The upper crust is moving into the centre of the city and booting out the poor," the reporter wrote. "The rooming house is becoming the professional man's home."[49]

The trend continued throughout the 1970s, bringing a change in the tenor of city politics. In the late 1960s, wrote Eudora Pendergrast, political rhetoric had stressed the importance of maintaining working-class neighbourhoods for working-class households.[50] The rhetoric of the 1970s, on the other hand, suggested the "suburbanization of the central city" with its emphasis on "local autonomy, community control, the exclusion of through traffic ... opposition to new development. In short, central city residents insisted on the city's role as primarily an amenable living environment."

The other side of the picture was presented in detail in two reports issued by the Metropolitan Toronto Social Planning Council (SPC) in 1979 and 1980.[51] They showed that Metro's post-war suburbs were no longer made up primarily of traditional two-parent families with young children living in

---

48. These credits, administered through the income tax system, reimburse low-income taxpayers for a portion of their property tax payments.

49. Martin Dewey, "Can Toronto be big *and* beautiful?" *Toronto Star*, October 23, 1971.

50. Pendergrast 1981, 146.

51. Social Planning Council of Metropolitan Toronto 1979 and 1980.

single-family homes. Suburban populations were aging, which meant that there were more couples without children and more people living alone. They were also experiencing an increase in the proportions of single-parent, usually mother-led, households; newly arrived immigrant families; unemployed adults; children with special learning needs or in need of care; and unemployed and alienated youth.

The study conveyed a picture of a metropolitan area that differed markedly from the one being depicted by U.S. writers at the time, in which older inner cities were suffering physical and social decline as businesses and middle-class residents moved to the suburbs. It also challenged the traditional view that immigrants to the Toronto region followed a settlement pattern considered typical of all immigrants to North America, whereby newcomers stayed in the core city until they adjusted to their new circumstances and moved to the suburbs.[52] What it showed, in fact, was that the number of recent immigrants living in Metro's outer municipalities (Scarborough, North York, and Etobicoke) exceeded the number in the inner municipalities (East York, Toronto, and York). Together with other non-traditional suburban residents, these new immigrants were making the suburbs more like the city in their population characteristics and levels of social need.[53]

There was more to the story, however, than gentrification in older city neighbourhoods and the transformation of some suburban districts into socially mixed enclaves. Many City of Toronto districts retained their predominantly working-class character and some of them contained large numbers of low-income households and recent immigrants. The core city also had a preponderance of people released from custodial institutions. Many suburban districts, on the other hand, consisted mainly of middle-class households living in single-family homes on individual lots. Residents of these districts often mobilized to protect their lifestyles from the social changes associated with the higher density housing being built in other parts of their municipalities. City politicians for their part continued to invoke suburban stereotypes as arguments against investing more money in Metro services (particularly public transit) that, they said, suburban residents would not use.

DEBATING A ROLE FOR METRO IN HOUSING

The principal agents of change in the Toronto housing market during this period were individuals and families, many of them immigrants, who bought and renovated homes in older neighbourhoods in or near downtown Toronto. Nonetheless, the dispersal of public and other types of low-rental

---

52. City of Toronto Planning Board 1974, 25.
53. Royal Commission on Metropolitan Toronto 1977(a), 236–237.

housing throughout Metropolitan Toronto in the 1960s and early 1970s was an important reason for the socio-spatial changes documented by the SPC. Not only did it make housing available in the suburbs for poor households displaced by residential upgrading near the core, but such households were less likely to crowd into the city's remaining low-rental stock. The public housing program ended in the 1970s, however, to be replaced by non-profit and co-operative housing programs and the inclusion of rent-supplement units in private buildings. The Ontario government left it up to municipal governments, both local and regional, to decide whether they would participate in these programs.

The City of Toronto responded to changes in federal and provincial housing policies by creating a housing department and a city-owned Non-Profit Housing Corporation (Cityhome) as part of a multi-faceted housing policy adopted in 1973. Its policy aimed to preserve and improve existing neighbourhoods, produce new rental housing, acquire existing housing for rental purposes, and reserve a substantial portion of this housing stock for senior citizens and families with low to moderate incomes.[54] Underlying these objectives, according to City staff, was a desire to retain "the social and economic diversity of the City's population," increase "the vitality and the range of uses of the central core," maintain "the amenity and stability of existing residence areas," and "ensure that all residents, including families with children, could continue to find affordable housing in all areas of the city."[55] In setting up the program, City of Toronto politicians and staff worked directly with federal government officials to tailor the national non-profit and co-operative housing programs to the city's needs.[56] Until 1983 the city received additional help in pursuing its housing goals from the federal Neighbourhood Improvement Program.

Rapidly rising real estate prices in the 1970s brought new pressures on governments to increase the supply of affordable housing both for middle-class buyers and low-income renters. In response, the government appointed an Advisory Task Force on Housing Policy to study all aspects of housing in the province.[57] Under pressure from the NDP, it also passed rent control legislation in 1975, right after an election had reduced it to minority status.[58]

---

54. For a more detailed treatment of the scope and outcomes of City of Toronto policy-making during this period, see Frisken 1988.

55. City of Toronto Planning and Development Department, Policy Section, *Confronting the Crisis,* January 1982, 1.

56. David Crombie, private communication, April 28, 1997.

57. Ontario Advisory Task Force on Housing Policy 1973.

58. The party could continue to form the government and remain in office, in other words, only with the support of one of the two opposition parties, the Liberals or the NDP.

A government looking for ways to cut costs and shore up electoral support, had little reason, however, to pressure local governments to add to the supply of rent-geared-to-income (RGI) housing. Building new assisted housing not only required immediate capital outlays, but also meant an increase in rent subsidies.

Public housing was also unpopular, and its unpopularity had made the Ontario Housing Corporation (OHC) a political liability. In the mid-1970s, therefore, the OHC began to decentralize administrative responsibility for its stock of public housing to local housing authorities, saying that it wanted to put "social housing in every community in the hands of local citizens who live and work in the community, and thus are sensitive to particular needs in the area."[59] There was little scope, however, for community participation and initiative in the authorities that OHC set up. Not only were most of their members appointed by the federal and provincial governments, but they were authorized only to administer the existing stock of RGI housing, not to add to it. Only non-profit agencies, housing co-operatives, and private developers could do that.

While Toronto was launching its housing program and the Ontario government was redefining its role in assisted housing, Metro Council was debating a draft housing policy issued by Metro planners in 1974. At issue in these debates were the role that Metro would have in providing government-assisted housing, the number of units it should provide (the draft planning document suggested 20,000 new RGI units, to be built over a three-year period), and how these units would be distributed among Metro's six municipalities. OHC's plan to delegate responsibility for public housing to municipal councils or local housing authorities was an important element of these discussions. Initially, Metro Chairman Paul Godfrey said that Metro Council should take over this function from OHC. The Robarts Commission endorsed the idea, saying that a Metro takeover would promote a more even distribution of low-cost housing among Metro municipalities and better coordination of housing with community and social services.[60] There was strong opposition, however, from every Metro municipality except the City of Toronto, which said it would support a Metro role in housing, but only if Metro agreed to delegate some of its responsibility to the local municipalities. Nonetheless, the city was willing to manage only some of its public housing because it did not want to "adversely affect the image of its non-profit program, which is geared to fulfilling the needs of middle- as well as low-income groups."[61]

59. Ontario Ministry of Municipal Affairs and Housing 1984, 42.
60. Graham Fraser, "Godfrey's private dealing angers Council," *Globe and Mail,* June 17, 1974; Royal Commission on Metropolitan Toronto 1977(b), 238.
61. Ontario Ministry of Treasury, Economics and Intergovernmental Affairs 1978, 41.

Table 4.2 Distribution of assisted households within Metropolitan Toronto, 1976

	Per cent of all households, 1976	Per cent of assisted households
East York	5.9	1.3
Etobicoke	13.0	10.9
North York	24.3	25.4
Scarborough	16.2	28.7
Toronto	33.7	28.3
York	6.9	5.4

Source: Metropolitan Toronto Planning Department, *The Assisted Housing Study, Final Report* (first draft, November 1976), Figure 4.

By 1977 the city's non-profit housing program was adding more units to Metro's stock of assisted rental housing than any other provider. It was also adding to Metro's share of subsidized rents. Godfrey quickly lost interest in the idea of a Metro takeover, therefore, and Metro and the city joined forces to pressure the federal and provincial governments to pay the entire cost of rent subsidies. The province said it would do so in 1980 as long as Metro agreed to having its stock of public housing assigned to an appointed authority directly accountable to the Ministry of Housing. Metro readily agreed to do this. The financial gain, said one Metro official, was more than worth the sacrifice. "They thought we'd be very opposed. We made a big stink about it, but we didn't care. It was a very costly trade-off for the province."[62] The Housing Statement included in Metro's 1980 Official Plan made no mention of assisted housing targets.

Metro Council housing debates also dealt with complaints that some municipalities got more assisted rental housing than others relative to their shares of Metro's total housing stock (Table 4.2). This too was a contentious issue. Suburban politicians did not want Metro deciding how much assisted housing they should have; City of Toronto officials feared that strengthening Metro's role in the allocation and distribution of housing would siphon federal and provincial housing grants away from city programs. In the end, Metro's Official Plan said that Metro Council would pursue a "fair share" distribution of low-income assisted housing, but only through consultation with area municipalities.[63]

By the time the plan was approved, there was little danger that Metro Council would be challenging municipalities to act on the "fair share" principle. Not only had the public housing program ended, but none of Metro's

---

62. Interview notes (name of interviewee withheld).
63. Municipality of Metropolitan Toronto 1980, 46.

lower-tier municipalities followed Toronto's lead in creating a housing department or a non-profit housing corporation. In the late 1970s Metro Council did authorize the Metropolitan Toronto Housing Company, which hitherto had built housing only for seniors, to build a limited amount of family housing.[64] Area municipalities could still use their land-use planning powers, however, to determine what types of housing they would allow and where new housing would go.

The distribution of rent-geared-to-income family housing units among Metro municipalities changed little in Metro between 1973 and 1985. Moreover, the number of family units actually declined, from more than 28,000 in 1974 to just under 23,000 in 1985.[65] By 1985, assisted rental housing for families accommodated only 3.7 per cent of Metro's non-senior households. The outer municipalities (Etobicoke, North York, and Scarborough) accounted for more than twice as many units as the inner ones (Toronto, East York, and York), with Scarborough having the largest number relative to its total number of households.

Metro's seniors fared much better than low-income families, with the number of units allocated to seniors nearly tripling, from 8,659 to 27,605, between 1973 and 1985.[66] By 1985, rent-geared-to-income units were able to accommodate nearly one-fifth of Metro's senior households. Like low-rental family units, however, many of these units were located in the outer suburbs, often on sites that were isolated from public transit, commercial districts, and major institutions.

SITUATING GROUP HOMES: ANOTHER "FAIR SHARE" ISSUE

The "fair share" concept was also raised in debates triggered by the efforts of community-based organizations to establish group homes for persons released from custodial institutions. This issue first emerged in the City of Toronto, where group homes tended to concentrate in older, less affluent neighbourhoods. As these neighbourhoods became gentrified, new homeowners complained that the presence of group homes threatened property values or neighbourhood safety and security. In response, Toronto City Council passed an "as-of-right" bylaw; that is, a bylaw to allow group homes to be located anywhere in the city. City officials also insisted, however, that such facilities should be distributed on a "fair share" basis throughout Metro—a challenge

64. McMahon 1990, 100.
65. The decline occurred because the owners of private rental buildings converted rent-geared-to-income units to private rental status after they had paid off their debts to the federal and provincial governments.
66. Klein and Sears 1975, Figure 7; Metropolitan Toronto Planning Department, Policy Development Division 1987, Table A6.

to municipalities that were using zoning bylaws and building regulations to restrict group homes to a few districts or to exclude them altogether.

Although the provincial government took little interest in Metro debates about the distribution of low-rental housing, it took a keen interest in the group homes issue. After endorsing the city's 1978 "as-of-right" bylaw, it recommended that all provincial municipalities adopt a similar policy, and laid out a model bylaw for them to follow.[67] A Metro Council majority voted within a year for a policy favouring "as-of-right" zoning for group homes anywhere in Metro. It also asked the government to take action against municipal bylaws that excluded group homes or allowed them for some types of residents but not others.[68]

Metro's action presented the provincial government with a dilemma. The closing of custodial institutions would proceed more smoothly if former residents could move into supervised settings rather than into unregulated boarding houses or onto the streets. On the other hand, the province had been advocating policy and procedural changes to give municipal councils and municipal residents a greater say in policy formation. While applauding Metro Council's action, therefore, the province's Secretary for Social Development told Metro that it was provincial policy to "encourage" municipalities to amend their planning regulations but not to "force" them to do so. "[I]t is extremely important to the successful integration of the residents into their neighbourhood," it said, "that there be community acceptance first."[69] Nonetheless, Metro Council decided in an unrecorded vote to incorporate the group homes policy into its draft Official Plan before sending it to the province for approval.

Provincial approval of the Official Plan would require all Metro municipalities to bring their bylaws into conformity with it, something that some suburban councils were clearly unwilling to do. Moreover, the OMB had been approving suburban bylaws that violated the "as-of-right" principle. The Minister of Municipal Affairs and Housing[70] approved only parts of the Metro

67. Dear and Laws 1986, 7.

68. Metropolitan Toronto Planning Department, "Proposed Amendment to the Group Homes Policy in the Metropolitan Toronto Official Plan," memorandum to the Metropolitan Chairman, January 31, 1983, 1.

69. Letter from Margaret Birch, Provincial Secretary for Social Development, to Paul V. Godfrey, Metropolitan Chairman, July 13, 1979.

70. Responsibility for local government organization, municipal planning, and local housing policy moved around within the Ontario government bureaucracy after 1970. The government did away with the Department of Municipal Affairs in 1972 and transferred responsibility for local government organization and community planning to the Ministry of Treasury, Economics and Intergovernmental Affairs (TEIGA). In 1974 it made a newly-created Ministry of Housing responsible for local government while leaving TEIGA in charge of community planning. TEIGA was divided into a Ministry of

plan, therefore, to give Metro time to reconsider its position. Metro Council held firm, leaving the group homes policy intact in a revised version of the plan it approved in 1981. The minister approved that plan within two days, leaving it up to disgruntled municipalities to appeal the decision to the OMB.

The OMB delayed its hearing until after Metro Council had agreed to a compromise amendment that won approval from all Metro municipalities except Etobicoke. Based on a policy already adopted by North York, the amended policy would allow Metro municipalities to specify the type of building in which a group home could operate, set distance requirements between group homes, and restrict homes for persons released from correctional institutions to properties on arterial roads. By the time the matter was argued before the OMB in 1984, therefore, only Etobicoke, one ratepayers' group, and several individuals spoke against it. The OMB approved the amended Metro policy, citing as a "principle ... of ordinary fairness" that individuals requiring group home accommodation should be able to find it in municipalities with which they were familiar.[71]

The decision essentially established a provincial policy for siting group homes throughout Ontario. It was a compromise between two extreme and seemingly irreconcilable local positions—one favouring the right of any type of group home to locate in any residential neighbourhood; the other upholding the right of municipal governments to control land uses in any way they saw fit. As with the decision-making process that had determined the location and distribution of assisted rental housing in Metro, it was arrived at without reference to the needs or convenience of the persons most affected by it—in this case group home residents and the community workers who shared their living quarters. Nonetheless, it probably resulted in more housing for such persons than there would have been if local preferences had prevailed.

SPATIAL INEQUALITIES IN THE PROVISION OF SOCIAL AND COMMUNITY SERVICES

More than 10 years after the provincial government had shifted responsibility for welfare from local councils to Metro Council, the Social Planning Council criticized Metro's social service system for failing to respond adequately to the Metro-wide dispersal of socially disadvantaged groups. It also noted that suburban governments had been slow to recognize or respond to

---

Treasury and Economics and a Ministry of Intergovernmental Affairs in 1978. In 1981 a new Ministry of Municipal Affairs and Housing became responsible for community planning as well as local government and housing policy. Then in 1985 the government once again assigned Housing and Municipal Affairs (meaning local government organization and community planning) to separate ministries. The NDP government combined the two functions once again into a single Ministry of Municipal Affairs and Housing after it took office in 1990.

71. Dear and Laws 1986, 13.

social change in their communities. Moreover, it pointed out, voluntary social service agencies tended to be heavily concentrated in the core city, and those in the suburbs were often poorly funded.[72] The SPC also found fault with both Metro and local officials for not considering the social implications of their land-use and transportation policies.

Initial reactions to the study were negative, even hostile. "For most of us, politicians as well as bureaucrats," observed Don Richmond, Metro's Deputy Commissioner of Social Services, "that study didn't tell us something that we didn't know, but it was something that we didn't want to hear."[73] Metro Chairman Paul Godfrey interpreted it as an attack on Metro's Social Services Department and its staff. The Department in turn charged the Social Planning Council with failing to give adequate credit to agencies (many of them voluntary) working in the suburbs, and failing to acknowledge that the city as well as the suburbs was experiencing "the economic, political and social changes ... operative throughout Metropolitan Toronto."[74] Moreover, it insisted, "a replication in the suburban areas of the traditional forms of social support which have been found in the City of Toronto is not necessarily the appropriate solution." Nonetheless, Metro's Coordinator of Multicultural Relations paid a visit to the suburbs and reported that the SPC was right: the suburbs were indeed badly in need of help.[75] The governments of Metro's three outer suburbs also set up special committees to look at social needs in their communities.[76]

In principle, Metro had the power to do anything it wanted for its resident poor, as long as it paid the full cost of items that were not eligible for provincial grants. In practice, it was Metro's policy not to expand existing programs beyond the limits imposed by provincial cost-sharing agreements. It also did not initiate new programs until agreements were in place. With the provincial government unwilling to increase its contributions to Metro's social services, Metro's response to the SPC challenge was primarily bureaucratic. The Social Services Department decentralized some functions, such as welfare, housing, and child care, to suburban or "regional district" offices. It also assigned Community Development Officers to suburban neighbourhoods to help community groups define local needs and apply for government funds to run their programs. Richmond defended his Department's approach as the

---

72. Social Planning Council of Metropolitan Toronto 1979, 79–83.
73. Don Richmond, "Social Services in a Time of Restraint," in Frisken 1982, 47–51.
74. The Municipality of Metropolitan Toronto Department of Social Services, "'Metro's Suburbs in Transition,' Report of the Social Planning Council of Metropolitan Toronto," December 7, 1979, 9 and 2.
75. David Lewis Stein, "The new social planners," *Toronto Star*, June 15, 1980.
76. Social Planning Council of Metropolitan Toronto 1980, 13.

best way to deal with Metro's growing social and cultural diversity, saying that groups rooted in communities knew what was best for those communities.[77]

Metro's policy changes gave existing community-based organizations (CBOs) a recognized role in Metro's social service delivery system and encouraged the creation of new ones. Consequently, the changes added to the fragmented and uncoordinated nature of Metro's social service delivery system—a characteristic that the Robarts Commission had already identified as the system's principal weakness. Robarts had also written that "public concern about the present levels of government spending and taxation," meant that "the recent rate of increase in human services costs cannot be sustained in the years ahead."[78] Nonetheless those costs would continue to rise throughout the 1980s.

ADAPTING TO ETHNOCULTURAL DIVERSITY

Metro and local government responses to the Social Planning Council report were among early efforts by governments in Canada to adapt to the arrival and settlement of large numbers of immigrants. The federal government had taken the lead in these efforts in the late 1960s with a policy to promote multiculturalism in its immigrant settlement programs. The goal was "to preserve and enhance the multicultural heritage of Canadians while working to achieve the equality of all Canadians in the economic, social, cultural and political life of Canada."[79] Initially federal grants supported language training programs offered by municipalities or local agencies. Gradually, however, federal programs had expanded to support a wide range to activities performed by agencies with immigrant clienteles.

In 1977 Ontario adopted its own multiculturalism policy, which acknowledged both the diverse nature of Ontario society and the rights and responsibilities of citizens of different backgrounds. It also set up Welcome Houses in different parts of the province to provide such services as translation, interpretation, and the publication of information brochures in various languages. Thus the policies of both senior governments provided a legal and philosophical context for the development or restructuring of municipal services both to aid immigrant settlement and to promote respect for and understanding of cultural differences within local populations.

In the Toronto region, school boards were the first local political bodies to initiate programs to aid immigrant absorption. By the early 1970s, however, the City of Toronto Council had begun to adopt policies to aid immigrant settlement, foster good race relations, and promote equal opportunity both in

---

77. Don Richmond, "Social Services in a Time of Restraint," op. cit., 49.
78. Royal Commission on Metropolitan Toronto 1977(b), 297.
79. Tator and Henry 1991, 38.

Table 4.3 Spending on public health in Metropolitan Toronto, 1975

Municipality	Assessed population	Public health spending per capita	Per cent of spending not cost-shared with prov. govt.
East York	104,102	5.64	3.54
Etobicoke	293,464	6.63	3.23
North York	558,067	6.56	20.42
Scarborough	380,931	6.03	6.76
Toronto	678,103	12.63	0.88
York	139,612	9.01	13.10

Source: Royal Commission on Metropolitan Toronto 1977(b), 142, 243.

employment and in access to municipal services.[80] By the end of the decade, Metro Council had adopted multicultural and equal opportunity policies of its own. Other GTA municipalities, both inside and outside Metro, would not begin to adopt similar policies until the late 1980s.

INTERMUNICIPAL DIFFERENCES IN THE FUNDING OF PUBLIC HEALTH

As had been the case with social assistance, public health was character-ized by large differences in spending within Metro, particularly between the City of Toronto and the suburban municipalities. The city spent roughly twice as much per capita as four of the five other municipalities in 1977, with the provincial government sharing virtually all of the city's costs (Table 4.3). Moreover, a larger share of the city's spending was eligible for provincial cost-sharing grants than was the spending of any other municipality.

Public health had remained a local responsibility in Metro Toronto, despite provincial government efforts, begun in the early 1960s, to persuade Metro to establish a single "district health unit" to achieve economies of scale and better coordination of services. Metro's local councils had always resisted these efforts, claiming they were better able to design services to meet distinc-tive local needs. They also pointed out that the populations served by their boards of health were larger than those of most of the consolidated health dis-tricts that had already been formed. Nonetheless, the province gave Metro's local boards a lower level of support (25 per cent) than district or county health boards in the rest of the province (75 per cent).[81] The Robarts Commission agreed with Metro's local boards and recommended not only that they remain in place, but also that they receive the same provincial funding as district

---

80. Wallace and Frisken 2000, 17–22.

81. Ontario Ministry of Treasury, Economics and Intergovernmental Affairs 1978, 46–49.

boards. The government left the local boards alone, but did not increase their share of provincial funding.

With the initiation of provincial transit subsidies in 1971, Metro Council did away with the zone-fare system that the TTC had used since it became a metropolitan agency. Metro residents who depended on transit could then travel anywhere in Metro for the same fare—an important change from an equity standpoint. Nonetheless, the subway system was designed mainly to carry passengers from suburban districts to downtown Toronto and back again, and the bus system was designed primarily to bring passengers to subway terminals. This core-city orientation meant that lower income residents who lived or worked in outer districts had to choose between long and time-consuming trips by transit or spending some of their limited resources on automobiles. The decentralization of jobs to suburban industrial districts only partly relieved the problem, because such districts were usually isolated from residential areas and poorly served by transit. These trends prompted the Social Planning Council to observe that

> It is somewhat easier for those living downtown, with more than half a million jobs within 20 minutes accessibility by public transit, to formulate the principle that people should seek out jobs in proximity to where they live. The principle becomes somewhat tarnished in suburban districts where the pool of available jobs within 20 minutes accessibility by public transit might be less than 5 per cent of the downtown.[82]

This kind of argument seldom found its way into discussions about transportation planning and policy at the Metropolitan Toronto or regional government level. Instead, such discussions tended to emphasize the potential of transit both to encourage and to serve high-density nodes of office and commercial development or to reduce the negative impacts of automobile use on the physical and natural environment. Prospects for more suburban rapid transit lines had seemed good in the early 1970s, however, not only because the province and local governments were helping to subsidize transit, but also because of persistent political opposition to urban highways. The bitterly fought campaign to stop the Spadina Expressway was just the first in a series of battles about additions or improvements to Metropolitan Toronto's road and highway network. Anti-highway sentiments persuaded Metro planners to

---

82. Social Planning Council of Metropolitan Toronto 1979, 171–173.

remove road links from the transportation plan and to propose a considerable expansion of Metro's transit network and a more compact urban structure to support it.

It turned out, however, that support for transit in principle did not translate into substantial transit improvements in practice. Apart from extensions to existing subway lines, the only new rapid transit line opened in Metro between 1966 and 1986 was an elevated light rail line connecting the east–west subway to Scarborough Town Centre. The transportation component of the Official Plan approved by Metro Council in 1980 (Figure 4.3) did not include any other new transit lines, even though Metro Council had agreed in principle to support high-density nodes of development in all parts of Metro. As the planners' proposed system became bogged down in disputes among Metro Toronto municipalities, the provincial government did not push Metro to approve a transit plan and start building new lines. It was trying to save money, not find new ways to spend it.

It took five years after Metro Council approved its Official Plan for Metro and TTC planners, in consultation with local municipalities, to hammer out a transit plan that Metro council would approve. That plan, Network 2011, bore little resemblance to the integrated system the planners had originally proposed (Figures 4.4a and 4.4b). Instead, it consisted of several disjointed lines linked to the existing subway system but having little relationship to each other. All of them ended well short of Metro's boundaries.[83] Thus it promised to do little to improve transit travel either among Metro's outer districts or between Metro and the burgeoning municipalities outside its boundaries. "We did Network 2011 without connecting to housing or employment," one planner later admitted.[84]

As Metro Council dithered, the opportunity to create a much-improved public transit system began to recede. By 1982, polls showed that public support for expressways was growing once again, while support for transit was declining. Provincial contributions to transit were also beginning to fall as a proportion of total transportation spending.[85] Moreover, the government was preoccupied with recovering from a recession that had hurt the rest of the province much more than Metro, and thus had little incentive to pour money into Metro services.

---

83. Metropolitan Toronto Planning Department and Toronto Transit Commission 1986.
84. Interview with John Livey, August 17, 1989.
85. Hoy 1985, 225-26.

Figure 4.3 Metropolitan Toronto Transportation Plan, 1980

Source: Municipality of Metropolitan Toronto, Metropolitan Planning Department, *Official Plan for the Urban Structure*, Figure 7 (October 10, 1980) [scanned reproduction].

Figure 4.4a Nodal concept proposed by Metro Toronto planners in 1976

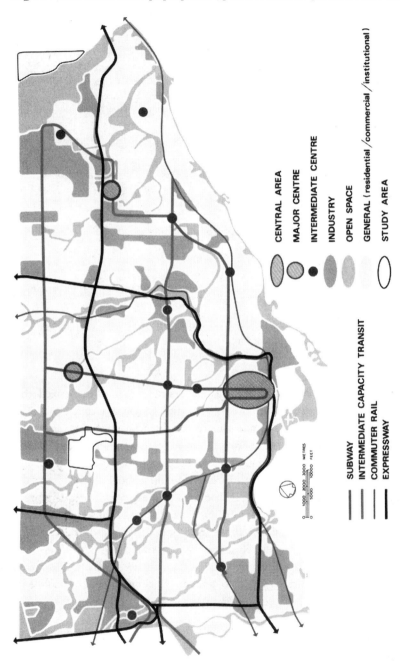

Metropolitan Toronto Planning Department, *MetroPlan: Concept and Objectives, a Summary for Public Discussion in the Metropolitan Plan Programme* (1976), 2 [scanned reproduction].

Figure 4.4b Rapid Transit Plan (Network 2011) as adopted by Metro Council in 1986

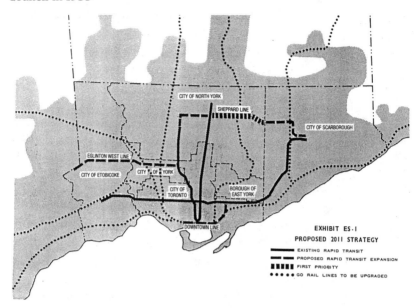

Metropolitan Toronto Planning Department and Toronto Transit Commission, *Network 2011, Final Report* (1986) [scanned reproduction].

THE TWO-TIER EDUCATION SYSTEM UNDER ATTACK

The growing emphasis on financial restraint that characterized this period placed severe strains on Metro's two-tier system of public education. These could be traced to the much-increased financial powers given to the Metropolitan Toronto School Board (MTSB) in 1967, together with the ceiling on local school board spending imposed by the provincial government in 1971. Because Metro's local boards were already spending above the ceiling at the time it was imposed, the MTSB staff had the thankless task of trying to bring local board budgets in line with the ceiling. That task involved trying to reduce the overall budget while shifting funds from richer to poorer boards so as to keep per pupil spending relatively uniform across Metro. At the same time, representatives of the local boards were struggling to maintain or increase their shares of the shrinking Metro budget. Declining school enrolments added to the tensions, because they brought a lowering of the spending ceiling and a decline in provincial grants.

Conflict about school board financing became so intense in Metro that the provincial government appointed a special commission in 1973 to review the situation. The Ministerial Commission on the Organizing and Financing of the Public and Secondary School Systems in Metropolitan Toronto looked for ways to balance the competing claims of equity and local autonomy (which it described more generally as "the tension between centralization and decentralization").[86] Although it commended the achievements of Metro's two-tier educational system and said it should be retained, it recommended several ways to give the six local boards more operating and financial autonomy.[87] The government acted on some of these recommendations in 1976 when it began to revise school finance as part of its more general effort to control spending. It backed away from its commitment to cover 60 per cent of total school board expenditure in the province, but it also removed the absolute ceiling on school spending. School boards could increase their spending on items eligible for provincial assistance as long as they could raise extra funds out of local property taxes. They could use a discretionary levy (up to a specified mill rate) to raise still more money to pay for activities that were not eligible for provincial assistance. These changes guaranteed that differences in school board spending in Metro would persist and probably increase because of large differences in the size and composition of the six municipal tax bases.

One year later, the Robarts Commission decided that Metropolitan Toronto's two-tier educational system was more trouble than it was worth. It recommended that the province gradually phase it out and make local boards responsible for most of their own funding. The province could then use alternative ways (like a Metro-wide property tax levy or provincial grants) to reduce disparities in local board wealth.[88]

The Metro Board said it would accept this recommendation if the province agreed to pool property taxes in Metro for the capital costs of schools, increase its grants to ensure equality of educational opportunity and taxation equity throughout Ontario, and find a way to get local boards to co-operate on matters of mutual interest.[89] The government decided instead to leave the two-tier system in place. The Robarts Commission had taken "the principle of autonomous and strong Area Boards ... to the extreme," the Ministry of Education concluded. Although "autonomy, accountability, and the voters' understanding of local government" were important, the organization of education in Metropolitan Toronto had to observe three other principles: "equality of educational opportunity, fiscal equity and the centralized coordination of issues of metrowide concern."[90] The government showed no interest, however, in applying these principles to all of Ontario.

86. Ontario Ministry of Education 1974, 15.
87. Ibid., 15, 25–30, 47–48.
88. Royal Commission on Metropolitan Toronto 1977(b), 317; 323–324.
89. Ontario Committee on the Costs of Education 1978, 49.
90. Ontario Ministry of Education 1978, 13, 14.

Table 4.4: Per pupil spending on public education
in Metropolitan Toronto, 1980

	Elementary ($ per pupil)	Secondary ($ per pupil)
East York	2,360	2,990
Etobicoke	2,415	3,158
North York	2,418	3,093
Scarborough	2,224	3,119
Toronto	2,821	3,518
York	2,516	3,301

Source: Based on data compiled by the Metropolitan Toronto School Board, private communication, November 1980.

Metropolitan Toronto's two-tier education system survived, therefore, but it continued to be wracked with dissension about financing. The City of Toronto, Scarborough, and York were the only Metro boards to use the discretionary levy between 1976 and 1983. York used it only once and Scarborough ended the practice in 1980, whereas Toronto used it on a regular basis.[91] Consequently, the Toronto board was able to spend considerably more than the other boards on both elementary and secondary schools (Table 4.4). Critics charged that the city used most of this money to hire additional teachers in order to decrease classroom sizes, in violation of an informal Metro agreement to keep board–teacher negotiations Metro-wide.

The City of Toronto also qualified for extra funds from the Metro board under a formula that took special educational needs into account, although the number of suburban schools that met the MTSB's criteria for these funds was growing. Nonetheless, the Toronto school board insisted that the MTSB funding formula did not adequately account for the city's unique needs, such as its larger poverty and immigrant populations and its aging schools. For much of this period, in fact, several members of the Toronto board engaged in a well-publicized campaign not only against the MTSB, but also against the entire Metro system and the provincial Ministry of Education.

Fuelling the Toronto board's complaints was the fact that the city's share of the MTSB budget was always much lower than its percentage contribution because of its high commercial and industrial assessment. Nonetheless, that same assessment allowed the Toronto board to supplement its ceiling-prescribed budget out of local taxes without leaning heavily on residential taxpayers. In fact, the city's residential mill rate for school purposes was lower in 1983 than that of every other Metro municipality except Etobicoke (Metro's wealthiest suburb).[92]

91. Ontario Ministry of Education 1983, 39.
92. Ontario Ministry of Education 1983, 39.

The government sought to ease the growing tensions in the Metro board by introducing special grants to help boards deal with the impacts of declining enrolments, and to fund programs such as special education, French as a first and a second language, English as a second language (ESL), and heritage language instruction for immigrant children—programs that supported city initiatives. The Chairman of the Toronto board dismissed them, however, as "a masterful piece of politics."[93] By the late 1970s his board had adopted a policy of open defiance, refusing to make its share of the Metro budget cut and departing from an informal agreement not to use funds raised from the discretionary levy to increase teachers' salaries above the limit prescribed by the MTSB.

The battle waged by the City of Toronto School Board against the Metro board, other local school boards, and the Ministry of Education cannot be characterized in conventional ideological terms. Although it was a Progressive Conservative government and the more conservative members of the Metropolitan Toronto School Board who tried to impose constraints on city spending, they did so not only to avoid tax increases, but also to maintain equity in school board spending and educational opportunity across Metro Toronto. The City of Toronto trustees who fought them most vigorously tended to be members of the left-leaning New Democratic Party, who insisted on the Toronto board's right to raise and spend as much money as possible to enhance programs for the city's poor and immigrant populations, even if it meant taking money away from other Metro schools.[94] On an issue of importance to local voters and taxpayers, in other words, an ideologically based concern for the needs of the disadvantaged ended at the city's boundaries.

Matters came to a head in the early 1980s, when the government decided to legislate joint salary negotiations for all Metro teachers and reduce the amount that local boards could raise by using the discretionary levy. The goal, according to Education Minister Bette Stephenson, was to support "the underlying principle of the two-tier form of educational governance in Metropolitan Toronto" and the principle that "there should be a comparable level of educational service and comparable access to resources through municipal taxes across the Metro area."[95] The bill passed after a bitterly fought parliamentary battle in which some of the government's own members supported the city's

---

93. Toronto Board of Education, "The Chairman's Letter #70," April 21, 1978.
94. Maggie Siggins, "Bothersome Bette: Bette Stephenson's Bill 127 could inflict serious damage on the city's school system!" *Toronto Life*, November 1982; Bob Spencer, "The Chairman's Letter," Toronto Board of Education, October 30, 1981.
95. Honourable B.M. Stephenson, Minister of Education, "Re Bill 127, An Act to Amend the Municipality of Metropolitan Toronto Act," Debates of the 2nd Session of the 32nd Parliament, March 9–July 7, 1982, and September 21, 1982, to February 23, 1983, 2099.

position. Stephenson compromised by increasing the size of the discretionary levy, after which she froze the amount that local boards could raise in this way at 1982 levels.[96]

AN UNSUCCESSFUL ATTEMPT TO INTEGRATE
SOCIAL CONCERNS INTO THE PLANNING SYSTEM

Issues related to the distribution of housing, social services, and public transit underlay the criticism, voiced by the Social Planning Council and others, that decisions affecting the physical development of Metro Toronto and other cities were typically made without thought being given to their social consequences. The provincial Planning Act Review Committee acknowledged this criticism by looking into the possibility of integrating social and land-use planning. It concluded, however, that "[h]ealth, safety, and welfare are broad municipal responsibilities ... which transcend the scope of the municipal planning system."[97] The primary purpose of municipal planning was "to establish and carry out municipal policies and programs for the rational management of the municipality's physical development." It should, however, "have regard for" the community's social and economic concerns and "the social and economic consequences of municipal development policies and programs."

The government included the "equitable distribution of educational, health and other social facilities" in the list of "matters of provincial interest" included in the revised *Planning Act* of 1983. Nonetheless, the Minister of Housing told Metro Council that it could not commit itself in its Official Plan to preparing a human services plan that recognized "the essential linkage between physical and social planning."[98] All it could do, said the minister, was insert a general statement committing Council to the pursuit of "human services policies that will meet people's changing needs and promote and maintain a healthy community in keeping with the economic resources of the municipalities." Such policies, said the government, should not be part of the Official Plan, but could only be worked out "in consultation with the [provincial] social policy field ministries and/or their agencies," and should respect "existing legislation or other jurisdictional limitations." In other words, the province did not want Metro to commit itself to social policies that the province did not favour or did not want to pay for.

---

96. Robert Matas, "Parents sway Stephenson on controls," *Globe and Mail*, October 21, 1982.

97. Ontario Planning Act Review Committee 1977, 14–15.

98. Municipality of Metropolitan Toronto Department of Social Services, "Agenda for the Eighties; Metro's Suburbs in Transition," Part II: Report of the Social Planning Council of Metropolitan Toronto, February 27, 1981, 14–15.

THE REGIONAL PICTURE

Outside Metro, the creation of regional governments had meant the centralization of both social services and public health in regional departments, all of which provided the same provincially mandated programs that Metro did. They offered fewer optional services, however, because of their relatively early stage of development, and different regional governments offered different programs. The suburban regions also lacked the extensive network of community-based organizations that had grown up in Toronto and was gradually spreading to other parts of Metro. Moreover, regional social service and public health departments were often a long way from many of their clients.[99]

The two matters of GTA-wide significance that attracted most attention, however, were the distribution of low-rental housing and the fragmentation of the regional transit network. Low-rental housing became an issue because the costs of acquiring land and buildings in most parts of Metro Toronto were higher than social housing providers were willing or able to pay. Moreover, the four regional municipalities had 31 per cent of the region's population in 1971, but only 2.3 per cent of its supply of family public housing.[100] For these reasons, Metro planners and the Robarts Commission urged the provincial government to promote a more equitable distribution of low-rental housing throughout the region.[101] The Planning Act Review Committee went further, urging the province to disallow the land-use practices that some municipalities were using to exclude it.[102] The province ignored both recommendations.

A fragmented and uncoordinated regional public transit network was the second regional issue to receive attention. Partly because of provincial operating subsidies, 14 local municipalities in the region, in addition to Metropolitan Toronto, had some form of transit service by 1973.[103] Each local transit operator had its own fare and service policies. There was also a confusing array of fare and service arrangements between GO and local transit operators. Some local companies served GO Transit stations; others did not. Local bus operators provided services across some municipal boundaries but not others, despite provincial subsidies to encourage cross-boundary links.[104] For persons who depended on transit, therefore, getting from one part

99. W. Douglas Johns, "Serving a Scattered Population," in Frisken 1982, 44–46.

100. Klein and Sears 1975, 59.

101. Municipality of Metropolitan Toronto 1976, 66; Royal Commission on Metropolitan Toronto 1977(b), 231–234.

102. Ontario Planning Act Review Committee 1977, xii, 129–130.

103. Steering Committee to Develop an Implementation Plan for the Creation of a Transit Operating Authority for the Toronto Centred Region, *T.A.T.O.A.: Report on the Organization of the Toronto Area Transit Operating Authority*, January 1974, B16–B42.

104. Paterson Planning and Research Limited 1983, 1–32.

of the region to another, if it was possible at all, could be time-consuming, frustrating, and often expensive.

As early as 1967 a Metropolitan Toronto and Region Transportation Study technical report had urged the government to create a single agency to provide and coordinate transit services in the Toronto region.[105] Shortly thereafter, the TTC proposed itself as the logical agency to operate a regional system.[106] That proposal went nowhere, but in 1973 the premier conceded that a transit system composed of disconnected regional and local operations stood in the way of achieving "an efficient user-oriented system" that would "encourage people to leave their cars at home."[107] His government created a Task Force to "study the need for and implications of a Regional Transit Authority in the Toronto Centred Region."[108] It told its Steering Committee, however, that the Authority should have "operating responsibilities only"—in other words, it should not be given powers to plan or initiate new services.

Acting on that recommendation, the provincial government created a Toronto Area Transit Operating Authority (TATOA) with a mandate to design and operate the regional (GO) transit system, coordinate the planning and operations of transit systems in the regional municipalities (which would plan and operate their own systems), and help coordinate them with GO. The mandate assumed that the provincial government would make regional governments responsible for transit, just as Metro was. Municipal governments in the suburban regions were strongly opposed to that idea, however, and the province decided to leave transit in local hands. Transit in the Toronto region not only remained fragmented, therefore, but TATOA was never able to perform the regional coordination and advisory roles assigned to it. It quickly became an agency devoted solely to operating GO rail and bus services. Responsibility for coordination reverted to the province, which took no further action.[109] By 1980 only half of the region's local transit system connected with GO train and bus lines.[110]

105. Metropolitan Toronto and Region Transportation Study, Technical Advisory and Coordinating Committee 1967, Recommendation C.3.

106. Toronto Transit Commission, "A Submission from the Toronto Transit Commission to the Government of the Province of Ontario re the MTARTS Proposal," January 1969.

107. Harold F. Gilbert, "Review of the Roles and Responsibilities of the Toronto Area Transit Operating Authority (T.A.T.O.A.)," (Toronto: Ontario Ministry of Transportation and Communications, March 1980), 7.

108. Steering Committee to develop an implementation plan for the Creation of a Transit Operating Authority for the Toronto-Centred Region. *T.A.T.O.A.: Report on the Organization of the Toronto Area Transit Operating Authority*, January 1974, 3.

109. Paterson Planning and Research 1983, 8.

110. Michael Keating, "Roads vs. transit: cars still lead rush into Metro," *Globe and Mail*, March 4, 1980.

The persistent absence of a regional voice

Arguments for a regionally based organization that could address region-wide concerns or give the Toronto region a stronger political voice were not high on local or provincial political agendas after 1974. Moreover, despite insisting that it alone was responsible for matters that transcended municipal or regional boundaries, the provincial government was highly selective in deciding which matters belonged in that category. In general, it took a stand on regional matters only when it had a clear interest in the outcome, as in the case of the distribution of group homes, or when there was a danger that decisions of regional or local municipalities would impose new costs on the province.

For the most part, the provincial government preferred to let local governments resolve regional issues on their own, a position that coincided with growing demands from local governments for more autonomy to manage their own affairs. For the local politicians making those demands, autonomy meant freedom both from provincial control and from control by any other government, such as an upper-tier council. Far from inspiring municipal governments to search for common solutions to shared problems, therefore, the province's retreat from regionalism encouraged them to emphasize their differences.

Intermunicipal differences were particularly evident in Metro, despite its two decades of experience as a metropolitan federation. Differences between the City of Toronto and other Metro municipalities, as played out on Metro Council and in the MTSB, were the most common causes of friction. In the case of the MTSB, disputes focused largely on the allocation of the Metro budget; in the case of Metro Council they arose out of deep-seated differences of opinion about how Metro should develop and what role the core city should play within it.

The strongest opposition to Metro policies came from members of Toronto City Council's neo-reform majority, many of whom had entered local politics as members of community groups that had fought the Spadina Expressway and urban renewal. The city government was itself divided, however, among radical reformers, moderate reformers, and surviving members of a pro-development "old guard." An inability to resolve these internal differences made the City of Toronto the only Metro municipality that did not make a submission to the Robarts Commission while it was reviewing Metro's governmental system between 1975 and 1977.[111]

One thing on which city and suburban politicians could agree, however, was that they did not want any increase in Metro's powers at the expense of

---

111. Alden Baker, "Briefs submitted to Robarts from all areas but Toronto," *Globe and Mail*, February 27, 1976.

the municipalities. While this consensus did not help to overcome other differences, it did mean that all parties took positions that precluded the formation of a common Metro interest. Disputes about the management and distribution of assisted rental housing, the distribution of group homes, additions to the rapid transit system, the administration of public health, and the distribution of funds for public education exemplified the way the concerns and priorities of individual municipalities conflicted with the ideal of a regional community.

Political infighting nonetheless resulted in a few partial accommodations, most of them reached in the prolonged negotiations that went into the production of a Metropolitan Toronto Official Plan. These negotiations produced a Metro-wide consensus on the idea of a nodal urban structure, in which some office and commercial activities would be distributed among a variety of suburban sites. They also included Metro's adoption of "fair share" policies for social housing and group homes, a decision to allow the Metropolitan Toronto Housing Company to play a limited role in the provision of government-assisted family housing, and an acknowledgement that Metro and its local governments had to pay more attention to the social implications and consequences of Metro's changing social structure.

At the regional level there was no forum, other than the provincial cabinet, where compromises about regional issues could be worked out and acted on. The only organization with a legal mandate to act for the entire region was the Toronto Area Transit Operating Authority. Not only did it have a limited mandate, but its structure made co-operation and coordination unlikely. Local representatives on the TATOA board were the chairs of the regional councils and, except for Metropolitan Toronto's representatives, had no responsibility for local transit. They also had little influence over the local planning decisions that determined the contexts in which transit systems operated.

Several groups of provincial and local politicians or civil servants met informally to discuss ways to deal with matters such as extending water services across the boundaries of regional municipalities, rebuilding a capacity for data collection for the whole Toronto region, and finding ways to coordinate transportation and land-use planning. These organizations had no formal status, however, and no formal connections to provincial policy-making. The only persons who had both an awareness of regional issues and direct access to elected officials were members of the provincial staff who had worked on Toronto-Centred Region and related initiatives in the late 1960s and early 1970s. Some of these individuals would stimulate the government to revisit the regional agenda in the mid-1980s.

FIVE
1985–1995
Regionalism Revisited

The Re-emergence of Regional Issues

Population growth slowed down after 1975 in the city-region containing Metropolitan Toronto and four suburban regional municipalities (Durham, York, Peel, and Halton), dropping from an average of 52,000 persons per year between 1971 and 1976 to 47,500 persons per year between 1976 and 1981.[1] It was soon on the rise again, however, with 315,000 people, or 63,000 people per year, added to the region's population between 1981 and 1986. Of the total 15-year increase of slightly more than 800,000 people, Metro Toronto accounted for just 12.6 per cent. The rest went into the suburbs. By the early 1980s, therefore, provincial staff and the business community were warning the government that the region's infrastructure was becoming seriously over-burdened. If nothing was done, they said, the region's economy would suffer, and with it the economic well-being of the entire province.

Persistent growth in the financial and corporate sectors had enabled the region to weather a recession in the early 1980s better than the rest of Ontario.[2] Consequently, most provincial cabinet members initially opposed doing anything that would benefit the Toronto region, particularly Metro Toronto, at the expense of the rest of the province. When several major employers threatened to leave the region, however, the government cautiously began to address the more urgent infrastructural needs.[3] Nonetheless, regional issues still tended to be overshadowed by financial concerns, as they had been in the 1970s.

Even when the economy was doing well, the government's search for ways to accommodate regional growth competed with efforts to control spending and to compensate for reductions in federal government transfers. Then in 1989 Canada entered its most serious economic downturn since the 1930s, a trend blamed on a variety of factors: the Canada–U.S. Free Trade

---

1. Based on Statistics Canada census data compiled for Metropolitan Toronto Planning Department, Research and Special Studies Division 1995, 1.4.
2. John Britton, "The Urban Economy in Context," in Goldrick and Holmes 1981, 48–49.
3. Gardner Church, personal communication, April 6, 1993.

Agreement signed in January 1989; global economic restructuring more generally; anti-inflationary policies adopted by the federal government; and the sudden collapse of an inflated real estate market.[4] The impacts of this recession, unlike those of the previous one, were felt more severely in the Toronto region than in many other parts of Canada.

In addition to having to work within financial constraints, government policy-makers had to deal with the uncertainties of a volatile political system. In 1985 the long-governing Progressive Conservatives were replaced by a minority government headed by the Liberal Party, which had hitherto opposed regional government and regional planning. The Liberals governed for two years with the support of the New Democratic Party (NDP) before winning a clear majority in 1987. Then in 1990 the New Democrats defeated the Liberals, also with a clear majority. Each new government first had to be persuaded that the Toronto region needed attention. It then began to devise regional policies that were consistent with its own priorities.

Both the provincial and municipal governments were also under persistent pressure to ensure that their policy deliberations allowed for participation by a regional population that was becoming increasingly diverse. As the region continued to absorb approximately one-third of Canada's yearly influx of immigrants, newcomers were replacing Canadian-born persons who were moving elsewhere. Because these newcomers came from all over the world, they were not only changing the region's demographic character, but were also presenting its governments with new and unfamiliar challenges.

Meanwhile, the environmental movement was becoming more politically assertive while being internally divided on questions of regional policy. The movement as a whole attacked urban sprawl for the threats it posed to agricultural land and to air and water quality. Some of its adherents, however, argued for more compact forms of urban development; others promoted policies that would slow growth significantly or stop it altogether.

In this climate of change, uncertainty, and conflicting policy preferences, the three governments that held office between 1985 and 1995 proceeded cautiously, avoiding the impulse to innovate that had characterized government responses to regional issues in the 1960s. Renewed attention to the regional agenda therefore brought only minor and incremental changes in institutional arrangements for addressing regional issues. Nonetheless, the period was important in the evolution of Toronto region governance because of its focus

---

4. Rachlis and Wolfe 1997, 342; Royal Bank of Canada Economics Department, "Outlook for Metro Toronto: Diagnosis of an Ailing Economy," 1995; Enid Slack, "Is There an Economic Crisis in the GTA Core?" (paper prepared for the GTA Task Force, August 31, 1995), 20.

on issues that would be addressed much more forcefully by the Progressive Conservative government that replaced the NDP government in 1995.

Incremental Regionalism

Although the provincial government became more involved in regional policy-making after 1985, its members often stated that the government had no interest in creating yet another unit of government with authority to act on behalf of the whole Toronto region, or even in restructuring local governments at all. It made an exception, however, in the case of Metropolitan Toronto, where the Council frequently became mired in unproductive debates about property tax, transportation, and housing issues.

After receiving the 1986 report of an appointed Task Force on Representation and Accountability in Metropolitan Toronto, the provincial government asked Metro's municipal members to recommend a way to restructure Metro's electoral system to make Metro Council more accountable to Metro residents. Metro Council did no more, however, than decide "to inform the province of its doubts and concerns."[5] The government then decreed that Metro Council members would be directly elected to serve Metro wards, a procedure that the City of Toronto had already adopted. Only municipal mayors would continue to represent municipal (lower-tier) councils at the Metro level.[6]

In general, however, the government's first response to a regional problem was either to ask regional and municipal government officials to work out agreements among themselves, or to ask a private consultant or an appointed committee to study the problem and offer advice. The focus of these studies was the Greater Toronto Area, or GTA, which different provincial ministries defined in different ways. According to the Ministry of Municipal Affairs, the GTA consisted of Metropolitan Toronto and the Regional Municipalities of Durham, York, Peel, and Halton; Ministry of Transportation and Communications officials usually included the Regional Municipality of Hamilton-Wentworth in their definition (see Figure 4.1, page 151).

The committee with the most comprehensive regional mandate was the Greater Toronto Coordinating Committee (GTCC), which was created in 1987, 10 years after the Robarts Committee had advised the government to create such a body "because the integrated development of the Toronto region

---

5. Mellon 1993, 50.

6. Metro councillors had hitherto been selected by a process of indirect election, whereby mayors and other persons elected to individual municipal councils either became members of Metro Council automatically or were selected by their councils to serve on that body.

is too important to be left to chance."[7] Made up of provincial, regional, and municipal government staff members and headed by a provincial deputy minister, the Committee was asked to evaluate competing demands for all types of infrastructure assistance coming from the GTA's municipal and regional governments.[8] On the advice of that Committee, the government also set up an Office for the Greater Toronto Area (OGTA) to provide the GTCC with staff support and a direct link to the provincial cabinet.

A matter that cried out for immediate attention was solid waste management. Even though the Robarts Commission had said that this issue was "quickly approaching crisis proportions" in 1977,[9] it was still a serious problem 12 years later. It was particularly acute for Metropolitan Toronto, which was running out of capacity in its principal landfill site in the Town of Vaughan, to the north of Metro, and could not find alternative sites elsewhere in the region.[10] Recognizing Metro's difficulty, the Robarts Commission had advised the province to assume responsibility for finding new sites. The government had instead assigned this task to Metro and the regional governments. By the late 1980s their council chairs were ready to acknowledge that waste disposal was a problem that they all shared, and constituted themselves as a steering committee to study it.[11] When they failed to agree where new dumps should be located, the provincial government appointed an Interim Waste Authority (IWA) to choose a site in each of Durham, York, and Peel.

The IWA exemplified another common way of addressing municipal or regional problems during this period: creating new crown agencies (special-purpose authorities) with appointed governing boards to address specific issues. Other examples were the Ontario Clean Water Agency, formed to construct new and replacement municipal sewage and water systems; the Ontario Transportation Capital Corporation, formed to find new sources of capital for roads and transit; and the Ontario Realty Corporation, formed to manage and if necessary dispose of the province's real estate holdings. To the extent that these agencies assumed tasks previously assigned to provincial ministries, they distanced the government from activities that were either politically controversial or likely to be costly. The NDP government, which

---

7. Royal Commission on Metropolitan Toronto 1977(b), 131.

8. Sean Fine, "Toronto area gets deputy minister," *Globe and Mail*, August 1, 1988.

9. Royal Commission on Metropolitan Toronto 1977(b), 261.

10. Metro Council selected the site in southern York county while it had planning jurisdiction over sparsely populated peripheral districts. By doing so, it was able to resolve a dispute among Metro's original 13 municipalities (Kaplan 1982, 698).

11. Michael Valpy, "New tier emerging in regional politics," *Globe and Mail*, March 15, 1989; Eric Skelton, "New utility should control garbage plan, regions say," *Globe and Mail*, August 28, 1989.

quickly became preoccupied with battling the recession, also justified them as contributions to deficit control, economic growth, and job creation.[12]

The government continued to respond directly, however, to political pressures for better environmental management. Its preferred response was to impose increasingly stringent environmental regulations on municipal and regional development. These offered some protection to environmentally sensitive areas, but frequently resulted in lengthy public hearings and appeals, which critics accused of adding to the time and costs of securing approval for new infrastructure or for the construction of new homes and workplaces. They also claimed that community groups were using the environmental appeal process to delay or kill projects (such as new rapid transit lines and affordable or higher density housing), even after they had received planning approval, for reasons that had little to do with their environmental impacts. When used in this way, the critics maintained, environmental regulations were making it more difficult to achieve desired regional development objectives or (especially after the recession began in 1989) create new jobs.

Dissatisfaction with the environmental review process contributed to a sense that it was time to revise the *Planning Act* once again. Acting on that sentiment soon after taking office in 1990, the NDP government created a three-person Commission on Planning and Development Reform in Ontario, headed by former Toronto Mayor John Sewell. The Sewell Commission conducted a comprehensive review of the *Planning Act* in the interest of making the planning process more responsive to public concerns, more sensitive to the natural environment, and more "timely and efficient."[13] By the early 1990s, the government had also exercised its right to act on "matters of provincial interest" by issuing four policy statements dealing with the protection of mineral aggregate resources, flood plain planning, wetlands policy, and land-use planning for housing. It had also quietly changed its planning legislation to allow it to "declare any matter to be of provincial interest, whether or not there is an approved provincial policy statement on that matter."[14]

The work of the Sewell Commission and the policy statements were the basis for a major revision of the Ontario *Planning Act* in 1994. They also complemented work begun in 1989 to devise and build region-wide consensus on a long-range land-use strategy for the Greater Toronto Area. The outcomes of these activities for regional policy are discussed in more detail later in this chapter. Taken together, they implied that the Ontario government was preparing to take a more active and decisive role in managing the

---

12. Colin Vaughan, "Rae not doing much for the greater good," *Globe and Mail*, February 15, 1993.

13. Commission on Planning and Development Reform in Ontario 1993, 1.

14. Farrow 1989.

region. The NDP government strengthened that impression in April 1995 when it appointed a Task Force on the Greater Toronto Area (the GTA Task Force or the Golden Task Force, after its head, Anne Golden) to carry out a comprehensive study of the region's system of governance and what could be done to improve it.

At the same time as it was revising its planning system and deciding what to do about the GTA, the provincial government was starting to deal with criticisms of the province's public education system.[15] There were taxpayer complaints that the high costs of education were not yielding the outcomes required by a competitive and changing job market, as well as charges of extravagance levelled at some local school boards. There was growing dissatisfaction among school board officials with provincial interventions in school administration, particularly in places like Metropolitan Toronto, where the province no longer paid a share of education costs. There were also complaints about growing disparities in the resources available to regional and district school boards.

Discussions about GTA governance and public education intersected only occasionally. Nonetheless, they were closely related by their importance to the well-being of the Toronto region's population and economy, to the management of local and provincial finance, and to the nature and scale of demands made on the provincial government. Government decisions to become more involved in these two areas implied that it was ready to exercise its responsibilities for both municipal affairs and education more firmly than it had done in the previous 20 years. It occurred, however, at a time when financial concerns had gained ascendancy over all others in every branch of provincial policy-making. It was financial concerns, in fact, that usually prompted the government to take action.

The Financial Challenges: Grappling with Declining Federal Government Support and a Major Recession

Shifting provincial spending priorities

Despite a gradual improvement in the provincial economy in the mid-1980s, the two governments headed by the Liberal Party (1985–87 and 1987–90) continued to emphasize the need to control spending because of reductions in federal government contributions to cost-sharing programs. These had begun in

---

15. Kelly Toughill, "Have Toronto trustees left the classroom for political arena?" *Toronto Star*, November 3, 1991; "Trustees forced to trim pay hike," *Financial Post*, January 6, 1993, 35; Gidney 1999, 194–195.

the late 1970s, when the federal government placed limits on its contributions to federal–provincial health care and post-secondary education programs. In 1985 Canada Mortgage and Housing Corporation (CMHC) reduced support for homeownership and mixed rental housing programs and began to target most of its housing assistance to very low-income groups. Federal housing support ended entirely in 1993. In 1990, just as the recession was getting under way, the federal government placed a ceiling on its contributions to social assistance in Ontario, British Columbia, and Alberta. By 1994–95 federal payments covered about 28 per cent of Ontario's welfare costs, as compared to 50 per cent in the country's seven poorer provinces.[16]

The federal government capped its contributions to welfare assistance immediately after the Ontario government announced sweeping and costly reforms to its welfare system in 1989.[17] Nonetheless the NDP government legislated a 7 per cent increase in welfare payments soon after coming to office in 1990. The NDP had already persuaded the minority Liberal government to increase its support for socially assisted housing in 1985, and it increased housing support still more after it took office. By 1994, Ontario's was the only provincial government still building affordable housing on a large scale.[18]

To find new money for social services, the provincial government curtailed spending in other areas. The Liberal government froze unconditional grants to municipal governments and reduced capital grants for school construction. Although the province was still committed to paying 75 per cent of the capital costs of public transit, the Liberals announced early in their first term that they were placing a ceiling on these contributions. They were not willing to pay the kinds of cost overruns that had occurred in the construction of the Scarborough Rapid Transit Line, the most recent addition to Metro's rapid transit system.[19]

By 1990, according to Gardner Church, Assistant Deputy Minister for the Greater Toronto Area, the province was insisting that money to fund new services in the Toronto region had to come from the region, where the principal

---

16. Margaret Philp, "Alberta driving out welfare recipients," *Globe and Mail*, February 9, 1995. This ceiling was extended to all provinces in 1995–96, when there was no increase in the Canada Health and Social Transfer over the previous year.

17. Mary Janigan, "Demise of a 'fat cat.' Bob Rae blames Ottawa for his province's fiscal woes," *Maclean's*, April 14, 1994, 10.

18. William Walker, "Housing minister discusses return of social housing plan," *Toronto Star*, November 12, 1994.

19. Cecil Foster, "Liberals to cut budgets for transit capital projects," *Globe and Mail*, July 17, 1985. The Chair of the TTC immediately pointed out that the province had only itself to blame, because it had insisted that the TTC use light rapid transit equipment built by a provincially sponsored firm.

beneficiaries of those services lived.[20] Alluding to recent consultations with municipal and regional government officials, Church noted that "it was not difficult to build a consensus about what an ideal city should look like," but it was difficult "to raise the capital plan that people can buy into." Nonetheless, he said, it was the Treasurer's position that there would be no major investments in regional infrastructure until such a consensus was reached. Withholding money for infrastructure was "the price of noncooperation."

The Liberal government came to office before Metro and the TTC adopted Network 2011. During the 10 years that Metro politicians argued about their transit preferences and priorities, the Toronto region gained more than 550,000 people, and fewer than 70,000 of these new residents moved into Metropolitan Toronto. Yet Network 2011 made no provision for linking TTC lines to the rest of the region. This lack of regional focus was one reason why the provincial government decided to hold up funding for new rapid transit lines in Metro while it conducted its own study of the Toronto region's transportation needs. It undertook that study, the Transportation Minister explained, because "transportation will continue to be a cornerstone of the economy and quality of life of the Greater Toronto Area," which "provides the focus for Ontario's competitiveness in world markets and underpins a strong provincial economy."[21]

The government apparently had decided that the Toronto region's transportation system was too important to be left in the hands of municipal and regional governments that were unwilling to adapt their transportation systems to regional needs. It also wanted to coordinate and rationalize its separate investments in four different and costly transportation programs in the region: provincial highways, GO Transit, municipal transit, and municipal roads. The aim was to spend less on the region's transportation system, not more; or at least to allocate transportation funds more efficiently and effectively.

While it looked for ways to bring transportation costs under control, the government ended its support for new trunk sewer and water services as soon as the York–Durham Servicing Scheme reached its planned limits in the mid-1990s. Regional governments became fully responsible for adding and funding new facilities in their own jurisdictions. Ministry of the Environment grants and loans went mainly to municipalities that wanted to clean up existing water and sewer systems, not build new ones.[22]

20. Elizabeth Grove-White, "Toronto the eleventh province," *Toronto*, February 1990, 23–27, 58.

21. Ontario Ministry of Transportation, "Transportation Directions for the Greater Toronto Area," May 1988, 2–3.

22. Jock Ferguson, "Ontario creates new agency to finance sewage systems," *Globe and Mail*, April 4, 1990.

Apart from its investments in social housing and transportation, the government's most direct financial contributions to GTA governance during this period were the funds it used to finance the many committees and task forces set up to study the region's infrastructure requirements. The costs of such studies could be high. The Interim Waste Authority, for example, reportedly spent $80 million on its unsuccessful search for waste disposal sites.[23]

Renewed interest in financial restructuring

The impacts of financial restraints on the provincial and municipal budgets helped to revive interest at both levels of government in restructuring the provincial–municipal financial relationship. Provincial and local officials, however, had different reasons for wanting change.[24] The province hoped that financial restructuring would allow it to reduce its share of municipal costs; municipal officials wanted less provincial regulation and interference, but as much or more provincial money. They also wanted the province to stop giving them new responsibilities without new funds to pay for them.

Despite their different objectives, participants in provincial–municipal discussions agreed on the words that best expressed their objectives. They sought

- disentanglement, or a clearer division of roles and responsibilities between the province and its municipalities;
- subsidiarity, whereby individual services were delivered by the lowest level of government able to deliver them; and
- government accountability to the citizens whose taxes paid for those services.

Those who subscribed to these objectives could often agree, at least in principle, as to what needed to be done. The provincial government, they said, should assume full financial responsibility for services (such as social services, public health, and education) that either entailed a redistribution of income among individuals and households or that benefited the province as a whole. Local governments should be fully responsible for services of a local nature, using property taxes and user charges to pay for these services. The province

---

23. John Barber, "Tory change to waste bill could cost Metro a lot," *Globe and Mail*, November 7, 1997.

24. Advisory Committee to the [Ontario] Minister of Municipal Affairs on the Provincial–Municipal Financial Relationship 1991; Association of Municipalities of Ontario 1995, "Disentangling the provincial-municipal relationship: AMO submission to the Provincial Cabinet," Toronto 1991; Ontario Fair Tax Commission 1993.

should also reduce the number of conditional grants it gave to municipalities and increase the percentage of assistance given in the form of unconditional grants or revenue sharing. Finally, there should be a province-wide property assessment system using a common standard.

There was nothing new about any of these ideas; they had been the subjects of discussion and recommendations since the early 1950s. Their underlying purpose was always to give municipal governments more freedom to set spending priorities for services that were primarily of interest to local constituencies while relieving them of responsibility for services that provided benefits to the larger society. And their emphasis on the need for property tax reform simply highlighted the failure of some regional and local municipalities, Metropolitan Toronto the most prominent among them, to carry out a responsibility that the government had handed back to them in 1978.

Increasing emphasis on private-sector funding

The pursuit of disentanglement, however, did not point to obvious ways to fund services that crossed municipal boundaries in the GTA and other city-regions. To deal with this challenge, the government tried to shift more of these costs to the private sector. The creation of crown corporations was part of this effort. To the extent that such organizations were able to finance their activities out of tolls and user fees or by entering into partnerships with private companies, they helped to relieve both provincial and municipal governments of some of the costs of supporting regional growth.

A second way of privatizing the costs of servicing growth was to allow municipal and regional governments to use development charges to pay for a broader range of services. Before 1989, provincial law restricted the use of such charges to the so-called "hard services," such as sewer and water facilities and roads; after that date, municipal governments could charge developers for some of the capital costs of such amenities as theatres, museums, libraries, parks, recreation centres, and tourism facilities.[25] School boards could also levy development charges to help pay the capital costs of new schools.

A third attempt to privatize regional costs was a controversial annual tax on large commercial structures and on commercial parking lots and garages in the GTA. When the government introduced the tax in 1989, it claimed that it would use money raised in this way to improve the region's transportation infrastructure. It did not, however, earmark these funds for that or any other purpose.[26] The government also looked for ways to involve private companies

25. Slack and Bird 1991, 1294.
26. Jim Byers, "Nixon won't drop tax on offices, parking lots," *Toronto Star*, October 27, 1989.

in the funding and construction of transportation infrastructure, promising that in return they would receive a share of profits from land development along subway routes or of tolls charged to highway users.[27]

The NDP government's controversial 1992 decision to authorize Ontario's first gambling casino was another attempt to tap private income for public purposes. Located in Windsor, immediately across the U.S. border from Detroit, the casino was intended to stem the flow of Ontario dollars into similar facilities in the United States A new crown agency, the Ontario Casino Commission, would own it and a consortium of private companies would operate it, but proceeds after payouts were to go to the government.

Consequences for Regional Governance: Much Discussion but Few Accomplishments

Limited progress on regional infrastructure

The provincial government's reliance on consensus building to address regional problems, together with its unwillingness to spend more provincial money on regional services, meant that there was little progress in dealing with infrastructure issues over the 10-year period. Solid waste disposal was a particularly intractable and divisive issue. The Interim Waste Authority created in 1991 quickly identified 57 possible dumping sites in the GTA and set out to whittle that number down to 3 through intergovernmental and public consultations. By the time it had brought the number down to 6, its work was completely bogged down in acrimonious public meetings and Metro was talking about shipping garbage to less-populated parts of Northern Ontario. The NDP government insisted, however, that Metro had to dispose of its garbage within the region, a position that was so intensely opposed in the outer suburbs that the Conservative Party said it would abolish the IWA if it won the election in 1995.[28]

The declining capacity of trunk sewer and water facilities was also becoming an issue again. Durham region complained to the province in 1989 that York planned to use more than its share of the capacity allotted to it when the York–Durham Servicing Scheme was launched in 1974.[29] In Halton, which

27. Ontario Ministry of Transportation, "Province announces $5-billion rapid transit agenda for the 90s," News Release, April 5, 1990.

28. James Rusk, "Metro seeking fallback garbage plan," *Globe and Mail*, July 6, 1993; James Rusk, "Proposed dump option denied Metro," *Globe and Mail*, December 9, 1993; Peter Krivel, "City above Toronto holds its own," *Toronto Star*, June 19, 1995.

29. Jock Ferguson, "Battle over sewer use erupts between Durham, York regions," *Globe and Mail*, November 22, 1989.

Table 5.1 GO Transit operating statistics, 1975–1994

	Passengers carried (ooos)			Route kilometres			Kilometres of service provided (ooos)		
	Rail	Bus	Total	Rail	Bus	Total	Rail	Bus	Total
1975–76	8,396	4,316	12,712	143	992	1,235	1,445	7,002	8,447
1983–84	14,148	10,234	24,382	341	1,127	1,468	1,700	13,565	15,265
1992–93	25,309	8,927	34,236	426	1,384	1,810	2,582	14,366	16,948
1993–94	25,938	8,715	34,653	360	1,252	1,612	2,329	14,305	16,634

Source: GO Transit, Annual Reports, various years.

had not been included in major servicing schemes in the 1960s and 1970s, planners were looking for ways to support accelerating growth. Real estate developers and municipalities welcomed the 1990 creation of the Ontario Clean Water Agency for its potential to open up new lands for development on the urban fringe.[30] Environmentalists, however, complained that the agency implied more sprawl. Their objections indicated that political opposition to new urban infrastructure was no longer confined to already built-up areas.[31]

There was also dissatisfaction with the state of the region's transportation system, even though the provincial Ministry of Transportation and Communications and the regional governments went on building new highways throughout the period. The government also allowed GO Transit to expand its rail system, sometimes in response to political pressure from communities outside the GTA. Although the rate of expansion was not as great as it had been in the previous 10 years, GO provided rail service on nearly three times as many miles of track in 1993 as it had in 1975. It also served three times as many rail passengers (Table 5.1). Its bus route mileage had doubled. Nonetheless, provincial spending on all forms of transportation had dropped from 9.3 per cent of the provincial budget in 1974–75 to 5.6 per cent in 1989–90, and would continue to fall after that.

Financing regional infrastructure not a priority

The government's foray into regional transportation planning in the late 1980s brought sporadic and inconsistent promises to spend more money on transportation in the GTA. First, the Liberal government promised in 1988 to spend $130 million over three years on "strategic transportation initiatives" in the GTA, by which it meant repairs to existing provincial highways and Metro

30. Jock Ferguson, "Ontario creates new agency to finance sewage systems," *Globe and Mail*, April 4, 1990.

31. White 2003, 60–61.

roads.[32] In 1990 it announced a $5-billion plan (*Let's Move*) for improvements to the area's public transit system alone, although the Transportation Minister emphasized that some of the money would have to come from municipalities and the private sector.[33] Four months later, with an election looming, the Minister of Transportation and Communications said that the province planned to spend an additional $11.9 million on a massive expansion of the GO train commuter network.[34] The NDP won the election and nothing more was said about this proposal.

In 1993, however, the NDP government announced it would allocate $1.5 billion of a recently announced $6-billion infrastructure investment fund to public transit improvements throughout the province, with two-thirds of the money to be spent within the GTA.[35] It then told the TTC to proceed with construction of two Network 2011 lines: an Eglinton line running west into the City of York and a Sheppard line running east through North York toward Scarborough (see Figure 4.4b, page 180). It also committed funds to support the cost of five major provincial highways—three to be built within the GTA and two just outside it.[36] It reduced its financial support for GO Transit, on the other hand, which immediately cut back both rail and bus services. Nonetheless, the number of passengers using GO's rail services continued to increase.

Despite recurring government promises to increase spending on the GTA's transportation system, the percentage of the provincial budget that went to transportation declined overall during this period (Table 5.2).

Although total per capita spending on transportation increased, it did not increase as much as spending on other functions. As a result, according to a Ministry of Transportation and Communications report, "transportation demand [grew] faster than the infrastructure required to support it."[37] The situation, the report implied, was a result of the failure of both the provincial

---

32. Ontario Ministry of Transportation, "Transportation Directions for the Greater Toronto Area," May 1988, 8.

33. Margaret Polanyi, "Rail, TTC expansion part of $5-billion plan to improve rapid transit," *Globe and Mail*, April 6, 1990.

34. Campaign Ontario '90, "Premier David Peterson nearly doubles GO train commuter rail network," August 28, 1990.

35. "Notes for remarks by the Honourable Ed Philip, Minister of Municipal Affairs and Office for the Greater Toronto Area" (delivered at the Canadian Urban Institute, March 4, 1993).

36. Government of Ontario, "Province commits multi-year JobsOntario funding for QEW upgrading," Press release, February 10, 1993.

37. Ontario Ministry of Transportation and Communications, *Towards a Greater Toronto Area Transportation Plan*, Technical Report #7, "Transportation Infrastructure: Expenditure Trends and Preservation Requirements," October 1996, 9.

Table 5.2 Ontario government spending on selected functions, 1974–1995

Function	1974–75 ($,000s)	% of total prov. budget	1984–85 ($,000s)	% of total prov. budget	1989–90 ($,000s)	% of total prov. budget	1992–93 ($,000s)	% of total prov. budget	1994–95 ($,000s)	% of total prov. budget
Community and Social Services	674	7.7	2,604	9.9	5061	13.0	8591	15.9	9,436	16.8
Education (including Colleges & Universities)	2,476	28.4	5,151	19.5	8059	19.4	10,439	19.3	8,882	15.8
Environment and Energy	60	0.7	362	1.4	532	1.3	667	1.2	543	1.0
Health	2,530	29	8,340	31.6	13,787	33.1	17,758	32.7	17,848	31.7
Municipal Affairs & Housing			1,029	3.9	1496	3.6	2,087	3.9	1,797	3.2
Transportation	812	9.3	1,587	6.0	2310	5.6	2,575	4.8	2,355	4.2
Payment on Public Debt	589	6.8	2,922	11.1	4,284	10.3	5,293	9.8	7,832	13.9
Total Prov. Spending (Operating + Capital)	8,722		26,431		41,602		54,235		56,326	

Source: Based on data contained in Ontario Budget documents, 1985–1996. The figures are only rough indicators of spending trends because different governments organized ministries in different ways, shifting responsibilities around within the government. Between 1972 and 1974, for example, municipal affairs was a responsibility of the Ministry of Treasury, Economics and Intergovernmental Affairs while Housing had its own ministry. Then the two functions were combined into a new Ministry of Municipal Affairs and Housing, which was broken into two separate ministries in 1985. The two functions were consolidated once again into a single Ministry of Municipal Affairs and Housing in 1995. Between 1971 and 1987, transportation was combined with communications in a Ministry of Transportation and Communications.

and municipal governments to follow through on political decisions made in the 1970s.

Other large North American urban centres attempted to address capacity problems with a proliferation of expressway construction through the 1960's and 70's. The GTA did not, and remains an area with a low count of expressway kilometres per capita. Through this period in the GTA, there was also no offsetting expansion of its transit systems.

Spending on the environment and energy, which encompassed provincial spending on sewer and water facilities, also accounted for a smaller percentage of the provincial budget in 1995 than it had in 1985.

The largest shares of the provincial budget went to ministries responsible for social programs, such as community and social services, education, and health. Their combined share of the budget also increased, from 61 per cent in 1985 to a high of 67.9 per cent in 1993, after which it dropped off. There were shifts in emphasis among the three service areas, however. The share going to education dropped after 1975, while the proportion devoted to health rose and then fell slightly. The ministry responsible for community and social services experienced the largest gain, with its share of the budget almost doubling between 1974–75 and 1994–95. Most of the increase occurred after 1985. This trend made social services a conspicuous target when the government began to look for ways to trim its spending in the mid-1990s.

Another trend that would lead to substantial changes in the province's fiscal policies, especially after 1995, was the growing proportion of the budget used to pay interest on the provincial debt. Although the percentage share of the budget that went to debt repayment dropped slightly between 1985 and 1993, it was always above the 6.9 per cent allocated to this purpose in 1975, when debt first became a reason for spending restraints. In 1993 the Ministry of Finance was projecting that interest payments would rise to 14 per cent of the provincial budget by 1995.

A BRIEF FLIRTATION WITH DISENTANGLEMENT

To maintain or increase spending on community and social services, the government not only reduced its spending on transportation and other types of infrastructure while maintaining a high level of debt, but it also increased some taxes and introduced new ones. The recession brought all three fiscal strategies under intense political scrutiny from taxpayer and business organizations. The NDP government soon backed away from promises to increase social spending still more and began to adopt measures to revive the economy, cut government costs, and reduce government debt. To gain control over welfare costs, it said, it would take over responsibility for social assistance as part of a program to "disentangle" provincial services from municipal services. In return, it said, municipalities would take over services such as local highways and public transit. It backed away from the proposal, however, in the face of opposition from municipal officials, who feared that the switch would add to their costs.[38]

As an alternative, it moved three discretionary social programs into the "mandatory" category and ended its support for several others.[39]

UNSUCCESSFUL ATTEMPTS TO REFORM METRO'S PROPERTY TAX SYSTEM

The recession not only stimulated provincial investment in GTA infrastructure, but also made property tax reform a GTA-wide issue. As Metro continued to lose businesses, some of them to the surrounding regions, financial analysts drew attention to the fact that business properties were taxed at higher rates in Metro than in the neighbouring regional municipalities.[40] Metro's outdated property tax system, they argued, was no longer just a local problem; it now threatened Metro's ability to maintain a strong role in the regional economy.

Assessment and property tax reform had become increasingly complex and contentious issues in Metropolitan Toronto both during and after the provincial government's attempt to deal with them between 1969 and 1978. Not only did the values of properties in different Metro districts change at different rates during the 1970s and 1980s, but the values of residential properties increased faster than the values of commercial and industrial properties. Consequently, the government kept up pressure on Metro to come up with a plan for reforming its assessment and property tax systems. It also allowed provincial assessors to carry out "spot reassessments" in different neighbourhoods, using their own evaluation standards, a practice that added to existing inequities in Metro's property tax bills.

Metro's failure to work out a plan that satisfied the province was one reason for the government's 1988 decision to change Metro Council to a system of direct election. The directly elected Council addressed the issue immediately. To lessen the impact of reform on residential and industrial properties, and so win Council approval, proponents devised a reform plan that shifted a larger share of the tax burden to office and commercial properties. Metro submitted this "temporary" plan to the Liberal government in 1989. The Liberals lost the next election to the NDP, however, and the new government immediately came under intense lobbying from City of Toronto officials, tenants and landlords of rental properties, owners of businesses likely to experience

38. Ibbitson 1997, 235.

39. Metro Community Services, Social Development Division 1995.

40. Board of Trade of Metropolitan Toronto, "Killing the Golden Goose," October 1994; Metro Chief Administrator's Office, "Metro Toronto Matters: An Agenda for Fiscal Reform in Metro Toronto," January 1995; Board of Trade of Metropolitan Toronto, "For the Greater Good: An Action Plan for Making the Greater Toronto Area More Competitive Through Property Tax and Governance Reform," October 1995.

large tax increases, and the unions that represented their workers. The NDP government soon shelved the plan, telling Metro to revise and resubmit it. When Metro did so, however, the province said it would not consider any new scheme until it received the report of a Fair Tax Commission that was looking into ways to restructure Ontario's tax system more generally.[41]

That Commission rejected the idea of market value assessment and instead recommended a complex assessment system based on building and lot size and building type, to which various weighting factors could be applied.[42] Neither Metro nor the NDP government took any further action. Nonetheless, assessments in Metro were gradually changing because of successful appeals by individual taxpayers, which increased sharply after the government released assessment data to the public in 1992. Particularly threatening to Metro's financial stability were the many appeals mounted by the owners of large commercial properties, who could afford the legal costs and who could expect large financial gains if their appeals were successful. Successful appeals implied either lower tax returns for Metro and local councils and school boards, or higher taxes for the owners of residential properties and small businesses.

LIMITS ON INVOLVING THE PRIVATE SECTOR

Government measures to hasten the provision of new transportation infrastructure in the GTA included a contractual arrangement with a private company to build a toll highway, the 407, through the Regional Municipality of York. The Ontario Transportation Capital Corporation, a provincial crown agency, was to retain ownership for the province, but the company would maintain the highway and charge tolls to cover its costs until it was paid for, up to a maximum period of 30 years.[43] This arrangement, provincial officials claimed, meant that the highway would be finished 15 to 20 years earlier than if it were built with government funds.

There were limits, however, to the government's ability to privatize the costs of new infrastructure. Those quickly became apparent in the opposition to the commercial concentration tax from land developers, real estate interests, hotel owners, parking lot operators, and local politicians. Embedded in this opposition was the implicit or explicit threat that some businesses would go to other regions, where the cost of doing business was lower. Business losses during the recession helped to persuade the NDP government to suspend use of this tax in 1993. It left the *Development Charges Act* in place, however, even though it too was being criticized as a disincentive to new investment.

---

41. Jane Coutts, "Province blocks Metro tax plan," *Globe and Mail*, November 16, 1993.

42. Ontario Fair Tax Commission 1993, 92.

43. James Rusk, "Ontario takes a new road," *Globe and Mail*, March 28, 1994.

Promoting consensus on a growth management strategy

TRANSPORTATION PLANNERS TAKE THE LEAD ONCE AGAIN

Diagnoses of Toronto region problems between 1985 and 1995 typically included arguments for the need to manage or control the outward spread of settlement. As had happened in the past, transportation planners were among the first government officials to make those arguments. According to the Minister of Transportation and Communications, the ministry decided to prepare a regional transportation plan to ensure "that transportation services support the desired form of urban development throughout the G.T.A." and that "transportation planning is done in a full regional context with due consideration for affordability and fair distribution of benefits."[44]

As to what "the desired form of urban development" should be, the minister's statement favoured "responding to the growth occurring in downtown Toronto, but actively promoting development in the city centres and emerging sub-centres." It was an endorsement, in other words, of the multi-centred urban form favoured in the TCR strategy of 1971 and in Metro Toronto's 1980 Official Plan.

As part of its planning exercise, the Ministry of Transportation and Communications had created a provincial–municipal Transportation Planning Forum in 1986 to review "aspects of transportation in Metro, Durham, York and Peel."[45] That Forum established a Working Committee of provincial, metropolitan/regional, and municipal transportation officials to sort out and assign priority to the many applications for transportation funds coming from different parts of the Toronto region. Metro Toronto had only three of the group's nine municipal representatives, and the TTC refused to participate, having always opposed efforts to incorporate it into a regional transportation system. The Working Committee identified nine major unfunded initiatives, six of which it ranked as most worthy of provincial support.[46] Four were additions or improvements to the road system, including Highway 407, a street leading into downtown Toronto, and two regional roads. The three initiatives to which the committee gave lower priority were additions to Metro's subway system. The group also described transit fare and service integration as "an essential framework for the improvement of interregional transit services in the G.T.A."

---

44. Ontario Ministry of Transportation and Communications, "Transportation Directions for the Greater Toronto Area," May 1988, 4.

45. Ontario Transit Advisory Group to the Minister of Transportation for Ontario 1987, 18.

46. Transportation Planning Forum, Working Committee on Transportation Benefits, November 14, 1986.

The composition of the Working Group and the outcome of its deliberations were evidence of the growing influence of provincial and suburban
officials, who wanted the government to put more money into road building
and less into Metro's costly subway system. Nonetheless, the emphasis in provincial policy statements dealing with the GTA gradually shifted away from
roads and toward rapid transit. The policy statement issued by the Liberal
government in 1990 (*Let's Move*) included most of the TTC's Network 2011
plan, but with three lines extended to the Metro boundary, as well as additions
to GO Transit and improvements to regional roads. The NDP government
placed even more emphasis on public transit. Investing in regional transit, said
the minister, was part of a process "that knits the GTA closer together—and
that reinforce [*sic*] our vision of managing growth and economic development
within the area."[47]

By the end of the period, the government had begun to draw on a special
infrastructure fund to support the construction both of new rapid transit lines
in Metro and new roads in the suburban regions. Job creation and promoting
economic recovery, not managing regional growth, were by then its principal
reasons for spending money on the Toronto region's transportation system.
This approach seemed likely to perpetuate the existing dichotomy between
an automobile-oriented, low-density land-use pattern in the suburbs and
the higher density, more transit-oriented land-use pattern in the urban core.
Transportation officials maintained, however, that these were simply catch-up
projects, undertaken to make up for a long period of inaction.[48] They looked
to ongoing provincial–municipal consultations about a regional land-use
strategy to produce a coherent and cost-effective framework to guide future
infrastructure decisions.

SHAPING A REGIONAL VISION

The consultations to which transportation officials referred were the culmination of several provincial initiatives. One was the Urban Structure Concepts
Study commissioned in 1989 by the Greater Toronto Coordinating Committee
(GTCC). The study evaluated three alternative scenarios for the region's
future development: (1) "spread," that is, a continuation of low-density land-
use patterns outside Metropolitan Toronto; (2) "central," meaning further
concentration of growth around fully built-up areas in and near the core; and
(3) "nodal," which allowed for the dispersal of future growth throughout the

---

47. "Notes for remarks by the Honourable Ed Philip, Minister of Municipal Affairs
and Office for the Greater Toronto Area" (delivered at the Canadian Urban Institute,
March 4, 1993).
48. Interview with Bruce McQuaig, March 23, 1995.

region, but allocated it to compact centres or nodes linked by rapid transit.[49] The study implied that the "nodal" concept was the most feasible alternative to the status quo or "spread" pattern. While it would be more costly to service than the "central" model, it was likely to be more politically acceptable because it allowed for growth in the newer suburbs as well as in already built-up areas.

Two other initiatives emphasized environmental concerns. One was a Greenlands Strategy prepared by Ron Kanter, a former Liberal Member of the Provincial Parliament, which outlined "an integrated and linked GTA greenlands system and an approach ... to manage greenlands within a larger context."[50] Another was a government decision to co-sponsor a Royal Commission on the Future of the Toronto Waterfront. The federal government set up this body in 1988 in response to criticisms of intensive waterfront development sponsored by the Harbourfront Corporation, the organization it had created 12 years earlier to manage the Harbourfront lands (see Chapter 4). The man it chose to head the Royal Commission, David Crombie, had been Mayor of Toronto when the harbour lands were assigned to the city. (He was later elected to the federal parliament.) The Crombie Commission's report called on all levels of government to adopt an "ecosystem approach" to planning; that is, an approach that recognized the interrelationships among economic, social, and environmental issues and integrated all three factors into development plans and practices.[51]

In 1991 the NDP government appointed six working groups to help the GTCC develop a vision statement that reconciled the nodal scenario, the Greenlands Strategy, and the ecosystem approach with three values that it described as "key" to its policies: "*Social Equity, Enhanced Employment and Economic Vitality, and Achievement and Maintenance of a Healthy Environment.*"[52] It asked the working groups to build a region-wide consensus around a regional land-use strategy based on "compact urban form, a multi-centred urban structure, countryside protection, maximizing the use of existing infrastructure and a transit-oriented transportation system."[53]

Provincial staff members who took part in this exercise first had to convince local and provincial politicians to accept projections that the region was likely to grow from 4.2 million people in 1991 to 6 million in 2011. They then had to persuade the staff of 21 provincial ministries, 5 regional municipalities, and 35 local municipalities to subscribe to a "vision" that embraced planning principles that conflicted with the land-use practices that most of them were

49. IBI Group and Associates 1990.
50. Berridge Lewinberg Greenberg 1992, 11. See Kanter 1990.
51. Royal Commission on the Future of the Toronto Waterfront 1992, xix–xxii.
52. Ontario Office for the Greater Toronto Area 1992, 5. (Italics in original.)
53. Berridge Lewinberg Greenberg Ltd. 1992, 47.

used to following. Nonetheless, according to Gardner Church, 33 out of 35 local municipalities agreed to the vision in principle.[54]

While provincial staff worked with municipal officials to develop a regional vision, the government received the report of the Sewell Commission and amended the *Planning Act* in 1994–95 to incorporate some of its recommendations. A consolidated list of policy statements and guidelines issued at the same time gave the provincial planning system a comprehensive policy framework.[55] The new act specified that decisions of municipal councils, local boards, the Ministry of Municipal Affairs, and the Ontario Municipal Board should "be consistent with" those statements.[56] The wording replaced an earlier requirement that those making decisions under the *Planning Act* should "have regard to policy statements." It implied, therefore, that the government was prepared to give more direction to municipal and regional planning.

The Office for the Greater Toronto Area tried to give the province an explicit role in Toronto region planning by incorporating principles contained in the GTCC's "vision" document, together with a statement supporting "the continued role of the central core of Toronto as the economic, social and cultural core of the Greater Toronto Area," into a policy statement on "Managing Growth in the Greater Toronto Area."[57] It issued the statement in draft form in 1994, but the government neither adopted it nor released it to the public. Nonetheless, elements of the revised planning system were consistent with some of that statement's objectives. Chief among them were policy statements that promoted: (a) environmentally sensitive municipal planning; (b) the development of compact, transit-friendly communities; (c) the optimal use of existing infrastructure; and (d) a more balanced distribution of housing types throughout municipalities and regions.[58]

Although supporters of regional planning wanted the government to go further in supporting regional and environmental planning, others felt that it had gone too far. Developers and municipal officials in particular complained that the detailed regulations attached to the revised legislation had complicated rather than simplified the planning process, thereby adding to the time and

---

54. Interview with Gardner Church, April 16, 1993.

55. Ontario Ministry of Municipal Affairs, *Guideline Directory: A Listing of Provincial Policies and Guidelines Related to Land Development*, 1993.

56. Legislative Assembly of Ontario, *Bill 163: An Act to revise the Ontario Planning and Development Act and the Municipal Conflict of Interest Act, to amend the Planning Act and the Municipal Act and to amend other statutes related to planning and municipal matters*, 3rd Session, 35th Legislature, Ontario, 43 Elizabeth II, 1994, Part III, Art. 6 (5).

57. Ontario Office for the Greater Toronto Area and Ministry of Municipal Affairs, "Policy Statement: Managing Growth in the Greater Toronto Area" (First Draft for Discussion, February 4, 1994).

58. Ontario Ministry of Municipal Affairs 1995.

costs of getting new development under way. Municipal officials also depicted the policy statements as one more example of unwanted government interference in local affairs.[59]

VISION VERSUS REALITY

Those who promoted transportation and land-use plans for the Toronto region often said that the success of any regional strategy depended on the co-operation of regional and municipal governments. The municipal governments that best subscribed to regional planning goals were those of Metropolitan Toronto and some of its municipalities, particularly the City of Toronto. In December 1994 the provincial government approved a revised Metropolitan Toronto Official Plan that committed Metro to participating "with the other Regions of the GTA in accommodating population growth in a compact regional urban form based on Centres and Corridors, supporting transit, walking and cycling."[60] It favoured the redevelopment (or "reurbanization") of underused but fully serviced lands in already built-up areas.

The City of Toronto's revised Official Plan also favoured policies "to promote the more intensive development of the existing urban area, particularly through the process of residential intensification in the city."[61] While supporting the development or redevelopment of underused city lands, however, it also emphasized the importance of protecting existing low-rise neighbourhoods.

The Metropolitan Toronto plan called on Metro to accommodate 200,000 (or 10 per cent) of the GTA's projected 2,000,000 new residents over the next 20 to 30 years. The City of Toronto, with 655,000 people in 1991, aimed for a population of 725,000 by 2011. Both plans also emphasized the importance of attracting employers to central locations.

Metro's and the city's interest in promoting population and employment growth were reactions to regional growth trends that threatened to weaken the core. Metro's share of the region's population fell from 72 per cent in 1971 to 63 per cent in 1991 as the four regional municipalities absorbed 86 per cent of the region's population growth. Although the City of Toronto benefited from growth in the financial and corporate sectors, it had been losing manufacturing jobs to the suburbs. Office-based activities were also locating in the outer suburbs. As a result, between 1971 and 1991, Metro Toronto's share of jobs in the Toronto Census Metropolitan Area (CMA) had fallen from 82

59. John Barber, "Ban urban sprawl, Ontario urged," *Globe and Mail*, June 22, 1993; James Rusk, "Minefield of dreams for rural candidates," *Globe and Mail*, October 31, 1994; James Rusk, "Municipalities to get more leeway," *Globe and Mail*, January 3, 1997.
60. Municipality of Metropolitan Toronto 1994, 8.
61. City of Toronto 1994, 1.1.

to 64.5 per cent and the city's from 48 to 31 per cent.[62] Although the shares of regional employment in the two jurisdictions exceeded their shares of the region's population, they were nonetheless losing ground as the region's primary population and employment centres. It was therefore in both Metro's and the city's interest to try to counter the regional trends.

Outer suburban municipalities, on the other hand, were not only still growing, but still had undeveloped land. They were therefore less ready to change traditional planning practices. At the urging of the provincial government, however, the councils of York and Peel regions approved official plans for the first time. Other regional and local governments began to change their plans to make them more consistent with the new provincial policies.[63] Densities increased in some suburban districts, although often because builders began to place single-family homes on smaller lots.

Two provincially backed planning exercises during this period were also consistent with the growth management goals contained in the GTA vision. The first was a City of Toronto plan for a mixed-income, medium-density residential community (Ataratiri) on derelict industrial land to the east of downtown Toronto.[64] If built, the project would have provided housing for up to 14,000 people within a relatively short streetcar ride from the Central Business District. It would have entailed high start-up costs, however, both for removing contaminants from the soil and for protecting the area from potential flooding by the nearby Don River. Toronto City Council decided not to proceed with the project without a firm provincial commitment, which the NDP government refused to give.

The second planning exercise was conducted by a committee appointed by the NDP government to prepare a new concept for the proposed community of Seaton, outside Metro's northeastern boundary—the project that the Progressive Conservative government had initiated in the late 1970s as an adjunct to a new international airport, from which it then withdrew its support. The committee prepared a vision document incorporating many of the principles that were finding their way into provincial policy statements at the time: a compact community; a variety of land uses (including employment sites) within walking distance of each other; transit-supportive urban form; the preservation of natural assets and heritage landmarks; the protection of farm-

62. Metropolitan Toronto Planning Department, Policy Development Division 1986, 45; Frisken, Bourne, Gad, and Murdie 1997, 20.

63. Ray Tomalty, "Suburban Intensification in the GTA," Research Note, *The Intensification Report* (Toronto: Canadian Urban Institute, 1995), 37–42.

64. City of Toronto Planning and Development Department, *Ataratiri Principles, Directions and Strategies*, May 1990; *Ataratiri: Part II Official Plan Proposals. Summary and Recommendations*, September 1991.

Table 5.3 Median household income in different parts of the Toronto Region as a percentage of Toronto region median, 1981–1996

	1981	1986	1991	1996
Toronto Region[a]	100.00	100.00	100.00	100.00
Metro Toronto	92.8	90.21	86.57	82.21
East York	85.11	81.14	79.91	76.62
Etobicoke	106.32	101.77	95.63	91.72
North York	99.55	94.21	89.95	83.85
Scarborough	105.23	102.45	95.82	88.51
Toronto	79.12	79.00	78.01	77.74
York	79.64	75.27	73.44	69.19
Durham	103.09	107.24	109.05	115.69
Halton	117.47	118.47	120.77	128.08
Peel	116.25	115.75	115.50	118.52
York	119.12	125.34	129.76	128.89
Northern Fringe	97.76	97.87	106.49	112.02

Source: Bourne 2000, Table 6.1. Bourne's data covers 28 lower-tier municipalities outside Metro. Only three of those municipalities had median household incomes below the regional median in 1996.

a. Note: Bourne defines the region as including Metropolitan Toronto, four regional municipalities, and suburbanizing districts to the north of Peel and York regions.

land; and extensive public participation.[65] The NDP government received this document just before its 1995 election loss to the Progressive Conservatives, whereupon the project died.

Challenges to maintaining equity and how they were addressed

GROWING SOCIAL DISPARITIES

As had been the case with U.S. city-regions at various times in the past, the growth of the Toronto region was marked by a tendency for the population of the outer suburbs to become wealthier than the population closer to the urban core. Median household income in Metro Toronto fell from 92.8 to 82.21 per cent of the GTA median between 1981 and 1996, while it rose by varying percentages in the four suburban regional municipalities (Table 5.3).

This trend did not indicate, however, that the core City of Toronto was going the way of older U.S. cities. In some ways, in fact, the core city's condition improved during this period. Its average (as distinct from median) household income was higher in 1995, relative to the CMA average, than in 1980

---

65. Seaton Advisory Committee, *Seaton: From Vision to Reality*, June 1995.

Table 5.4 Changes in average household income in
Metropolitan Toronto and selected GTA municipalities, 1950–1990

	Ratio of Average Household Income to CMA Average (CMA = 100)				
	1950	1970	1980	1985	1995
Metro Toronto					
East York	107.4	89.2	85.3	80.9	82.8
Etobicoke	116.8	109	105.5	104.4	94.6
North York	116.6	110.7	103.4	100.1	92.4
Scarborough	103.2	99.7	97.7	95.3	84.9
Toronto	93.1	90.8	89	90.9	93.2
York	102.5	84.6	78.4	75.3	71.9
Newer Suburbs					
Mississauga	na	110.8	110.2	108.8	105.6
Brampton	na	103.8	106.3	105.4	105.7
Richmond Hill	na	98.2	107.7	116.2	115.9
Oakville	na	112.2	121.4	123.7	139.2
Vaughan	na	116.7	132.4	128.1	124.3
Markham	na	123.6	136.4	139.7	130.5

Source: Bourne 2000, Table 6.4.

(Table 5.4).[66] No other Metro municipality experienced a similar increase. In fact, Toronto was the only core city in Canada where average household income rose relative to the CMA average between 1980 and 1995 (Table 5.5), despite the fact that its 1995 population accounted for a much smaller percentage of the CMA population than did that of other large Canadian cities. Moreover, fully one-third of Toronto's families had incomes above the national average in 1991, a figure matched or exceeded in only eight of the twenty-four lower-tier municipalities in the suburban regions.[67] The percentage for Metro as a whole was 19 per cent.

There were still many middle- and upper-income residential districts scattered throughout Metro Toronto, therefore, and some of them were close to or within the downtown core. City streets were safe and lively, and the crime rate was low for a city of Toronto's size. Moreover, the core economy, while somewhat battered by the recession, was still strong. On the other hand, 29 per cent of the city's population was classified as low-income in 1996, a percentage exceeded only in the small City of York (Table 5.6). And poverty rates were considerably higher in all of Metro's municipalities than in the outer suburbs.

66. Bourne, Starkweather, and Basu 2000, Table 6.4.
67. City of York, *Managing the GTA as a Community, A Creative Response to the Challenge* (submission to the Greater Toronto Area Task Force, September 1995), 18.

Table 5.5 Average household incomes of Canada's 10 largest
central cities as a percentage of their CMA averages, 1971–1995 (CMA=100)

	1970	1980	1990	1995
Metropolitan Toronto			92	90
City of Toronto	91	89	91	93
Montreal	89	81	79	77
Vancouver	94	90	89	89
Ottawa	102	95	90	89
Edmonton	100	96	95	94
Calgary	100	100	99	98
Quebec City	88	81	80	80
Winnipeg[a]	88	100	99	98
Hamilton	92	88	82	80
London	101	99	98	98

a. In 1972 the former City of Winnipeg was united with 11 suburban municipalities to form the new City of Winnipeg (Unicity). The figure used here for 1970 is for the former city; later figures are for the amalgamated city.
Source: Census of Canada, various years.

Metro planners insisted that Metro's higher incidence of low-income households

> should not become a caricature. Metro remains a very mixed-income community and the outer GTA is somewhat mixed-income. The outer GTA does have ⅓ of the GTA's low-income family households of each type [2-parent, 1-parent, childless couples], and ¼ of the GTA's low-income non-family households.[68]

Nonetheless, income trends sounded a warning to anyone who hoped that Metropolitan Toronto would remain an economically strong, socially integrated, and residentially attractive regional node.

Three questions arise. First, to what extent had government policies been responsible for the increasing percentage of households in poverty in the GTA and their distribution within the region? Second, were income trends symptomatic of a general decline in the well-being of the urban core and its importance in the region? Finally, were governments responding to income and other trends in ways designed to counteract the region's growing socio-spatial differences, or did their responses seem likely to reinforce them?

Several explanations for growing poverty rates in the Toronto region linked them to changes taking place across Canada, and not to trends occurring

---

68. Metropolitan Toronto Planning Department, Research and Information Services Division 1996, 24.

Table 5.6 Low-income population as a percentage of the total population
in Metropolitan Toronto and regional municipalities in the GTA, 1986–1996

	1986[a]	1991[a]	1996[b]
Metro Toronto	16.4	22.4	27.6
East York	14.8	16.4	26.6
Etobicoke	12.0	14.7	23.2
North York	15.3	18.6	28.0
Scarborough	13.5	17.2	27.4
Toronto	21.5	22.4	29.0
York	19.3	22.4	31.9
Durham	9.0	8.4	11.1
Halton	6.5	6.7	9.3
Peel	8.1	9.7	15.0
York	6.6	7.5	12.9
GTA	12.8	14.0	20.2

a. Metropolitan Toronto Planning Department, Research and Special Studies Division
1994.

b. Bourne 2000, Table 6.5. Bourne includes districts to the north of Peel and York in his
definition of the Greater Toronto Area.

in the region alone. They included changes in household and family composition (more single-parent families and more individuals living alone); changes
in the labour market (fewer jobs in manufacturing and more low-paying
jobs in service industries); and, after 1989, the loss of jobs during the recession.[69] None of these explanations, however, either alone or in combination,
accounted for the fact that poverty rates in parts of Metro exceeded poverty
rates in Ontario or in Canada as a whole. Nor did they explain differences
in the way poor households were distributed within the GTA. Explanations
for these particular trends directed attention to seven different public policy
areas, some of which implicated all levels of government in the shaping of the
GTA's socio-spatial character. The policy areas were immigration, immigrant
settlement, housing, public transit, social and community services, property
assessment, and education.

IMMIGRATION POLICY
A characteristic of the Toronto region that set it apart from other Canadian
metropolitan areas was its ongoing absorption of more than one-third of
Canada's annual intake of immigrants. As a result of this inflow, immigrants
increased from 34.5 per cent of the GTA's population in 1986 to 40 per cent 10

---

69. Bourne, Starkweather, and Basu 2000, 6.1.

years later.[70] In previous years, however, the average earnings of immigrants and non-immigrants had tended to converge as immigrants became more settled in Canada. But immigrants began to lose ground financially after 1989, partly because of the recession, but also because of recent changes in federal immigration policy.

Before 1986 the federal government had adjusted immigrant admission rates to the needs of the Canadian economy; from 1986 onward it used immigration as a way to offset a declining rate of natural increase in the Canadian population, regardless of the employment situation.[71] It removed a requirement (introduced in 1982) that made pre-arranged employment one of the criteria used to determine whether an independent applicant would be admitted to Canada. It also broadened the definition of persons who could be sponsored by family members living in Canada; that is, those who could come without satisfying criteria applied to non-sponsored immigrants.

Immigrants fell into three broad categories: family-sponsored immigrants, independent immigrants (including immigrants with money to invest in a business), and refugees. In the early 1990s further changes in federal immigration policy shifted the emphasis away from family-sponsored immigrants toward immigrants in the independent and businesses classes. Another policy change gave preference to applicants who were capable of filling one of a list of "designated occupations."[72] As had been the case for independent immigrants since 1967, such persons also had to qualify under a point system that assessed applicants according to criteria such as age, education, and knowledge of a Canadian official language.

Because of the policy changes, the number of immigrants coming to Canada increased from 99,325 in 1986 to 212,859 in 1996, and totalled 2 million during that period.[73] The largest number came between 1991 and 1996, despite the recession that began in 1989, and more than 40 per cent of them came to the Toronto CMA. More people came, but fewer jobs awaited them. Immigrants also faced other barriers to employment, including the need to have their qualifications recertified by professional organizations in Canada and to meet employer requirements for Canadian experience. Immigrants who could not find work, or who could not find work to match their skills, became part of the region's low-income population.

---

70. Metropolitan Toronto Planning Department, Research and Special Studies Division 1994, 23; Frisken and Wallace 2000, Table I, p. 7. (Based on Statistics Canada data. Statistics Canada categorizes anyone who was not born in Canada as an immigrant, even if the person has become a Canadian citizen.)

71. Green and Green 1996, 24–25.

72. Ibid., 27.

73. Citizenship and Immigration Canada, *Recent Immigrants in Metropolitan Areas: A Comparative Portrait based on the 1996 Census*, May 2000, 3.

As for refugees, they tended to arrive with few or no resources and without family members to sponsor them. In 1993 the federal government separated the refugee class from other immigrant classes, which meant that the number of refugees no longer counted as part of the annual immigration target.[74] Nonetheless, provincial, regional, and municipal agencies still had to provide services to them. In fact, because they received less help from the federal government than did other immigrants, they were more likely to turn to provincial and local government agencies for help.

Ironically, therefore, poverty among immigrants was increasing at a time when a growing percentage of new arrivals seemed qualified to find well-paying employment soon after they arrived. Growing poverty among immigrants and refugees contributed to growing poverty rates in general. While the incidence of poverty among families headed by a person born in Canada increased from 12.5 to 13.2 per cent between 1986 and 1996, it rose from 11.6 to 21.2 per cent among families headed by a person born outside Canada.[75] Among families who immigrated after 1989, the poverty rate was 47 per cent in 1996.

Growing poverty among immigrants also contributed to growing city–suburban differences. Although all parts of the GTA except Durham region experienced an increase in poverty, Metro Toronto's larger proportion of recent immigrants implied a larger proportion of poor immigrant households. Metro accounted for 69 per cent of all immigrants who came to the GTA between 1981 and 1991, for example, but only 17 per cent of the region's total population growth during that period.[76] Metro also had the largest number of refugees.

Federal immigration policy was a direct contributor, therefore, to growing poverty in the GTA. All levels of government, however, were involved in other policies that influenced the distribution of poor households in the GTA and the services provided to them.

IMMIGRANT SETTLEMENT POLICIES

In addition to deciding who would be admitted to Canada, the federal government took primary responsibility for helping immigrants settle after they arrived. It exercised this responsibility mainly by funding agencies that

---

74. Green and Green 1996, 29.

75. Michael Mendelson and Andy Mitchell, with the assistance of Mikael Swayze, *Trends in Poverty in the New City of Toronto*, A Report to the City of Toronto Homelessness Task Force, July 21, 1998, 17.

76. Metropolitan Toronto Planning Department, Research and Special Studies Division 1994, 29; Metropolitan Toronto Planning Department, Research and Special Studies Division, 1995, Table 1.4.

provided different types of services to immigrants (such as counselling and job and language training). It also directly supported indigent immigrants (primarily refugees) for up to one year after they arrived. Ontario's Welcome Houses directed immigrants to agencies that provided the services they needed. Beginning in the mid-1980s, the Ontario government also adopted a Race Relations Policy (1985), a *Pay Equity Act* (1987), and an *Employment Equity Act* (1993).

Federal and provincial settlement policies made no distinction among immigrants according to place of residence, and thus had no obvious significance for regional governance. By directing support mainly to community-based agencies that catered to immigrants, however, these policies meant that the number and type of services available to immigrants depended on the number and type of agencies in immigrant-receiving communities. Metro Toronto had a much more extensive network of community agencies than did any of the suburban sub-regions, with the largest number based in the City of Toronto. This meant that immigrants living in Toronto had access to a broader range of services, while immigrants living outside Toronto had to come into the city for services they could not get in their own municipalities.

Because the federal and provincial governments did not formally acknowledge that municipalities had an important role in immigrant settlement, municipal and regional governments had to decide for themselves how to respond to new arrivals. Here again there were large differences among municipalities in the Toronto region.[77] Both Metro Toronto and the City of Toronto developed programs in the 1980s to promote accessibility and equitable delivery of social and community services to their diverse populations. In 1995 Metro Council consolidated its programs into an Access and Equity Centre, which looked after the interests of all "human rights protected groups."[78] Other municipalities in the region, including those with large and growing immigrant populations, tended to wait until the provincial government adopted legislation dealing with race relations and equity issues before developing programs of their own.

HOUSING POLICIES

An unintended effect of federal immigration policy was to create two classes of new immigrants: those who arrived with enough money to buy a home, and those who had to rely on the more limited rental housing market. Many of the former group settled in the suburban regions. In 1991, for example,

77. Frisken and Wallace 2003.
78. The term encompassed immigrants, refugees, and racial and religious minorities as well as gays, lesbians, and the transgendered, persons with disabilities, women, and Aboriginals.

Table 5.7 Distribution of housing by tenure among Metropolitan Toronto and four regional municipalities in the GTA, 1996

Regional Municipality	Total Households[a]	% Housing Owned[b]	% Housing Rented[b]
Metropolitan Toronto	903,565	47	53
Durham	152,755	76	24
Halton	117,750	75	25
Peel	265,620	69	31
York	176,680	82	18
Total GTA	1,615,530	59	41

a. Statistics Canada Census data, 1996.
b. Ranu Basu and Larry Bourne, private communication.

Table 5.8 Rent-geared-to-income housing, regional municipalities in the Greater Toronto Area, 1996[a]

Municipality	Rent supplement housing	Non-profit housing	OHC-owned housing	Other	Total RGI units	As % of local housing	As % of GTA total
Metro Toronto	6,061	25,217	29,403	12,902[b]	73,583	8.1	77.8
Durham	449	2,947	1,275	0	4,671	3.1	4.9
Halton	215	1,549	1,404	8[c]	3,176	2.8	3.4
Peel	1,421	6,394	1,016	0	8,831	3.3	9.3
York	125	3,270	872	0	4,267	2.4	4.5
Total GTA	8,271	39,377	33,970	12,910	94,528	5.9	100

a. Table lacks data on market units contained in housing built with government assistance. RGI units made up 58 per cent of the total social housing stock in 1993; the rest were rented at market rates (Metropolitan Toronto Planning Department, Research and Special Studies Division 1995, 3.0).
b. With municipal assistance from the Metropolitan Toronto Housing Company Limited. Source: Province of Ontario, CHUMS Database, August 16, 1996.
c. Native

only one-fifth of new immigrants in Metropolitan Toronto owned their own home, while half of new immigrants settling in the outer parts of the GTA were homeowners.[79] Immigrants who relied on the rental market were more likely to settle in Metro simply because Metro had more rental housing. It was the only GTA jurisdiction, in fact, where more than half the population lived in rental units in 1996 (Table 5.7).

---

79. Metropolitan Toronto Planning Department, Research and Information Services Division 1996, 76.

Intra-regional differences were even more pronounced for the small proportion of rental housing available to households eligible for rent-geared-to-income (RGI) units. With 56 per cent of all households in the GTA in 1996, Metro Toronto had nearly 78 per cent of RGI units (Table 5.8).

The growing number of individuals released from custodial institutions added to pressures on the region's low-rental housing stock. Many of them looked for accommodation in boarding or rooming houses, which were found principally in the City of Toronto, or in group homes operated by community organizations. Not only did the number of such units fall short of demand, but gentrification in some of Toronto's older neighbourhoods, together with stricter housing bylaws, was reducing the supply.[80]

Private builders withdrew from the rental market in the 1980s, blaming rent controls for their loss of interest in producing this type of housing. Housing built by municipal and community agencies with government assistance became the principal source of new rental housing in Metro Toronto.[81] Nonetheless, it constituted only a small proportion of the GTA's supply of rental housing, much of which consisted of second suites in private homes, rented condominium apartments, and rented houses.[82] Of the three, second suites were usually the most affordable. This source of housing was also more heavily concentrated in Metro than in the suburbs, partly because of Metro's older housing stock, and partly because some suburban governments had passed bylaws to discourage or exclude it.

Municipal governments were largely responsible for the way private and government-assisted rental housing was distributed within the region. Municipal official plans, zoning bylaws, and bylaw amendments specified the purposes for which land could be used, the types of housing that could be built, and the way housing could be used. This was true even for housing built or sponsored by the region's three municipal non-profit housing agencies—Cityhome, the Metropolitan Toronto Housing Company, and Peel Living—and by community agencies that ran housing for persons with special needs.

In principle, the Ontario government had always been able to ask municipal governments to plan for a balanced distribution of housing types within their communities. In practice, it had let municipal governments decide what kind of housing mix they wanted to accommodate. During the 1980s,

---

80. City of Toronto Alternative Housing Subcommittee, "Off the Streets: A Case for Long-Term Housing," September 1985, 2.

81. Metropolitan Toronto Planning Department, Research and Information Services Division 1996, 57.

82. According to figures compiled by Metro planners, such housing accounted for between 11 per cent and 15 per cent of the rental supply in 1991 (Metropolitan Toronto Planning Department, Research and Information Services Division 1996, Appendix A, 5).

however, the province's position gradually changed as rapidly rising house prices resulted in a sharp decline in the supply of housing that low-income households could afford.

Both the provincial and the City of Toronto governments initially responded to the affordability "crisis" by commissioning studies and adopting measures to deal with its most obvious symptom: increasing homelessness, especially among persons with psychiatric problems. Much of this work focused on the City of Toronto, where homelessness was most evident.[83] With help from both senior governments, the City of Toronto opened hostels and emergency shelters for homeless individuals. The provincial government also put more money into other types of social housing.

As demand for affordable housing rose, however, so did criticisms of outer suburban municipalities for not adding to the region's supply of affordable rental housing.[84] The Liberal government responded in 1989 with a policy statement that required all municipalities to adopt planning policies that would enable "at least 25 per cent of New Residential Units resulting from New Residential Development and Residential Intensification" to be affordable to "households within the lowest 60 per cent of the income distribution for the Housing Region"—a very vague definition. In addition, the statement asked for zoning provisions "to permit rooming, boarding and lodging houses, and Accessory Apartments as-of-right where they are permitted uses in the [municipal] official plan."[85] The government also amended the *Planning Act* to prevent municipalities from passing bylaws to exclude group homes from residential areas.[86]

The NDP government strengthened the Housing Policy Statement by increasing the target for affordable units from 25 to 30 per cent of all new housing. It also specified that half these units should be for households in the lowest 30 per cent of the income distribution; that is, for the neediest households in the region. (It was not clear whether this stipulation applied to the entire Toronto region or just to the regional municipality to which the local municipality belonged.) It incorporated this statement, along with five others, into a Comprehensive Set of Policy Statements that accompanied the revised *Planning Act* of 1995.[87] A few GTA municipalities adopted housing policies that were consistent with the statement. Even if they were committed to such

83. Lisa Orchard, "Prior Recommendations on Homelessness in the City of Toronto 1983–1997," prepared for the City of Toronto Homelessness Task Force, May 1998.

84. Sean Fine, "Suburban housing policy defended by mayor," *Globe and Mail*, January 25, 1988.

85. Ontario Government, "Land Use Planning for Housing," Policy Statement issued under the authority of Section 3 of the *Planning Act* 1983, 1989.

86. Wilson 1990, 8.

87. Ontario Ministry of Municipal Affairs 1995.

policies, however, they still had to overcome the opposition that commonly greeted any plan to build lower priced rental housing, whether public or private, in most suburban municipalities. There were also the uncertainties associated with potential appeals to the Ontario Municipal Board, which tended to rule on contested planning decisions according to its own standards of what constituted "good planning."[88] These standards did not always conform to goals contained in provincial policy statements, despite *Planning Act* requirements that the planning decisions of provincial and local agencies should "have regard to" and then (after 1993) "be consistent with" provincial policies.

There seemed to be little likelihood, therefore, that suburban efforts would result in a substantial increase in low-rental family housing outside Metro. Thus Metro's Planning Department concluded at the end of the period that Metro had no choice but to meet most of the growing GTA demand for rental housing. It could do so in one of two ways, it said: by enabling the construction of new rental housing, or by "letting unfettered market forces bring rapid neighbourhood change to Metro" through the ongoing conversion of private housing to rental use.[89]

A FRAGMENTED PUBLIC TRANSIT SYSTEM

The relatively large amount of low-rental housing within Metro and the movement of jobs, particularly manufacturing jobs, to the suburbs implied a growing spatial mismatch between unskilled or entry-level jobs in the GTA and the residential choices of the people who could fill them.[90] Existing transit service could also be costly for people travelling relatively short distances across a municipal boundary.[91] Yet this period saw little progress toward coordinating fares and services between the GO commuter system and local transit operators or between individual local operators, even though governments headed by all three parties took steps to address the problem.

In 1984, the Progressive Conservative government asked a private consultant to study the problems of coordinating the region's commuter and local transit systems and ways to overcome them. The study identified four possible ways of proceeding and advised the government to choose the one that suited it best.[92] After taking office in 1985, the Liberal government asked the study's author to work with an Advisory Group to help it make the appropriate choice. The group concluded that the government had to take a leader-

88. Chipman 2002, 177–179.

89. Metropolitan Toronto Planning Department, Research and Information Services Division 1996, 61–62.

90. Frisken, Bourne, Gad, and Murdie 1997, 17–31.

91. Ontario Transit Advisory Group to the Minister of Transportation for Ontario 1987, 34.

92. Paterson Planning and Research Limited 1983.

ship role in inter-regional transit planning and coordination, and that it should establish an Inter-Regional Transit Coordinating Agency to assist with that task.[93] The government agreed in principle, but took no action, because transit coordination implied new costs that it did not want to incur.[94]

The NDP government tried again in 1993 by appointing a Transit Integration Task Force composed of municipal officials, representatives of transit operators, and private consultants. The Task Force recommended the creation of a limited-purpose federation of transit operators, with no operating responsibility, as "the best framework to achieve transit integration while maintaining local autonomy."[95] Again the government did not act. The Task Force's principal achievement was the production of a regional "ride guide" to help transit users navigate the GTA's regional and local transit systems.

DIFFERENCES IN SOCIAL AND COMMUNITY SERVICES

As mentioned earlier, there were substantial differences between Metro and the suburban regional municipalities in the number of community-based organizations operating within their boundaries, and thus in the extent to which their populations had access to community services. There were also substantial differences in the per household amount spent on social and community services in Metropolitan Toronto and the four regional municipalities. In fact, Metropolitan Toronto and its local governments were spending much more per household than governments in the suburban regions in all service categories except environmental services (sewer, water, and waste management) and planning and development in 1994 (Table 5.9).

Metro's larger population of low-income households was one explanation for its higher social spending. Another was that Metro provided more provincially assisted optional programs than did regional governments and the number of community agencies eligible for Metro funding was increasing all the time. As Metro's Commissioner of Community and Social Services described Metro's situation in 1991, "[W]e have a tradition of segregating services by race and religion. This means that new groups representing a huge diversity of ethnic and racial groups are making 'legitimate' demands to provide their own services."[96] His department's work, he claimed on another occasion, placed Metro "at the cutting edge in the world in dealing with a multicultural society where demands are based on a concept of 'rights.'"[97]

93. Ontario Transit Advisory Group to the Minister of Transportation for Ontario 1987, 82–84.

94. Ontario Ministry of Transportation, "Transportation Directions for the Greater Toronto Area," May 1988, 7.

95. Ontario Transit Integration Task Force 1994, 8.

96. Richmond 1991, 18–19.

97. Canadian Urban Institute, "A Discussion with Don Richmond," May 3, 1991, 5.

Table 5.9 Average per household spending by local governments in the Greater Toronto Area, 1994

Dollars Spent Per Household on Upper-tier and Lower-tier Services Combined

	Total $ spent per household	General Govt.	Environment (Sewer, Water, Waste Mgt)	Health & Social Services	Parks, Recreation, and Libraries	Planning & Development	Protection	Transportation
Metro Toronto	5,998	640	570	2,095	545	81	912	1,156
Durham	3,644	339	572	1,143	348	85	636	520
Halton	3,219	387	618	577	404	87	640	506
Peel	3,579	488	593	798	325	61	732	582
York	3,590	528	709	737	424	89	625	479
Four suburban regional municipalities	3,536	448	621	822	368	77	669	530
All Ontario municipalities	4,094	434	570	1279	370	88	607	744

Source: Based on data contained in Ontario Ministry of Municipal Affairs and Housing, Municipal Financial Information 1994, Chapters 2, 3, and 4. Toronto: Queen's Printer for Ontario, 1996.

The Commissioner of Social Services in Peel Region had a different philosophy. He described the work of his department as based on a "hands-up" philosophy that focused on helping first-time applicants find alternatives to welfare.[98] While he did not formally describe it as a "work-for-welfare" program (which federal funding rules did not allow), its purpose was similar. Recipients were told they would lose benefits if they did not try to find work, and the department offered some forms of training, education, and guidance to help them do so.

Whatever the merits of the different approaches to social service delivery, Peel's approach was more in tune with emerging ways of thinking about social assistance than was Metro's. This was a period of intense debate about the role of governments in the lives of citizens, as well as growing disillusionment with programs and policies that were seen to perpetuate poverty or encourage dependency. The emphasis was increasingly on finding ways to improve individual autonomy and self-reliance.[99] Even the NDP government described its unsuccessful attempt at disentanglement as a first step toward implementing "reforms designed to help people get off welfare."[100]

It had always been Metro's policy to offer only those programs that were eligible for provincial assistance. Its response to provincial welfare cuts, therefore, was to end or curtail programs for which provincial assistance was reduced or eliminated.[101] Nonetheless, Metro was spending more than one-third of its budget on health and social services in 1994, up from 20 per cent in 1986.

SPENDING AND TAX-BASE DIFFERENCES

Intra-regional differences in spending on municipal services were partly the result of local circumstances: more poverty in Metro; a greater need for new infrastructure in the suburban municipalities. They also attested to differences in the size and composition of regional and local government tax bases.

Metro's total assessment per household in 1994, as determined by the province's equalizing formula, was higher than that of all other regional municipalities except York. Metro differed from its neighbours, however, in having a larger percentage of its assessment in the commercial/industrial category and a smaller percentage in the residential category (Table 5.10). Moreover, Metro's local governments applied higher tax rates to commercial properties

---

98. Gary Webb-Proctor, "'Hands-up' policy in Peel breaking welfare cycle," *Globe and Mail*, December 31, 1986.

99. Melchers 1999, 32–33.

100. Richard Mackie, "Ontario plans to take sole responsibility for welfare," *Globe and Mail*, December 17, 1992.

101. Metro Community Services, Social Development Division 1995.

Table 5.10 A comparison of total equalized assessments
and total revenues in GTA regional municipalities, 1994

	Total assessment per household	Residential assessment as % of total assessment	Total revenues per household	Property taxes as % of total revenues
Metropolitan Toronto	311,261	57.3	5945	43.5
Durham	183,404	76.0	3639	52.4
Halton	242,051	74.7	3218	60.7
Peel	257,587	67.9	3569	57.1
York	327,014	73.0	3613	54.5
Ontario	182,764	67.8	4082	46.3

Source: Based on data contained in Ontario Ministry of Municipal Affairs and Housing, *Municipal Financial Information 1994*, Chapters 2, 3, and 4. Toronto: Queen's Printer for Ontario, 1996.

(including rental apartment buildings) than did local governments in the suburbs.[102] The differences meant that Metro governments had more property tax revenues to spend while still taxing homeowners at similar or lower rates than those used in the suburbs. There was little reason, in other words, for middle-class residents to move to the suburbs as a way to reduce their tax bills.

Despite Metro's relative affluence, Metro and its municipalities still received more than one-third of provincial conditional grants and nearly 27 per cent of capital grants in 1994 when Metro had only 22 per cent of the provincial population, largely because of Metro's high public transit, social services, and social housing costs, and relatively high local government spending on public health. Metro received a smaller share of unconditional grants, but these accounted for only 11 per cent of all provincial grants going to municipalities in 1994.

Differences in the size of commercial/industrial tax bases also affected the ability of lower-tier governments to spend on their own services. For example, the City of Toronto, which had the largest ratio of non-residential to residential assessment in Metro, spent more per household than other Metro municipalities on all the services it provided (Table 5.11).

Disparities in school board spending

By 1995 the provincial share of education costs had fallen to 45 per cent of total spending in the province, down from 61 per cent in 1975, and the province was contributing nothing toward education in Metropolitan Toronto. School boards had to make up the difference out of local property taxes. At the same time, Metro's high non-residential assessment allowed its boards to spend well

---

102. Slack, "Is There an Economic Crisis in the GTA Core?", op. cit. 24.

Table 5.11 Per household spending by local governments in Metropolitan Toronto, 1994

Municipality	# Households	Total spending ($000s)	Spending per household on local services ($)[a]
East York	45,877	54,376	1185
Etobicoke	121,865	181,287	1488
North York	211,083	326,384	1546
Scarborough	183,432	223,428	1218
Toronto	290,038	676,987	2334
York	58,254	54,376	933

a. Spending figures do not include spending by local school boards.
Source: Based on data contained in Ontario Ministry of Municipal Affairs and Housing, *Municipal Financial Information 1994*, Table 4-1-1 and Table 4-1-7. Toronto: Queen's Printer for Ontario, 1996.

above the spending ceilings on which the province based its grants. In fact, Metro spending on education exceeded that of almost every other board in the province, including all other boards in the Toronto region (Table 5.12).

Meanwhile, some of the province's poorer school boards were spending below the provincial ceilings. These intermunicipal disparities were of particular concern to the provincial government, which had frequently said it was committed to preserving equality of educational opportunity throughout Ontario.

Metro's public school boards justified their higher levels of spending by pointing to their disproportionately large populations of low-income and recent-immigrant families. The growth in separate school enrolments weakened that argument, however. Not only did the Metropolitan Toronto Separate School Board serve the same population as the Metropolitan Toronto School Board, but its schools attracted a larger share of immigrant students. Yet separate school boards remained underfunded relative to their public school counterparts, despite receiving equivalent provincial grants after 1984, because they received a smaller share of locally generated property taxes, particularly non-residential taxes. Public school boards in assessment-poor communities were also disadvantaged. Moreover, immigrants were beginning to settle in large numbers in the suburban regions, prompting officials in those municipalities to complain that they were disadvantaged relative to Metropolitan Toronto in their ability to respond to the changing needs of their populations.[103]

---

103. Craig McInnes, "Community [York Region] can't make good on Utopia pledge," *Globe and Mail*, December 22, 1992; Lila Sarick, "A region [Peel] grown like a gawky adolescent," *Globe and Mail*, December 30, 1994.

Table 5.12: School board spending per pupil in the GTA and the rest of Ontario, 1994

School Board	$ per secondary school pupil[a] above (or below) provincial grant ceiling	Rank in province	$ per elementary school pupil above (or below) provincial grant ceiling	Rank in province
Durham Bd. of Ed.	1,370	28	802	37
Durham RCSSB	292	99	298	99
Halton Bd. of Ed.	1,710	18	1,004	19
Halton RCSSB	1,197	42	850	59
Metro Toronto SSB	1,298	31	972	21
Metro Toronto SB	3,174	2	2,549	1
Dufferin Peel RCSSB	545	89	350	93
Peel Bd. of Ed.	1,785	11	1,330	9
York Reg. Bd. of Ed.	1,506	21	1,052	15
York Reg. RCSSB	1,260	34	440	86
Lowest spending (Horne-payne Bd. of Ed.)	(1,804)	115		
Lowest spending (Chapleau Panet Caverly Dist. SSB)			(347)	122

a. The grant ceilings set by the provincial government for 1996 were $4,028 for elementary pupils and $4,290 for secondary pupils. The standard varied for individual boards, however, because the province adjusted this amount, "to recognize that [some boards] face added costs (considered to be beyond the control of the local board) in delivering this level of education because of their geographic location, the social or economic conditions in their community, linguistic or demographic considerations, or the particular needs of their students." The province also gave program-specific grants "to encourage boards to extend education programs and services into areas that respond to local needs and meet provincial priorities" (Working Group on Education Finance Reform 1996, 9).

Source: Working Group on Education Finance Reform, Report to the Minister of Education, June 1996, 57–58, 60–61.

In response to complaints from the separate school boards, the government decreed in 1989 that commercial and industrial taxes for education would be pooled at the regional municipality level. The change meant that separate school boards in Metro Toronto, regional municipalities, and other consolidated school districts would receive shares of commercial and industrial taxes that matched their shares of the school population. Disparities in school board spending persisted, however, among different regional municipalities and other school districts. Poorer boards therefore began to ask the government to pool commercial/industrial assessment for education on a province-wide basis.

A committee of school board and municipal officials tackled the issue in 1992 as part of a larger study of property taxation. It described the idea of pooling commercial and industrial assessment as "perhaps the most divisive issue in education funding over the past 20 years."[104] A majority of the committee turned down the proposal, saying that it would undermine local accountability and autonomy and would mean a decrease in provincial grants. These, they said, should instead be increased.

A minority, which consisted of representatives of separate school boards and one rural board, dissented. This group argued that the amount of autonomy enjoyed by school boards was directly related to the size of their assessments, which meant that only the wealthier boards could offer programs over and above what the province required of them.[105] Moreover, the wealth of local school boards depended on the size of their commercial and industrial assessments, which, the group insisted, should therefore be viewed as "a provincial resource to be used in funding provincially mandated programs." That was the "fundamental issue." Students should not be penalized because of the way "accidents of geography and history," together with provincial subsidies to private investors, had affected the distribution of commercial and industrial assessment among different school districts. Moreover, "[t]he rest of the province ... [should not] be treated as a colony or hinterland for the urban areas to exploit especially in respect to a social good and basic entitlement such as education." The dissenters also dismissed the majority's recommendation for increased provincial grants as unrealistic and "calculated to delay essential change."

The equity issue was raised by the Royal Commission on Learning, which the government appointed in 1993 to chart a new course for Ontario's education system. The Commission concluded that the province should exercise strong leadership in curriculum development, educational administration, and the allocation of funds for school purposes. If it did so, it said, the government would assume the redistribution function being performed by the Metro Toronto Board of Education, thereby reducing its role "to the point that the costs would not warrant its existence."[106] It pointed out that large property tax bases gave the Metropolitan Toronto and Ottawa school boards so much independence that they could act without provincial approval, or even ignore provincial directives. The growing emphasis on fiscal restraint, however, and the need for a standardized curriculum, meant that the ministry should set priorities for Ontario education, clarify goals, and define the desired outcomes.

Overview: Intermunicipal equity as a multi-faceted problem
Returning to the questions asked at the beginning of this section, it is evident that the policies of all levels of government, and not just changes in the econ-

---

104. Ontario Fair Tax Commission, Property Tax Working Group 1992, 105.
105. Ibid., Appendix A, 16–21.
106. Ontario Royal Commission on Learning 1994, vol. 4, 116–117.

omy and in social mores, affected the GTA's socio-spatial structure, including the size and circumstances of its low-income population. Some of these policies had helped give Metropolitan Toronto a disproportionately large share of the region's neediest residents, while others had made it easier for Metro's governments to deal with increasing socio-economic diversity. In 1995 Metro was still a financially strong city and showed no signs of serious physical or social decay, even though its economy was somewhat battered by the recession. It provided its socially diverse communities and its business sector with a rich blend of social and community services, on which its governments cumulatively spent more per household than the governments of any of the surrounding regional municipalities.

Metro's relative financial strength within the Toronto region depended on two things: its strong business sector and the grants it received from the provincial government. By the end of the period, however, Metro's ability to maintain these advantages faced several threats. One was the decline in the number of business establishments and in the number of jobs that had occurred during the recession. Office building and residential construction had slowed almost to a halt. While these trends affected the entire GTA, they were much more pronounced in Metro, with the result that commercial, industrial, and business assessment declined in all of Metro's municipalities between 1989 and 1994, whereas it grew substantially in some of the outer suburbs.[107] Meanwhile, the number of people and organizations looking for assistance from municipal agencies was increasing.

A second threat to Metro's finances was growing political pressure on the province to recognize the changing needs of other Ontario municipalities, several of them in the GTA, that were either undergoing substantial social or economic change or that claimed that the province was ignoring their needs. The provincial government, however, was determined to limit, not increase, its spending in the municipal sector. Consequently, non-Metro officials had begun to look enviously at Metro's large commercial and industrial tax base, claiming that it should be used to support local services, particularly education, in all parts of the province. Their voices in provincial–municipal discussions were growing stronger as Metro's shares of the region's and the province's population and employment declined.

The third threat to Metro's financial stability was a move by various interests to persuade the province to eliminate differences in the taxes paid by businesses in Metro Toronto relative to those paid by businesses in the suburbs. Although Metro staff joined others in arguing for tax reform, the issue posed a dilemma for Metro's elected councillors. If they maintained Metro's

---

107. Slack, "Is There an Economic Crisis in the GTA Core?", op. cit., 8.

relatively high taxes on the business sector, they risked driving businesses to the suburbs. If they lowered taxes on the business sector and raised taxes on homeowners, they risked losing votes or driving middle-class homeowners away. If they cut services to save money, they not only risked angering voters, but also endangering Metro's quality of life.

Maintaining equity in the distribution of the costs and benefits of urban growth among Toronto-region municipalities was becoming an increasingly complex challenge for any government. Moreover, measures taken to achieve that objective were likely to affect the social and economic future of Metropolitan Toronto and its suburban neighbours. It is not surprising, therefore, that distributional issues were among the more serious barriers to building a sense of regional identity and promoting a political consensus on how regional issues should be addressed.

Regional unity remains elusive

PERSISTENT DISUNITY WITHIN METROPOLITAN TORONTO
Dissatisfaction with financial arrangements persisted in Metropolitan Toronto throughout this period. As Metro's suburban politicians saw it, the City of Toronto's high tax returns from non-residential properties allowed it to tax its homeowners at lower rates while providing higher quality services. In 1986, for example, some Metro politicians and local newspapers argued that commercial and industrial assessment should be pooled on a Metro-wide basis for locally provided as well as for Metro-provided services. Toronto Mayor Art Eggleton objected that this would "penalize Toronto for its own success" in building a fine city that was attractive to office and other development. He also pointed out that Toronto had not only paid a large share of the costs of public works that had aided suburban growth, but that it still paid 40 per cent of Metro's costs, even though it contained only 30 per cent of Metro's population. Anyone suggesting more tax pooling, he said, would be "more honest if he recommended total amalgamation" of Toronto and the Metro suburbs to form one big city.[108]

The Toronto Board of Education also engaged in this debate, launching a campaign in 1990 to use public meetings and mailings to make the city's taxpayers more aware that school costs were being paid almost entirely out of local property taxes, and that city taxpayers were paying a disproportionate share of Metro's education costs.[109] Nonetheless, school board politics became

---

108. Michael Best, "Mayors square off on tax sharing," *Toronto Star*, December 27, 1985.

109. Orland French, "Public trustees worried Toronto may be cash cow," *Globe and Mail*, March 22, 1990.

less fractious as the period wore on. Pressures on the province to pool com-mercial and industrial assessments for education on a province-wide basis, together with the end of provincial grants, posed common threats to Metro's relatively well-funded boards. They were incentives to school board officials to present a more united front on financial issues than in the past.

Nonetheless, the City of Toronto remained firmly opposed to any kind of property tax or assessment reform, insisting that it would mean hardships for city homeowners on fixed incomes and deprive the city of the money it needed to serve its diverse population. Moreover, if the assessed values of City of Toronto properties increased, so would the city's share of Metro costs. From the city's perspective, there was also a danger that property tax increases resulting from reform would make homes in the city less attractive, thereby slowing or reversing gentrification in older neighbourhoods and driving middle-class homeowners to the suburbs. Small businesses might also close or move away, reducing the variety and vitality of the city's streets.[110]

Transportation and housing were also divisive issues in Metro. Toronto officials typically took a strong pro-transit, anti-road stance while still allowing intensive downtown development, which added to automobile congestion on existing streets. They also insisted that suburban municipalities inside Metro should do more to ease the affordable housing crisis.[111] Suburban officials were unwilling to support new rapid transit lines anywhere in Metro unless they were assured that their municipalities would also benefit directly from Metro's transit investments.

The province's answer to Metro Council deadlocks—switching Metro to a system of direct election in 1988—did not end disputes between the city and Metro governments. In fact, according to Richard Gilbert and Don Stevenson in a report for the Canadian Urban Institute, there was "more tendency for confrontation rather than compromise" in Metro politics in 1994 than there had been in the past.[112] Their study was a commentary on a City of Toronto deci-sion to ask its electorate to vote in a non-binding referendum on the question: "Are you in favour of eliminating the Metro level of government?" Fifty-eight per cent of voters said yes. While few people expected the provincial govern-ment to act on this verdict, Metro's critics hoped it would help to persuade the

---

110. Don Stevenson and Richard Gilbert, "Background paper with respect to the question on the ballot, City of Toronto Municipal Elections" (Toronto: Canadian Urban Institute, August 31, 1994), 6; Peter Tomlinson, "Metro Reassessment: the Provincial Interest" (presentation to the Social Development Committee, Ontario Legislature, December 5), 1992.

111. Sean Fine, "Metro muscle: New powers could wake up quiet senior council," *Globe and Mail*, October 21, 1988.

112. Stevenson and Gilbert, "Background paper with respect to the question on the ballot," op. cit., 7.

province to review local government either in Metropolitan Toronto or in the whole of the GTA.

Clearly, by the mid-1990s Toronto's much-lauded experiment in two-tier metropolitan government seemed to be on the verge of collapse. The least contentious activity was planning, but not because local planners adhered to the hierarchical model suggested by the original two-tier concept. Rather, many planners in Metro, the City of Toronto, and the suburbs subscribed to the principle of promoting future development at office and commercial nodes with good access to rapid transit. Metro planners also provided services, such as compiling information or conducting research, that were useful to both levels of government.

EFFORTS TO RAISE REGIONAL CONSCIOUSNESS

As had happened in the late 1940s and again in the 1960s, the period from the mid-1980s to the mid-1990s was marked by the vigorous efforts of some senior provincial officials, interest groups, community organizations, and local media to convince the government of the need for a new mechanism to address regional issues on a GTA-wide basis. Some of them argued for a two-tier government for the entire GTA; others urged the province to act more vigorously itself. Nonetheless, the provincial government continued to try to engage municipal and regional government staff and sometimes the general public in discussions about regional policy alternatives. The goal, it insisted, was to build region-wide consensus on how regional issues might be addressed, not to create new units with authority to deal with them.

Consensus-building efforts had some modest successes, such as the list of transportation priorities compiled by the Transportation Planning Forum and the willingness of most municipal officials to subscribe in principle to a regional "vision" statement. Studies produced by the Office for the Greater Toronto Area (OGTA) also helped raise awareness of regional trends and issues both inside and outside the government.

Despite these accomplishments, however, consensus-building efforts highlighted sources of regional disunity. Local mayors, for example, often objected to the province's tendency to ask regional government politicians and staff to represent local viewpoints on GTA organizations as a way to limit the size of such organizations. Municipal governments in the more urbanized parts of the regional municipalities objected to paying for services in the less urbanized districts. The City of Mississauga in Peel Region felt particularly aggrieved, because the province had given it less than half the votes on Peel council, even though it had nearly two-thirds of Peel's population. The governments of rural areas and small towns objected to the higher taxes they paid to support regional services. They not only opposed regional government activities that impinged on their rights to make decisions for their own communities, but also strongly resisted any suggestion that the province might give the GTA yet another level of government.

These anti-regional sentiments surfaced in 1992 when word went around that the province might launch a study of the region's future. Several local mayors formed their own committee, the Mayors' Task Force on Economic Development, to look after their interests in the region. "Changes in the GTA can't be legislated from the province down," said Mississauga Mayor Hazel McCallion, an instigator of the Task Force. "[They have] to happen from the grassroots up, and we are the grassroots."[113] The Task Force said it would promote the entire GTA to potential investors as a single economic entity. It limited its activities, however, to conducting a study of tax disparities, agreeing on the need for a coordinated regional economic development policy, and sending representatives to several North American trade shows. As a general rule, local officials remained focused on their own concerns, or on sorting out their differences with regional councils. At the same time, many Metro Toronto officials did not want to become too involved in any organization dominated by the suburbs.[114]

Financial concerns also stood in the way of regional consensus-building. The pooling of taxes for regional services had not ended the tendency of local governments to compete with each other for new assessment. Most of them had established economic development programs, some of which were devoted to attracting business away from Metro Toronto.[115] Such programs also caused disagreements between regional governments and their local municipalities. The Region of Peel had no economic development program, because Mississauga had managed to end it in the early 1980s. Economic development offices in other regional municipalities tended to limit their activities to strategic planning and infrastructure development, and left business attraction in local hands.

Officials in all the regional municipalities could often agree, however, that Metropolitan Toronto was their principal rival for economic investment, and that it received too much provincial help. They tried to persuade the province to put more money into infrastructure to support development in their parts of the GTA. Doing so, they argued, would be less costly than putting money into expensive projects (like new subways) in Metro. Metro officials countered that they were being treated unfairly relative to the suburbs, point-

113. Lynda Hurst, "30 mayors put GTA on map," *Toronto Star*, January 20, 1995.
114. Jane Armstrong, "GTA mayors push new regional body," *Toronto Star*, June 17, 1995.
115. Wolfson and Frisken 2000.

ing to the larger education grants given to the regional school boards and, after 1993, to the fact that Metro received no education grants at all.

Transportation posed another severe challenge to the development of a sense of regional purpose. Metro wanted the province to spend its transportation money on transit; suburban officials wanted more roads. Nonetheless, Metro councillors opposed additions to the TTC system that would serve outer suburban commuters unless suburban governments paid their full costs.

On the issue of transit integration, the TTC did not want to participate in a regional transit federation in which it would be only one local operator among several. It was willing to serve as transit supplier to the entire region, but only if the province provided adequate funding. Some TTC staff members argued that the province should not subsidize local transit in the suburbs, where ridership was low, but should direct all transit subsidies to the Metro system, which carried most of the region's transit riders (83.2 per cent in 1985).[116] Municipal politicians and transit operators outside Metro not only resisted a TTC takeover, but also opposed any organizational change that would mean higher costs for their own taxpayers or transit users.[117]

Metro's insistence that the outer suburbs should accommodate more affordable rental housing was another divisive issue. Most suburban governments were not interested in housing more of the region's neediest families. The Regional Municipality of Peel was the only suburban municipality to operate a non-profit housing program before 1990, when York Region set up its own non-profit corporation to build housing, most of it for seniors.

THE PROVINCIAL GOVERNMENT STEPS IN

Faced with so many conflicting perspectives on governance in the Toronto region, the Ontario government was little inclined to take action. There were political dangers in coming down too strongly on one side or another. Moreover, municipal officials usually insisted that the price of their co-operation was a larger financial commitment from the province. Thus municipal disagreements provided the government with reasons not to act at a time when it wanted to control its spending, not increase it.

---

116. In 1985 the TTC accounted for 93 per cent of the users of local transit systems in Metropolitan Toronto and the regional municipalities of Durham, York, Peel, and Halton, or 88 per cent of all transit users in those five jurisdictions, including users of the GO commuter system (Ontario Transit Advisory Group to the Minister of Transportation for Ontario 1987, 23). By 1996 the figures were 90 per cent and 82 per cent respectively (Bill Dawson, Superintendent of Route and System Planning, Toronto Transit Commission, personal communication, April 3, 2003).

117. These comments are based on my own observations while serving as a member of the Transit Advisory Group (1986–87) and the Transit Integration Task Force (1993–94).

There were costs to doing nothing as well, however, as a growing body of critics pointed out when the GTA economy faltered in the early 1990s. Among them was the Canadian Urban Institute, a think-tank set up in 1989 with initial funding from Metro and the City of Toronto to "enhance policy making" and "to serve as a window for decision makers in the Toronto Region."[118] It conducted research and seminars, sometimes with the support of the OGTA, to raise awareness of city–regional issues and promote GTA-wide approaches to dealing with them. The cause was also taken up by some of the Toronto media. *The Toronto Star* in particular ran frequent articles, editorials, and special features that argued the need for a GTA government.

The Minister of Municipal Affairs and Housing eventually responded to these pressures by creating a GTA Task Force with a mandate that encompassed most of the objectives commonly found in the regional agenda. It was to "define a system and a style of governance, appropriate to the Toronto [region] of the next century, that promotes economic health and competitiveness, community well-being and a high quality urban environment."[119] The system should "be founded on a solid base of municipal finance, ... promote effective and efficient urban management, ... be accountable to and representative of the diverse Toronto of the future, ... promote the broadest civic engagement" and "be founded on an ecosystem approach." Leading the list of questions the government asked the Task Force to address was one that had often appeared in earlier discussions of regional trends: "How do we best organize ourselves to avoid the urban problems of many U.S. cities and maintain the secure and satisfying quality of life we now feel under threat?"

The creation of the GTA Task Force coincided with NDP government measures to completely restructure the province's public education system. These measures included initiating a program to develop a common curriculum for Ontario schools, creating a task force to recommend ways to reduce the number of school boards in Ontario, and appointing a working group to recommend ways to reform public school finance. Thus the government seemed to be on the verge of making changes in Toronto region governance and public education that would match those legislated in 1953 and again between 1968 and 1974. It acted, however, just before a provincial election, in which the NDP lost to the Progressive Conservative Party. The government that decided what to do with these initiatives had a very different ideology and a different set of priorities from the one that had set them in motion.

---

118. Don Stevenson, private communication. January 9, 2005.
119. GTA Task Force 1996, 229.

SIX

1995–2003
Charting a New Course
for Regional Governance

The GTA Task Force began its work just before a provincial election returned the Progressive Conservative Party to office with a large majority. Thus it faced the immediate challenge of convincing a new government, many members of which had never held elected office, that the Greater Toronto Area (GTA) was important enough to provincial well-being and that its problems were serious enough to justify government action. In making that case, the Task Force compared the situation in the GTA to that of the much smaller Toronto region in the early 1950s, but it also emphasized that the region faced "stark new realities." "The GTA's challenge," it said, "is to reinvent itself into a city-region that is economically and socially sustainable in today's global context."[1]

There were certainly similarities between the two time periods. In both, for example, the region had recently gone through a serious economic downturn that had shaken the confidence of its governments and business communities. And in both periods, serious infrastructure deficiencies stood in the way of the region's ability to make a full economic recovery. There were also important differences, however. The Toronto region of the mid-1990s contained nearly three times the number of municipalities (including regional municipalities), four times the population, and more than eleven times the land area of the one studied by the Ontario Municipal Board (OMB) in the early 1950s. In 1951, Metropolitan Toronto had contained 25 per cent of Ontario's population, whereas the GTA in 1996 accounted for 43 per cent of the population of Ontario, and that percentage was creeping upward year by year. Whatever the economic arguments for a unified governance structure—and the GTA Task Force stated these eloquently—the provincial government had a clear, if unspoken, interest in allowing the region to remain politically fragmented in order to protect its own jurisdictional supremacy and its political importance in Canada.

---

1. GTA Task Force 1996, 34.

The structure of the regional economy also differed from that of the 1950s. The Toronto region no longer consisted of a prosperous, highly urbanized, and financially strong core city surrounded by residential suburbs that could not afford to provide even the most basic services. Economic activity was now dispersed widely throughout the GTA. Although both the City of Toronto and Metropolitan Toronto still had strong economies, they had been losing manufacturing industries for some time to the suburban regions and more distant locations. Some suburbs had also begun to compete successfully for investment in the office and commercial sectors. Moreover, Metro's economy had suffered more during the recession than had the economies of its suburban neighbours, and it was recovering more slowly.[2]

Finally, the Government of Ontario, like the governments of many other national and sub-national jurisdictions, was moving away from the principles that had dominated Canadian public policy-making for nearly three decades after the Second World War. Those principles had supported a strong role for governments not only in managing their economies, but also in developing social welfare programs, both to alleviate poverty and to satisfy the basic needs of all citizens.[3] The growing importance of multinational corporations in economic affairs, the signing of free trade agreements first with the United States and then with the United States and Mexico, and rising government debt, much of it to international lenders, had eroded support for such ideas. There was a growing sense that governments were losing the ability to control their countries' economic destinies. There was also growing disillusionment with some of the outcomes of government intervention, particularly rising taxes and the growth of large and expensive public bureaucracies.

All Ontario governments, even the one headed by the left-leaning New Democratic Party, had tried to reduce government spending on urban infrastructure and social programs from the mid-1970s onward. None did so with as much ideological fervour, however, as the Progressive Conservative government elected in 1995. Commonly referred to as the Harris Tories, after leader Mike Harris, this government came to office on a neo-conservative election platform—"The Common Sense Revolution" or CSR—in which it promised to balance the provincial budget while reducing provincial income taxes by 30 per cent over a three-year period. To fulfill these promises, the Conservatives said that they would cut the size of government and reduce non-priority spending (defined in the CSR to include everything except health

2. Metropolitan Toronto Planning Department, "Metro Facts: Employment in Metropolitan Toronto—1995," July 1996.
3. Manzer 1985, 61.

care, law enforcement, and "education spending in the classroom") by 20 per cent.[4]

While the Conservatives promised to implement a Job Creation Plan that would "generate economic growth and investment in Ontario and create more than 725,000 new jobs," their platform made no mention of the Greater Toronto Area, site of nearly half of the province's jobs, where infrastructure deficiencies were being blamed for a slow economic recovery. Once elected, however, they embarked on a program of municipal restructuring that substantially changed the way services in the Toronto region were provided, but left its system of governance almost as fragmented and uncoordinated as it had been when they took office.

Institutional and Policy Adjustments Affecting the GTA

One of the first acts of the new government was to cut the budget of the GTA Task Force and ask it to complete its work in six months instead of eighteen. The Task Force decided not to hold public hearings, but it did consult widely with experts on city–regional issues. Even so, the government paid little attention to its recommendations on regional governance, which was not an issue it considered important. Although the government was not able to ignore the city-region agenda for long, it dealt with it in ad hoc, piecemeal, and politically expedient ways, and only after it had dealt with other matters to which it gave priority. The results for GTA governance were very different from those that the Task Force had envisioned.

What the GTA Task Force recommended

The GTA Task Force released its report in January 1996, six months after the Conservative government took office. In the report, it linked its work to the Conservatives' electoral platform by emphasizing the importance of the GTA to the province's economy and the annual savings that its recommendations would mean for governments and the private sector. These recommendations rested on the argument that Greater Toronto was "a highly interdependent region whose whole is greater than the sum of its parts, and whose overall health is dependent on the prosperity of those constituent parts."[5] Not only was this an argument being made by many contemporary writers on city-regional issues,[6] but it also evoked Lorne Cumming's 1953 conclusion that the

4. Ontario Progressive Conservative Party, "The Common Sense Revolution," Pamphlet, May 1994, 2.
5. GTA Task Force 1996, 9.
6. Barnes and Ledebur 1998; Dodge 1996; Peirce, Johnson, and Hall 1993.

"underlying social and economic unity" of the Toronto region (as it was then defined) justified uniting its municipalities into a metropolitan federation. In fact, the Task Force cited the creation of Metropolitan Toronto as an important reason for the Toronto region's widely acclaimed success.[7]

The system of governance recommended by the Task Force was similar to, although less centralized, than the one that had presided over Metropolitan Toronto since 1953. It would mean replacing the Metropolitan Toronto and suburban regional councils with a single Greater Toronto Council (GTC) made up of representatives of the GTA's large municipalities and combinations of small ones. The GTC would have fewer powers than the existing upper-tier councils, but would coexist with several "flexible service districts" (that is, special-purpose authorities) with responsibilities for region-wide services such as conservation, public transit, policing, water and sewer facilities, and waste disposal. It would be responsible for producing a regional plan to guide local planning decisions (particularly those related to investment in new infrastructure), overseeing and coordinating services provided by the service districts, and working with provincial agencies to develop and co-finance regional policies. Lower-tier governments would have more responsibilities than they did under existing two-tier arrangements.

None of these things happened.

What the Ontario government did, and why

A FRACTIOUS END TO METROPOLITAN TORONTO
AS AN OUTCOME OF MUNICIPAL RESTRUCTURING

The new government's lack of interest in regional governance contrasted sharply with its intense interest in reorganizing virtually every other type of provincial responsibility. In fact, the Conservative government made so many changes to the structure and financing of Ontario's public services during its first two years in office that one writer would describe that period as "the most extensive reworking of the economic, social, and institutional infrastructure by a subnational government … anywhere or any time."[8] Of all the changes it made, however, the one that attracted most attention from the Toronto media and urban analysts was the amalgamation of Metropolitan Toronto with its six member municipalities into a new, greatly enlarged City of Toronto (the Toronto Megacity, as it was quickly named by the media).

Amalgamation was not a new idea for Metropolitan Toronto. It was the institutional arrangement that the City of Toronto had asked the OMB to

---

7. GTA Task Force 1996, 31.
8. Courchene 2000, 170.

approve in 1953 and had continued to advocate until the mid-1960s. No other Metro municipality had ever asked for it, however, and Toronto politicians had ceased to support it after the city's share of Metro's population and membership on Metro bodies declined. Nonetheless, the decision to amalgamate Metro's six municipalities could be seen as just another step in a prolonged process of adjusting Metropolitan Toronto's governmental system both to circumstances impinging on its performance and to immediate provincial priorities.

Unlike earlier changes, however, the 1996 decision was not preceded by well-publicized debates and detailed studies that helped to build awareness of the issues at stake and how they might be dealt with. Instead, discussions leading to amalgamation occurred largely within the provincial cabinet and caucus, or between individual cabinet members and a few outside advisers, and lasted only a few months. Thus the decision prompted a variety of explanations based on hastily gathered evidence or different political perspectives, each of which provided different insights into the pressures on Metropolitan Toronto at this time in its history. Taken together, they make Toronto's amalgamation a good example of how economic and political motives can interact to produce outcomes for urban governance that were neither prescribed nor foreseen when policy discussions began.

A CONFUSING DECISION TO AMALGAMATE

The most simplistic explanation of Metro's amalgamation was that Conservative leaders wanted to punish the left-leaning Mayor and Council members of the City of Toronto for recent acts of defiance against elements of the government's cost-cutting program. Although this explanation was attributed to an "observer close to the premier's office," and widely circulated at the time, it was later dismissed as "nonsense" by John Matheson, Chief of Staff to Al Leach, Ontario's Minister of Municipal Affairs and Housing and an early proponent of amalgamation.[9] Whether or not it was justified, however, it did capture the antipathy felt by some provincial politicians toward Toronto and its government. It also highlighted the fact that the provincial government could antagonize the city at little political cost. Toronto in 1996 had only 6.1 per cent of Ontario's population and 14 per cent of the population of the Toronto region. It had 9 of the 130 seats in the provincial legislature in 1995, and only 4 of those were held by Conservatives.

The provincial government had also acted against the wishes of Toronto City Council, however, when it created Metro Toronto in 1953, at which time Toronto had only 15 per cent of the population of Ontario. Toronto, in other

---

9. Ibbitson, 1997, 242; interview with John Matheson, Chief of Staff to Ontario Minister of Municipal Affairs and Housing from 1995–98, April 26, 2005.

words, had never been able to count on population size alone to give it a strong political voice in provincial deliberations. On the other hand, Toronto still occupied an important place in the provincial economy, and the government was under strong pressures to ensure that it would go on doing so. The City of Toronto alone had accounted for nearly one third of GTA jobs in 1991, and Metro had accounted for nearly two-thirds. Both units had lost jobs during the recession, however, and were still trying to regain them. Metro's failure to reform its property tax system was a frequently cited reason for the economic difficulties of the GTA core, and the City of Toronto's opposition to reform helped to account for that failure.

Trends in the Metro economy and how they were explained tied into a second explanation for the province's decision: that amalgamation would bring an end to costly and unproductive competition for economic development both among Metro's individual municipalities and between those municipalities and the directly elected Metro Council.[10] By doing so, it would strengthen the area's ability to compete against other large cities in the international arena. "We're a global city," said Al Leach. "And if we're going to be a player in this global area that we've got, we're going to have to become a player."[11] As mentioned earlier, however, this type of argument did not persuade the government to give the entire region a government with authority to act on regional issues. It was willing to allow competition to continue between Metro and other municipalities in the GTA rather than take the political risks that such a decision entailed.

Although there is evidence to support both explanations, therefore, they suffer from an implicit assumption that either the City of Toronto or Metro Toronto was high on the list of government preoccupations when the Conservatives took office. The more comprehensive explanation, and the one that is most consistent with government statements, is that Metro's amalgamation was only one element of a broadly based municipal and institutional revolution aimed at strengthening the ability of the entire province to function more effectively in a global setting.[12] Although previous governments had taken steps in that direction, the recession of the early 1990s had intensified pressures on the government to reduce taxes, cut government costs, and reduce the deficit in order to free up money for private investment

---

10. For example, according to John Matheson (ibid.), the premier was annoyed that the City of North York had decided to compete against Toronto in trying to attract the 2008 Olympics.

11. Stuart Green and David Nickle, "Exclusive talk with minister on amalgamation," *East York Mirror*, November 15, 1997.

12. Courchene 2000; Keil 1998.

and consumer spending. Far from driving government efforts to pursue these objectives, Metro's amalgamation occurred almost as a reluctant afterthought.

EXTRANEOUS OBJECTIVES

There were contradictions nonetheless between what Conservative candidates and advisers initially said should be done about Metropolitan Toronto and what the Conservative government actually did. There were also contradictions between the government's insistence that it wanted to cut costs and a decision that many people said would make local government more costly, at least in Metro Toronto. To make sense of the decision, therefore, it is necessary to look in some detail at the political process that led to it. It was a process driven not only by the government's financial goals but also by a determination to realize two other objectives that made achieving those goals more complicated.

One of the government's financially driven objectives was to replace welfare with a new program ("workfare") that would help to move people into the labour force, a goal that could be pursued only with the co-operation of the municipal governments that administered social assistance programs. Those units would also have to be large enough and financially strong enough both to administer the "workfare" and other social programs and to pay a substantial share of their costs.

The other objective was to regain control of and reform the public education system, the problems of which (high school board costs, the growing dependence of local school boards on property taxes, and comparatively poor indicators of student performance) the government blamed mainly on wasteful spending by some local trustees, on the symbiotic relationship that had developed between school boards and teachers' unions, and on the unstructured approach to curriculum development and classroom teaching that the Robarts government had instituted in the 1960s. School boards, on the other hand, blamed most of their problems on a decline in provincial government support, which had fallen from 61 per cent of provincially mandated costs in 1976 to 45 per cent in 1995.

No matter how they were explained, trends in school board financing were making school boards increasingly unequal in the amount they had to spend and in the types of programs they could offer. The boards serving low-assessment communities, which relied heavily on provincial grants, tended to be in the smaller, more rural parts of the province. Metropolitan Toronto, with its rich assessment base, received no provincial grants at all. Nonetheless, its politicians complained that the provincial grant formula treated Metro un-fairly, and wanted the province to adapt its grant programs to Metro's special needs.

The Conservatives had no interest, however, in making new funding commitments. In fact, they estimated that to keep their election promises they would have to cut $6 billion out of an annual budget of $56 billion without taking anything away from the health care sector, which accounted for 32 per cent of that budget in 1994 (see Table 5.2, page 202). They had also promised to maintain "education spending in the classroom." Nonetheless, they soon heard from John Sweeney, Chair of the Ontario School Board Reduction Task Force,[13] that savings in the education sector could be achieved by cutting the costs of school infrastructure and administration.[14] The Task Force had also concluded, however, that simply reducing the number of school boards would not solve problems of school board financing and educational inequalities. What was needed was a uniform system of funding "that gave each student equal access to education." Minister of Education John Snobelen told Sweeney "to complete his report, and not to hesitate to mention the funding concerns."

Apart from health and education, the municipal sector accounted for the largest share of provincial transfers (mainly for social and community services, but also for urban roads, public transit, and other functions). Conservative leaders quickly concluded, therefore, that they would have to give special attention to municipal finance and the provincial–local relationship. Only a few brief sentences in the Common Sense Revolution statement hinted at this conclusion. They spoke of ensuring "that municipalities and regional governments do everything possible to deliver services more efficiently"; of rationalizing "the regional and municipal levels to avoid the overlap and duplication that now exists"; and of "reducing government entanglement and bureaucracy with an eye to eliminating waste and duplication as well as unfair downloading by the province."[15] That same party platform also promised that a Conservative government would work "closely with municipalities to ensure that any actions we take will not result in increases to local property taxes."

The municipal sector's importance to the government's strategy meant that the Ministry of Municipal Affairs and Housing (MMAH) had an important role to play in helping the new government achieve its objectives.[16] Al Leach, the man chosen to head this ministry, was one of the four Conservative members elected in Toronto ridings. He was a former Manager of the TTC and before that Managing Director of the GO Transit commuter system, so he was knowledgeable about both Metro and GTA politics. Before the election,

---

13. The NDP government had appointed this Task Force shortly before leaving office (see Chapter 5).

14. Ibbitson 1997, 226–227.

15. Ontario Progressive Conservative Party, "The Common Sense Revolution," op. cit., 5, 17.

16. See note 70 on p. 171–72.

he had served on a task force created by Conservative Party leader Mike Harris to consider the future of Metro. Although it had never submitted a formal report, its chair, Joyce Trimmer, a former Mayor of Scarborough, was known to favour doing away with the metropolitan level of government.[17]

CONFRONTING AN UNFINISHED MUNICIPAL AGENDA

The ministry that Leach took over had a province-wide mandate and a good deal of unfinished business, some of it dating as far back as the reforms in municipal government and finance that the province had initiated in the 1960s but never completed. Property tax reform had occurred in some parts of the province, including some parts of the Toronto region, but not in others. There were still nearly 100 separate provincial grant programs, all with their own rules and administrative procedures.[18] The province's municipal sector was still highly differentiated and only partly reorganized. For example, much of southern Ontario had been restructured into two-tier regional municipalities in the early 1970s, but parts of the province were still under the old county system, and some remote areas lacked municipal organization altogether. From the ministry's standpoint, therefore, restructuring the province's financial relationship with municipal governments implied restructuring the municipal sector itself.

After the regional government program ended in the mid-1970s, the ministries responsible for local government had continued to encourage locally initiated attempts to restructure county governments or to amalgamate small local governments into larger units in order to broaden local tax bases and make it easier to coordinate provincially assisted services. Few restructurings occurred, however. By the early 1990s, about 600 of the province's more than 830 municipalities still had populations of less than 2,000.[19] The province either provided or substantially supported many of the services that these municipalities received. In addition there were numerous agencies, boards, and commissions performing a large number of local functions, obscuring lines of accountability and the way government money was spent, as well as complicating the delivery of local services. The Association of Municipalities of Ontario (AMO) had long been urging the government to simplify the municipal system and the municipal grant structure in the interest of giving municipal governments more control over their own affairs.

---

17. Sancton 2000, 143–144.

18. Don Stevenson and Richard Gilbert, "Restructuring Municipal Government in Greater Toronto" (a report prepared for the city of Montreal 1999), 4.

19. Interview with Marcia Sypnowich, Assistant Deputy Minister for Policy Development, Ontario Ministry of Municipal Affairs, May 18, 1994. My thanks to Robert Whelan for sharing his interview notes with me.

The MMAH's long history of trying to rationalize the municipal sector set it apart from other provincial ministries, the staff of which traditionally worked closely with the specialized agencies to which they gave grants and applied regulations—arrangements sometimes characterized as "vertical silos" that operated independently and with little knowledge of each other.[20] Municipal restructuring, in other words, was as much about reducing the size and costs of the provincial civil service, and making it easier to control, as it was about making municipal governments more financially viable and efficient.

A HEADLONG LEAP INTO MUNICIPAL RESTRUCTURING

Changes in provincial policies with significant implications for GTA governance began to occur soon after the Conservatives took office. The incoming government ended financial support for the construction of new social housing (although it honoured commitments already made); cancelled several infrastructure projects, including most of the subway lines planned for Metro Toronto; and reduced the size of welfare payments by more than 20 per cent.[21] In November 1995 it launched a full-scale assault on the municipal system with a *Savings and Restructuring Act* (Bill 26) that laid out procedures for freestanding municipalities and unrestructured counties to reorganize voluntarily, using various forms of annexation or amalgamation.[22] While the legislation was directed at those parts of the province where local governments had not yet been reorganized, some of its provisions had implications for any municipal institutions to which the government might turn its attention. On the one hand, it said that municipal restructuring plans would have to be approved by a majority of the affected electorate, a majority of councillors in each town affected, and a majority of towns themselves. On the other hand, it gave the government the right to appoint a commission to draw up a restructuring plan for any area where municipalities could not agree to one themselves.

Also in November the government said that it planned to make the municipal planning system "faster and less bureaucratic," with a view to lessening "the weight of the province's hand on municipalities."[23] Revisions to the *Planning Act* quickly followed. The government also began to rewrite the *Municipal Act*, the legal basis of Ontario's municipal system since 1849. The goal, said the MMAH in announcing these initiatives, was to free

20. Stevenson and Gilbert 1999, op. cit., 4; Interview with Gardner Church, April 6, 1993.

21. Isin and Wolfson 1999, 61.

22. Sancton 2000, 137-139.

23. James Rusk, "Tories have plans for Planning Act," *Globe and Mail*, November 17, 1995.

"municipalities from bureaucratic red tape and the need to comply with numerous provincial laws" and to give them "the flexibility the private sector already has to get things done."[24]

In addition, the government announced cuts in its grants to school boards. The cuts did not affect Metropolitan Toronto and other wealthy boards, which relied entirely on property taxes. The boards that were affected accused the government of violating its promise to maintain full funding for "education spending in the classroom," and some boards raised property taxes once again. Inter-board spending differences increased still more. "From that moment on," according to John Ibbitson, "the days of the boards were numbered," because they "had committed the cardinal sin of passing on cuts from the provincial level in the form of increased property taxes."[25] All that was left for the government to decide was whether it would abolish the boards altogether or whether it would just take away most of their powers.

The restructuring bill (with its implicit threat of provincially imposed amalgamations), the changes to the *Planning Act*, and cuts in school board grants generated a strong political backlash in various parts of the province, including municipalities that had elected Conservatives in 1995. While the government was deciding how to proceed, the GTA (Golden) Task Force published its report. Not only did it recommend the changes in GTA governance described earlier, but it also argued the need to disentangle provincial from municipal responsibilities, as earlier studies had done, and to make municipal governments more cost-effective. The Task Force, however, showed little enthusiasm for amalgamations or consolidations of services either in Metro or the GTA, noting that their cost-saving benefits "are often overstated." It did advise the government, however, to investigate "the possible amalgamation of ambulance and fire services, with a view to achieving greater efficiencies and improving response times.[26] It also came down emphatically on the side of property tax reform based on something very like market value assessment, saying that it was essential to the GTA's continued economic stability.

The School Board Reduction (Sweeney) Task Force issued its report one month later. In contrast to the GTA Task Force, it concluded that school board amalgamations were necessary to achieve a more cost-effective and accountable public education system.[27] Its recommendations included the amalgamation of the York, East York, and Toronto boards into a single board, and the dissolution of the Metropolitan Toronto School Board. (These

---

24. Ontario Ministry of Municipal Affairs and Housing, "Province releases proposal for new Municipal Act," News release, March 10, 1997.

25. Ibbitson 1997, 231.

26. GTA Task Force 1996, 212, 179.

27. Ontario School Board Reduction Task Force 1996, 28.

changes would have reduced the number of school boards in Metro Toronto from seven to four.) The Task Force also recommended changes in the way education was financed, attaching particular importance to the idea of pooling all commercial and industrial property taxes for education purposes.

By the time these two reports came out, the premier was beginning to fear that some of his cabinet ministers were being captured by their civil servants and losing sight of Common Sense Revolution priorities.[28] He and other cabinet members also realized that changes in the organization of municipal governments, in the funding of municipal services, and in the property tax system would have serious impacts on the distribution of local revenues and local costs across the province, and thus on Conservatives' political popularity.

To give its restructuring efforts more legitimacy, therefore, the government appointed a Who Does What (WDW) panel made up of municipal officials, representatives of the business community, and private consultants to advise it "on ways to eliminate duplication, over-regulation and blurred responsibility for the delivery of local and provincial services, and to help the government implement the changes."[29] The panel's chair was David Crombie, an old-style "progressive" Conservative, a former Toronto mayor, former cabinet member in a Conservative federal government, and head of both the Royal Commission on the Future of the Toronto Waterfront and a Waterfront Regeneration Trust that the Ontario government had set up in 1992 to implement some of the Commission's recommendations. Although he and other panel members were expected to buttress the government's case for municipal reforms, they had their own ideas about how urban issues should be addressed, and these did not always coincide with the views of the Harris government. Nonetheless, they sometimes persuaded that government to make decisions that were not part of its original plan.

The WDW panel broke up into sub-panels, each of which looked at different aspects of municipal governance or finance and reported its findings in a letter to the Minister of Municipal Affairs and Housing.[30] Its first task was to review work already done "on Ontario's patchwork property tax assessment system, and recommend a new system that [could] be applied across the province."[31] Change was urgently needed, Leach told the panel, because of "wide variations across the province and the rapid erosion of Metro Toronto's assessment base." The panel sent Leach five separate letters dealing with this

---

28. Interview with John Matheson, April 26, 2005.

29. Ontario Ministry of Municipal Affairs and Housing, "Panel to sort out 'who does what,'" News release, May 30, 1996.

30. The government published these letters separately. There was no final report.

31. Ontario Ministry of Municipal Affairs and Housing, "Panel to sort out 'who does what,'" op. cit.

topic alone, drawing on and adding to the numerous studies of property tax reform that the government had sponsored over the previous 30 years. Like most of those studies, it concluded that properties in the province should be assessed at their current market values and that assessments should be updated on a regular basis, but it added that municipal governments should have some latitude to decide how the tax burden would be distributed among different types of property.[32]

In its work on local government structures and organization, the WDW panel concentrated mainly on those parts of the municipal sector that had not been restructured in the 1960s and 1970s: northern communities, many of them unincorporated, and predominantly rural counties that had not been merged with the cities they either surrounded or adjoined. Although the panel also looked at regions and large urban centres, it recommended only that the government consider consolidating two-tier regions into single-tier cities or amalgamating small municipalities into larger ones when restructuring would enhance efficiency. It did not discuss Metropolitan Toronto at all, because panel members could not agree on what should be done with it. A few (Crombie among them) favoured making Metro into a single city; others argued for doing away with the Metro level of government, but consolidating Metro's six municipalities into four; still others defended the status quo.

WEIGHING THE ALTERNATIVES FOR METRO

WDW panel debates about Metro's future echoed debates that had been going on in the Conservative Party cabinet and caucus for some time. Not only had Joyce Trimmer, chair of the "Mike Harris Task Force on Bringing Common Sense to Metro," advised Harris to do away with the Metro level of government, but some of Harris's close advisers were still urging him to take that step.[33] Harris himself had seemed to agree, at least before the election. The GTA Task Force had recommended replacing the GTA's five upper-tier councils with a single council for the entire Toronto region. The City of Toronto was pushing for Metro's dissolution, and a majority of its electorate had supported the idea in the 1993 referendum. North York's submission to the Golden Task Force also favoured doing away with Metro. In fact, as soon as the Task Force released its report, North York Mayor Lastman joined the mayors of Toronto, Mississauga, and Oshawa in an alliance (soon nicknamed the Gang of Four) to urge the government to abolish the regional governments

---

32. Letter from David Crombie, Chair, Who Does What Panel, to the Honourable Al Leach, Minister of Municipal Affairs and Housing, "Assessment and Property Tax Reform—Tax Governance," December 20, 1996.

33. Interview with John Matheson, April 26, 2005.

and return most of their responsibilities to local governments.[34] "We believe," they wrote, "that local government preserves local community identity for residents and businesses and promotes the efficient use of resources."

Others argued differently, however. Metro's less affluent municipalities (East York, Scarborough, and York) told the GTA Task Force that they favoured Metro's retention. Etobicoke sat on the fence. Metro Council's submission insisted that "metropolitan government had already brought [benefits] to the Toronto area," citing an efficient transit and road system, a network of green spaces, cost-effective water and sewer systems, a full range of housing opportunities, and a thriving downtown core. Those benefits would persist, it implied, only if Metro and the regional governments were either retained or replaced by a government for Greater Toronto with similar powers. And David Crombie was arguing the advantages of moving to a single city not only within the WDW panel, but also in private discussions with Minister of Municipal Affairs and Housing Al Leach.

The dilemma, which Metro staff members pointed out to both Metro and provincial politicians and civil servants whenever they could, was deciding what to do about the services that Metro provided if Metro institutions were eliminated. If the government simply handed them back to the six local governments, as Toronto and North York proposed, there would be large differences in the ability of those governments to pay for them. The alternatives were to create new institutional arrangements (such as special-purpose districts) to take over and finance at least some Metro services; do away with Metro, but reduce the number of municipalities from six to four, as Goldenberg had recommended in 1965; or keep Metro, but do away with the lower-tier units. The first option did not fit with the government's pledge to reduce the number of municipal governments and make local governance simpler and easier to understand. The second was unlikely to end the intergovernmental bickering and competition among Metro municipalities that some commentators blamed for Metro's economic problems. And the third (having Metro take over everything) was certain to meet strong resistance from Metro's local governments, especially those (like Toronto's) that had been in open conflict with Metro Council for some time.

Once he had looked at the options, Leach concluded that consolidation under one government was the best course to take. Knowing that it would be politically unpopular, however, he hesitated to recommend it. He did so only after Crombie assured him that Metro's local communities would continue to exist as self-defined entities, as they had done after the 1967 restructuring,

---

34. Mayor Hazel McCallion, Mayor Mel Lastman, Mayor Nancy L. Diamond, and Mayor Barbara Hall, "Moving Forward Together: A Discussion Paper," January 1996.

even if they were not distinguished by political boundaries.[35] Premier Harris accepted Leach's recommendation, having come to the conclusion that an amalgamated city would help the Toronto region compete more effectively for international investment. His recent travels abroad had told him that "Toronto" and not "Ontario" was the name that gave his province visibility on the world stage.[36]

THE POLITICS OF AMALGAMATION I: TAKING POSITIONS

To reconcile its decision with the Common Sense Revolution platform, the government asked the consulting firm KPMG to show how amalgamation would save money by eliminating duplication of effort, reducing the number of politicians and local employees, and helping to make local administration more efficient. It then used the KPMG study in its campaign to persuade Conservative Party sceptics and the Metro population of the benefits of amalgamation.[37]

First, however, Leach gave Metro's six disgruntled mayors a month to devise an alternative plan that would meet provincial objectives. The mayors' proposal called for the complete elimination of the Metro level of government and the return of all municipal services except social services to the six local governments, which would then establish a thirteen-member Local Municipal Coordinating Board "to oversee the delivery of regional services within Metropolitan Toronto."[38] This body, said the mayors, could be replaced at some later time by a similar coordinating board for the entire GTA.

The mayors' proposal promised cost savings and an end to some service duplications, but showed little willingness to address other concerns, such as preserving cost-sharing arrangements within Metro or achieving Metro-wide property-tax reform. It also assumed that the provincial government would take over financial responsibility for social services. The government ignored it, therefore, and on December 17, 1996, brought to the Legislature a *City of Toronto Act* (Bill 103) that called for the dismantling of the governments of both Metro and the six local municipalities, and their replacement with a newly constituted government for a new City of Toronto. That city's Council would have 44 elected members (62 fewer than the existing system), one from

35. Interview with John Matheson, April 26, 2005. Crombie had grown up in the Village of Swansea, which became part of the City of Toronto in 1967.
36. Ibbitson 1997, 241.
37. Al Leach, Ontario Minister of Municipal Affairs and Housing, "Toronto for all of us," Pamphlet, December 1996.
38. Mayor Frank Faubert, Mayor Barbara Hall, Mayor Doug Holyday, Mayor Mel Lastman, Mayor Frances Nunziata, and Mayor Michael Prue, "Change for the Better. A Vision for the Future of our Communities; a Framework for Restructuring Local Government," November 1996.

each of 44 newly formed wards, and would serve a population of 2.4 million. In other words, the government had decided to start afresh, instead of handing over more powers to Metro Council.

At this early stage, Bill 103 specified that the province would appoint a transition team of one or more members and give it virtually unlimited powers to draw up new ward boundaries and appoint department heads and senior civil servants for the new city government. It also provided for a provincially appointed board of trustees to approve all municipal spending over $50,000 until the new Council took office on January 1, 1998. The decisions of both bodies would be final; they could not be appealed to the courts.

The plan met with both opposition and support. Critics charged that the government was seriously undermining the principles of local democracy. They also questioned its claim that amalgamation would save money.[39] Supporters echoed the government's arguments and added that amalgamation would help to strengthen Toronto's position within the GTA and that it would result in better, more equitable services for the growing low-income population in Metro's five suburban municipalities.[40] In addition, members of the development industry welcomed its potential for ending the confusion and delays associated with having to deal with two levels of local government.[41]

THE POLITICS OF AMALGAMATION II: THRASHING ABOUT IN MUDDIED WATERS

Despite the attention it attracted, the decision to amalgamate Metro Toronto was still only one element of the government's much larger effort to restructure its relationship with municipal governments. Many of those who participated in that effort believed that it would lead to the province's taking over full financial responsibility for both education and welfare, leaving municipal governments completely responsible for most other services. The Who Does What panel initially recommended this type of tradeoff. At the same time, it assumed that the outcome would be "revenue-neutral"—that is, that each level of government would be contributing as much to local services after it occurred as before.

It was soon apparent, however, that the provincial government could not take over both education and welfare without a large increase in its own costs, an outcome that it clearly would not accept. In a final letter to the pre-

39. John Barber, "Amalgamation sure to be costly," *Globe and Mail*, December 10, 1997; Michael Grange, "Amalgamation follows Tories' philosophy," *Globe and Mail*, December 18, 1997; Jane Jacobs, Deputation to Standing Committee on General Government, *City of Toronto Act*, 1996, Bill 103, February 3, 1977.

40. Barber, "Amalgamation sure to be costly," op. cit.; "Megaforum," *Globe and Mail*, February 15, 1997.

41. Colin Vaughan, "Developers support megacity for bureaucratic neatness," *Globe and Mail*, February 24, 1997.

mier, therefore, Crombie insisted that any changes had to be contingent on the ability of municipal governments to absorb their costs. If there had to be "a choice between placing education or health and welfare on the property tax," he insisted, "it is clearly preferable to continue to rely on the property tax for the funding of education."[42]

The argument did not appeal to a government that not only wanted to reduce its own costs, but was also determined to regain control over public education. Less than a month after introducing Bill 103, therefore, it introduced sweeping changes in municipal administration and municipal finance that differed substantially from the recommendations it had received. Within the space of a single week (January 12–15, 1997) it introduced *The Fewer School Boards Act* (Bill 104), which made the province fully responsible for managing and funding public education. It also substantially increased the amount that municipal governments would pay for most local services, social as well as non-social. (The specific changes are discussed in the section "Financing the New Arrangements.") An important aim of restructuring—which the government referred to as "local service realignment" and critics as "downloading" or "offloading"—was to enable the province to pay a larger share of public education costs. To round out the week, the government announced that it would reassess all properties throughout the province, using a common standard.

Coming as it did only weeks after the Megacity announcement, financial restructuring was soon being closely coupled with the plan to amalgamate Metro Toronto. Opposition to amalgamation escalated, therefore, soon drowning out the voices of support. Although the province had said it would create an $800-million fund to help municipal governments adapt to the new system, critics charged that the government either wanted to use the new city as a source of funds for services (particularly education) in the rest of the province, or that it wanted to load more costs (particularly the costs of social services) onto Metro taxpayers. Even some Conservative politicians openly criticized their party. House Speaker Chris Stockwell, a Conservative member from Etobicoke, found the government in contempt of the legislature for issuing pamphlets touting the benefits of Toronto's amalgamation without mentioning that the legislation had not yet been approved.[43] He also criticized the government for using public money in an advertising campaign when the opposition lacked access to similar funding.

---

42. David Crombie, Letter to the Honourable Al Leach, Minister of Municipal Affairs and Housing, "Re: Who Does What Panel's recommendations on taxation and assessment, disentangling provincial–municipal responsibilities and governance," December 23, 1996.

43. Martin Mittelstaedt, "Pamphlet puts Ontario in contempt," *Globe and Mail*, January 23, 1997.

Opposition in Metro soon coalesced into a loosely organized protest movement calling itself Citizens for Local Democracy (C4LD). Spearheaded by middle-class homeowners in downtown Toronto, among them the respected author Jane Jacobs, and led by John Sewell, a former Toronto mayor, a former chair of the Metropolitan Toronto Housing Authority, and the former chair of the NDP government's Commission on Planning and Development Reform, C4LD set out to build a Metro-wide coalition against amalgamation.[44] Sewell's past attacks on suburban development patterns and suburban lifestyles, which he had aimed primarily at post–Second World War suburbs within Metro, made this effort more challenging. Nonetheless, C4LD attracted large turn-outs to community meetings in all parts of Metro Toronto. It also helped to persuade Metro's six municipal governments to hold a referendum that asked the area's local voters one question: "Are you in favour of eliminating [name of municipality] and all other existing municipalities in Metropolitan Toronto and amalgamating them into a megacity?" About 25 per cent of the electorate participated (a higher percentage than had voted in the most recent municipal elections) and more than 76 per cent of these voters said no.

In their campaign against amalgamation, C4LD defended the values of local democracy against the threat of takeover by large, impersonal, heavily bureaucratized institutions. Its campaign overlapped, therefore, with the interests of local mayors, councillors, and public servants in saving their communities and protecting their jobs. The powers the province proposed to give to the Transition Team and the Board of Trustees were particularly offensive to all defenders of existing local governments. Scarborough took the province to court, charging that the government did not have the right to appoint trustees to oversee municipal spending (that is, to take away powers it had already given to municipal governments) before Bill 103 had been passed. The court agreed.[45] Other municipalities hired their own consultants to discredit the KPMG study by showing why costs in the new city were likely to rise, not fall, because of higher administrative costs and a levelling up of the costs of salaries and benefits.[46]

---

44. For detailed accounts of the anti-amalgamation fight waged by C4LD, see Boudreau 2000 and Horak 1998.

45. James Rusk and Donn Downey, "Toronto mayor warns of amalgamation chaos," *Globe and Mail*, February 7, 1997; Ijeoma Ross and James Rusk, "Megacity trustees ruled illegal," *Globe and Mail*, February 26, 1997.

46. Andrew Sancton, "Toronto's Response to the KPMG Report, 'Fresh Start: An Estimate of Potential Savings and Costs from the Creation of Single-Tier Local Government for Toronto,'" prepared for the Board of Management, City of Toronto, December 17, 1996; Deloitte and Touche, Letter to Mr. Glenn Kippen, Treasurer, Borough of East York, February 2, 1997; Wendell Cox Consultancy, "Local and Regional Governance in the Greater Toronto Area: A Review of Alternatives," Report prepared for the City of Toronto, January 10, 1997.

Metro's was the only Council to take a different stance. Faced with the threat of extinction, it passed a motion after two days of heated debate asking the government to eliminate the six lower-tier municipalities and merge their responsibilities into the Metro administration, saying that this would lessen the costs of moving to a unified city.[47] Not all Metro Council members supported the motion, but all of them did support a motion opposing the downloading plan, which estimates said would add $500 million dollars to the costs of governing Metro Toronto.

Shaken by the intensity of the opposition, the government reconsidered. It could not abandon amalgamation without jeopardizing municipal restructuring altogether, including its plans both to consolidate local and regional municipalities in other parts of the province and to cut the costs of municipal and other services.[48] Moreover, its own polls had told it that opposition to amalgamation was closely tied to voter worries about what it would mean for their tax bills.[49] What the government did, therefore, was try to make amalgamation more palatable to local voters. It said it would look for ways to ensure "that Metro mill rates would not increase in the first year after amalgamation," a proposal attributed to North York Mayor Mel Lastman.[50] Lastman would later run a successful campaign to become the new city's first Mayor on a promise that a council he headed would not increase property taxes.[51] The government also changed both the amalgamation and the downloading bills before sending them back to the legislature for final reading.[52]

The version of *The City of Toronto Act* approved on April 26, 1997, allowed the Transition Team to hire senior executives for the new city, but otherwise made its role solely advisory; the City Council would make final decisions. The Board of Trustees also became an advisory body. The number of wards in the new city was increased from 44 to 56, to be based on existing ward boundaries (it would be reduced to 44 once again in 2000 with the majority support of the new Council). The legislation also provided for the creation of community councils and possibly for neighbourhood committees, their powers to be decided by the City Council. Other changes in provincial

47. Ijeoma Ross, "Metro votes for unified city," *Globe and Mail*, February 14, 1997.

48. James Rusk, "Harris sticks to Metro merger: rejection in vote to bring changes," *Globe and Mail*, March 5, 1997.

49. James Rusk, "Tories' reaction likely to be more flexibility," *Globe and Mail*, March 4, 1997.

50. Rusk, "Harris sticks to Metro merger," op. cit.

51. Lastman's opponent, Barbara Hall, mayor of the old Toronto, refused to make such a promise. In fact, Lastman could not guarantee that the City Council would abide by his promise, because Canadian mayors do not have the authority to dictate City Council policy. They can only try to persuade other Council members to accept their advice.

52. Ontario Ministry of Municipal Affairs and Housing, "We've listened—Bill 103 Proposed Amendments (City of Toronto Act, 1997)," Backgrounder, March 27, 1997.

legislation, discussed in more detail in the section "Financing the New Arrangements," sought to reduce the financial impacts of downloading on the new Toronto and other large municipalities.

A REAFFIRMATION OF PROVINCIAL AUTHORITY

The battle was not yet over. All Metro municipalities except North York, together with a coalition of residents' associations, immediately challenged Bill 103 in the courts, claiming that it not only violated the Canadian *Charter of Rights and Freedoms* in at least four ways, but that it also violated a guarantee of local democracy that was implicit in the *British North America Act* of 1867.[53] Justice Stephen Borins of the Ontario Court's General Division ruled, however, that the province was fully within its legal rights to make the changes it had made.[54] The arguments he had heard, he said, were political, not legal arguments. Although he suggested that the government might have paid more attention to public opinion, he also pointed out that it was not the court's job to pass judgment on the wisdom of legislation. "'It may be,' he said, 'that the government displayed *megachutzpah* [brazen effrontery] in proceeding as it did, and in believing that the inhabitants of Metro Toronto would submit ... without being given an opportunity to have a real say in how they were to live and be governed.'" Nonetheless, "'the [Canadian *Charter of Rights and Freedoms*] does not guarantee the individual the right to live his or her life free from government *chutzpah* or imperiousness.'"[55]

Some amalgamation opponents vowed to seek changes in provincial legislation that would guarantee the Toronto government (and perhaps other city governments in Ontario) more financial and legislative autonomy, and more protection from provincially imposed changes in local boundaries and institutional structures.[56] For the time being, however, the amalgamation battle had reaffirmed the provincial government's constitutional authority to create or dissolve municipal institutions to suit its own purposes. At the same time, it had demonstrated that there were both legal and political limits on how far the province could go. Legally, the provincial government could take powers away from municipal governments only if there were laws in place allowing it to do so. Politically, it had to pay some attention to municipal concerns, if only to ensure

53. Donn Downey, "Megacity law violates Charter, court told," *Globe and Mail*, July 8, 1997; John Barber, "Contempt for local government goes back long way," *Globe and Mail*, July 11, 1997.

54. Thomas Claridge and Chad Skelton, "Megacity law survives court challenge," *Globe and Mail*, July 25, 1997.

55. John Barber, "Court's authority not good enough," *Globe and Mail*, July 25, 1997.

56. John Barber, "Parliamentary system defeated megacity foes," *Globe and Mail*, April 23, 1997.

support for elected members of its own party. Nonetheless, the government continued with municipal restructuring in other parts of the province, sometimes in the face of strong opposition. By 2001 it had amalgamated three other regional municipalities (Hamilton-Wentworth, Ottawa-Carleton, and Sudbury) into single cities and reduced the number of lower-tier municipalities from 815 to 447, an accomplishment to which it pointed with pride.[57]

The political costs of amalgamation and disentanglement were not as high as some critics had predicted. The Conservatives were returned to power in 1999 with 57.3 per cent of the seats in a restructured 103-seat legislature, slightly less than the 63 per cent of legislative seats they had captured in the 130-seat legislature elected in 1995. The party won 8 out of 22 seats in the new Toronto, a smaller percentage than the 16 out of 30 seats it had won in Metro in 1995, but not the wipe out that some of its critics had predicted. The Conservatives lost all their Toronto seats in a 2003 election, while the Liberals won a healthy majority, but local government restructuring was not an important issue in that campaign.

AND FOR THE GTA ... A COUNCIL OF GOVERNMENTS

Although the Conservative government was willing to tamper extensively with municipal institutions in all parts of the province, it was not willing to give the whole Toronto region a government of its own. In fact, according to one newspaper account, its leaders rejected the proposal for a GTA Council almost as soon as it received the GTA Task Force report, saying that it would be like creating "a small country, let alone a small province."[58] Nonetheless, the cabinet set up a review panel to "determine the level of [GTA-wide] consensus" on that report's contents. After consulting with municipal officials, the panel reported that there was "almost no support for the creation of a Greater Toronto Area with a 'big box' governing body."[59]

The government seemed ready to let the regional question drop. The WDW panel insisted, however, that a Greater Toronto Services Board was "of overwhelming importance," and should be "a first priority."[60] Such a Board, it said, could help to maintain a strong urban core by encouraging future development to concentrate within an urban zone, beyond which services would not be extended for at least 25 years. In response, Leach appointed Special Advisor

---

57. Ontario Ministry of Municipal Affairs and Housing, "New municipalities mean better government for Ontario's taxpayers," News release, January 2, 2001.

58. William Walker, "The inside story: How Harris built Megacity," *Toronto Star*, December 21, 1996.

59. Review Panel on the Greater Toronto Area Task Force 1996, 24.

60. David Crombie, Letter to the Honourable Al Leach, Ontario Minister of Municipal Affairs and Housing, re: "WDW Panel recommendations on Local Governance," December 6, 1996.

Milt Farrow (a former Assistant Deputy Minister of Municipal Affairs) to ask municipal politicians what such a Board should look like and what it should do. Like the review panel before him, Farrow found little support for a body with GTA-wide responsibilities.[61] He therefore advised the government to create a Board with a relatively weak mandate, but one that could develop and adopt strategies for coordinating infrastructure and for long-term waste management. It should also be able to implement its decisions, he said, and apportion their costs among local municipalities.

The Board the province created lacked even those limited powers. Essentially, the Greater Toronto Services Board (GTSB) was a council of governments of the type that had proliferated in the United States in the 1960s. Its principal function was to approve the capital and operating budgets of the Greater Toronto (formerly GO) commuter transit system, allocate their costs among GTA municipalities, and "promote and facilitate coordinated decision making among the municipalities in the Greater Toronto Area" on transit-related matters.[62] A six-person committee consisting of representatives of Toronto and the regional municipalities of Durham, York, Peel, Halton, and Hamilton-Wentworth, all members of the GTSB, would oversee the operation of the GO commuter system.[63] Beyond that, the Board could adopt strategies for infrastructure development or countryside protection, but only if two-thirds of its members were in favour of its doing so.

Financing the New Arrangements

Biting the bullet on property tax reform

Although the Conservative government never strayed far from its financial objectives (reducing government costs, paying down the deficit, cutting taxes), its efforts to appease its many critics made this a confusing time for anyone trying to understand what was happening. What became clear early in the process, however, was that the government could not go very far with municipal restructuring without reforming the property tax system—an issue that earlier governments had grappled with and then dropped. There were at least three compelling reasons for going ahead with reform. The first was to

61. Special Advisor to the Minister of Municipal Affairs and Housing [Milt Farrow], "Developing the Framework for a Greater Toronto Services Board," Discussion paper, February 1997.

62. Ontario Government, *Greater Toronto Services Board Act*, 1998. Office Consolidation Statutes of Ontario 1998, Chapter 23, December 3, 1999.

63. The Regional Municipality of Hamilton-Wentworth, located to the west of Halton, was consolidated as the new City of Hamilton in 2001. Representatives of this region sat on the GTSB only when transit matters were discussed.

assist with the process of realigning service responsibilities between municipal governments and the province. If the provincial government wanted to use local property taxes as a source of funds for education or shift more responsibilities to municipal governments, it needed a standard basis for measuring and comparing the relative taxable wealth of different municipalities.

The second reason was to get rid of a Business Occupancy Tax that had been in place since 1903. This tax, which was based on the assessed value of business-occupied properties but levied on business owners, was difficult to administer and collect. It was also difficult to rationalize because, for historical reasons, different types of business were taxed at different rates. Undoubtedly it was also a source of irritation to the business community from which the Tories drew much of their support.

Differences in the way properties in Metro and the suburban regions were assessed and taxed, particularly the higher taxes paid by commercial properties in Metro, was the third argument for property tax reform. Those differences could not be addressed until inequities and inconsistencies were removed from Metro's property tax system and its outcomes made comparable with property tax outcomes in the rest of the region.

The government decided, therefore, that all properties in the province would be reassessed at their "current value," which in practice differed only slightly from the "actual value" standard proposed by the GTA Task Force and the contentious "market value" measure that the government had backed away from in 1978.[64] To carry out this task, it created the Ontario Property Assessment Corporation (OPAC), a non-share-capital, not-for-profit organization to which all municipalities in Ontario would belong. Twelve members of its fourteen-member board of directors were municipal officials; two were provincial appointees.[65]

As soon as it had set property tax reform in motion, the government began to make adjustments in tax law to accommodate objections, many of them from the new Toronto, that the new system would mean large tax increases for single-family homeowners and small businesses. It gave municipal governments the right to create new property classes, to tax different classes at different rates, and to shift tax burdens among property classes within provincially prescribed limits. These accommodations enabled Toronto to continue to tax commercial and industrial properties at higher rates than those being applied to similar properties in the suburbs.[66]

64. Sancton 2000, 151–152.

65. Ontario Property Assessment Corporation, "What is OPAC," Public information leaflet," n.d.

66. Slack 2000, 25–26.

Juggling property taxes and provincial grants

As first announced in 1997, "local services realignment" meant taking education off the residential property tax and funding this service entirely out of provincial revenues and provincially prescribed portions of commercial and industrial property taxes.[67] Municipal governments would then become completely responsible for some services that the province had been fully or partially funding, including regional and municipal public works, roads that served local needs (including some that had been classified as provincial highways), public transit (including GO), public health, libraries, ambulance services, group homes for the mentally ill, "domiciliary beds" (that is, beds in shelters and hostels), and the capital costs of social housing. Municipal governments would also become responsible for 50 per cent of the costs of social services (up from approximately 20 per cent), including some services (such as rent subsidies and family benefits) that the province had fully funded in the past. Provincial grants to municipalities were to be eliminated, although the government created several special funds to assist with community reinvestment and to help cover the costs of restructuring.

The resulting outcry from municipal governments and property owners persuaded the government to shift some of the costs of education back to the residential tax base. It was then able to reduce the municipal share of welfare and several other social services from 50 per cent to 20 per cent of program costs, although municipal governments would continue to pay 50 per cent of the costs of administering the workfare program. The province also decreed that the municipal share of welfare and social housing would be pooled across the GTA, and that the province would collect the money and redistribute it among Toronto and the four regional municipalities. Once again there were strong objections, this time from regional councils. The government immediately removed public health, child care, and ambulances from the pool, leaving only welfare and social housing costs to be shared.

Changes in social service financing were only the first of a series of adjustments that saw the government restore provincial grants for hostels, public health services, public libraries, and some types of local transit service, and take back full responsibility for long-term care. It lent money to Toronto to help defray the costs of restructuring. By the end of the period it had also agreed to cover GO Transit's operating deficits once again and pay a share of its capital costs.

---

67. Ontario Ministry of Municipal Affairs and Housing, "Where Will the Changes Be?" Background information, January 17, 1997.

Funding arrangements for education also went through several itera-tions. At first, the government said that properties throughout the province would be taxed for education at a uniform rate. Next it decided to tax com-mercial and industrial properties in Toronto at a higher rate than it used in the rest of Ontario, as Metropolitan Toronto had done. When Toronto protested, it agreed to bring education taxes on Toronto's business sector into line with the rest of the province over an eight-year period.

Strengthening the role of the private sector

Following the lead of its Liberal and NDP forerunners, the Conservative government looked for ways to shift the costs of new infrastructure to the private sector, and encouraged municipal governments to do the same. In 1998 it sold the partly finished provincial Highway 407 to a private corporation to complete and operate. A year later, it created a new special-purpose authority (the SuperBuild Corporation) within the Ministry of Finance to "address Ontario's infrastructure needs and meet the economic challenges of the new millennium."[68] SuperBuild's job was to review and coordinate the capital spending plans of provincial ministries and major institutions, and advise the government on which ones it should support. The agency received $20 billion from the government in start-up funds, but was expected to "identify opportunities for private sector involvement in the delivery of government programs and services."

While trying to enlist the private sector in infrastructure development, the government also sought to protect it from higher municipal taxes. It repealed the legislation that had permitted municipalities to levy a "commercial concentration tax" on large commercial structures and parking lots, restricted the right of municipal governments to increase taxes on non-residential properties, and reduced the number of purposes for which municipal govern-ments could impose charges on developers.[69] These tax changes, together with the adoption of a more permissive *Planning Act,* signalled the government's determination to encourage new construction, both within urban areas and on the urban fringe, as a way to promote economic growth. At the same time, the changes deprived municipal governments of potential sources of revenue to fund their new obligations.

Development charges remained important, nonetheless, as sources of funds for new infrastructure in the suburban regional municipalities. They

68. Ontario Ministry of Finance, "Ontario SuperBuild Corporation: History," online at: www.superbuild.gov.on.ca/english/history/htm.

69. Ontario Ministry of Municipal Affairs and Housing, "New Development Charges Act to aim at Jobs, Affordable Homes," News release, November 25, 1996.

were not an option for the new Toronto, however, as its Council discovered when it decided to impose a uniform charge on new residential developments in the city. Developers and construction unions objected, saying that development charges were intended only to fund new infrastructure in the suburbs, where "growth should pay for growth," not to provide revenues to cities where infrastructure was already in place. After two large developers appealed the bylaw to the OMB and one of them won its case, Toronto's Council reinstated the former city's practice of negotiating agreements with developers on a project-by-project basis.[70]

Government-regulated gambling was also gaining grounds as a way to shift costs to the private sector. The Windsor casino generated $316 million for the province in its first year of operation,[71] and the Conservative government wasted no time in approving three more casinos in different parts of the province. It used some of the revenues from these and other gambling sources to fund social and community services and the arts, as a way to offset reductions in provincial grants. The job of administering the funds went to the Trillium Foundation, hitherto "an obscure funder of social work,"[72] which used them to make grants to community organizations involved with arts and culture, the environment, human and social services, sports, and recreation.

Outcomes for the Toronto Region

Economic growth a priority, but not the infrastructure to support it

Provincial policy statements throughout this period, including statements relating to GTA governance, consistently emphasized economic growth as the goal of government policies, no matter what their substance. The Minister of Municipal Affairs and Housing declared that the amalgamation of Metropolitan Toronto would strengthen the Toronto economy by ending costly duplication of services and unproductive competition among Metro municipalities, and by

---

70. Such agreements had allowed individual developers to increase building height or density in exchange for land or cash for the city's housing program, or for including amenities such as daycare centres or recreational spaces in their buildings. Gay Abbate, "Developers challenge city's policy on fees," *Globe and Mail*, August 28, 2000; Gay Abbate, "Deal brings peace with developers as 30-per-cent levy quashed," *Globe and Mail*, January 22, 2001.

71. Shafer Parker Jr., "Canada's fastest-growing industry (outside of Alberta, Ontario is the province deriving most revenue from gambling, chiefly through casinos)," *Alberta Report*, 24 (5), 10 (January 13, 1997).

72. Ray Conlogue, "Shaking the old pros to the foundations: Established arts groups are finding they simply don't meet the mandate of Ontario's Trillium Foundation," *Globe and Mail*, March 30, 2002.

enabling the core to play a stronger role in the global arena.[73] His ministry also claimed that GTSB efforts to coordinate services would "pay big dividends in terms of business investment, which means more jobs and a better economic climate all across the GTA."[74]

MOVING SLOWLY ON TRANSPORTATION

An interest in economic growth did not mean, however, that either the provincial government or the GTA's municipal governments were willing to invest large sums in services to accommodate it, particularly during the Conservatives' first years in office. Although road congestion continued to increase, the government's most important transportation initiative was the sale of Highway 407 to a private consortium, which agreed to maintain it, extend it east and west, and build seven interchanges in exchange for the right to charge tolls for 99 years.[75] The decision had less to do with improving mobility in the region than it did with getting rid of an expensive responsibility.

By the end of 2001, the government was ready to support extensions to two other major highways in the Toronto region. Because these would speed up travel for outer suburban residents, they were likely to add to congestion in the region's heavily populated core, not relieve it. There was little possibility, however, of adding capacity to the road network in built-up areas, at least not without expensive land expropriations and prolonged political battles. The only way to relieve congestion in those areas was to greatly improve the region's public transit systems and convince more people to use them.

Recognizing these challenges, the Who Does What panel strongly advised the government to retain control of GO Transit. The commuter system, it said, was "critical in reducing congestion on the existing road network, thereby reducing the cost of doing business and enhancing our competitiveness—and in providing the private sector ready access to a mobile and professional labour force."[76] Ignoring this advice, the government made municipal governments fully responsible for the capital and operating costs of both GO and municipal transit. Before ending its contributions to municipal

---

73. Stuart Green and David Nickle, "Exclusive talk with minister on amalgamation," *East York Mirror*, January 15, 1997; Michael Grange, "Amalgamation follows Tories' philosophy," *Globe and Mail*, December 18, 1996; Ontario Ministry of Municipal Affairs and Housing, "Toronto for All of Us," Pamphlet, December 1996.

74. Ontario Ministry of Municipal Affairs and Housing, "Service coordination in the Greater Toronto Area," Background information, December 17, 1996.

75. Michael Valpy, "Transit gridlock just a traffic-light away," *Globe and Mail*, May 4, 1999.

76. Letter from David Crombie, chair, and William F. Bell, chair of transportation and utilities sub-panel, Who Does What panel, to the Honourable Al Leach, Minister of Municipal Affairs and Housing, December 12, 1996.

transit, however, it agreed to honour an existing commitment to support the 6.4-kilometre Sheppard subway, a line that had been vigorously promoted by North York Mayor Mel Lastman, who argued that it would generate new development in the northern part of Metro, including around the North York City Centre. At the same time, it ended support for a short east–west line connecting the City of York to the subway system, thereby ending York's aspirations to develop its own commercial node and leaving west and northwest Metro poorly served by rapid transit. (Both lines had been elements of the much-debated Network 2011 that Metro had approved in 1986. See Figure 4.4b, page 180.)

The withdrawal of provincial support ushered in an acrimonious period in transit politics in the GTA. Within Metro, there were public disagreements between TTC Manager David Gunn, who insisted that the transit system should be self-supporting, and TTC Chairman Howard Moscoe, other local politicians, and community group members, who insisted that transit was an essential community service. Disputes died down after Gunn left in 1998, to be replaced by Rick Ducharme, a former General Manager of GO Transit. Ducharme agreed that the TTC could not maintain its equipment, expand its facilities and services, or even provide enough services to sustain existing ridership without more support from the city or subsidies from senior levels of government.

At the GTA level, disputes often centred on a provincially imposed funding formula that required the City of Toronto to pay half the cost of the GO system, even though most GO riders lived in the suburbs.[77] Participants in such disputes had little interest in looking for ways to expand existing transit services throughout the region or move people and goods more efficiently across municipal boundaries. Nonetheless, the GTSB worked with the GTA's regional and local planners to devise a Strategic Transportation Plan for the GTA (including Hamilton-Wentworth) that emphasized public transit "as the key to reducing congestion, especially during rush hours."[78] Instead of proposing a comprehensive and integrated regional transit system, however, the strategy combined existing and proposed rapid transit systems and corridors into a single map. It also identified "the programs needed to integrate local feeder transit services with interregional transit."

The Strategic Transportation Plan did not assign priority to specific routes or facilities, because the GTSB did not want to seem to favour some parts of the region over others. Instead, it depicted the evolution of regional

---

77. Jennifer Lewington, "GTA transit plan inching forward," *Globe and Mail*, June 26, 1999.

78. Greater Toronto Services Board 2000, 6.

transit as an incremental, locally directed process. Individual municipalities would add to their own systems in their own time, and adopt policies (such as planning for higher densities in transit corridors) to promote increased transit ridership. The Board adopted this strategy by consensus in June 2000 as "a basis for discussions with potential funding partners," by which it meant the federal and provincial governments and the private sector.

COMPROMISING ON SOLID WASTE DISPOSAL

There was also little progress during this eight-year period toward finding publicly acceptable ways to dispose of solid waste, another infrastructure issue that the Harris government turned back to the GTA's city and regional governments after disbanding the Interim Waste Authority. In the process, the government removed constraints imposed by its NDP predecessor on two much-debated alternatives: incineration (although it issued guidelines to govern incinerator use), and shipping garbage north by rail for disposal in an abandoned mine near the town of Kirkland Lake. The changes were especially significant for Toronto, which faced the imminent closure of the large landfill site in the City of Vaughan in York region. Environmentalists strongly opposed both alternatives, however, and the private company involved in the mine disposal scheme refused to delete a clause from its contract that could make the city liable for environmental problems.[79] Toronto Council decided, therefore, that it would ship its waste by truck to landfill sites in Michigan, immediately increasing its waste disposal costs from $13 to $55 per ton.[80] At the same time it stepped up an already active program to divert wastes to other uses.

EXPANDING SEWER CAPACITY: A NEW ANTI-GROWTH FLASHPOINT

One infrastructure project that did move forward was a plan for a trunk sewer system to support development in York region. Although bitterly opposed by many residents of King Township, an enclave of large estate homes and residual rural uses, and by a majority of Township councillors, the new system was supported by the Township's mayor and by the council, planners, and health commissioner of York region. Opponents wanted to protect their communities from concentrated suburban settlements like those springing up to the south; supporters argued that a piped sewer system was necessary to community health, because leakage from septic tanks posed a danger to

79. "Council votes overwhelmingly to scrap Adams Mine project," *Globe and Mail*, February 2, 2001.

80. Interview with Bob Davis, Supervisor of Public Consultation, City of Toronto, October 2004.

local wells.[81] Although the Township council voted for further study, it was the government of York region that would build and pay for the system. It decided that the facility should go ahead, and that it had to be large enough to serve 40,000 or more people.

The York region dispute was symptomatic of the type of issue that was likely to become increasingly prominent in GTA politics in the years ahead. In pushing for the new sewer, York's regional government was simply doing the job the province had assigned to it during an earlier period of local government restructuring (1969–74). In that sense it was acting as an agent for the provincial government, which frequently favoured new residential development not only as a type of economic investment but also as a way to absorb the 100,000 added to the regional population every year. To build infrastructure to support new growth, however, the regional government also had to have the backing of a majority of its members, most of whom represented heavily populated, highly urbanized southern municipalities. Clearly, the urban–rural fault lines that had divided the region from the beginning were still present and perhaps widening. The issue also highlighted the role of regional governments as buffers between the provincial government and irate residents who found themselves in the path of urban expansion.

FINANCING REGIONAL SERVICES TAKES A
BACK SEAT TO OTHER FUNDING PRIORITIES

The two Conservative government decisions of most immediate relevance to regional finance were the amalgamation of Metropolitan Toronto and property tax reform. Although the government justified amalgamation simply as a way to save tax dollars, there was the implicit possibility that the city might use some of the tax revenues it saved to enhance services of regional benefit, such as the rapid transit system or low-cost housing. That possibility remained both hypothetical and unlikely in 2001, however, because the costs of servicing the new Toronto went up during its early years, just as critics had predicted they would.[82]

Some of the increases resulted from one-time transition costs, such as the costs of updating office equipment and hiring staff to run it, and the costs of severance packages. Others, however, resulted from bringing services in

81. John Barber, 2001, "King mayor uses sewer-pipe issue to strike blow," *Globe and Mail*, May 16, 2001; Wallace Immen, "York determined to build King sewer," *Globe and Mail*, May 12, 2001; "King township in battle royal over growth," *Globe and Mail*, October 30, 2001.

82. Anne Golden and Enid Slack, "Urban Governance Reform in Toronto: A Preliminary Assessment" (paper presented to the 8th Biennial Jerusalem Conference in Canadian Studies, Jerusalem, June 25–29, 2000).

Metro's poorer municipalities up to higher standards and harmonizing the salaries of municipal employees, and thus were lasting additions to the new city's budget. There were also the extra costs imposed by provincial downloading. Instead of saving the province money, therefore, the city absorbed a $50-million grant and $113 million in interest-free loans from the province during its first two years alone. With its higher servicing costs and its debt to the province, the city was in no position to invest in new infrastructure.

The government had also justified amalgamation as a way to help Toronto remain a strong and effective competitor for economic investment in the global economy. Looked at from this perspective, amalgamation might result in new property tax revenues that the city government could use to improve city services and contribute to services of regional importance. It would be many years, however, before anyone could determine whether amalgamation had marked a turning point in the fortunes of this urban core, for better or for worse, or analyze the role it played in the regional economy.

The second provincial decision with important implications for regional finance was property tax reform. Here the government succeeded where many previous governments had failed. Reassessment of properties throughout the province using the "current value" standard gave both the provincial and local governments a common basis for comparing local wealth and spending capacity. What reform did not do was end tax rate differentials between Toronto and the suburban regions, although provincial restraints on tax increases prevented the gap from growing. Toronto continued to tax large commercial properties at higher rates than other types of property in the interest of preserving a social mix in city neighbourhoods and protecting small businesses. The province's decision to tax commercial properties in Toronto for education at a higher rate than it applied to similar properties in other municipalities also helped to maintain the city–suburban differential.

Local government restructuring helped the Conservatives to achieve the financial goals that drove their legislative program, but only to a limited extent. The government managed one round of tax reductions, but put off a promised second round. By shifting substantial social service and infrastructure costs to municipalities and cutting the size of the provincial civil service, it also achieved some reductions in its own spending. Thus the provincial budget increased by a smaller percentage between 1996 and 2003 than during the previous six years (Table 6.1). The percentage of the budget allocated to debt repayment had fallen to 11.2 per cent in 2002–03 from a high of 14.5 per cent in 1995–96. Community and social services, environment and energy, municipal affairs and housing, and transportation also accounted for smaller budget shares than when the Conservatives took office. Only the shares going to education and health had increased. Health accounted for nearly 38 per cent

Table 6.1 Ontario government spending on selected functions, 1989–2003

Function	1989–90 ($000s)	% of total provincial budget	1994–95 ($000s)	% of total provincial budget	% change 1989–90/ 1995–96
		1989–1995			
Community & Social Services	5,061	13.0	9,436	16.8	86.5
Education (including Colleges & Universities)	8,059	19.4	8,882	15.8	10.0
Environment & Energy	532	1.3	543	1.0	2.1
Health	13,787	33.1	17,848	31.8	34.3
Municipal Affairs & Housing	1,496	3.6	1,797	3.2	20.1
Transportation	2,310	5.6	2,355	4.2	2.0
Payment on Public Debt	4,284	10.3	7,832	13.9	82.8
Total Prov. Spending (Operating + Capital)	41,602		56,168		35.0

Function	1995–96 ($000s)	% total provincial budget	2002–03 ($000s)	% total provincial budget (op.+cap.)	% change 1995–96/ 2000–03
		1995–2003			
Community & Social Services	8,830	15.2	5,803	8.5	−34.3
Education (including Colleges & Universities)	8,949	15.4	12,550	18.3	40.2
Environment & Energy	477	.8	440	.6	−7.7
Health	17,775	30.5	25,888	37.8	45.6
Municipal Affairs & Housing	3,049	5.2	656	1.0	−78.5
Transportation	2,441	4.2	1,379	2.0	−43.5
Payment on Public Debt	8,475	14.5	7,694	11.2	−9.2
Total Prov. Spending (Operating + Capital)	58,273		68,492		17.5

Source: Ontario Budget documents, 1989–2006.

of the provincial budget in 2003, making it the largest expenditure item by far. Nonetheless, the government was still being accused of starving the health care system of funds.

The share of the provincial budget going to education was also higher in 2001 than in the government's first year of office. This was not surprising, given that the province now had a new source of revenue—commercial/industrial property taxes—to spend on this service. Even so, it had managed to keep education costs down by making substantial cuts in the budget of the Toronto District School Board.

The service areas for which budget shares declined (such as community and social services, municipal affairs and housing, and transportation) were all important to the Toronto region's economic performance and social well-being. The declines were not surprising, given that the government had targeted these spending areas when it set out to reshape the municipal sector. Regional and municipal governments were supposed to step in to fill funding gaps with local taxes. This did not happen, however, especially in the case of services of GTA-wide importance.

Even if municipal governments had wanted to contribute to regional services (and there was little indication that they did), the province made it difficult for them to do so by restricting their ability to increase property taxes or pass on costs to developers. It had also bowed to local pressures by specifying that the Greater Toronto Services Board could levy a charge on its member municipalities (over what was needed for operating expenses) only if it had the approval of "a majority of the municipalities against which the levy is made," and then only if those municipalities represented "at least two-thirds of the total weighted assessment" of those members.[83] This provision virtually guaranteed that the GTSB could not initiate new infrastructure programs.

Although it transferred responsibilities to the municipal property tax while placing constraints on how it could be used, the government turned down repeated municipal requests for new sources of revenue, such as shares of the provincially collected gasoline and sales taxes to fund local and regional transit. To take this approach, said one provincial official, would mean that one level of government would collect the money while another level spent it and got the "kudos."[84]

By constraining the ability of municipalities to raise new funds, the government avoided taking the blame for higher local taxes, which would have conflicted with the tax-cutting image it wanted to portray. It also guaranteed, however, that little new infrastructure was built, and that the provincial government would face growing pressures to do more for the region. It also brought similar pressures on the federal government, which responded in March 2001 by allocating $2 billion to improvements to urban infrastructure, including public transit, on the understanding that the money would be matched by provincial and municipal contributions.[85] In May 2001, Prime Minister Jean Chrétien also appointed a Liberal Party Caucus Task Force on

83. Ontario Government 1999, 15.

84. Jennifer Lewington, "Province rejects sharing fuel-tax income," *Globe and Mail*, March 3, 2001.

85. Wallace Immen, "Federal dollars could ease traffic gridlock," *Globe and Mail*, March 9, 2001.

Urban Affairs, stirring hopes that the federal government might become an active player in the urban policy field once again.

That same month, the Ontario government earmarked $250 million of SuperBuild money for inter-regional transit in the GTA and the Golden Horseshoe, a territory stretching along Lake Ontario beyond the boundaries of the GTA in both directions. It took back responsibility for GO Transit's operating deficit at the same time, and said it would contribute money toward system improvements, provided that the federal and municipal governments did the same. "While there has been considerable effort over the last two years to improve co-operation among GTA municipalities," said its budget statement, "it is clear that provincial leadership is necessary."[86] To suggestions that the government had made a U-turn from its earlier position, the Finance Minister replied that, in his view, "The job wasn't getting done."[87]

Downloading had apparently failed, in other words, as a means of shifting the costs of regional services to the property tax base. Nonetheless, by the time the period ended, there had been several important changes in financial arrangements for servicing the GTA. The provincial government had imposed tax pooling for some social services on Toronto and four suburban regions, and was requiring Toronto and the regions to share some of the costs of GO Transit (a service to which they had not contributed before 1997). In addition, the federal government had become a conspicuous presence in discussions about service financing for the first time since the early 1970s. Moreover, the province seemed more than willing to secure federal government help, although it still insisted that federal agencies should channel money through the province and not give it directly to local or regional governments.

The creation and mandate of the SuperBuild Corporation signified other important changes in the funding of GTA services. GTA municipalities, including the new City of Toronto, had to compete for infrastructure funds with municipal governments throughout Ontario, making it more difficult for them to make a case that they had unique needs. The government created a similarly competitive environment for GTA arts and community service organizations in the mandate it gave to the Trillium Foundation, which by 2002 was making grants totalling approximately $100 million a year.[88] Although these grants partly made up for cuts in provincial funding, the Foundation made them on

---

86. Richard Brennan, "Province fights traffic gridlock with $250 million for transit," *Toronto Star*, May 10, 2001; Ontario Ministry of Finance, "Ontario government has a plan to address gridlock," News release, May 14, 2001.

87. Jennifer Lewington and Richard Mackie, "Ontario to give transit $3-billion," *Globe and Mail*, September 28, 2001.

88. Ray Conlogue, "Shaking the old pros to the foundations: established arts groups are finding they simply don't meet the mandate of Ontario's Trillium Foundation," *Globe and Mail*, March 30, 2002.

an annual, one-time-only basis. Their purpose was to help community organizations become self-sufficient. This mandate made no distinction between organizations that served Toronto's resident and tourist populations and organizations that operated in small towns and rural communities. For example, large professional theatrical companies in the Toronto region had to compete for funds every year with amateur theatre groups in other parts of Ontario. Even if their grant applications were successful, the funds they received did not compensate for the provincial grants they had lost. Yet these organizations were becoming increasingly important to the Toronto economy.

SuperBuild and the Trillium Foundation shared another characteristic that distinguished them from earlier modes of providing urban services: governing boards that were appointed by the provincial premier's office and were therefore isolated from the provincial electorate and from provincial and local political processes. SuperBuild's board consisted of senior executives of large corporations, senior provincial civil servants, and private consultants.[89] It had no municipal representatives. The Trillium Foundation's 19-member board, according to one report, included 14 Conservative Party donors in 2000.[90] The government also appointed the volunteers who recommended how grants should be awarded in each of the province's 18 catchment areas.

The Conservative government's preference for having appointed boards administer public funds partly fulfilled its promise to reduce the role of government and increase the role of the private sector in the management of public services. Nonetheless, the premier's office and a few senior cabinet members approved all grant recommendations made by these authorities. The government also instructed these boards to encourage the organizations they dealt with to enter into financial partnerships with the private sector and to look for ways to pay all or more of their costs out of private donations and user fees. It did the same with other public institutions, such as hospitals and universities. In the case of Highway 407, it went further—giving private firms complete control of a facility that seemed likely to play a crucial role in shaping regional development and regional character.

What happened during this period, in short, was a substantial shift of financial control over regional infrastructure away from elected officials and toward appointed authorities and the provincial cabinet. Only time and the decisions of later governments would determine how lasting these changes in financing would be, and what effects they would have on the region, however its boundaries were defined.

---

89. Government of Ontario, "Ontario SuperBuild: About Us," Ontario government internet bulletin, February 27, 2004, site not longer operating.

90. Conlogue, "Shaking the old pros to the foundations," 2002, op. cit.

In the eyes of some of the government's critics, all policies adopted during this period were the actions of a government that was so blinded by ideology that it failed to recognize its responsibility for municipal and regional well-being. A change of government, they implied, would bring a change in approach. Not just ideology, however, but also politics influenced the way the Harris government made financial decisions. By instructing appointed boards to treat all parts of the province equally, it acknowledged the complaints of those parts of Ontario that had always felt that the Toronto region received too much provincial largesse. Moreover, the government was unable to ignore the preferences of a voting public that wanted it to tax less but spend more on health care and education. Putting money into regional infrastructure did not have the same political advantages as putting money into services that the population valued more highly.

Municipal governments also preferred to spend their money on the services that mattered most to their own taxpaying voters. While the GTSB was working on a regional transportation strategy, for example, municipal officials were pressuring the provincial and federal governments to fund new transit in their own communities, even if it would do little for the rest of the region. And, as will be discussed in a later section, municipal governments in the Toronto region disagreed about how they wanted the region to develop, and thus about what services they wanted and might be willing to help pay for. There was no guarantee, therefore, that the politics of regional financing would change if a different party took office.

Retreat from regional growth management

According to its proponents, regional growth management helps to keep down the costs of urban and regional services by limiting the extent of the territory needing to be serviced. This argument carried little weight with the Harris government, however, especially during its early years in office. Instead, the changes it made in the province's planning and land-use management systems were designed to remove constraints on private investors, including private land developers, as a way to promote "economic recovery by cutting red tape and getting rid of obstacles to growth."[91]

A MORE DEVELOPMENT-FRIENDLY PLANNING SYSTEM
In rewriting the *Planning Act* in 1996, the new government did away with the requirement for planning decisions to "be consistent with" provincial policies

---

91. Ontario Ministry of Municipal Affairs and Housing, "New Planning System Now the Law," News release, May 22, 1996.

and restored the "have regard to" principle that had been in place before 1993. The Conservative government also compressed all provincial policies into a single Provincial Policy Statement from which many restrictions on development and redevelopment had been removed.[92] The new planning process allowed municipal governments a shorter time in which to announce and hold public meetings and to process applications before the applicant could appeal to the Ontario Municipal Board. Applicants could also appeal to the OMB if a municipal council did not act on a request for a planning amendment within a stated period of time.

Changes in the planning system also gave municipal governments the right to adopt their own plans without seeking approval from the Ministry of Municipal Affairs and Housing or an upper-tier (regional or county) government. Thus they allowed the province to dismantle much of the planning approval apparatus that had evolved within the MMAH since the 1960s. The government also decreed that only the MMAH could appeal to the OMB on behalf of the province. Thus the changes strengthened the role of the OMB as the final arbiter of municipal land-use decisions.

The removal or reduction of restrictions on municipal planning and a weakened environmental assessment system met with cautious approval from the development industry, although some developers said the government had not gone far enough. Environmental groups, on the other hand, insisted that the government had gone much too far; that its actions would inevitably lead to environmental degradation and more urban sprawl. The government dismissed the latter arguments as the pleadings of "special interests," and thus irrelevant to its own agenda.[93] Nonetheless, the activities of these groups were partly responsible for a piece of legislation—the *Oak Ridges Moraine Conservation Act* of 2001—with considerable potential for shaping long-term growth patterns in the GTA's northern sectors.

A PARTIAL VICTORY FOR ENVIRONMENTAL PROTECTION

Passage of the *Oak Ridges Moraine Conservation Act* ended a prolonged political battle that had pitted environmental groups, rural property owners (including those who commuted to Toronto from rural residential estates), and anti-development politicians against private developers and pro-development municipal and provincial officials. At issue was a 160-kilometre strip of forested sand and gravel on the built-up edge of Toronto's northern suburbs. Those who lived near the moraine wanted to protect it as natural open space. The City of Toronto sided with environmentalists who argued that development on the moraine would contaminate waters flowing out of it toward Toronto.

---

92. Ontario Government 1997.
93. Walkom 1997, 414–415.

The province at first tried to distance itself from the fight, saying that it had given municipal governments the authority to protect their own critical environmental features. Affected municipal governments retorted that the OMB could always overturn their zoning decisions, and that they could not afford to buy land for the purpose of conserving it.[94] Planners and environmental groups pointed out that the moraine crossed nine regions and dozens of different jurisdictions, making it unlikely that municipal governments would adopt a cohesive strategy for protecting the land.[95] Only the province could do what was necessary.

The government, well aware of the political dangers of angering suburban voters who had helped to bring it to office, not only stepped in, but also took the OMB to court for refusing to hear the testimony of an expert witness on "how housing on the … [m]oraine would affect drinking water."[96] It was able to avert an expensive OMB hearing by working out an agreement among the parties involved, which became the basis for the *Oak Ridges Moraine Conservation Act.*[97] Developers agreed to confine their activities to designated "settlement areas," and to exchange their lands in the most environmentally sensitive parts of the moraine for provincially owned land elsewhere in the Toronto region. The government set up a foundation to raise funds for land acquisition, and donated $15 million and some land to get it started.

Although the agreement did not satisfy those who wanted the entire moraine protected from development, it did give the GTA a large outdoor recreation area and wildlife sanctuary in its rapidly growing northern sector. Moreover, the legislation included strong protections for "natural core and natural linkage destinations" covered by the plan, and established a public process for deciding whether other lands within the conservation area would be opened for development. What it did not do was establish a special Commission, as the *Niagara Escarpment Act* had done and environmentalists had asked for, to administer moraine lands and fight for their protection. Nor did the moraine legislation place an outer limit on urban sprawl. Because land to its south was filling up, development pressures were already moving further to its north,

94. Richard Mackie, "Ontario says it won't protect moraine," *Globe and Mail*, February 26, 2000; Wallace Immen, "Developers plan OMB appeal over Oak Ridges," *Globe and Mail*, March 17, 2000.

95. Wallace Immen, "Groups trying to drag province into moraine fight," *Globe and Mail*, March 9, 2000.

96. Gay Abbate, "Province wins case on moraine housing," *Globe and Mail*, February 22, 2001.

97. Ontario Ministry of Municipal Affairs and Housing, "Ontario Government Protects Moraine Water Resources and Natural Features," News release, November 1, 2001.

where they were likely to intensify if there was little or no change in the types of housing developers wanted to build and people wanted to live in.

REMOVING IMPEDIMENTS TO BROWNFIELDS DEVELOPMENT

The government adopted another piece of legislation, however, with the potential to encourage developers and municipalities to accommodate more growth on underused but already-serviced lands in the southern, urbanized part of the region. The *Brownfields Statute Law Amendment Act 2001* was designed to reduce legal and financial impediments to the redevelopment of vacant or underused commercial and industrial lands in built-up areas. Although these impediments had always existed, the Conservative government had made them more onerous soon after coming to office, first by giving municipal governments more responsibility for ensuring that provincial guidelines were adequately followed, and then by saying that it would no longer back up municipal decisions. These actions deterred both municipal governments and private landowners from trying to redevelop contaminated land.

The impetus for reconsidering brownfields policy came largely from the provincial bureaucracy, particularly staff members of the Ministry of Municipal Affairs and Housing. After consulting with municipalities, developers, and the public, reviewing practices and policies in 50 U.S. states, and compiling a series of "success stories," the ministry issued documents that emphasized the advantages of brownfields renewal for economic development, government finances, and the environment.[98] In other words, they recast what had earlier been an environmental cause into an economic one. They also pointed out that municipal governments already had several planning and financial tools that they could use either to encourage the remediation and reuse of contaminated properties or to do the work themselves.[99] What they needed was provincial assistance or encouragement.

The outcome of these efforts was legislation that gave municipalities and lenders more time to deal with brownfield sites, allowed the province and municipal governments to freeze taxes on eligible properties for negotiated periods, and partially protected those involved in brownfield redevelopment projects from future liability. Some liability issues remained, however, for later governments and the courts to resolve.

---

98. Interview with Lynnne Peterson, Ontario Ministry of Municipal Affairs and Housing, April 29, 2004.

99. See, for example, Ontario Ministry of Municipal Affairs and Housing, "Brownfields showcase: Realizing the environmental, economic and community building benefits of brownfields development," Summer 2000.

MADE-IN-ONTARIO "SMART GROWTH"

By the end of this six-year period, the government was linking both the Oak Ridges Moraine and the brownfields legislation to its emerging interest in promoting "smart growth," a term borrowed from American sources. Like the concepts of "regional planning" and "regional growth management" to which it was closely related, the "smart growth" concept attracted a variety of champions, ranging from those who wanted to slow down or stop suburban expansion altogether to those who simply wanted to reduce some of its costs or avoid some of its more harmful effects.[100] Ontario's government occupied the latter end of the spectrum. Although Premier Mike Harris linked the idea of "smart growth" to three broad principles ("a stronger economy, strong communities, and a healthy environment"), he created a Central Ontario Smart Growth Panel to "focus on finding working solutions for central Ontario's most urgent growth problems—gridlock and waste disposal."[101] The Panel was empowered to look at infrastructure needs in all of the Golden Horseshoe—a region that extended well beyond the boundaries of the GTA in all directions (Figure 6.1).

The Central Ontario Smart Growth Panel was the first of five such units put in place throughout Ontario. It consisted of provincially appointed members drawn from public and private organizations and the municipal sector, although municipal officials were not there to represent specific municipalities. Its job was to prepare a long-term vision for economic growth that included strategies to integrate local and regional services, protect "significant natural systems," and increase housing choice.[102] It was to report to the premier and cabinet through the Ministry of Municipal Affairs and Housing.

By folding both the Oak Ridges Moraine conservation strategy and the brownfields legislation into its "smart growth" initiative, the government made it difficult to determine whether it was looking for fundamental changes in the GTA's sprawling development pattern. Keeping urban development off the moraine implied either pushing it further north, and further away from Toronto, or persuading municipalities south of the moraine to accommodate a larger share of the region's population growth at higher densities. The brownfields legislation would aid the latter objective if it encouraged municipal governments to promote redevelopment of declining industrial areas for residential and commercial uses.

---

100. For an overview of the "smart growth" debate and its participants, see Downs 2001.

101. Ontario Ministry of Municipal Affairs and Housing, "Ontario's Growing Fast— Smart Growth will make it Last: Harris," News release, February 11, 2002.

102. Ontario Smart Growth Secretariat 2001.

Figure 6.1 Central Ontario Zone, Smart Growth Study Area, 2003

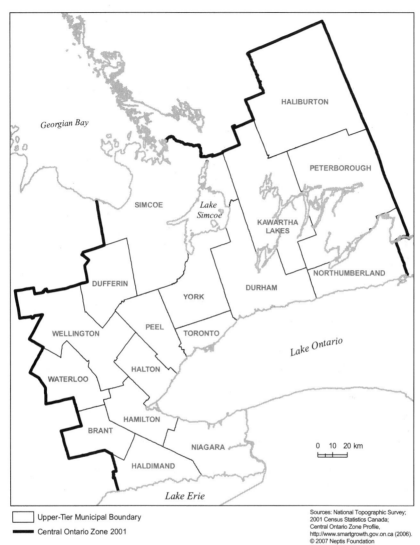

HALIBURTON

Georgian Bay

PETERBOROUGH

SIMCOE

Lake Simcoe

KAWARTHA LAKES

NORTHUMBERLAND

DUFFERIN

DURHAM

YORK

WELLINGTON

PEEL

TORONTO

Lake Ontario

HALTON

WATERLOO

HAMILTON

BRANT

NIAGARA

0 10 20 km

HALDIMAND

Lake Erie

☐ Upper-Tier Municipal Boundary

━━ Central Ontario Zone 2001

Sources: National Topographic Survey;
2001 Census Statistics Canada;
Central Ontario Zone Profile,
http://www.smartgrowth.gov.on.ca (2006).
© 2007 Neptis Foundation

Much of the onus for interpreting and implementing "smart growth" ideas fell on regional and municipal governments (which had had little direct involvement in developing the initiative or in establishing the Central Ontario Smart Growth Panel) and the Ontario Municipal Board. Several regional and municipal governments in the GTA had begun to plan more compact, transit-related, mixed-used districts even before "smart growth" became a provincial slogan, principally because they hoped to attract a larger share of the office and commercial development coming to the region. Others remained firmly wedded to conventional suburban development patterns, although a few of them were looking for ways to combine subdivision planning with measures to preserve environmentally sensitive areas.[103]

The municipality that took the strongest stand against urban sprawl during this period was the amalgamated City of Toronto, where planners worked on an Official Plan that built on the earlier plans of Metropolitan Toronto and its former municipalities. It designated 25 per cent of the city's area for intensive redevelopment.[104] For the plan to succeed, the city would have to accommodate 20 per cent of the GTA's population growth (or a minimum of 537,000 new residents) and 30 per cent of its employment growth over the next 30 years. Because the plan also committed the city to strengthening "the existing character of our neighbourhoods, ravines, valleys and ... open space system" that occupied the remaining 75 per cent of its territory, new development or redevelopment would have to occur in the downtown core, around sub-centres in the former suburbs, along arterial roads, and in aging employment districts.

In summary, the Toronto region entered the 21st century with a regional growth management system headed by a provincial government that equated growth management ("smart growth") with encouraging or supporting economic investment, a core city that hoped to increase its share of that growth without detracting from neighbourhood and environmental amenities, and a collection of regional and municipal plans indicating varying degrees of municipal interest in or commitment to growth management principles. Regional growth management, in other words, faced an uncertain future.

Reducing some intermunicipal inequities while adding others

Reducing inequalities among GTA municipalities was seldom given as a reason for changing Ontario's municipal policies after 1995. The emphasis was always on cutting costs. Nonetheless, this objective did appear in documents and discussions both before and after changes were announced. It also influenced the government to modify parts of its restructuring program. Because there were so many changes affecting so many aspects of municipal policy, however, the period had mixed results for intermunicipal equity in the GTA.

---

103. "Planning departments identify priorities," *GTA/905 Development News*, July 7 1999, 1–5.

104. Toronto Urban Development Services 2002, 1.

CENTRALIZED EDUCATION FUNDING AND ADMINISTRATION

The province's takeover of financial and administrative responsibility for public education implied greater equity in education funding, not just in the GTA, but in all of Ontario. In principle, the Ministry of Education would collect property taxes for education and redistribute them, together with provincial grants, among municipal school boards according to the size of the school populations and measures of special need. The change created two kinds of hardship for the new City of Toronto, however. Not only would it have to turn over a larger share of its commercial and industrial assessment to the province than would other provincial municipalities, but its own schools would be less well funded than they had been in the past. As a result, the province's takeover of education ushered in a period of intense political friction between a provincial government determined to make the Toronto District School Board cut costs, and local groups (school board trustees, teachers' unions, parents' organizations) intent on keep existing programs and facilities in place. The government's opponents contended that provincial regulations and provincial funding formulae failed to take account of the vast differences between school boards serving diverse populations and those that served more homogeneous communities. The cuts also forced local schools to impose or greatly increase charges for the use of school property or for non-classroom activities, thereby straining the budgets of community organizations that used the schools for their activities, or forcing them to eliminate programs altogether.

Political strife over issues of public school funding persisted to the end of the period, creating uncertainty about what government-imposed changes implied for the long-term quality and stability of Toronto's public school system. The province added to this uncertainty in 2001 when it announced a plan to give a tax rebate to parents who sent their children to private schools. (This controversial measure was repealed by the Liberal government that replaced the Conservatives in 2003.) What was clear, however, was that the ability of the region's public school system to deal with the challenges of rapid demographic and social change depended almost entirely on the decisions of the provincial Ministry of Education and the provincial cabinet.

RELUCTANT COST-SHARING

Metropolitan Toronto Council was one of only a few municipal governments in the GTA to support the pooling of municipal taxes for regional purposes. In its statement to the GTA Task Force, it argued that

> [t]he social costs and responsibilities of growth and change in the entire Toronto region, particularly with respect to the most disad-vantaged in society, must be shared. The fact that the poor may be

disproportionately concentrated in a few jurisdictions does not absolve other jurisdictions in Toronto from sharing the social burden. These poor belong to the entire urban region.[105]

It was partly on this basis that the Metro statement argued that the province should dissolve Metro and the four regional governments and replace them with a multi-purpose regional government for the southern, most urbanized part of the GTA (which then contained 90 per cent of the region's population). This unit, it said, should be responsible for all the services then being provided by Metro and the regional governments, and should be able to finance them out of a variety of revenue sources, including pooled local taxes. Such a tax pool, it went on, was "especially important for education, policing and community services" because it would contribute "to the long term health of the core" and prevent "the downward spiral of the more socio-economically depressed parts of the Toronto region."

Noting that the City of Toronto had already "suggested pulling out of the Metro tax pool," the Metro submission warned that the city was risking long-term difficulties for short-term benefit, in much the same way as OMB Commissioner Lorne Cumming had described Toronto's refusal to annex its suburbs as "short-sighted" in 1953. "If the City of Toronto found itself in financial difficulties," Metro argued, "it would be left like almost every inner city in the United States, spiralling downwards and wishing it could pool resources regionally."[106] Moreover, it added, "Once the tax pool has been eliminated and municipalities have been financially 'unbundled' from one another, it will be almost impossible to put them back together again."

The city was able to demand an end to tax pooling because it had fared so well under the Metro system. Not only did it still have a strong tax base, but many of those who benefited most from pooled services were now living in the suburbs, while older city neighbourhoods were undergoing a renaissance. Nonetheless, all of Metro's suburban mayors joined Toronto Mayor Barbara Hall in signing a proposal to the Ministry of Municipal Affairs and Housing (as their alternative to amalgamation) that included only a vague commitment to "maintain a system that shares our economic wealth in providing region-wide services,"[107] even though three of them represented communities that clearly benefited from tax pooling. Nor did the provincial government express

---

105. Metropolitan Toronto Council 1995, 6.

106. Ibid., 25.

107. Mayor Frank Faubert, Mayor Barbara Hall, Mayor Doug Holyday, Mayor Mel Lastman, Mayor Frances Nunziata, and Mayor Michael Prue. *Change for the Better. A Vision for the Future of our Communities; a Framework for Restructuring Local Government.* Toronto: City of Toronto Information Services, 1997, 3.

an interest in preserving equity in local service provision among its reasons for amalgamating Metro. One Conservative politician who did allude to the issue, however, was a member from Scarborough, one of Metro's tax-poor municipalities. Amalgamation, he said, "has nothing to do with the downtown core withering and dying and becoming a hole in the doughnut; it's the doughnut that's dissolving."[108]

Whatever the government's motives, Metropolitan Toronto's amalgamation undoubtedly led to more cost-sharing and service harmonization among its wealthier and poorer districts than its local municipalities would have agreed to among themselves. At the same time, it did not signify that the government was concerned with reducing intermunicipal inequalities in general. Such an interest was not present either in the mandate given to the GTSB, nor in the way the government wanted to fund services of region-wide importance. It was only after hearing vigorous objections on behalf of Toronto that it decided to pool social service costs across the GTA.

SOCIO-ECONOMIC POLARIZATION ON THE INCREASE

The government justified its tax pooling decision as a way to "avoid the problems that have plagued large urban areas in the United States—polarization into 'have' and 'have not' areas, and the hollowing out of the downtown core."[109] Other Conservative government policies seemed likely to increase social polarization, however. Shortly after taking office in 1995, the government reduced the size of welfare payments and other forms of assistance (including rent subsidies) and tightened eligibility requirements for welfare. At a time when poverty among recent immigrants was increasing, it also eliminated or cut back programs to assist immigrant settlement. It not only ended capital assistance for the construction of new low-rental housing, but it also replaced the *Landlord and Tenant Act* with legislation that made it easier for landlords to raise rents and evict tenants.[110] Its revised planning system restored the right of municipal governments to disallow accessory apartments in private homes. The government also removed specific targets for "affordable housing" from the Provincial Policy Statement, thereby

---

108. Steve Gilchrist, Conservative MPP for Scarborough East and Parliamentary Assistant to Minister of Municipal Affairs and Housing Al Leach, in "Megaforum," *Globe and Mail*, February 15, 1997.

109. Ontario Ministry of Municipal Affairs and Housing, "Cost Equalization in the GTA," Background information, August 6, 1997.

110. Linda Lapointe, "Options for Eviction Prevention," November 1998; Michael Mendelson, Andy Mitchell, and Mikael Swayze, "Trends in Poverty in the New City of Toronto," Background papers prepared for the Mayor's Homelessness Action Task Force, July 1998.

making it less likely that suburban municipalities would try to accommodate a larger share of the region's low-income households.

The new City of Toronto and Peel region were the only GTA municipalities to continue to support the creation of additional social housing, usually in the form of hostels or emergency shelters for homeless individuals. Decisions to open new hostels and shelters often met with vigorous community opposition, not only from neighbourhoods that had never had social housing, but also from those that claimed to have more than their "fair share." Housing proponents sometimes charged objectors with social elitism or racism (when immigrants were involved) but city councillors, even those holding left-wing views, could not ignore the preferences of middle-class homeowners if they wanted their votes.

By 2001, Toronto and Peel region had waived or reduced city-imposed charges on non-profit and private rental housing or provided other incentives to developers who produced it. These and other regional governments insisted, however, that they could not meet the demand for additional low-rental housing on their own, especially now that they had to bear the full costs of operating and maintaining the existing stock. They needed help from the federal and provincial governments.

For most of this period, the housing assistance available in Ontario took the form of rent supplements administered by city and regional social service departments as part of the welfare system. The Ontario government also helped to fund housing for people with mental illness or developmental disabilities. To stimulate private-sector activity, the province made public land available, offered tax incentives to developers willing to build affordable housing (and allowed municipalities to do the same), adopted measures to reduce "red-tape barriers" to the construction of rental units, and offered limited financial support for municipal housing initiatives.[111] It persuaded the federal government to recognize these programs, together with money spent by municipal governments and community groups, as Ontario's contributions to a new federal–provincial housing partnership announced by Ottawa in 2001.[112] There were signs, therefore, that a new period of low-rental housing construction might soon begin.

Growing spatial mismatch

Even as Metro and the City of Toronto absorbed a growing share of the region's poor households, many of them headed by immigrants, job oppor-

---

111. Ontario Ministry of Municipal Affairs and Housing, "Removing barriers to rental housing," News release, November 30, 2001.

112. "New National Housing Program," *Housing Again*, Bulletin #46, December 4, 2001.

tunities were increasing faster in the suburbs than in the urban core.[113] These trends highlighted the importance of a well-integrated regional public transit system that could move city residents to suburban jobs and bring suburban residents into the city. GTA-wide transit integration remained an elusive goal, however, although York region made some progress toward integrating its own transit systems. GTA residents without a car remained seriously disadvantaged if they needed to travel across municipal boundaries to work or attend classes.

Little support for a regional voice

Strengthening the Toronto region's ability to participate in national and international affairs, or even to look after its own needs, was seldom an explicit objective in Ontario government policy statements or legislation during this period. For the Toronto region to have a unified voice in the development of regional policies, therefore, it had to have an organization that could persuade municipal politicians of the benefits of unity. The only organization that might have done so was the Greater Toronto Services Board, and the province had ended that possibility when it took back operating responsibility for GO Transit in May 2001. The new GO Transit Board of Directors that replaced the GTSB included members from municipalities well outside the GTA boundary. Many of them were former municipal officials with some business experience. There was only one City of Toronto representative on the Board.

There were two contradictory explanations for the GTSB's demise, both suggested by people who were closely associated with it. The first came from former GTSB Chair Alan Tonks and former Executive Director Lynn Morrow. They maintained that the GTSB became a threat to the province's ability to control events as soon as it showed signs of success in building regional consciousness and formulating policy positions.[114] As evidence of the GTSB's growing effectiveness, they cited its approval of a regional transportation strategy and the willingness of local and regional politicians to take a co-operative approach to protecting the Oak Ridges Moraine. They also credited the organization with making municipal representatives more aware of the particular problems of the City of Toronto and of the region's smaller, more rural municipalities. Out of this awareness came a decision to sponsor work on a Countryside Strategy to preserve the character of rural municipalities and protect them from urban development. Thus, according to

---

113. James Rusk, "The business of taxing office towers," *Globe and Mail*, January 21, 2002.

114. Interview with Alan Tonks, January 23, 2002; Interview with Lynn Morrow, February 28, 2003.

its defenders, the GTSB had evolved to a point where the province either had to empower it to move forward or take back responsibility for managing the region itself. The province chose to do the latter.

The opposing explanation, suggested by the GTSB's critics in various media reports, was that the GTSB had moved too slowly to resolve critical issues, and had lost provincial support as a result. This explanation focused on those matters on which the Board had not taken action, or about which its members could not agree. Although the Board was able to reach consensus on the need for a regional transportation strategy, for example, it voted down a proposal by a Toronto councillor to link that strategy to a regional land-use plan.[115] Raising money for GTSB activities (whether legally mandated or proposed by Board members) was also a persistent source of dissension. For its first year, the GTSB was largely funded by the province, because Board members did not want to contribute to it. From then on, municipal representatives typically turned down initiatives that would have required larger contributions from their councils and taxpayers.

The most divisive financial issue was tax-pooling for social services and regional transit. Politicians in the regional municipalities argued that they should not have to contribute to city services over which they had no control. Toronto's mayor, never a supporter of the GTSB, objected just as strongly to a provincially imposed formula that assigned half the costs of the GO Transit commuter system to the city.[116] The city did not need the commuter system, he said, because suburban commuters could transfer to TTC vehicles at city boundaries.

There was one GTA-wide initiative, however, that did bring local politicians together for a narrowly defined purpose. The Greater Toronto Marketing Alliance emerged in 1997 out of discussions among staff members of the Office for the Greater Toronto Area, municipal mayors and economic development officers, and members of the Toronto Board of Trade and local Chambers of Commerce. Its aim was to attract new, mainly international, investment to the GTA by marketing the region abroad and acting as a central contact for potential investors. It kept a low profile and always insisted that it was there to provide support for municipal economic development offices, not to usurp their role. It did not associate itself with the GTSB and continued to exist after the GTSB was dissolved. What it indicated was that the region's local politicians were able to work together if they believed their own communities might benefit from their doing so, or might be disadvantaged if they stayed away.

---

115. Jennifer Lewington, "Political sparring set aside to get transit moving," *Globe and Mail*, July 1, 2000.

116. James Rusk, "Changes to GO anger Lastman," *Globe and Mail*, May 27, 1998.

THE ROOTS OF REGIONAL DISUNITY

Divisions within the GTSB, especially when local tax dollars were at stake, arose partly from anxiety about the consequences of downloading for municipal budgets and partly from an absence of that sense of interdependence and common destiny that infuses writings on city-region issues. They showed that politicians in the Toronto region fell roughly into four camps, each having a distinct set of interests and aspirations that diverged from those of other sectors.

Only one of the four came out clearly in favour of taking a coordinated approach to GTA-wide issues, particularly transportation, while still opposing the creation of a strong regional government. It consisted of representatives of large, rapidly growing suburban municipalities and was headed by Mississauga Mayor Hazel McCallion, a long-time foe of the regional municipalities created in the 1970s. This group wanted the province to eliminate the regional municipalities, reduce the number of local municipalities in the suburban ring by consolidating them into a few large units, and give a restructured GTSB the authority to establish policies, set service standards (including standards for tax pooling), and coordinate (but not provide) municipal infrastructure. This model for GTA governance was similar to the one proposed by Special Advisor Milt Farrow in 1997, but it was not one to which other municipal governments subscribed.

The second group consisted of representatives of small towns and rural areas who were anxious to preserve a way of life threatened by the relentless expansion of suburban development. For some, that way of life was primarily agricultural; for others it meant large homes on estate lots or renovated homes in carefully preserved rural villages, far removed from the densely settled urban core. Members of this group were strongly against giving the GTSB (or any other regional organization) powers like those granted to Metro in the 1950s, which they blamed for Metro's evolution into one large and undifferentiated city. According to the GTSB's first chair, the organization was able to make members of this group the "most supportive" members of the GTSB by emphasizing a need to focus on "sustainable development" in its Countryside Strategy.[117] Representatives of smaller municipalities were also more likely to favour the retention of regional governments than were representatives of the larger suburban cities.

Those who worked for regional governments made up the third group. They had little reason to support the GTSB or any other GTA-wide organization because of the widespread assumption that any GTA-wide organization

---

117. Interview with Alan Tonks, January 23, 2003.

with meaningful responsibilities would bring an end to the regional units, and therefore to their jobs.

Finally, there was the new City of Toronto, which constituted a fourth group on its own, and one that many other GTA politicians regarded warily. Before amalgamation, the larger municipalities outside Metro had viewed the old core city as an almost equal match in the competition for population and jobs. With amalgamation, the core city became a monolithic unit of 2.4 million people, more than four times the size of the City of Mississauga, its largest suburban rival. The province added to fears of Toronto domination when it asked Alan Tonks, a former Metro Toronto chair, to chair the GTSB. Provincially imposed tax pooling for social services had the same effect. An interest in offsetting Toronto's power was one reason why the mayors of large suburbs tried to convince the government to consolidate suburban governments and strengthen the GTSB, something the province decided not to do.[118]

Toronto's lack of interest in the GTSB was not surprising, given that the new City Council and the GTSB got under way at about the same time. For its first few years, Toronto's Council had to grapple with the challenges of harmonizing local services and developing a budget in a fiscally constrained environment.[119] It was also embroiled in persistent squabbling among former city and suburban councillors, and headed by a mayor who thought that municipalities outside Toronto had nothing in common with the city and no understanding of its needs.[120]

*A brief retrospective: From disentanglement
to re-entanglement in only five years*

The vision of the provincial–municipal relationship underlying changes in Ontario's municipal policies in the later 1990s adhered in some respects to the principles of *disentanglement* and *subsidiarity* discussed in Chapter 5. The rewriting of the *Municipal Act*, at least as the government first presented it, was intended to enshrine that vision in provincial law.[121] The structure and mandate of the Greater Toronto Services Board were also compatible with the vision. They implied that regional or local governments would provide virtually all the services needed to support population and economic growth in the

118. James Rusk, "Province plans to stop forcing cities to merge," *Globe and Mail*, February 8, 2001.

119. The services were public health, public libraries, land-use planning, public works, fire fighting, and parks and recreation.

120. James Rusk, "Lastman critical of city's neighbours," *Globe and Mail*, Friday, May 18, 2001.

121. Ontario Ministry of Municipal Affairs and Housing 1996.

GTA. It was up to the GTSB to persuade these governments to recognize the regional significance of their decisions, coordinate their activities to achieve GTA-wide goals, and negotiate cost-sharing arrangements.

Even at the beginning, however, municipal restructuring did not adhere strictly to the principles of disentanglement. For example, the Conservative government ignored the argument that senior governments should assume full financial responsibility for services that redistributed income and pay for them out of income taxes, not municipal property taxes. It also limited municipal discretion by issuing or strengthening administrative regulations and guidelines for general welfare assistance, public health, and other services, and by placing constraints on the ability of municipal governments to raise more money themselves.

In the process of revising the *Municipal Act*, the government shifted its focus away from promoting municipal autonomy and flexibility toward ensuring municipal accountability and financial prudence. Its initial proposals included "health, safety, protection, and the well being of people" and "the natural environment," among the spheres of jurisdiction for which it planned to give municipal governments broad authority. The version of the act that went to the legislature in 2001, however, declared the "natural environment, health, safety and nuisance" to be "matters ... of significant provincial as well as local interest," which therefore called for detailed provincial regulation.[122] Municipal governments gained increased powers to regulate those activities that pertained strictly to the physical character of their communities, but only as long as their actions did not conflict with provincial laws. Clearly, the province had decided that it wanted to remain in control of the municipal sector.

Changes to the municipal restructuring program between 1996 and 2001 were reactions to concerns raised by diverse interests, including municipal officials, the business community (such as the Toronto Board of Trade, property development and real estate interests, and the owners of small businesses), members of the government's own party, senior government staff, external advisors, the staff of provincial and local service agencies and their clients, and community and environmental groups. In many cases, these were not groups that the government had looked to for advice; in fact it had emphasized on taking office that it intended to distance itself from the "special interests" that had influenced the policies of earlier governments. Environmentalists and social activists were high on its list of those whose opinions it did not welcome. Nonetheless, the government could not safely ignore the concerns of these or any other groups if they overlapped with the concerns of the voters who

---

122. Ontario Ministry of Municipal Affairs and Housing, "A New *Municipal Act* for Ontario," Backgrounder, October 18, 2001.

had brought them to office or the municipal officials whose co-operation they sought.

Some of the consequences of municipal government restructuring may also have persuaded provincial politicians to question the wisdom of giving municipal governments more responsibility for key services. For example, in 2000 a serious outbreak of illness caused by E. coli contamination of the water supply in the small town of Walkerton, in southwestern Ontario, not only raised questions about the competence of local officials, but also of the provincial government, which had given them responsibility for monitoring water quality.[123] And the GTSB's unwillingness to tackle the Toronto region's transportation needs without large financial commitments from senior governments implied that municipalities would not or could not take on responsibilities that were important to the provincial economy. Not to be overlooked was an increase in provincial revenues after 1998 that allowed the government to be a little more generous with municipalities.[124]

Apart from the amalgamation of Metropolitan Toronto, however, the upheavals of the late 1990s left institutional arrangements for governing the Toronto region remarkably unchanged. After reducing the number of lower-tier municipalities from 815 to 447,[125] the government decided that the benefits of amalgamating local governments were no longer worth the associated political costs.[126] Further amalgamations would go ahead, it said, only if municipal governments asked for them.

The decision to end restructuring seemed intended mainly to allay the fears of local politicians in the GTA's four suburban regional municipalities, where the Conservatives had strong electoral support, but where restructuring proposals had become matters of intense political debate.[127] The government brought an end to the GTSB only a few weeks later. It also shut down the Office for the Greater Toronto Area and transferred its staff to the Central Ontario Smart Growth Panel, which reported directly to the province. The GTA had essentially ceased to exist as an entity recognized in provincial law or policy documents.

123. "Scathing words for Ontario's government," *Maclean's,* January 28, 2002, 16.

124. James Rusk, "High revenue brings Ontario's deficit in below projection," *Globe and Mail,* February 11, 1998.

125. Ontario Ministry of Municipal Affairs and Housing, "New municipalities mean better government for Ontario's taxpayers," News release, January 2, 2001.

126. James Rusk, "Province plans to stop forcing cities to merge," *Globe and Mail,* February 8, 2001.

127. Wallace Immen, "Durham area communities resist amalgamation push," *Globe and Mail,* October 12, 1999; Jennifer Lewington, "Talk of merger stirs up emotions in communities." *Globe and Mail,* March 13, 2000; "Restructuring study stokes fiery debate at Vaughan meeting," *Globe and Mail,* March 17, 2000.

Whatever its reasons for changing its policies, the provincial government was still as involved in municipal affairs in 2003 as it had been when it took office eight years earlier. Where regional governance was concerned, its involvement was almost total. Nonetheless, governance arrangements for the Toronto region (however defined) remained fragmented among a disparate collection of provincial agencies, municipal governments, and special-purpose bodies serving jurisdictions of widely varying sizes and characteristics (Figure 6.2). This bewildering assortment of decision-makers would take the region into the 21st century.

Figure 6.2 Toronto region governance, 2001[a]

Function	Ontario government	Toronto Region (GTA or larger)	Regional Municipalities	Municipalities	Intergovernmental
Economic Development	**Ontario SuperBuild Corporation**[b]	**Greater Toronto Area Marketing Alliance** (municipal government & private sector)	Durham Economic Development and Tourism Dept.; Halton Business Development Department	Toronto Economic Development, Culture and Tourism Department; Municipal Economic Development or Planning and Development Departments; **Toronto Economic Development Corporation**; **Mississauga Economic Development Board**	**Moving the Economy** (Toronto, federal government, and non-profit sector)
Education	Ministry of Education		**Public and Separate school boards**	**Toronto District School Board**; **Toronto Separate School Board**	
Finance	**Ontario Property Assessment Corporation**		Departments of Treasury and/or Finance	Toronto and other municipal departments of Finance or Treasury	
Housing			**Regional Housing Authorities**; **Peel Living**; **Housing York Inc.**	Toronto Community and Social Services Department; **Toronto Community Housing Corporation**	
Infrastructure	**OntarioSuperBuild Corporation**; **Ontario Clean Water Agency**		Works or Environmental Services Departments	Toronto Works and Emergency Services; Municipal Works, Engineering, and/or Environmental departments	

Function	Ontario government	Toronto Region (GTA or larger)	Regional Municipalities	Municipalities	Intergovernmental
Libraries				Municipal Departments and/or **Public Library Boards**	
Parks	Ministry of Natural Resources (provincial parks)	**Toronto and regional Conservation Authorities**[c]		Toronto Economic Development, Culture and Tourism Department; other municipal Parks or Parks and Recreation departments	**Harbourfront Corporation**
Planning/Land Use	Ministry of Municipal Affairs and Housing (Policy Statements) **Ontario Municipal Board** **Ontario Realty Corporation**		Planning or Planning and Development departments	Toronto Urban Development Services Department; other municipal Planning or Planning and Development departments	**Central Ontario Smart Growth Panel** (provincial, municipal, private sector) **Harbourfront Corporation** **Toronto Harbour Commission** **Toronto Waterfront Revitalization Corporation**
Protection	**Ontario Provincial Police**			Toronto Works and Emergency Services Department; municipal fire departments	**Police Services Boards** (province and City of Toronto or regional governments)

Function	Ontario government	Toronto Region (GTA or larger)	Regional Municipalities	Municipalities	Intergovernmental
Public Health	Ministry of Health and Long Term Care		Departments or **Boards of Health**	Toronto Department of Community and Neighbourhood Services; **Toronto Board of Health**	
Social and Community	Ministry of Community and Social Services (GTA tax-pooling arrangements); **Children's Aid Societies**		Departments of Social or Community and Social Services	Toronto Department of Community and Neighbourhood Services	
Transportation	Ontario Ministry of Transportation		Public Works or Environmental Services departments	Toronto Works and Emergency Services Department; municipal Works, Engineering or Transportation departments; **Toronto Transit Commission**	**GO Transit Board of Directors** (Ontario government; Toronto, four regional municipalities); **Greater Toronto Airports Authority** (Toronto, four regional municipalities; Ontario government; federal government)

a. This figure includes only those departments and agencies engaged in activities of particular importance to regional development and well-being. As interpreters and administrators of provincial laws, provincial departments influenced the content and delivery of all services provided to municipal populations. This figure shows, moreover, that many provincial agencies were still directly involved in GTA governance in 2001 despite the changes made by the province in the name of disentanglement. It also shows the increasing use being made of special-purpose bodies. The inclusion of Economic Development, a function not found in Figures 2.2 and 4.2, recognizes the importance that municipal governments now attached to this activity.

b. All units in bold type were special-purpose bodies. Regional and City of Toronto school boards differed from other special-purpose bodies in being directly elected by local voters. Members of other special-purpose bodies were appointed by regional or municipal councils, and sometimes by the provincial and/or federal governments.

c. Boundaries of Conservation Areas did not coincide with regional government boundaries.

Sources: Canadian Urban Institute, "Inventory of Existing Government Structures in the Greater Toronto Area," a report prepared for the GTA Task Force, 1995; Government Internet sites.

SEVEN

Fifty Years of Regional Governance under Provincial Stewardship

This study has looked at the evolution of governance in the Toronto city-region from 1924 to 2003. In it, "governance" has been used to mean more than "government," a word reserved for a set of institutions with legal authority to make and implement policies for a defined territory (a national, state, or provincial government, for example). As used here, the term "regional governance" encompasses the many institutions and public policies used by one or more governments to address issues related to population growth and territorial expansion in a large city-region over an extended period.

Of the many issues that may arise as a city-region expands, the ones that are most likely to generate calls for government action are the rate at which new territory is absorbed on the urban fringe, rapid changes in the physical and socio-demographic characteristics of different parts of the region (particularly its urban core), and changes in the magnitude and the distribution of different types of social need. For that reason, this study has focused principally on arrangements for providing three types of services: (1) basic infrastructure to support population and economic growth, particularly water supply, sewage treatment, waste disposal, and transportation facilities; (2) strategies to plan or manage spatial organization and outward expansion; and (3) services that affect the ability of a city-region's less affluent residents to participate in its economic and community life (social housing, public education, local public transit, and social and community services).

For regional governance to have lasting and influential consequences, it must be linked to a government with the authority either to empower institutions to act on regional issues or to do so itself. Although four levels of government (federal, provincial, metropolitan/regional, municipal) influenced the development and character of the Toronto region during the period covered by this study, only the Government of Ontario was able both to decide how regional issues would be addressed and to make its decisions legally binding. This is because the Ontario government, like all of Canada's provincial governments, has constitutional responsibility for "municipal institutions" and for the powers and revenue sources it assigns to them.

First and foremost, then, this has been a study of Ontario government policies for Canada's largest city-region; it has not been a study of a government created specifically to preside over that region. The Toronto region did have such a government during part of the study period—that of the federated Municipality of Metropolitan Toronto (Metro) created in 1953—but its importance to regional governance steadily declined as urban settlement spread beyond Metro's boundaries. As early as 1962, in fact, the Ontario government was beginning to find other ways to deal with issues related to regional expansion. In 1997 it ended the metropolitan government experiment entirely by consolidating Metropolitan Toronto institutions with those of Metro's six lower-tier municipalities to form a new, greatly enlarged City of Toronto, which by then had less than half the population of the much larger region surrounding it.[1]

Different approaches to regional governance often overlapped, however, which meant that governance arrangements in the region became increasingly fragmented and complex as the period wore on. Moreover, a noteworthy feature of the period were the many changes that occurred in the way the Toronto region was defined (Figure 7.1). Regional boundaries changed not only in response to trends in regional development, but also according to changes in the composition and priorities of the provincial government. In fact, it was not unusual for provincial agencies to work with more than one definition of the region at the same time. Metropolitan Toronto coexisted with a much larger Metropolitan Toronto Planning Area (MTPA) for nearly 20 years, and the MTPA coexisted with a provincially organized Metropolitan Toronto and Region Transportation Study (MTARTS) between 1962 and 1967. From the mid-1980s onward, most provincial agencies were focusing on a Greater Toronto Area (GTA) made up of Metropolitan Toronto and four two-tier regional municipalities (Durham, Halton, Peel and York) containing 30 lower-tier municipalities. The Ministry of Transportation, however, added a sixth regional municipality (Hamilton-Wentworth) to its definition (GTA+H), bringing the total number of regional and local municipalities to 37. At the end of the period, a Central Ontario Smart Growth Panel was looking for ways to address transportation and waste management for an area of southern Ontario containing 99 single-tier and 17 two-tier (regional and county) municipal units. This Central Ontario Smart Growth Zone covered nearly five times as much territory as GTA+H. Moreover, all of the province's definitions of the Toronto region differed from the way Statistics Canada defined the Toronto Census Metropolitan Area (CMA) for data-gathering purposes.

---

1. Because the region was being defined in several ways, it is impossible to be more precise about the new city's relative position within it.

Figure 7.1 Alternative definitions of the Toronto city-region, 1953–2003

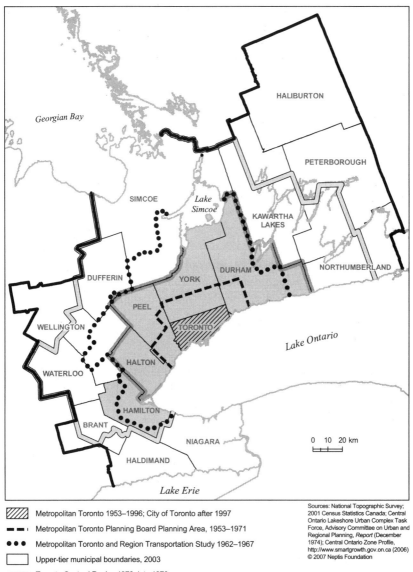

Metropolitan Toronto 1953–1996; City of Toronto after 1997

Metropolitan Toronto Planning Board Planning Area, 1953–1971

Metropolitan Toronto and Region Transportation Study 1962–1967

Upper-tier municipal boundaries, 2003

Toronto-Centred Region 1970–late 1970s

Greater Toronto Area, mid-1980s

Greater Toronto Area plus Hamilton-Wentworth, mid-1980s–2001

Central Ontario Zone 2001–2003

In addition to looking at the institutional characteristics of governance in the Toronto region at successive stages of its development, this study examined the political and financial dimensions of institutional arrangements and institutional restructuring. A city-region typically consists of many different units (municipal councils and school boards, appointed boards or commissions, and professional, community, and public service organizations) whose interests and responsibilities may be affected by actual or proposed changes in arrangements for providing regional services and managing regional development. Choosing a mode of governance for such a region, therefore, involves more than creating new institutions or assigning tasks to those that already exist. It also means deciding which units and community interests will have greatest influence on regional development and character, or trying to work out compromises among competing viewpoints. The Ontario government found these tasks increasingly difficult and politically more hazardous as the Toronto region expanded and its population became more socially and ethnically diverse.

The financial challenges of regional governance also increased as the region grew. Throughout the period, the Toronto region played a pivotal role in both the national and the provincial economies, making its well-being a matter of considerable interest to senior governments. At the same time, its persistent growth generated relentless demands for new or expanded public services. Finding ways to pay for those services was not just one among several challenges confronting the Ontario government; it was the one that most often prompted provincial officials to acknowledge that regional problems existed and then to look for ways to address them.

Even though the Ontario government experimented with different modes of regional governance and regional finance for more than half a century, the Toronto region still faced serious challenges in 2001. This study provides a historical context for understanding the nature of those challenges, evaluating the different ways in which similar challenges were addressed in the past, and understanding the consequences of past responses for the region's spatial and social character.

Because the Toronto region is often compared (both positively and negatively) to city-regions in the United States, the study also pointed out some similarities and differences between approaches taken to governance in the Toronto region and approaches that are regarded as typical of city-region governance in most of the U.S. For the study period as a whole, the most obvious difference in modes of city-region governance was the fact that the Ontario government never surrendered any of its powers to shape the region either to the federal government or to municipal governments, as state governments did at various times in their history. In fact, it exercised its right to create and re-create municipal institutions in ways that many state governments had made legally impossible before the period began. It also maintained full control over legal arrangements for municipal administration and finance, sometimes down to the smallest details.

Despite the difference in legal context, however, Toronto region governance evolved in a way that was similar to the way governance had evolved in most large U.S. city-regions. It began in the early years of Toronto-related expansion with the annexation of suburban districts to the core city. The City of Toronto Council turned against this approach in 1912, however, because it did not want to pay the extra costs of extending services to newer districts. Little changed until 1953, when the Ontario government united the area's 13 municipalities into a metropolitan federation and empowered its institutions (the Metropolitan Toronto Council, the Metropolitan Toronto School Board, and the Toronto Transit Commission) to provide selected services for all of the territory most immediately affected by Toronto-related growth.

As the region continued to expand, the province used more specialized or geographically limited arrangements (such as provincial departments or agencies, special-purpose authorities, and two-tier regional governments) to provide services to different geographic versions or different sectors of the region. By the end of the period, it was relying heavily on intergovernmental or public–private forums to define and assign priority to regional issues and advise governments what to do about them. It was also looking to the private sector to pay for services it had previously financed either on its own or in partnership with local governments.

Institutional arrangements, however, are not the only important characteristic of regional governance. Just as important is what institutions are able to do for the region and its residents. Consequently, the study examined the ways in which different modes of regional problem solving dealt with five objectives (referred to collectively in this work as "the regional agenda") that often appear in campaigns for regional governance reform: (1) to provide infrastructure to support population and economic growth; (2) to control or minimize the costs of providing regional services; (3) to manage or contain territorial expansion; (4) to equalize the distribution of regional costs and benefits among the municipalities included in the region; and (5) to give local officials a stronger, more effective voice in the formation and implementation of regional policies. The next section summarizes how these objectives fared over the period covered by the study.

Assessing the Results of Provincial Stewardship for the Regional Agenda

Providing infrastructure to support regional economic growth

An interest in sustaining or promoting economic growth was the catalyst for most of the changes made by the Ontario government in its own and in local arrangements for regional policy-making. Of all those changes, the most effective at providing growth-supportive infrastructure was the government of Metropolitan Toronto (Metro) in its early years. Metro owed its successes to its clear legal mandate, its authority to borrow money for its own and local capital investments, its assured access to a pool of local tax revenues, and determined local leadership. It also benefited from a widespread consensus that all parts of the region would benefit from the services it provided.

Provincial agencies were also effective infrastructure providers after they became directly involved in delivering regional services in the 1960s. So were the governments of two-tier regional municipalities created outside Metro between 1969 and 1974, various special-purpose authorities, and private corporations— as long as the province gave them money or the authority to raise money to do their jobs. The least effective approach to regional governance was to ask the region's municipal governments to work out mutually acceptable strategies for improving regional services. The times when the province relied heavily on this consultative approach were times when little got done and problems tended to multiply, eventually pushing the province to take action itself. Nonetheless this approach became the government's preferred and sometimes only way of dealing with regional issues after the mid-1970s.

The reasons why intergovernmental consultation was an ineffective approach to regional governance were the same as the reasons why the provincial government hesitated to exercise its own authority more vigorously. Finding solutions to regional problems often implied finding ways to raise a good deal of money to pay for them, a challenge that neither the provincial nor local governments tackled with much enthusiasm. Moreover, the process of choosing among alternative ways to address regional issues often aroused intense differences of opinion among municipal governments and community groups with stakes in the outcomes. These differences of opinion not only stood in the way of intermunicipal agreement, but they also implied political hazards for any provincial government that decided to intervene. Although it was easier for provincial and local politicians to agree about the need for new infrastructure than about other regional objectives, even proposals to build new infrastructure often became the subject of heated controversy.

TRANSPORTATION

Inadequacies in the region's transportation system were usually the first regional problems to attract widespread attention and then to spur the province to take action. A prominent issue in transportation debates was the appropriate allocation of funds between roads and public transit. Metropolitan Toronto Council resolved this debate in 1964 by approving a so-called "balanced" plan that favoured the construction of major highways to support the growth of suburban districts while giving transit an important role in the heavily populated urban core. Over the next decade, however, the tide gradually turned in favour of transit. Financial help from the metropolitan and provincial governments allowed the TTC to extend subway lines into Metro's three outer municipalities (Scarborough, North York, and Etobicoke). By 1974 the TTC was operating one of the most successful transit systems in North America in terms of ridership and cost recovery. Meanwhile, community opposition in Toronto had brought the construction of urban highways to a stop, and Metro Toronto planners were working on a plan for an urban structure featuring compact clusters of development in five of Metro's six municipalities, all of which would be linked by rapid transit.

At the regional scale, the provincial government instituted the Government of Ontario (GO) rail and bus commuter system in 1967 and assumed responsibility for all its capital and operating deficits. In 1970, it adopted a regional planning strategy to channel new development in the southern part of the Toronto region into clearly defined, transit-connected communities. Over the next two years it began to share the capital and operating costs of local transit systems, including the TTC, with municipal governments.

The results of provincial and municipal subsidies were disappointing. Automobile use continued to increase more rapidly than population in all parts of the region. At the same time, transit use failed to keep up with population growth, falling from 16 per cent to 12 per cent of all trips between 1986 and 1996 alone.[2] Even in Metropolitan Toronto, TTC ridership fell from 25 per cent to 22 per cent of Metro's daily trips during that period, despite an increase of nearly 200,000 persons in Metro's population. Ridership on GO Transit increased, but still accounted for only 1 per cent of total trips in the region during this 10-year period.

The gradual but apparently relentless ascendancy of automobile over transit travel followed a trend occurring throughout North America. Some explanations for this trend, such as a decline in transit use among women

---

2. Figures derived from University of Toronto Joint Program in Transportation, *The Transportation Tomorrow Survey 1986, 1996 and 2001, Summaries of the GTA*, online at: http://www.jpint.utoronto.ca/GTA.html.

and increased use of automobiles for home-to-school trips, had nothing to do with regional governance.[3] Also implicated, however, were the land-use and transportation policies of senior and local governments, which seldom assigned transit an important role in building or strengthening local and regional economies, or in serving other objectives, such as ensuring GTA-wide mobility for people without cars.

Only in Metropolitan Toronto was transit linked to economic development objectives for most of the period. Early in Metro's history, transit officials and Metro planners had justified subway construction as a way to bring suburban commuters to downtown Toronto and relieve severe traffic congestion on inner-city streets. Metro planners promoted new rapid transit lines in the 1970s as support for the development of suburban office and commercial sub-centres. GO Transit was established to bring commuters into downtown Toronto, a role reinforced by special provincial subsidies to local bus companies that carried riders to and from GO terminals. Not until late in the period did some provincial and local officials begin to regard GO and suburban transit systems as potential aids to the building of suburban economies.

The primary purpose of the Toronto region's transit systems, therefore, was to help maintain the urban core as the focal point of the regional economy. As the region expanded and economic activities gradually decentralized, transit's usefulness to the economy became less obvious and therefore less appreciated. Typically, suburban jobs were widely dispersed among relatively low-density office and industrial parks, making them difficult to serve by public transit. The regional economy also came to rely increasingly on road transport for commercial purposes (for just-in-time delivery, for example). Moreover, the automobile industry was always "a key component of the manufacturing sector" in the Toronto region,[4] and its importance increased after Canada signed an automobile trade agreement with the United States in 1965.

Low and declining transit use, particularly in the suburbs, apparently persuaded the Conservative government that it could end all forms of support for both local and regional transit systems in the late 1990s without jeopardizing its pledge to "generate economic growth and investment in Ontario."[5] Only four years later, that same government renewed support for some types of GO and local transit services, after it was warned that increasing highway congestion was threatening the GTA's economic potential. Thus, the question of whether government policy should emphasize roads or transit was still being framed almost entirely in economic development terms. Nonetheless, a

3. Miller and Shalaby 2000, 84–87.
4. GTA Task Force 1996, 50.
5. Ontario Progressive Conservative Party, "The Common Sense Revolution," Pamphlet, 1994, 3.

growing public recognition of the close link between transportation and land use (see "Managing Regional Growth," below) was also making urban transportation policy an important target of environmentalists looking for ways to combat urban sprawl. Environmentalists were also major players in political disputes about how to handle two other pressures for infrastructure improvements: the growing difficulty of disposing of solid waste, and the declining capacity of the region's trunk sewer systems.

SOLID WASTE MANAGEMENT

Solid waste management became a regional rather than a local function after 1966, when the province shifted it from local governments to the restructured Metropolitan Toronto and to the regional governments created between 1969 and 1974. Metro Council was able to avoid conflict with its municipal members by disposing of solid waste at sites in the lightly populated outer-ring suburbs within the Metropolitan Toronto planning area, as long as those sites had been approved by the relevant municipal councils or, failing that, by the Ontario Municipal Board (OMB).[6] By the 1980s, however, these waste disposal sites were approaching capacity, and vacant land in the suburban regions was rapidly disappearing. Moreover, Metro no longer had any planning control over the outer districts. A sense of urgency began to build, and from the late 1980s onward, provincial and metropolitan/regional governments engaged in expensive and time-consuming efforts to deal with the problem.

Strong political opposition persuaded governments to back away from the three options they most preferred: opening new waste disposal sites within the region; trucking waste to Northern Ontario for burial in an abandoned mine; and burning it in incinerators. Instead the City of Toronto opted for two costly alternatives: shipping solid waste to a disposal site in the State of Michigan, a practice that made the city vulnerable to political decisions in another country, and an ambitious program to recycle (or divert to other uses) virtually all its solid waste by 2010.[7]

TRUNK SEWER AND WATER FACILITIES

The institutions created by the provincial government to increase water and sewage capacity in the Toronto region were more effective in some sectors than others in keeping up with development pressures at the edge of the region. Peel region still had unused capacity at the end of the period, but growth pressures were increasing in neighbouring Halton, which had not been included in

---

6. Kaplan 1982, 698.

7. Interview with Bob Davis, Supervisor, Public Consultation, City of Toronto, September 28, 2004.

the trunk servicing schemes begun in the 1960s. Halton had therefore begun to develop a lake-based water and sewage disposal system of its own.

To the north and east of Metro Toronto (the consolidated City of Toronto after 1997), 80 per cent of the sewage flow into the York Durham Servicing System (YDSS) came from York region,[8] leading officials in Durham region (the GTA's slowest-growing sector) to complain that they would not be able to accommodate the development pressures that were just beginning to occur there. In fact, the YDSS had reached its limits by the late 1990s "and required major increases of capacity, while the Metro water and sewer systems built in the 1950s were reaching both the end of their useful life and the limits of their capacity."[9] Moves to expand that capacity, however, were beginning to encounter strong opposition from residents and elected politicians in the small towns and rural areas outside existing urban boundaries.

Managing the costs of regional services

Whether and where to build new infrastructure to support economic and population growth, and often what type of infrastructure to build, were clearly divisive questions in discussions about how best to govern the expanding Toronto region. Just as divisive was the question of how to pay for any new infrastructure that got approved. The answer to this question depended on the answer given to another one: Who benefits from the investment of public money in city-regional services? Some persons identified the principal beneficiaries of urban growth as "the provincial economy" or "the whole society," and used this answer to argue for provincial and national government contributions to regional services. Others, however, claimed that the benefits of Toronto region development flowed mainly to the people who lived, worked, and did business in the region, and who should therefore pay most of the costs of maintaining it.

The Ontario government vacillated between these two points of view. More often than not, however, it favoured the second one, which helped to justify efforts to minimize or reduce its own spending in the region by making local property owners and businesses pay most of the costs of servicing it. The creation of Metropolitan Toronto in 1953 and of regional municipalities between 1969 and 1974 were outcomes of these efforts. This meant that metropolitan or regional institutions could use property taxes raised in built-up municipalities to finance major infrastructure in developing districts. The right given to municipal councils to levy development charges was another way of keeping the costs of serving regional growth within the region.

8. White 2003, 64.
9. Ibid., 60.

In the 1960s, however, the provincial government began to treat development in the Toronto region as an important contributor to the entire provincial economy, and therefore as an important provincial responsibility. It put more money (either directly or in the form of grants-in-aid) into the kinds of regional services that it had earlier expected Metropolitan Toronto institutions to build and finance, such as trunk water and sewer facilities, arterial roads, both rapid and bus public transit, and assisted rental housing. It also increased its contributions to education and social and community services. It was able to do these things both because it was experiencing a prolonged period of prosperity and because of federal–provincial agreements that committed the federal government to paying large shares of provincially administered social assistance, health, housing, education, and other programs. Also during this period the province became entitled to gradually growing shares of the federally collected income tax. Some of this new revenue went into regional services; some helped to finance conditional and unconditional provincial grants to municipal governments.

Provincial largesse did not last, however. In the mid-1970s high inflation resulting from rapidly rising oil prices, together with an economic slowdown, raised government concerns about the effects of rising debt and new funding commitments on the provincial budget. The federal government added to the province's financial worries by curtailing its own social spending (leaving provincial and municipal governments to deal with the consequences) and by placing caps on its contributions to social programs. To compensate for declining federal support, the Ontario government increased its spending on social programs while trying to reduce its costs in other areas. As a result, the share of the provincial budget devoted to regional infrastructure and municipal services levelled off or declined during the 1980s and 1990s.

To justify its lower levels of support, the government reverted to the idea that city-regional services should be provided and paid for by those who lived, worked, and paid taxes in the region. This perspective was particularly pronounced in the approach taken to regional and local finance by the Conservative government elected in 1995. It had begun to emerge before 1980, however, in the form of caps on the size of provincial contributions to education, public transit, and other municipal services.

Caps on provincial subsidies were also a response to rapid increases in local government spending after provincial grants became available. Their goal, in other words, was not only to reduce provincial costs but also to force local governments and local school boards to operate more efficiently. A third, less obvious, goal was to accommodate a provincial electorate that was more aware of and concerned about health and education than about the functional requirements of the Toronto region. A large component of that electorate was

Table 7.1 Greater Toronto Area revenue sources in comparative perspective, 1994

	Assessed population	As % of Ontario population	Equalized assessment ($ooos)	As % of Ontario total	Ontario govt. grants[a] ($ooos)	As % of Ontario total
GTA	4,004,567	41.5	393,255,000	52.5	2,632,192	42.5
Metropolitan Toronto	2,151,430	22.3	215,261,000	28.8	1,957,431	31.6
Four regions	1,853,137	19.2	176,927,000	23.7	674,761	10.9
Ontario	9,653,837		747,590,000		6,197,620	

a. Data includes conditional, unconditional and capital grants

Source: Based on data contained in Ontario Ministry of Municipal Affairs and Housing, *Municipal Financial Information 1994*, Chapters 1 and 4.

also becoming increasingly resistant to tax increases, as were the businesses to which the province looked for new investment. The Conservatives responded to these sentiments by making tax cuts its highest priority after coming to office in 1995, a decision that left the government with even less money for regional services than it had had before.

The GTA's relationship to the rest of the province was also a political barrier to the investment of provincial tax dollars in the Toronto region. By 1996, the GTA contained 43 per cent of the provincial population, up from 38.5 per cent in 1976. It occupied less than 1 per cent of the province's land area, however, and contained only 30 of the province's 815 municipalities. Consequently, its representatives were likely to make up a minority of local officials taking part in provincial–municipal discussions.[10] Moreover, local politicians in other parts of the province undoubtedly saw the region as being well able to look after itself. In 1994, for example, the GTA had 52.5 per cent of the province's total assessment (after assessment data had been subjected to provincial equalization formulae) but only 41.5 per cent of its assessed population (Table 7.1). Its share of provincial grants was also slightly larger than its share of the provincial population.

Politicians in the GTA also differed in the way they perceived the financial needs and circumstances of their own municipalities relative to those of others in the region. Although Metropolitan Toronto accounted for disproportionately large shares of the region's equalized assessment and provincial grant revenues, Metro politicians insisted that their governments needed all the money they could raise (and more) to cover their disproportionately high

---

10. In 2001, after a period of intensive municipal restructuring, the five-unit GTA consisted of 44.5 per cent of the provincial population but only 30 of the province's 447 lower-tier municipalities.

social costs. They also claimed that the rest of the region benefited from many of the services that Metro's local governments provided. Suburban officials countered that their governments could not provide the most basic services fast enough to accommodate the demands of their rapidly growing populations, let alone spread their limited resources over a wider area.

There were other political obstacles to shifting the costs of regional services to the local tax base. Noticeable increases in residential taxes tended to alienate those who were most likely to vote in provincial and local elections. They could also impose hardships on people on low or fixed incomes. If municipal governments tried to avoid these problems by shifting a larger share of the tax burden to the non-residential sector, they risked driving businesses to other municipalities, or away from the region altogether. Consequently, municipal governments, both rich and poor, tended to object to any use of local taxes for regional purposes, unless such use implied obvious and immediate benefits for their own communities or constituents.

Adding to the difficulties of working out ways to use local tax dollars to finance regional services were the many disparities and inequities in Ontario's property tax system caused by past accommodations with different types of property owners. These differences included the way in which properties were evaluated in different municipalities, and also the amount of taxes levied on similarly valued properties in the same local or regional municipalities, particularly Metro Toronto. To overcome these problems, the provincial government embarked in 1969 on a program to reassess all property taxes in the province at market value as a first step toward reforming the property tax system. Its efforts met with strong opposition from some municipalities and local taxpayers, and in 1978 it abandoned the attempt, telling regional and local governments to devise their own plans for reform. Metropolitan Toronto (which had the most severe assessment and taxation discrepancies in the province) grappled with the issue for more than 10 years. Its Council, however, was unable to win provincial approval for its reform proposals, which invariably tried to protect homeowners and small businesses from large tax increases by imposing disproportionately high taxes on large commercial properties.

The Conservative government elected in 1995 finally imposed a system of "actual value" (essentially market value) assessment on the entire province in 1997. Like its predecessors, it allowed Toronto to tax large business properties at rates that were higher than those levied in the rest of the region, at least for several years. This concession was intended to soften city objections to assessment reform and to allow the provincial government to use a disproportionately large share of Toronto's commercial taxes to help fund public education, for which it had assumed financial responsibility.

The provincial government also made increasing use of alternative financial strategies as a way to avoid the political and financial costs of using provincial and municipal taxes to fund city and regional services. It appealed to the federal government for financial help, although it always insisted that federal dollars should flow through provincial agencies. It backed away from costly transit and community-building initiatives, even when they were consistent with its stated objectives for the region. It created new special-purpose authorities with some potential for raising their own revenues. And it shifted or allowed municipal governments to shift some servicing costs to private developers, other private corporations, and individual users.

Many of these devices upheld or added to the complexity of the regional governance system. They also helped to highlight the absence of a coherent regional development strategy either to guide or to justify the decisions that were made. From time to time, however, the government did take steps to control the pace and pattern of regional growth in the interest of lowering the costs of regional services, guiding the decisions of local and provincial agencies, or achieving the objectives of environmental advocates, which gained a growing constituency in all parts of the region as the study period wore on.

Managing regional growth

The Ontario government's efforts to manage growth in the Toronto region began with the 1946 appointment of a Toronto and Suburban Planning Board (soon to be replaced by a Toronto and York Planning Board) to look for ways to provide the region with badly needed infrastructure. The matters addressed by these units were dealt with more comprehensively by the Metropolitan Toronto Planning Board (MTPB), appointed in 1953, which had planning jurisdiction over an area three times the size of Metropolitan Toronto. The government began to reduce the MTPB's role as a regional planner in 1962, however, when it appointed a Metropolitan Toronto and Region Transportation Study and asked it to recommend a transportation strategy for a region five times Metro's size. It reduced it still further a few years later when it empowered its own agency, the Ontario Water Resources Commission (OWRC), to develop sewer and water infrastructure in suburban districts outside Metro.

Metro lost its role as a regional planner altogether between 1969 and 1974, when the province grouped outer suburban municipalities into four regional municipalities and told them to produce "regional" plans of their own. By that time it had also authorized provincial staff to devise a transportation/land-use strategy for a part of south-central Ontario (the Toronto-Centred Region, or TCR) nearly 36 times as large as Metro. It adopted the TCR concept in 1971 as a guide for future development, depicting it as a first step in the development of a province-wide land-use strategy to which the plans of Metropolitan Toronto and the regional governments would have to conform. No sooner were the TCR strategy and regional governments in place, however, than the province began to ignore them, letting the TCR initiative quietly die. Only two of the four regional municipalities (Halton and Durham) produced plans within a few years of their creation. The other two (York and Peel) waited until the province pressured them to adopt plans in the early 1990s.

The government restored regional growth management to the provincial agenda in the late 1980s when it commissioned a study of three options for the physical development of the GTA. In combination with several other planning initiatives, the Urban Structure Concepts Study served as the basis for a government-sponsored effort to persuade municipal officials to subscribe to a regional "vision," which would have required them to work toward a more compact, transit-supportive, and environmentally sensitive urban structure. The visioning exercise ended after the Conservative government took office in 1995 and rescinded or relaxed policies that would have supported it. Only six years later, however, the same government appointed the Central Ontario Smart Growth Panel and asked it to "provide a vision for sustainable economic growth backed by strategies to improve the quality of life and protection of the environment" in a zone containing 38,000 square kilometres of southern Ontario.[11] That initiative was still being pursued when the study period ended.

Despite its recurring interest in exercising control over Toronto region development, the provincial government typically ascribed less importance to managing regional growth than to ensuring that growth continued to occur. Regional planning exercises lost momentum, therefore, as soon as growth in the province or the region slowed down and the government began to look for ways to stimulate new investment. Similarly, Metro Council moved quickly in its early years to approve plans for trunk sewer and water mains and an integrated transportation system to support suburban growth, but did not adopt a comprehensive "Official Plan" until 1980, by which time Metro was almost fully built up and no longer had authority to plan for its suburban fringe.

Regional planning exercises had only a few lasting consequences, therefore, for the way the Toronto region developed. One was an infrastructure plan adopted by Metro in the 1960s that called for the construction of trunk sewer and water lines only to Metro's outer boundaries. Together with provincial government restraints on septic tank development, that plan helped to control the rate of outward expansion during Metro's early years. As a result,

---

11. Ontario Ministry of Municipal Affairs, "Ontario's Growing Fast—Smart Growth will make it Last: Harris," News release, February 11, 2002.

Metro's three outer municipalities (Etobicoke, North York, and Scarborough) developed at densities that were high relative to those of most North American suburbs, and thus somewhat better able to support public transit. Metro's ability to contain outward expansion ended in the 1960s, however, when the province empowered the OWRC to build sewer and water facilities in Peel, York, and Durham regions.

The transportation plan that Metro adopted in 1964 was less influential on Metro's development than the sewer and water plan, because some of its highway and rapid transit elements never got built. Nonetheless, in favouring a "balance" between highways and public transit, it differed from most metropolitan transportation plans being produced in North America at the time. There was still some hope of achieving this balance, in fact, because the province was paying only 50 per cent of the costs of urban highways, as compared to the 90 per cent share being paid by the U.S. government for urban links to the interstate highway system. The province had also begun to contribute the same share of the costs of subway roadbeds. These transit-supportive moves paved the way for the transit-oriented urban structure plan that Metro planners produced in the 1970s. Metro Council adopted that plan, however, only after it had removed designations for new transit lines to support it. The transit plan it eventually adopted was not the integrated system of interconnected lines that Metro planners had proposed, but a system of disjointed lines connecting individual Metro municipalities to the subway system.

Growing political support for public transit had disappointing results, therefore, for the development of Metro's public transit system. After the mid-1960s, additions to that system depended principally on the outcomes of Metro Council debates in which Council members evaluated proposed rapid transit lines in terms of the costs and benefits they would bring to their own communities, and not in terms of the benefits they would bring to all of Metro Toronto or to the Toronto region.

PLANNING IN THE SUBURBAN REGIONS

The nodal development idea also gained support from municipal governments outside Metro—so much so, in fact, that by 1995 there were 33 proposed nodal sites in the plans of the four suburban regions and their lower-tier munici-palities—or 18 more than had been suggested in a land-use concept prepared for the provincial Office for the Greater Toronto Area.[12] There was a discon-nection, however, between the planners' concept of nodal development as a contributor to a more compact, transit-supportive urban structure and the way

---

12. Ray Tomalty, "Suburban Intensification in the GTA," Research note, *The Intensification Report*, November–December 1995, 41.

municipal councils interpreted the idea. Municipal councils saw high-density activity nodes as a way to attract the types of office and commercial development that had traditionally located in downtown Toronto, not as a way to encourage their residents to make more use of public transit. Consequently, the plans they approved did not depart very much from the strong automobile orientation that characterized other types of suburban development. The three nodes that were under development by the end of the study period were all within easy access of major highways and all had ample provision for parking.[13] Only one of the three seemed likely to promote increased transit use and more pedestrian activity. Located in the former Metro city of North York, this node was built directly over a Metro subway station and had more indoor and less outdoor parking space than the other two centres.

In general, therefore, the most important influences on suburban land-use patterns during the study period were decisions made by private land developers, the municipal officials with whom they negotiated for subdivision approval, and individual members of the Ontario Municipal Board who ruled on disputes between supporters and opponents of planning proposals. The cumulative results of their decisions tended to be subdivisions consisting mainly of single-family homes on individual lots, low-density office and industrial parks, curvilinear street patterns designed to slow down car traffic and keep out trucks and buses, and a separation of residential areas from all other types of activity.

Suburban land-use choices meant that Metro's three outer municipalities (Etobicoke, North York, and Scarborough) achieved lower densities than its two inner ones (York and East York) during Metro's first 25 years (Table 7.2). With the exception of Mississauga, suburban municipalities immediately outside Metro's boundaries achieved even lower densities in their first 25 years as components of regional municipalities than did suburbs within Metro. Yet the GTA's population increase of 1.9 million between 1976 and 2001 was slightly higher than the 1.8 million increase registered in the previous 25 years. Moreover, poor integration of public transit with other aspects of the GTA's physical development meant that the region entered the 21st century with a transit system that had not adapted well to the movement of people and jobs within Toronto and the region as a whole. The GTA was an automobile-dominated region, and becoming more so all the time.

---

13.   Filion, McSpurren, and Huether, 2000.

Table 7.2 Changes in gross population density (persons per square kilometre) inside and outside Metropolitan Toronto during two rapid-growth periods, 1951–1976 and 1976–2001

	Metropolitan Toronto, 1951–1976	
	1951	1976
Metropolitan Toronto	1,173	3,371
Inner Three	6,287	5,903
East York	3,803	4,796
Toronto	7,196	6,168
York	4,757	5,807
Outer Three	465	2,544
Etobicoke	686	2,398
North York	486	3,157
Scarborough	300	2,063

	GTA and six close-in outer suburbs, 1976–2001	
	1976	2001
Greater Toronto Area	447	720
Six outer suburbs (all)	361	1,127
Ajax	307	1,089
Brampton	390	1,228
Markham	266	977
Mississauga	913	2,238
Pickering	123	385
Vaughan	65	661

Source: Calculated using Statistics Canada Census data.

TWO PLANNING SUCCESSES

Nonetheless, there were noteworthy achievements in two areas often included in arguments for regional growth management: the preservation of undeveloped land for parks and natural open space, and the maintenance of a financially strong and socially vibrant urban core. Areas set aside as natural open space in the GTA included Toronto's (the former Metropolitan Toronto's) extensive ravine-based and Toronto Island park system, the Niagara Escarpment, a Waterfront Trail, sections of the Oak Ridges Moraine, and many regional conservation areas and provincial parks. The region owed these achievements partly to chance events, including Hurricane Hazel in 1954, and partly to the hard work of dedicated provincial and local officials and environmental interest groups. The provincial government always had to approve conservation plans, however, and in doing so it helped to give the Toronto region a system of parks and conservation areas that residents of many North American regions would find enviable.

The second achievement, a core city that avoided the decline that afflicted many U.S. cities during the study period, occurred despite the rate and scale of suburban expansion. At the time of Metro's creation, the former City of Toronto contained 77 per cent of the metropolitan population; by 1996 that percentage had fallen to 27 per cent of Metro's population and 12 per cent of the population of the GTA. It still contained 31 per cent of all jobs in the CMA in 1991,[14] however, and its population had been growing since 1981, after declining in the 1970s. Its average household income also rose between 1980 and 1995. A city council policy to encourage all types of housing in the city was one explanation for these population and income trends. A housing policy cannot sustain a city's well-being, however, if there is no demand for the kinds of housing a city government tries to protect or encourage. The former Toronto remained a healthy city because people wanted to live there.

Maintaining a viable urban core, however, did not mean escaping urban poverty and problems related to it. By the 1990s it was clearly evident that (Metro) Toronto was absorbing a growing share of the region's poorest residents, and the number of poor neighbourhoods in the city was increasing even while others were becoming wealthier. Moreover, even though (Metro) Toronto gained 206,000 residents between 1991 and 2001—more than twice the number it had gained in the previous 20 years—it was losing jobs, particularly in manufacturing and wholesale trade (see Table 7.3). These trends highlighted the growing importance of the ways in which Toronto region governance had both affected and responded to the distribution of the benefits and costs of urban growth among the region's different municipalities.

Reluctant sharing of regional assets and regional costs

Ontario's experiments with regional governance began in the early years of the development of the Canadian welfare state, one feature of which was a federal–provincial equalization program recommended by a Royal Commission on Dominion– [i.e., Federal–] Provincial Relations in the 1930s, but not adopted until 1957. As described in the Canadian Constitution in 1981, the program committed the Government of Canada "to the principle of making equalization payments to ensure that provincial governments have sufficient revenues to provide reasonably comparable levels of public services at reasonably comparable levels of taxation."[15] Although municipalities were never included in equalization agreements, the Toronto region evolved in

---

14. Frisken, Bourne, Gad, and Murdie 1997, 18.
15. *Constitution Act*, 1981, Part III, Section 36(2).

Table 7.3 Population and employment changes in the Toronto Census Metropolitan Area, 1971–1991

	Population			
	% CMA population 1991	% increase 1971–91	% CMA population 2001	% increase 1991–2001
CMA		48.4		20.1
(Metropolitan) Toronto	58.4	9.1	53.0	9.0
Outside Metro Toronto	41.6	199.5	47.0	35.6

	Employment			
	% CMA employment 1991	% increase 1971–91	% CMA employment 2001	% increase (decrease) 1991–2001
CMA		73.7		10.5
(Metropolitan) Toronto	63.8	34.9	56.2	(2.7)
Outside Metro Toronto	36.2	26.4	43.8	33.7

Sources: Calculated using Statistics Canada population and place-of-work data. Place-of-work data for 1971 to 1991 was compiled by Gunter Gad for Frisken, Bourne, Gad, and Murdie 1997, 18; Place-of-work data for 2001 was provided by Gunter Gad in a private communication, April 12, 2004.

a context where inter-jurisdictional equity was debated and then formally recognized as an appropriate activity for a democratic state.[16]

The equal treatment of municipalities was a relatively minor objective in provincial–municipal grant and subsidy programs, but it did influence Ontario's municipal policies in other ways. Government members or their advisors often evoked it, for example, in explaining changes in public education and municipal taxation policies. The equalization principle also appeared in provincially legislated arrangements for financing infrastructure, social services, and public education in Metro Toronto and the regional municipalities. Although those arrangements applied only to sectors of the region and not to the region as a whole, the extensive use made of local revenue sharing within two-tier municipalities distinguished governance in the Toronto region from governance in most American city-regions during the period covered by this study.[17]

---

16. For more on the influence of welfare-state ideas on government programs that impinged on Toronto region governance, see Donald 2002, 2138–2139, and Frisken 1986.

17. Efforts to change the distribution of costs and benefits among municipalities in U.S. city-regions were often undermined by determined local resistance. State governments sometimes circumvented the problem by transferring responsibility for some redistributive services, such as welfare, to county governments.

METROPOLITAN TORONTO

Within Metropolitan Toronto, the benefits of cost-sharing were initially most apparent in the newer suburbs of Etobicoke, North York, and Scarborough, where Metro quickly built new infrastructure to support population and industrial growth. The city later benefited, however, from the successful efforts of Metro Chairman Frederick Gardiner and Metro planning staff to persuade within-Metro suburbs to accept a share of low-rental housing, including housing built with government assistance, and from Metro's decision to help the TTC extend core-oriented subway lines into the suburbs. The transfer of social services to Metro in the mid-1960s also helped the city and its poorer suburbs by reducing differences in the types of social services available to poor residents living in different parts of Metro. Metro ensured that some differences in social and community services would persist, however, when it decided in the early 1980s to fund volunteer and non-profit agencies to deliver a large range of optional services. Because Toronto had the largest number of such agencies, its residents had a larger number of services from which to choose. Suburban residents either had to do without or look for what they needed in the city. The same differences in types and variety of community services existed at the end of the study period between the new Toronto and the suburban regional municipalities.

Toronto also gained financially in 1966 when it was consolidated with two inner suburbs, one of which (Forest Hill) was Metro's wealthiest municipality. The suburbs also benefited indirectly, however, because a larger city tax base meant larger city contributions to Metro services, including public education. Even before restructuring, Toronto had also benefited directly and the suburbs indirectly from the city's disproportionately large amount of non-residential assessment. That assessment continued to grow faster in the city than in the suburbs in the 1970s and 1980s because of large-scale growth in the downtown office sector. The core city still had a disproportionately large share of Metro's non-residential assessment when it was absorbed into the amalgamated City of Toronto in 1998.

The city's population also became wealthier on average after Metro was restructured in 1967–68. Apart from the Borough (later City) of York, Toronto had the lowest average family income in Metro in 1961.[18] Because of extensive gentrification in downtown neighbourhoods and the construction of new housing (mainly condominiums) in the city, Toronto's average family income and average per capita income gradually rose, to become the highest

---

18. Based on data contained in Social Planning Council of Metropolitan Toronto, *Metropolitan Profile, 1966* April 1970, 52–53. Data not available for all Census tracts.

in Metro by 1991.[19] On the other hand, Toronto's poverty rate was higher in 1991 than that of any other Metro municipality except the City of York, indicating that the city's population was becoming more polarized economically.[20] Poverty rates in suburbs inside Metro were also high, however, relative to those in the outer suburbs (see Table 5.6 on page 215).

Under the Metro system, therefore, Metro's member municipalities became more alike socio-economically, with the city of Toronto becoming richer and suburbs becoming poorer. It is debatable, however, whether the system made life significantly better for the area's poorer residents. The dispersal of low-rental housing throughout Metro probably made more subsidized housing available to eligible low-income tenants than there would have been if all such housing had gone into the inner city. It also meant, however, that many of Metro's neediest households were situated in remote suburban locations that lacked many of the services available in the inner city. And the challenge of serving these districts became increasingly complex after they began to absorb large numbers of the new immigrants who settled in the Toronto region every year from the 1950s onward.

The gradual extension of TTC bus services and the adoption in the 1970s of a single fare for travel within Metro gave persons who lived or worked in Metro's outer districts an affordable transportation alternative to the automobile. The core-orientation of the transit system meant, however, that transit travel between dispersed suburban residential districts, employment sites, shopping centres, and public institutions (such as hospitals and universities) was often difficult and time-consuming. Metro Council did not adopt planners' proposals for east–west rapid transit lines to serve Metro's northern districts, and the TTC did little to promote them. Instead, according to Juri Pill, General Manager of Planning in the 1980s, TTC management took the position that the TTC was not a "social service," even though it performed a "social function."[21] It was a business that had to be marketed and operated like a business, with cost-effectiveness as the ultimate goal. This corporate philosophy served the TTC well as long as most jobs and other activities were concentrated in downtown Toronto and near subway terminals. It gave TTC management little incentive,

---

19. For figures on family income, see City of York, *Managing the GTA as a Community: A Creative Response to the Challenge*, Submission to the GTA Task Force, September 1995, Table 3.2, 18. Data used in this table were derived from "Canadian Markets," *The Financial Post*, 1994. For data on average annual per capita income, see Board of Trade of Metropolitan Toronto, *Toronto Business and Marketing Guide, 1996/97*, Mary deReus, Publisher/Editor, Table 4.10, 132.

20. Metropolitan Toronto Planning Department, Research and Special Studies Division 1994, 77.

21. Luther S. Miller, "What Makes Toronto Transit Different," *Railway Age*, October 1986, 68–71.

however, to consider what the decentralization of low-income households implied, not only for the people most likely to value and use transit, but also for the agency's ability to sustain ridership as the region evolved.

The restructuring of the provincial–municipal relationship in the late 1990s, together with Metropolitan Toronto's amalgamation, had mixed implications for equity within the urban core. Amalgamation not only preserved tax sharing within (Metro) Toronto, but also extended it to services (such as public health, recreation, and public libraries) that Metro's local municipalities had formerly provided. Actual value reassessment helped to reduce property tax inequities in Toronto, although it did not eliminate them altogether. Provincial takeover of public education financing implied more equal funding for schools in different parts of (Metro) Toronto, but it also meant a substantial reduction in the new city's total education budget and raised questions about the ability of Toronto schools to deal effectively with the educational needs of a diverse and rapidly changing population. The downloading of public transit costs on local governments put Metro's public transit system at the mercy of locally elected politicians, many of whom represented outer districts with few transit users. It certainly did not make local politicians more willing than they had been in the past to pay the full costs of new rapid transit lines out of local taxes.

THE REGIONAL PICTURE

Within the larger Toronto region, provincial government policies reduced financial inequalities among municipalities in the suburban regions, but helped to preserve or increase disparities across the region as a whole. The province allowed both regional and local governments to decide whether or not to include a component of "affordable" or government-assisted housing in their residential districts, and only a few of them did so. Thus, like most U.S. cities, Toronto seemed destined to be the region's principal provider of low-rental housing for the foreseeable future. Municipal governments were also free to decide whether to integrate their transit services with the GO commuter system and other municipal transit systems; again, only some of them did so. Transit in the region therefore remained fragmented and uncoordinated, making it difficult or impossible for GTA residents without a car to travel to or among residential, employment, institutional, and recreational districts outside (Metro) Toronto.

The Conservative government elected in 1995 rescinded measures, only recently adopted by its NDP predecessor, to promote a wider distribution of "affordable" housing and a more integrated public transit system within the region. It did not ignore equity issues entirely, however. For example, it justified its takeover of public education finance as a way to reduce the large disparities in school board spending throughout the province. The takeover had nothing to do with helping beleaguered inner-city schools, because Metro's school system drew on one of the wealthiest tax bases in the province. Rather the government wanted to transfer property tax dollars from Metro and other wealthy school districts to rural, northern, and Separate (Roman Catholic) school districts with fewer resources. The alternative was to increase its own assistance to poorer boards, and that it was not willing to do.

The Conservative government also required that property taxes in the GTA be pooled for social services and social housing. At the same time it made Toronto pay a much larger share of GO Transit costs than its share of GO Transit riders. Because Toronto had the largest share of social service needs, these two decisions injected into regional finance the kind of quid pro quo that had helped to maintain the Metro system. As had been the case in Metropolitan Toronto four decades earlier, however, cost-sharing arrangements met with strong opposition from both the city and the suburbs. Toronto insisted that it should not have to contribute to the capital costs of a transit system managed by the province and used mainly by people who lived outside the city, especially as the province no longer paid a share of the TTC's operating deficit.[22] Suburban governments argued that they should not have to help Toronto deal with its social service needs when their own service costs were increasing, especially since provincial assistance was levelling off or declining. Moreover, suburban populations were becoming more diverse, both ethnically and economically, putting pressure on suburban governments to spend more on local social and community services.

Disputes about regional cost-sharing in the GTA highlighted the political and administrative difficulties of pursuing intermunicipal equity in a large and growing urbanized territory where different municipalities have different tax bases and social characteristics, and are at different stages in their development. Such efforts have to contend both with private-sector decisions either to invest or not to invest in different parts of the region, and with the general tendency of local governments to put the immediate interests of their own municipalities ahead of all other interests. In the Toronto region, that tendency usually outweighed arguments for the fifth objective often found in the regional agenda: that of engaging a region's municipalities in the task of developing common approaches to regional issues.

---

22. Toronto announced in 2001 that it would no longer contribute a share of GO costs. It changed its position after the provincial government decided in 2001 to give municipal governments a share of the gas tax, at the same time making Toronto's share contingent on the city's contributing to GO. Interview with Michael Roschlau, President and CEO of the Canadian Urban Transit Association, July 6, 2005.

*Building a capacity for local governments
to participate in regional policy-making*

The idea of strengthening the capacity of local institutions to take an active role in regional policy-making commanded little support from either provincial or local officials after 1953, despite the early successes of Metropolitan Toronto. There were several reasons for this lack of government interest.

From the provincial standpoint, the Toronto region was not only Ontario's largest city-region, but was also growing faster than the rest of the province. Thus any change that strengthened the region's ability to govern itself would weaken the province's authority over municipal affairs and its status in federal–provincial negotiations. Moreover, a stronger, more united region could mean substantially higher provincial costs. In the case of public transit, for example, a more united Metro Council would have allowed the TTC to move ahead faster with the planning and construction of new rapid transit lines in the 1970s and 1980s, thereby forcing the province to pay higher capital and operating subsidies. A GTA-wide transit authority would have raised expectations for more and better transit in the regional municipalities, again implying more provincial subsidies. A successful effort to promote a regional social housing program would have had similar results for the province.

There was also little municipal support for a unified local response to regional issues. Even though municipalities lacked the "home rule" protections that had been granted to municipal governments in many U.S. states, local politicians in the GTA resisted moves to create or strengthen regional organizations by depicting them as infringements on local autonomy. Provincially imposed municipal consolidations did not weaken this tendency. After short periods of adjusting to their new situation, politicians in consolidated municipalities fought just as vigorously for the interests of their new communities as had politicians who had served the old ones.

Political and financial as well as ideological reasons contributed to a lack of local interest in participating in formal arrangements for regional governance. Local officials tended to resist proposals for structural changes that threatened their political or professional positions. Moreover, the heavy dependence of municipal governments on the property tax for much of their funding motivated them to compete for those types of development that were likely to yield the best returns in taxes, and to resist developments that implied higher local costs. The Conservative government strengthened this competitive impulse after 1997 by shifting new responsibilities to the local tax base and reducing the number of services that municipal governments could finance out of development charges or by other means.

Local governments in the region were also deeply divided about how they wanted the region to develop and the role they wanted to play within it. Metropolitan Toronto officials, confident that the core would always dominate the region's economy, often treated the rest of the region as if it were irrelevant to Metro's interests. Officials in some of the faster growing, close-in suburbs were bent on building the economies and status of their own municipalities, even if it meant weakening Metro. Those who spoke for municipalities in the outer parts of the region disagreed among themselves about regional issues. Some shared the growth aspirations of the more urbanized municipalities; others reacted with horror as suburban development crept relentlessly outward, threatening to swallow up the rural landscape and small communities. They opposed any institutional changes that might promote that process.

BASES FOR AGREEMENT

Even when the province encouraged municipalities to address contentious issues co-operatively, differences in municipal aspirations and priorities stood in the way of regional consensus-building. Nonetheless, there were a few bases for agreement. One grew out of a shared reluctance to spend local property taxes on services that would not bring immediate or obvious benefits to donor municipalities. Thus local officials could usually agree that senior governments should pay most or all of the costs of regional services.

Most local officials could also agree on the need for more and better transportation facilities. They often disagreed, however, about what the most pressing transportation needs were and how they should be addressed. As a general rule, Metro officials wanted the province to spend more money on public transit; suburban officials wanted provincial transportation money to go to roads. Many Metro politicians, however, did not want Metro tax dollars spent on rapid transit lines that would serve outer suburban commuters unless outer suburban governments paid a large share of the local costs. Discussions about transportation issues tended to proceed slowly, therefore, and often ended in a stalemate. In the face of municipal unwillingness to co-operate, the provincial government sometimes acted on its own, as it did when it established GO Transit in 1967. In doing so, it reduced the ability of municipal governments to participate in the development of a service with substantial potential for shaping the region.

A third basis for intermunicipal agreement was a widespread interest among regional residents in preserving as much green space in the region as possible. Governments were reluctant to contribute tax dollars to this effort, however, which meant that political support for the creation of regional parklands usually outpaced the commitment of funds to acquiring and maintaining them. As a result, some protected natural areas remained vulnerable to changes in provincial laws and regulations or in local zoning bylaws when the study period ended.

As a general rule, therefore, the promotion of intermunicipal consultation and co-operation was seldom an effective way to further regional objectives. Nonetheless, it was an approach the provincial government frequently used because it served a number of useful purposes: it was a way to mute criticisms of government inaction; it allowed the government to postpone decisions that might be politically unpopular; and it helped to limit the size of government contributions to expensive infrastructure.

THE BENEFITS OF CONSULTATION

Consultative organizations provided some benefits nonetheless, although not usually the ones that proponents of regional government were looking for. They served as forums for debating regional issues, for acknowledging the legitimacy of different municipal positions and concerns, and for discussing possible compromises. Thus they sometimes helped to smooth the way for later provincial interventions. In addition, staff members attached to regional organizations compiled, processed, and disseminated data about regional trends and issues, thereby providing an information base for provincial and municipal plans and policies. They also promoted awareness of the regional context in which local decision-makers (particularly local planners) oper-ated. On occasion they were even able to persuade some municipal govern-ments to incorporate regional perspectives into land-use plans and other local programs.

The disbanding of the Greater Toronto Coordinating Committee (GTCC), the provincial Office for the Greater Toronto Area (OGTA), and the Greater Toronto Services Board (GTSB) in 2001 deprived the GTA of organizations able to perform these consciousness-raising and information-gathering functions. Municipal officials appointed to the Central Ontario Smart Growth Panel spoke for more than 100 urban and rural units that varied greatly in population size, economic base, social character, and stage of urban development. The new City of Toronto, by far the largest and most economi-cally important unit in the Central Ontario Zone, had no special place in its or-ganizational structure, either as a city, as a region, or even as part of its name. Yet development trends in Toronto and its suburban environs were just as challenging for governments in 2003 as they had been half a century earlier.

The Situation in 2003

There were still important differences between the Toronto region in 2003 and most older city-regions in the United States. The core city remained a major source of regional employment, particularly employment in professional and service occupations, as well as being home to a substantial share of the region's higher income residents. The costs of some services were being shared among local governments in that part of the region known as the GTA. The province's takeover of public education finance meant that the amount spent on education in different jurisdictions did not depend principally on the size of local tax bases. In fact, taxes raised in the wealthier school districts (including Toronto) were helping to pay for education in the poorer ones.

In other ways, however, the Toronto region's development patterns and characteristics were converging with those of other North American city-regions. Suburban development was spreading outward at declining densities, resulting in increased dependence on automobiles and declining transit use. Demands for new suburban infrastructure often emphasized the importance of suburban expansion to the region's economy. At the same time, the region's population was becoming more segregated into rich and poor districts, and the latter were not only increasing in number but also becoming poorer, especially in Toronto.

These trends meant that the agenda for regional governance reform was superficially the same as it had been at earlier stages in the region's development. It had become more difficult to find ways to pursue regional objectives, however, for both financial and political reasons.

Infrastructure needs had to be addressed on a much larger scale than in the past because of the region's much larger population and geographical size. Moreover, an increase in the number of municipalities included in the region had injected a greater variety of municipal viewpoints into discussions about what should or should not be done to secure its future.

Governments were less willing to spend money on new urban infrastructure because other matters, such as improving the national health care system and building security against terrorism, now headed policy priorities. Governments were also being urged to spend more on higher education to keep the Canadian economy competitive with the economies of other nations.

Persistent low-density development at the edge of the region had contributed to the growth of an environmental movement that argued passionately for growth management policies to promote more compact, transit-supportive forms of development. At the same time, however, the preference for traditional neighbourhoods dominated by single-family housing remained strong both within the development industry and among housing consumers. There were always local residents ready to organize and fight strongly to defend such neighbourhoods from the threats they associated with other types of housing, even if the proposed sites were some distance away. One Minister of Municipal Affairs put the case succinctly: "[T]here are only two things that people don't like about planning, and that's density and sprawl."[23]

There were growing inequities in the way some services and amenities were distributed among different municipalities and neighbourhoods. Those with the most worrying implications for the region's future were inequities between the inner and outer parts of the region in the distribution of affordable rental housing (both private and government-assisted), public transit, and immigrant settlement services. These inequities implied that Toronto and a few other municipalities would have to absorb growing shares of the costs of providing services to regional residents with multiple needs.

There was no organization with either legal or symbolic authority to engage the region's local governments in the tasks of making and implementing regional policies. Moreover, the region's growing size had made it harder to persuade senior governments that strong regional institutions were a good idea. The region defined as Metropolitan Toronto in 1953 had contained 24 per cent of Ontario's population and 8 per cent of the population of Canada. The Greater Toronto Transit Authority, which had replaced the Greater Toronto Services Board as manager of the GO Transit system, served a region containing at least half of Ontario's population and about 20 per cent of Canada's population in 2001. The Central Ontario Zone, as defined by the Ontario government that same year, contained 66 per cent of Ontario's population and 25 per cent of the population of Canada. Politicians in other parts of the province or the country were unlikely to respond favourably to policies that would give this one region more advantages than it already seemed to have.

Decision-making processes had also changed to allow for more participation by or inputs from members of the community than had earlier been the case. At the same time, changes in the national and global economies had weakened public confidence in the ability of governments to achieve positive change, and thus reduced public willingness to pay taxes to support new government programs. There had also been a decline in respect for expert opinion, which meant a weakening of the role of the public bureaucracy in regional decision making. For all these reasons, the task of developing workable regional policies had become more time-consuming and politically divisive.

Although the provincial government was still the only government with constitutional authority to decide how the region would be governed, all levels of government would help to determine whether the Toronto region could meet these challenges while retaining its claims to distinctiveness. There were in fact strong arguments for giving either the federal government or

---

23. Remarks by the Honourable Chris Hodgson, Ministry of Municipal Affairs and Housing, to the Toronto Summit, June 26, 2002.

local governments (or both) much larger roles in local and regional policy-making while reducing the role of the province. Such arguments not only restated long-standing municipal demands for more functional and financial independence, but also implied a loss of faith in the Ontario government's ability to make effective urban policy. When these arguments are examined in the light of this study's findings, however, it seems unlikely that giving the federal government a larger role in urban affairs or granting more powers to city governments would do much by themselves to further the goals of the regional agenda.

Arguments for a larger federal role in city-region governance often began with the observation that federal revenues were increasing faster than those of other governments. They also emphasized that cuts in federal transfers to the province had been partly responsible for provincial government decisions to offload services on municipalities. Instead of asking the federal government to contribute more to provincially run programs, however, those making such arguments wanted it to work directly with city governments, or to transfer some of its revenues (such as a share of gas or income taxes) to them, rather than channelling money through the provinces.

Appeals to the federal government had yielded some results by the end of the study period, including a commitment of federal funds to support municipal building projects and the appointment of a "Prime Minister's Caucus Task Force on Urban Issues." Previous federal governments had taken similar initiatives, however, only to reduce or abandon them during periods of budgetary restraint or when provincial governments strongly objected to federal interventions. The federal government could easily retreat again if it encountered similar constraints, or if federal leaders or federal priorities changed.

Nonetheless, federal funds for municipal building projects promised to provide relief for some of the regional problems that were causing greatest concern when the study period ended—infrastructure deficiencies and the high costs of addressing them. Different types of building projects, however, could have very different consequences for the social and physical character of the region. Federally supported projects on the urban fringe would help to bring about a more decentralized and disconnected regional development pattern than projects that strengthened the urban core as an economic, social, or cultural nucleus. Even short-lived federal programs could have long-lasting effects on regional character if they favoured one type of regional development pattern over another.

The federal government, however, still had little capacity to evaluate the impacts of its programs on regional character. This was apparent in the case of those federal policies that had already had important consequences for the character of the Toronto region. For example, federal immigration policy had been shaping (Metro) Toronto's demographic and social character for some time, and its impacts were spreading to other municipalities in the region. In addition, federally funded immigrant settlement programs were helping to determine how well immigrants were able to adapt to and play productive roles in their new society. Yet the federal government had paid little attention to the link between immigration and other trends in urban development, including increases in urban poverty and social polarization both within and among municipalities in this and other regions. The record showed, in fact, that the federal government was just as likely to withdraw as to increase support for social programs (such as social assistance, low-rental housing, and immigrant settlement) at those very times when social needs were on the rise.

What the federal government gave, in other words, it could just as easily take away, but not without leaving problems behind for other governments to cope with. The same was true of the provincial government, as Ontario's Conservative government had made abundantly clear in the late 1990s. In fact, that experience had been an important stimulus in the campaign for increased local autonomy.[24] That campaign actually had two separate components, one regional and one city-based, although the distinction was not always acknowledged. The regional component called for a charter that recognized the Greater Toronto Region as "an order of government that is a full partner of the Federal and Provincial Governments of Canada." [25] As proposed, that charter would empower the region and its municipalities to "govern and exercise responsibility over a broad range of issues ... with the exception of those matters as are mutually agreed upon with other levels of government that are best assigned to another level." Several suburban mayors had already endorsed this proposal as a useful step toward rethinking provincial–municipal relations.[26]

Toronto's Mayor Mel Lastman, however, framed the argument for local autonomy in more parochial terms. He asked the province for a new charter for Toronto alone "to protect it from further provincial offloading, give it new revenue sources and raise its legal status above that of a municipality."[27]

24. See, for example, Rowe 2000.
25. Avana Capital Corporation, "Towards a Greater Toronto Charter," 2001. The "broad range of issues" specified in this document included child and family services; cultural institutions; economic development and marketing; education; environmental protection; health care; housing; immigrant and refugee settlement; land-use planning; law enforcement and emergency services; recreation; revenue generation, taxation, and assessment; transportation; sewage treatment; social assistance; waste and natural resource management; and water supply and quality management.
26. Jennifer Lewington, "GTA mayors endorse regional charter," *Globe and Mail*, May 13, 2000.
27. James Rusk, "City needs charter status for protection: Lastman," *Globe and Mail*, June 23, 2000.

Although the city wanted more powers to make decisions without constantly seeking provincial approval, it especially wanted more money, preferably from sources that it controlled, both to carry out the responsibilities that the province had given it and to initiate new programs to deal with newly identified needs.

For the Toronto region, therefore, the 21st century began with campaigns for a loosening of central government constraints on local government powers that were much like the campaign for both municipal and county "home rule" in U.S. states a century earlier. The Toronto campaign was at an early stage, however, and there were many questions still to be addressed. From a regional governance perspective, the most important were those discussed below.

First, where should autonomous local decision-making powers reside—in a government for the whole Toronto region, in the government of the City of Toronto, or in the governments of all Ontario municipalities? To decide this question in favour of the region meant first having to decide how the region would be defined. Although advocates of regional self-government frequently referred to the GTA (by which they usually meant the City of Toronto and the regional municipalities of Durham, Halton, Peel, and York), the GTA no longer existed as a provincially recognized construct. Even the GO Transit service area included the new City of Hamilton and several other municipalities outside commonly recognized GTA boundaries. Nonetheless, advocates of regional governance reform tended to insist that the five-unit GTA still encompassed most of the needs and problems that had to be dealt with on a regional scale.

Second, if municipal and provincial politicians could agree on which municipalities to include in the region and which to leave out, they would then have to agree that it was in their mutual interests to create an authority that could speak for the region. There was little evidence, however, that either the province or municipalities wanted such an authority. The Ontario government had just done away with a regional organization (the GTSB) that it could have empowered to play a stronger role in regional governance. The same suburban mayors who endorsed the idea of a Greater Toronto Charter had neither been strong supporters of the GTSB nor had they tried to save it from the provincial axe.

Third, if the province decided against giving the region its own unit of government, but was in favour of strengthening the decision-making and financial powers of local governments, to which municipalities should it give those powers? Several members of the city charter movement initially claimed that enhanced powers should go only to the governments of Toronto and four other Canadian "hub cities" (Montreal, Calgary, Vancouver, and Winnipeg), a term used by Winnipeg Mayor Glen Murray and urban writer Jane Jacobs to emphasize the importance of these cities (the C5) to Canada's social and economic well-being.[28] Not surprisingly, as Jacobs herself conceded, other Canadian cities were "browned off" at being left out of the group, which she took to mean that the C5 should be expanded to C7, or even C10. The implication, however, was that only the core cities of Canada's largest city-regions had governments that were able to deal with their own problems in their own ways.

Demands for new relationships with federal and provincial governments were much more diffuse, however, than large city boosters acknowledged. They were also more difficult for senior governments to brush aside. Some of the dilemmas these governments faced in their dealings with the Toronto region can be deduced from Table 7.4, which lists all Canadian cities with populations of more than 100,000 in 2001 and distributes them according to size among the GTA, the rest of Ontario, and the rest of Canada. It reveals:

- Toronto and Montreal were in a class by themselves, being the only Canadian cities with populations of more than one million. If a federal government wanted to build a national base of support, however, it could not focus on these cities alone. To do so would mean offending the governments and residents of cities in eight other provinces.
- Of the 38 cities in Canada that qualified for this table, 9 were in the Greater Toronto Area. Four others (Hamilton, Kitchener, Cambridge, and Guelph), were also encompassed by the provincially designated Central Ontario Smart Growth Zone. In other words, nearly one-third of Canada's largest cities were having to decide how to deal with issues affecting the same city-region.
- Of the eight suburban municipalities in the five-unit GTA, one (Mississauga) was the seventh largest city in Canada. It was larger even than the City of Vancouver, one of the C5 cities, and almost as large as Winnipeg. It was also larger than seven of Canada's ten provincial capitals. In fact, three other GTA municipalities (Brampton, Markham, and Vaughan) were larger than six provincial capitals, only two of which (Regina and Quebec City) made it into the table. Four others were too small (Charlottetown, P.E.I., 32,245; Fredericton, N.B., 47,560; Victoria, B.C., 74,175; and St. John's, Nfld., 99,182). Yet their city and provincial governments were unlikely to respond well to a national urban policy that treated the country's largest cities as more important than provincial capitals.

---

28. "C5: Historic First Meeting of Canadian Mayors with Jane Jacobs," *Ideas that Matter*, 2 (1), 4–5 (2001).

Table 7.4 Canadian cities with more than 100,000 residents, 2001

Greater Toronto Area	Ontario	Rest of Canada
Toronto 2,481,4994		
		[a]Montreal, Que. 1,039,534
		Calgary, Alta. 878,866
	Ottawa 774,072	
		[b]Edmonton, Alta. 666,104
		[b]Winnipeg, Man. 619,884
Mississauga 612,925		
		Vancouver, B.C. 545,671
	Hamilton 490,268	
		[b]Halifax, N.S. 359,111
		[d]Surrey, B.C. 347,825
		[c]Laval, Que. 343,005
	London 336,559	
Brampton 325,428		
Markham 208,615		
	Windsor 208,402	
		Saskatoon, Sask. 196,811
		[d]Burnaby, B.C. 193,954
	Kitchener 190,399	
Vaughan 182,022		
		[b]Regina, Sask. 178,225
		[b]Quebec City, Que. 169,076
		[d]Richmond, B.C. 164,076
	Sudbury 155,219	
Burlington 150,836		
Oakville 144,758		
Oshawa 139,051		
Richmond Hill 132,022		
	St. Catharines 129,170	
		[c]Longueuil, Que. 128,016
		Abbotsford, B.C. 115,463
	Kingston 114,195	
		[d]Coquitlam, B.C. 112,890
	Cambridge 110,372	
	Thunder Bay 109,106	
	Guelph 106,070	
		Saanich, B.C. 103,654
		[e]Gatineau, Que. 102,898

a. Montreal's population jumped to 1.8 million late in 2001 when the Quebec government amalgamated the 28 municipalities on the Island of Montreal, all of them members of the two-tier Montreal Urban Community (MUC), into a much-enlarged City of Montreal.

b. Provincial capital
c. Suburb of Montreal
d. Suburb of Vancouver
e. Suburb of Ottawa

Source: Census of Canada, 2001.

The political perils inherent in catering to only a few large cities and ignoring all others was undoubtedly why federal government talk of "a new deal for cities" quickly changed to talk of "a new deal for municipalities" just after the study period ended. New federal money would go to large and small municipalities alike, as long as they could convince the federal government that they qualified for it. The Ontario government had behaved similarly toward its own municipal governments in the past, typically extending to all municipalities either the opportunity or the obligation to participate in programs instigated by Toronto or some other city. Although municipal governments did not always welcome such programs, especially if they had to pay some of their costs, local politicians typically objected to any indication that the province was singling Toronto out for special treatment. They were likely to raise similar objections to government decisions to give Toronto more freedom of action or new sources of revenue without giving other local governments the same rights.

This observation raises two additional questions with important implications for the future of Toronto region governance: To which of its municipal governments would the province give additional powers? And what powers would it give them? Even if the province decided to extend new decision-making autonomy only to the governments of cities that met certain criteria, such as population size, or types of economic activity, or rate of growth, or level of social need, it would have to include many of Toronto's suburbs in the changes it made. In doing so, it could easily add to the mechanisms that suburban governments already used to strengthen their own positions within the region, even at the risk of weakening other municipalities, including Toronto.

To raise these final two questions is to highlight a fundamental contradiction in the argument that Toronto and other cities should have more decision-making autonomy because of their importance to the national and provincial economies. It can just as easily be argued that the greater the importance of cities to their national, provincial, or state economies, the more interest central governments are likely to take in what city governments do and how well they do it. National governments will be most likely to support local government activities that promise to further national objectives. Similarly, provincial or state governments are most likely to surrender only those municipal responsibilities that they no longer consider important to their own economic or political interests. For this reason, increasing local autonomy would not necessarily mean that regional objectives would either be pursued or realized.

Nonetheless, municipal governments were still likely to play important roles in shaping the region, even if they did not acquire substantially greater powers. This study has provided numerous examples of ways in which municipal governments, while nominally constrained by provincial laws or regulations, used their legal powers, their financial resources, and their persuasive skills to influence the way services were provided in the region and the way the region evolved. In fact, municipal governments, particularly those of Toronto and Metropolitan Toronto, often took the lead in proposing or developing innovative programs to deal with new circumstances, and then persuading senior governments to support them.

Allowing municipal governments more freedom to innovate, therefore, could result in new and useful ways to address problems that confronted some or all of the region's local governments. As a general rule, however, municipal governments had always been more likely to use whatever means they could to enhance their own status and competitive positions within the region without considering what their actions might mean for other municipalities or the people who lived in them. They were likely to go on doing so unless they were constrained by provincial laws or regulations to act in ways that took regional as well as local interests into account.

Provincial government policies would remain critical, therefore, in deciding the future character of the region and the well-being of the people who lived there. Particularly important would be the way its policies addressed such matters as the rapid rate and declining density of new suburban development, the provision and siting of new infrastructure, the distribution of residential and employment opportunities among the region's different municipalities, the declining ability of regional residents to move about the region without a car, and the differing abilities of regional and municipal governments to fund social and community services. If the provincial government decided to leave such matters entirely in the hands of municipal governments, residential densities would probably go on declining, especially at the edge of the region; automobile use would continue to rise; and the gap between rich and poor communities would continue to widen. Moreover, the services available to the region's poorest residents would likely deteriorate as municipalities with large low income populations diverted more of their resources into efforts to protect or build their economies and to persuade middle-class residents not to move elsewhere.

At the end of the study period, several of the Toronto region's municipal governments were grappling with the challenges posed by growing poverty and rapid demographic change. The City of Toronto faced the most numerous and widespread challenges, however, and they seemed likely to increase. The city would also remain the region's most visible symbol of the ability of Canadian institutions to deal with some of the more intractable problems of urban life and global change. The answer to Toronto's problems did not seem to lie, therefore, in cutting the city adrift from the province and asking it to deal with its situation on its own. There was always a danger, however, that a future provincial government might decide to use this approach to its own advantage. What was needed, therefore, was a concerted effort by those concerned for the city's well-being to persuade all other governments, including the governments of other municipalities in the Toronto region, that helping to keep the city strong would be of benefit not only to the province but to the entire nation.

References

A note on sources: Information used in this study came from a large number of sources, including interviews with knowledgeable individuals and unpublished documents. These are cited only in the footnotes.

Newspaper and magazine articles are also cited only in the footnotes. This material came from the following publications:

Alberta Report
Canadian Railway and Marine World
City Magazine
East York Mirror
Financial Post
Globe and Mail
GTA/905 Development News (Novæ Res Urbis)
Housing Again (http://housingagain.web.ca)
Ideas that Matter
Maclean's Magazine
Municipal World
Railway Age
The Intensification Report (Canadian Urban Institute)
Toronto (published by *The Globe and Mail* from 1988 to 1991).
Toronto Life
Toronto Star
Toronto Telegram

Footnote citations to items in the following list of references give the author's last name, date of publication, and page number (e.g. Lemon 1996, 242).

Adams, Thomas, Harold M. Lewis and Theodore T. McCroskey. 1974. *Population, Land Values and Government. Volume II of The Regional Survey of New York and its Environs.* First published 1929. New York: Arno Press Reprint.

Advisory Committee to the [Ontario] Minister of Municipal Affairs on the Provincial–Municipal Financial Relationship [the Hopcroft Committee]. 1991. *Report.* Toronto: The Advisory Committee, January 3.

Alway, Richard M. 1965. *Mitchell Hepburn and the Liberal Party in the Province of Ontario.* Ph.D. diss., University of Toronto.

Axworthy, Lloyd. 1971. "The Housing Task Force: A Case Study." In *The Structures of Policy-Making in Canada*, 130–153. Edited by G. Bruce Doern and Peter Aucoin. Toronto: Macmillan.

Barnes, W.R., and L.C. Ledebur. 1998. *The New Regional Economies: The U.S. Common Market and the Global Economy.* Thousand Oaks, CA.: Sage.

Bell, George G., and Andrew D. Pascoe. 1988. *The Ontario Government: Structure and Functions*. Toronto: Wall & Thompson.

Benjamin, Gerald, and Richard P. Nathan. 2001. *Regionalism and Realism: A Study of Governments in the New York Metropolitan Area*. Washington, D.C.: Brookings Institution Press.

Berridge, Joe. 1999. *Reinvesting in Toronto. What the Competition Is Doing*. Prepared by Urban Strategies, Inc. Toronto: Canadian Urban Institute.

Berridge Lewinberg Greenberg Ltd. 1992. *Shaping Growth in the GTA*. Toronto: Greater Toronto Coordinating Committee.

Birkhead, Guthrie S. 1974. "Introduction." In *A Look to the North: Canadian Regional Experience*. Volume 5 in *Substate Regionalism and the Federal System*. Washington, D.C.: Advisory Commission on Intergovernmental Relations.

Bollens, John C., and Henry J. Schmandt. 1982. *The Metropolis*. 4th ed. New York: Harper & Row.

Boudreau, Julie Ann. 2000. *The Megacity Saga: Democracy and Citizenship in the Global Age*. Montreal: Black Rose Books.

Bourne, Larry. 2003. *Social Change in the Central Ontario Region*. Toronto: The Neptis Foundation.

——, with Sarah Starkweather and Ranu Basu. 2000. *People and Places: A Portrait of the Evolving Social Character of the Greater Toronto Area*. A report for the Neptis Foundation. Toronto: University of Toronto.

Bower, R.J. 1979. "The Influence of the Subway System on the Growth of Metropolitan Toronto." In *New Urban Rail Transit: How can its Development and Growth-Shaping Potential be Realized?*, 17–28. Report prepared for the Subcommittee on the City of the Committee on Banking, Finance and Urban Affairs, U.S. House of Representatives, 96th Cong., 1st. sess. Washington: Government Printing Office.

Cameron, David M., and J. Stefan Dupré. 1983. "The Financial Framework of Income Distribution and Social Services." In *Canada and the New Constitution*, edited by Stanley M. Beck and Ivan Bernier, 333–399. Montreal: The Institute for Research on Public Policy.

Central Ontario Lakeshore Urban Complex Task Force, Advisory Committee on Urban and Regional Planning. 1974. *Report*. Toronto: The Task Force.

Chipman, John George. 2002. *A Law Unto Itself: How the Ontario Municipal Board Has Developed and Applied Land Use Planning Policy*. Toronto: University of Toronto Press.

City of Toronto. 1994. *Official Plan*. As approved by the Minister of Municipal Affairs. Toronto: Planning and Development Dept., September 8.

City of Toronto Planning Board. 1959. "Draft History of Planning Organization in Toronto."

——. 1974. *Ethnic Change, 1951–1971*. Research Bulletin 8, Toronto: Planning Board, April 8.

City Planning Board of Toronto. 1943. *The Master Plan for the City of Toronto and Environs*. Toronto: Planning Board.

Clark, S.D. 1962. *The Developing Canadian Community*. 2nd ed. Toronto: University of Toronto Press.

——. 1966. *The Suburban Society*. Toronto: University of Toronto Press.

Colton, Timothy. 1980. *Big Daddy*. Toronto: University of Toronto Press.

Comay Planning Consultants; P.S. Ross & Partners; Proctor, Redfern, Bousfield and Bacon. 1973. *Subject to Approval: A Review of Municipal Planning in Ontario*. Toronto: Ontario Economic Council.

Commission on Planning and Development Reform in Ontario (John Sewell, Chair). 1993. *New Planning for Ontario. Final Report*. Toronto: The Commission.

Committee for Economic Development. Research and Policy Committee. 1970. *Reshaping Government in Metropolitan Areas.* New York: The Committee.

Cook, Gail C.A. 1973. "Effect of Metropolitan Government on Resource Allocation: The Case of Education in Toronto." *National Tax Journal,* 26, 585–590.

Courchene, Thomas J. 2000. "NAFTA, the information revolution, and Canada–U.S. relations: an Ontario perspective." *American Review of Canadian Studies,* 30 (Summer), 159–180.

Dakin, John. 1969. "Metropolitan Toronto Planning." *Town Planning Review,* 40, 3–24.

Danielson, Michael N. 1976. *The Politics of Exclusion.* New York: Columbia University Press.

Danielson, Michael N. and Jameson W. Doig. 1982. *New York: The Politics of Urban Regional Development.* Berkeley: University of California Press.

Dear, Michael, and Glenda Laws. 1986. "Anatomy of a Decision: Recent Land Use Zoning Appeals and Their Effect on Group Home Locations in Ontario." *Canadian Journal of Community Mental Health,* 5 (1), 5–18.

DelGuidice, Dominic, and Steven M. Zacks. 1969. "Why the Ontario Committee on Taxation Made its Excursion into Regional Government." In *Politics and Government of Urban Canada: Selected Readings,* 265–285. 3rd ed. Edited by Lionel D. Feldman and Michael Goldrick. Toronto: Methuen. (First published in Bureau of Municipal Research, "Regional Government—The Key to Genuine Local Autonomy," *Civic Affairs.* Toronto, May 1968).

———. 1972. "The 101 Governments of Metropolitan Toronto." In *Politics and Government of Urban Canada: Selected Readings,* 237–247. 2nd ed. Edited by Lionel D. Feldman and Michael D. Goldrick. Toronto: Methuen. (First published in Bureau of Municipal Research, "Regional Government—The Key to Genuine Local Autonomy," *Civic Affairs,* Toronto, May 1968).

Dodge, William R. 1996. *Regional Excellence: Governing Together to Compete Globally and Flourish Locally.* Washington, D.C.: National League of Cities.

Donald, Betsy. 2002. "Spinning Toronto's golden age: The making of a 'city that worked.'" *Environment and Planning A,* 34: 2127–2154.

Downs, Anthony. 2001. "What Does 'Smart Growth' Really Mean?" *Planning,* 67 (April), 136–156.

Dreier, Peter, John Mollenkopf, and Todd Swanstrom. 2001. *Place Matters: Metropolitics for the Twenty-first Century.* Lawrence, Kansas: University of Kansas Press.

Dupré, J. Stefan. 1972. "The Political Dimensions of Regional Government." In *Politics and Government of Urban Canada: Selected Readings,* 284–289. Edited by Lionel D. Feldman and Michael D. Goldrick. Toronto: Methuen.

Dyck, Rand. 1986. *Provincial Politics in Canada.* Scarborough, Ont.: Prentice-Hall, 1986.

Elazar, Daniel J. 1966. *American Federalism: A View from the States.* New York: Thomas Y. Crowell.

Ewing, Gordon O. 1992. "The Bases of Differences between American and Canadian Cities." *The Canadian Geographer* 36(3), 266–279.

Fallis, George. 1985. *Housing Economics.* Toronto: Butterworths.

Farrow, G.M. 1989. "Notes for Remarks ... at the 'Insight' Seminar, *The Planning Act*: Is Council in Control?" Toronto: Insight.

Federal Task Force on Housing and Urban Development. 1969. *Report.* Ottawa: Information Canada.

Feldman, Lionel D. 1963. "A Housing Project Wends its Weary Way." *Canadian Public Administration,* 6, 221–232.

Filion, Pierre, Kathleen McSpurren, and Nancy Huether. 2000. "Synergy and Movement within Suburban Mixed-Use Centres: The Toronto Experience." *Journal of Urban Affairs,* 22 (4), 419–438.

Fish, Susan A. 1976. "Winning the Battle and Losing the War in the Fight to Improve Municipal Policy-Making." In *Politics and Government of Urban Canada: Selected Readings*, 175–186. 3rd ed. Edited by L.D. Feldman and M.D. Goldrick. Toronto: Methuen.

Fisher, Harry K. 1972. "Local-Provincial Relations in Education." In *School Boards and Political Fact*, 24–32. Edited by P. Cistone. Toronto: Ontario Institute for Studies in Education.

Fox, Kenneth. 1977. *Better City Government*. Philadelphia: Temple University Press.

Frisken, Frances, ed. 1982. *Conflict or Cooperation. The Toronto-Centred Region in the 1980s*. Symposium Proceedings. Toronto: Urban Studies Program, York University, Division of Social Science.

——. 1984. "A Triumph for Public Ownership: The Toronto Transportation Commission, 1921–53." In *Forging a Consensus: Historical Essays on Toronto*, 238–271. Edited by Victor L. Russell. Toronto: University of Toronto Press.

——. 1986. "Canadian Cities and the American Example: A Prologue to Urban Policy Analysis." 1986. *Canadian Public Administration*, 29 (Fall), 345–376.

——. 1988. *City Policy-Making in Theory and Practice: The Case of Toronto's Downtown Plan*. London, Ont.: Department of Political Science, The University of Western Ontario.

——. 1991. "Local Constraints on Provincial Initiative in a Dynamic Context: The Case of Property Tax Reform in Ontario." *Canadian Journal of Political Science*, 24 (June), 351–378.

——. 1993. "Planning and Servicing the Greater Toronto Area: The Interplay of Provincial and Municipal Interests." In *Metropolitan Governance: American/Canadian Perspectives*, 153–204. Edited by Donald N. Rothblatt and Andrew Sancton. Berkeley: Institute of Governmental Studies Press; and Kingston, Ontario: Queen's University Institute of Intergovernmental Relations.

——, L.S. Bourne, Gunter Gad, and Robert A. Murdie. 1997. "Governance and Social Well-Being in the Toronto Area: Past Achievements and Future Challenges." Research Paper No. 193. Toronto: Centre for Urban and Community Studies, University of Toronto.

——, and Marcia Wallace. 2000. *The Response of the Municipal Public Service Sector to the Challenge of Immigrant Settlement*. Report prepared for Citizenship and Immigration Canada. (Revised 2002.)

——. 2003. "Governing the Multicultural City-Region." *Canadian Public Administration*, 46 (2) , 153–177.

Gainsborough, Juliet F. 2001(a). "Bridging the City-Suburb Divide: States and the Politics of Regional Cooperation." *Journal of Urban Affairs*, 23 (5), 497–512.

——. 2001(b). *Fenced Off. The Suburbanization of American Politics*. Washington, D.C.: Georgetown University Press.

Gelfand, Mark J. 1980. "How Cities Arrived on the National Agenda in the United States." In *Financing Urban Government in the Welfare State*, 28–49. Edited by Douglas E. Ashford. London: Croom Helm.

Gidney, R.D. 1999. *From Hope to Harris: The Reshaping of Ontario's Schools*. Toronto: University of Toronto Press.

Goldberg, Michael A., and John Mercer. 1986. *The Myth of the North American City: Continentalism Challenged*. Vancouver: University of Vancouver Press.

Goldenberg, Carl. 1939. *Municipal Finance in Canada: A Study Prepared for the Royal Commission on Dominion-Provincial Relations*. Ottawa: The Royal Commission.

Goldrick, Michael, and D. Holmes, eds. 1981. *Jobs and the Metro Toronto Economy*. Toronto: Urban Studies Program, Division of Social Science, York University.

Gomme, Ted. 1984. "Municipal Planning in Ontario." *Plan Canada*, 24 (December), 102–110.

Goodall, Leonard E. 1968. *The American Metropolis.* Columbus, Ohio: Charles E. Merrill.

Grad, Frank P. 1970. "The State's Capacity to Respond to Urban Problems: The State Constitution." In *The States and the Urban Crisis,* 27–58. Edited by Alan K. Campbell. Englewood Cliffs, N.J.: Prentice-Hall.

Graham, Roger. 1990. *Old Man Ontario: Leslie M. Frost.* Toronto: University of Toronto Press for the Ontario Historical Studies Series.

Greater Toronto Services Board. 2000. *Removing Roadblocks to Continued Economic Prosperity for the Greater Toronto Area, Ontario and Canada. A Strategic Transportation Plan for the GTA and Hamilton-Wentworth.* Toronto: Greater Toronto Services Board.

Green, Alan and David Green. 1996. "The Economic Goals of Canada's Immigration Policy, Past and Present." Research on Immigration and Integration in the Metropolis, Working Paper Series No. 96-04. Burnaby, B.C.: Simon Fraser University.

Greer, Scott. 1962. *Governing the Metropolis.* New York: John Wiley.

GTA Task Force. 1996. *Greater Toronto: Report of the GTA Task Force.* Toronto: The Queen's Printer.

Gulick, L.H. 1962. *The Metropolitan Problem and American Ideas.* New York: Knopf.

Gurr, Ted Robert and Desmond S. King. 1987. *The State and the City.* Chicago: University of Chicago Press.

Harrigan, John J. 1985. *Political Change in the Metropolis.* 3rd ed. Toronto and Boston: Little, Brown and Company.

Hawley, Amos H. and Basil G. Zimmer. 1970. *The Metropolitan Community.* Beverly Hills: Sage.

Hawley, Willis D. 1976. "On Understanding Metropolitan Political Integration." In *Theoretical Perspectives on Urban Politics,* 100–145. Edited by Willis D. Hawley, Michael Lipsky, Stanley B. Greenberg, J. David Greenstone, Ira Katznelson, Karen Orren, Paul E. Peterson, Martin Shefter and Douglas Yates. Englewood Cliffs, N.J.: Prentice-Hall.

Higgins, Donald J.H. 1986. *Local and Urban Politics in Canada.* Toronto: Gage.

Hobson, Paul A.R., and France St-Hilaire, eds. 1997. *Urban Governance and Finance: A Question of Who Does What.* Montreal: The Institute for Research in Public Policy.

Horak, Martin. 1998. *The Power of Local Identity: C4LD and the Anti-Amalgamation Mobilization in Toronto.* Research Paper No. 195. Toronto: Centre for Urban and Community Studies, University of Toronto.

Hoy, Claire. 1985. *Bill Davis.* Toronto: Methuen.

IBI Group and Associates. 1990. *Greater Toronto Area Urban Structure Concepts Study. Summary Report.* Toronto: The Greater Toronto Coordinating Committee.

Ibbitson, John. 1997. *Promised Land: Inside the Mike Harris Revolution.* Scarborough, Ont.: Prentice-Hall.

Isin, Engin F., and Joanne Wolfson. 1999. *The Making of the Toronto Megacity: An Introduction.* Working Paper No. 21. Toronto: York University Urban Studies Program.

Jacek, Henry J. 1985. "Regional Government and Development: Initiation, Implementation and Impact." In *Government and Politics of Ontario,* 100–118. Edited by Donald C. MacDonald. Scarborough, Ont.: Nelson.

Jackson, Kenneth T. 1972. "Metropolitan Government versus Suburban Autonomy: Politics on the Crabgrass Frontier." In *Cities in American History,* 442–462. Edited by Kenneth T. Jackson and Stanley K. Schultz. New York: Knopf.

Jarrett, Gould, and Elliott. 1975. *A Financial Profile of Metropolitan Toronto and its Constituent Municipalities, 1967–1973.* Background report. Toronto: The Royal Commission on Metropolitan Toronto.

Jones, Victor. 1942. *Metropolitan Government.* Chicago: The University of Chicago Press.

Kanter, Ron. 1990. *Space for All: Options for a Greater Toronto Area Greenlands Strategy.* Report submitted to The Honourable David Peterson, Premier of Ontario. Toronto: Government of Ontario.

Kantor, Paul. 1995. *The Dependent City Revisited: The Political Economy of Urban Development and Social Policy.* Boulder, San Francisco, and Oxford: Westview Press.

Kaplan, Harold. 1967. *Urban Political Systems.* New York and London: Columbia University Press.

——. 1982. *Reform, Planning, and City Politics: Montreal, Winnipeg, Toronto.* Toronto: University of Toronto Press.

Keating, Michael. 1995. "Size, Efficiency and Democracy: Consolidation, Fragmentation and Public Choice." In *Theories of Urban Politics*, 117–134. Edited by David Judge, Gerry Stoker and Harold Wolman. London: Thousand Oaks, and New Delhi: Sage.

Keil, Roger. 1998. "Toronto in the 1990s: Dissociated Governance." *Studies in Political Economy*, 56 (Summer), 151–167.

Kitchen, Harry M. 1977. *Public Finance in Metropolitan Toronto.* Toronto: The Royal Commission on Metropolitan Toronto.

Klein and Sears. 1975. *The Provision and Conservation of Housing in Metropolitan Toronto.* Background report. Toronto: The Royal Commission on Metropolitan Toronto.

Kozol, Jonathan. 1991. *Savage Inequalities.* New York: Crown Publishing.

Lemon, James. 1985. *Toronto since 1918: An Illustrated History.* Toronto: James Lorimer & Company.

——. 1996. *Liberal Dreams and Nature's Limits: Great Cities of North America Since 1600.* Toronto, New York, Oxford: Oxford University Press.

Lithwick, N.H. 1970. *Urban Canada: Problems and Prospects.* Ottawa: Central Mortgage and Housing Corporation.

Long, Norton. 1958. "The Local Community as an Ecology of Games." *The American Journal of Sociology*, 64, 3 (November), 251–261.

——. 1962. "Who Makes Decisions in Metropolitan Areas." In Norton E. Long, *The Polity*, 256–64. Edited by Charles Press. Chicago: Rand McNally.

——. 1972. The Unwalled City: Reconstituting the Urban Community. New York: Basic Books.

Magnusson, Warren. 1983. "Toronto." In *City Politics in Canada*, 94–139. Edited by Warren Magnusson and Andrew Sancton. Toronto: University of Toronto Press.

Manzer, Ronald. 1985. *Public Policies and Political Development in Canada.* Toronto: University of Toronto Press.

Markusen, Ann R. 1978. "Class and Urban Social Expenditure: A Marxist Theory of Metropolitan Government." In *Marxism and Metropolis*, 102–110. Edited by William K. Tabb and Larry Sawers. New York: Oxford University Press.

Martin, Joe. 1974. *The Role and Place of Ontario in the Canadian Federation.* Toronto: Ontario Economic Council.

Mary Collins Consultants Ltd. and Community Social Planning Associates. 1975. *Social Policy in Metropolitan Toronto.* Background report. Toronto: Royal Commission on Metropolitan Toronto.

McCordic, Wm. J. 1964. "Metro's Dilemma in Public Education." *Canadian Public Administration*, 7 (December), 464–478.

——. 1969. "Urban Education: An Experiment in Two-Tiered Administration." In *Politics and Government of Urban Canada: Selected Readings*, 86–98. 2nd ed. Edited by Lionel D. Feldman and Michael Goldrick. Toronto: Methuen.

McDougall, A.K. 1986. *John P. Robarts; His Life and Government.* Toronto: University of Toronto Press for the Ontario Historical Studies Series.

McGilly, Frank J. 1972. *The Functions of Conflict in the Council of Metropolitan Toronto, 1953–1966.* Ph.D. diss., The University of Pittsburg.

McKenzie, R.D. 1933. *The Metropolitan Community.* New York: McGraw Hill.

McMahon, Michael. 1990. *Metro's Housing Company: The First 35 Years.* Toronto: Metropolitan Toronto Housing Company Limited.

Melchers, Ron. 1999. "Local Governance of Social Welfare: Local Reform in Ontario in the Nineties." *Canadian Review of Social Policy,* 43 (Spring), 29–57.

Mellon, Hugh. 1993. "Reforming the Electoral System of Metropolitan Toronto: Doing away with Dual Representation." *Canadian Public Administration,* 36 (1): 38–56.

Metro Community Services, Social Development Division. 1995. *Filling in the Future: Social Prospects for Metro Toronto.* Toronto: Municipality of Metropolitan Toronto.

Metropolitan Toronto and Region Transportation Study, Technical Advisory and Coordinating Committee. 1967. *Transportation for the Regional City.* Toronto: The Committee.

Metropolitan Toronto Council. 1995. "There's No Turning Back: A Proposal for Change." Submission to the Greater Toronto Area Task Force. Toronto: Metro Chief Administrator's Office, Corporate Planning Division.

Metropolitan Toronto Council Minutes (Metro Minutes). Various years.

Metropolitan Toronto Planning Board. 1959. *The Official Plan of the Metropolitan Toronto Planning Area.* Draft. Toronto: The MTPB.

———. 1965. *Official Plan of the Metropolitan Toronto Planning Area.* Proposed. Toronto: The MTPB.

Metropolitan Toronto Planning Board, Research and Transportation Divisions, 1974. *Preliminary Impressions of the Urban Structure: To 1971.* Background study. Toronto: Metroplan: Plan for the Urban Structure of Metropolitan Toronto.

Metropolitan Toronto Planning Department, Policy Development Division. 1986. *The Changing Metropolitan Economy.* Toronto: Metropolitan Plan Review Report No. 2. Toronto: The Municipality of Metropolitan Toronto.

———. 1987. *Housing Trends 1976–1986.* Toronto: Metropolitan Plan Review Report No. 3. Toronto: The Municipality of Metropolitan Toronto.

Metropolitan Toronto Planning Department, Research and Information Services Division. 1996. *Housing Patterns and Prospects in Metro.* Toronto: The Municipality of Metropolitan Toronto.

Metropolitan Toronto Planning Department, Research and Special Studies Division. 1994. *1991 Census Atlas. Series B Data.* Toronto: The Municipality of Metropolitan Toronto.

———. 1995. *Metropolitan Toronto Key Facts 1995.* Toronto: The Municipality of Metropolitan Toronto.

Metropolitan Toronto Planning Department and Toronto Transit Commission. 1986. *Network 2011, Final Report.* Toronto: Metropolitan Toronto Planning Department.

Metropolitan Toronto Transportation Plan Review. 1973. *Strengths and Weaknesses, Part 1: Public Transport.* Toronto: Municipality of Metropolitan Toronto.

Miller, Eric J. and Amer Said Shalaby. 2000. *Travel in the Greater Toronto Area: Past and Current Behaviour and Relation to Urban Form.* Report prepared for the Neptis Foundation. Toronto: University of Toronto Joint Program in Transportation.

Milner, James B. 1957. "The Metropolitan Toronto Plan." *University of Pennsylvania Law Review,* 105 (February), 572–587.

Miron, John. 1988. *Housing in Postwar Canada: Demographic Change, Household Formation, and Housing Demand.* Kingston and Montreal: McGill-Queen's University Press.

Mogulof, Melvin. 1972. *Five Metropolitan Governments.* Washington: The Urban Institute.

Moore, Peter W. 1979. "Zoning and Planning: the Toronto Experience, 1904–1970." In *The Usable Urban Past: Planning and Politics in the Modern Canadian City.* Edited by Alan F.J. Artibise and Gilbert A. Stelter. Toronto: Macmillan.

Morton, Desmond, 1985. "Sic Permanet: Ontario People and Their Politics." In *Government and Politics of Ontario,* 1–16. 3rd ed. Edited by Donald C. MacDonald. Scarborough, Ont.: Nelson Canada.

Municipality of Metropolitan Toronto. 1976. *Metroplan. Concept and Objectives*. Toronto: Metropolitan Planning Department.

——. 1980. *Official Plan for the Urban Structure*. Toronto: Municipality of Metropolitan Toronto.

——. 1994. *The Official Plan of the Municipality of Metropolitan Toronto: The Liveable Metropolis*. As approved by the Minister of Municipal Affairs, December 30. Toronto: Metro Planning.

Neatby, H. Blair. 1972. *The Politics of Chaos: Canada in the Thirties*. Toronto: Macmillan.

Oliver, Peter. 1985. *Unlikely Tory: The Life and Times of Allan Grossman*. Toronto: Lester and Orpen Dennys.

Ontario Advisory Task Force on Housing Policy. 1973. *Report*. Toronto: The Queen's Printer.

Ontario Committee on the Costs of Education. 1978. *Final Report*. Ontario: The Committee.

Ontario Committee on Taxation. 1967. *Report*, Vol. II: *The Local Revenue System*. Toronto: The Queen's Printer.

Ontario Community Planning Branch, Department of Municipal Affairs. 1967. *Choices for a Growing Region*. Final Report, Metropolitan Toronto and Region Transportation Study. Toronto: Metropolitan Toronto and Region Transportation Study.

Ontario Fair Tax Commission. 1993. *Fair Taxation in a Changing World. Report of the Fair Tax Commission: Highlights*. Toronto: University of Toronto Press.

Ontario Fair Tax Commission, Property Tax Working Group. 1992. *Report: Property Tax*. Toronto: The Fair Tax Commission.

Ontario Government. 1938. *Statement to the Royal Commission on Dominion-Provincial Relations. Book II: General Statement*. Ottawa: The Royal Commission.

——. 1997. *Provincial Policy Statement*. Revised February 1. Toronto: Publications Ontario Bookstore.

——. 1999. *Greater Toronto Services Board Act*. Office Consolidation Statutes of Ontario 1998, Chapter 23. December 3. Toronto: The Queen's Printer.

Ontario Interdepartmental Advisory Committee on Regional Development, 1970. *Design for Development: the Toronto-Centered Region*. Toronto: Queen's Printer.

Ontario Ministry of Education. 1974. *Report of the Ministerial Commission on the Organization and Financing of the Public and Secondary School Systems in Metropolitan Toronto*. Toronto: The Ministry.

——. 1978. *Government Statement on the Review of Local Government in the Municipality of Metropolitan Toronto: Education*. White Paper. May 4. Toronto: The Ministry.

——. 1983. *Commission to Inquire into the Discretionary Local Levy for Education in Metropolitan Toronto*. Toronto: Toronto: The Ministry.

Ontario Ministry of Municipal Affairs. 1995. *Comprehensive Set of Policy Statements*. Toronto: The Ministry of Municipal Affairs.

Ontario Ministry of Municipal Affairs and Housing. 1984. *Ontario Housing Corporation 1964-1984*. Toronto: The Ministry of Municipal Affairs and Housing.

Ontario Ministry of Treasury, Economics and Intergovernmental Affairs. 1975. *The Report of the Special Program Review*. Toronto: Ontario Government Bookstore.

——. 1976. *Regional Government in Perspective: A Financial Review*. Ontario Tax Studies 11. Toronto: The Ministry.

——. 1978. *White Paper: Government Statement on the Review of Local Government in the Municipality of Metropolitan Toronto*. Toronto: The Ministry.

Ontario Municipal Board. 1953. *In the Matter of Sections 20 and 22 of "The Municipal Act" … Decisions and Recommendations of the Board*. Toronto: The Queen's Printer.

Ontario Office for the Greater Toronto Area. 1992. *GTA 2021—The Challenge of our Future*. Toronto: Ontario Office for the Greater Toronto Area.

Ontario Planning Act Review Committee. 1977. *Report.* Toronto: The Committee.

Ontario Provincial–Municipal Grants Reform Committee. 1977. *Report 1.* Toronto: The Committee.

Ontario Provincial-Municipal Relations Committee. 1953. *Progress Report.* Toronto: The Committee.

Ontario Royal Commission on Learning. 1994. *For the Love of Learning.* 4 vols. Toronto: The Commission.

Ontario School Board Reduction Task Force. 1996. *Final Report.* Toronto: Publications Ontario.

Ontario Smart Growth Secretariat. 2001. "Ontario Smart Growth." Consultation paper. Toronto: The Queen's Printer.

Ontario Transit Advisory Group to the Minister of Transportation of Ontario. 1987. *Crossing the Boundaries: Coordinating Transit in the Greater Toronto Area.* Ontario: Transit Advisory Group.

Ontario Transit Integration Task Force. 1994. *Beyond the Periphery. Coordinating Public Transit in the Greater Toronto Area.* Final Report. Toronto: Ontario Ministry of Transportation.

Orfield, Myron. 1997. *Metropolitics: A Regional Agenda for Community and Stability.* Washington, D.C.: Brookings Institution Press.

Owen, C. James, and York Wilburn. 1985. *Governing Metropolitan Indianapolis.* Berkeley: University of California Press for the Institute of Governmental Studies.

Painter, Joe. 1995. "Regulation Theory, Post-Fordism and Urban Politics." In *Theories of Urban Politics,* 276–295. Edited by David Judge, Gerry Stoker and Harold Wolman. London: Thousand Oaks, and New Delhi: Sage.

Paterson Planning and Research Limited. 1983. *Inter-regional Transit Coordination: A Working Paper.* Scarborough: Paterson Planning and Research Ltd.

Pearson, Norman. 1975. "Regional Government and Development." In *Government and Politics of Ontario,* 171–193. Edited by Donald C. MacDonald. Toronto: Macmillan.

Peirce, Neal, Curtis Johnson, and John Stuart Hall. 1993. *Citistates: How Urban America Can Prosper in a Competitive World.* Washington, D.C.: Seven Locks Press.

Pendergrast, Eudora S. 1981. *Suburbanizing the Central City: An Analysis of the Shift in Transportation Policies Governing the Development of Metropolitan Toronto, 1959–1978.* Paper No. 27. Toronto: University of Toronto Department of Urban and Regional Planning, Papers on Planning and Design.

Penner, Norman. 1978. "Ontario: The Dominant Province." In *Canadian Provincial Politics: The Party Systems of the Ten Provinces.* 2nd ed. Edited by Martin Robin. Scarborough, Ont.: Prentice-Hall.

Pickvance, Christopher. 1995. "Marxist Theories of Urban Politics." In *Theories of Urban Politics,* 253–275. Edited by David Judge, Gerry Stoker and Harold Wolman. London: Thousand Oaks, and New Delhi: Sage.

Pill, Juri. 1979. *Planning and Politics: The Metro Toronto Transportation Plan Review.* Cambridge, Mass.: The MIT Press.

Plumptre, A.W.F. 1935. *The Government of the Metropolitan Area of Toronto.* Report to the Hon. David Croll, Minister of Municipal Affairs in the Province of Ontario.

Rachlis, Chuck, and David Wolfe. 1997. "An Insiders' View of the NDP Government of Ontario: The Politics of Permanent Opposition Meets the Economics of Permanent Recession." In *The Government and Politics of Ontario,* 331–364. 5th ed. Edited by Graham White. Toronto: University of Toronto Press.

Regional Municipality of York. n.d. *Insights. Local and Regional Government in York Region.* Newmarket, Ont.: Regional Municipality of York Information Office.

Review Panel on the Greater Toronto Area Task Force. 1996. *The Report.* Toronto: The Review Panel.

Richardson, N.H. 1981. "Insubstantial Pageant: The Rise and Fall of Provincial Planning in Ontario." *Canadian Public Administration*, 24 (Winter), 563–585.

Richmond, Don. 1974. *The Economic Transformation of Ontario*. Toronto: Ontario Economic Council.

——. 1991. "Social and Community Services: Who's in Charge? Who Should Be?" In *Dialogue on Urban Issues*. Toronto: Canadian Urban Institute.

Rideout, E. Brock. 1974. "Equality of Educational Opportunity Versus Local Autonomy— the Dilemma Facing North American Education—the Ontario Experience." In *Futures in School Finance: Working Toward A Common Goal*. Proceedings of the 17th Conference of the National Conference on School Finance, Orlando, Florida.

Robarts, J.P. 1966. *Statement by the Prime Minister of Ontario re: the Report of the Royal Commission on Metropolitan Toronto*. Toronto: The Queen's Printer.

Rose, Albert. 1958. *Regent Park: A Study in Slum Clearance*. Toronto: University of Toronto Press.

——. 1972. *Governing Metropolitan Toronto: A Social and Political Analysis 1953–1971*. Berkeley: University of California Press.

——. 1980. *Canadian Housing Policies (1935–1980)*. Toronto: Butterworths.

Rowe, Mary W. 2000. *Toronto: Considering Self-Government*. Owen Sound, Ont.: The Ginger Press.

Royal Commission on Dominion–Provincial Relations. 1940. *Report*. 3 vols. Ottawa: J.O. Paderaude, Printer to the King.

Royal Commission on the Future of the Toronto Waterfront (Honourable David Crombie, Commissioner). 1992. *Regeneration: Toronto's Waterfront and the Sustainable City*. Final Report. Ottawa: Minister of Supply and Services; and Toronto: The Queen's Printer.

Royal Commission on Metropolitan Toronto (H. Carl Goldenberg, Commissioner). 1965. *Report*. Toronto: The Queen's Printer.

Royal Commission on Metropolitan Toronto (Honourable John. P. Robarts, Commissioner). 1977(a). *Report. Volume 1: Metropolitan Toronto: A Framework for the Future*. Toronto: The Commission.

——. 1977(b). *Report. Volume 2: Detailed Findings and Recommendations*. Toronto: The Commission.

Rusk, David. 2003. *Cities without Suburbs. A Census 2000 Update*. Washington, D.C.: Woodrow Wilson Center Press.

Sancton, Andrew. 2000. "Amalgamations, Service Realignment, and Property Taxes: Did the Harris Government have a Plan for Ontario's Municipalities?" *Canadian Journal of Regional Science*, 23 (1), 135–156.

——. 2001. "Canadian Cities and the New Regionalism." *Journal of Urban Affairs*, 23 (5): 543–555.

Sewell, John. 1993. *The Shape of the City: Toronto Struggles with Modern Planning*. Toronto: University of Toronto Press.

Sharpe, L.J., ed. 1995. *The Government of World Cities: The Future of the Metro Model*. Chichester, New York, Brisbane, Toronto, Singapore: John Wiley & Sons.

Simeon, Richard. 1985. "Ontario in Confederation." In *Government and Politics of Ontario*, 133–157. 3rd ed. Edited by Donald C. MacDonald. Toronto: Nelson.

Slack, Enid. 2000. *Municipal Finance and Governance in the Greater Toronto Area: Can the GTA Meet the Challenges of the 21st Century?* A report to the Neptis Foundation. Toronto: Programme in Planning, Dept. of Geography, University of Toronto.

——, and Richard Bird. 1991. "Financing Urban Growth Through Development Charges." *Canadian Tax Journal*, 39 (5), 1288–1304.

Smallwood, Frank. 1963. *Metro Toronto: A Decade Later*. Toronto: Bureau of Municipal Research.

Smith, Auld & Associates. 1975. *The Organization of Local Government in Metropolitan Toronto*. Background report. Toronto: The Royal Commission on Metropolitan Toronto.

Social Planning Council of Metropolitan Toronto. 1963. *A Study of the Needs and Resources for Community-Supported Welfare, Health and Recreation Services in Metropolitan Toronto.* Toronto: Social Planning Council of Metropolitan Toronto.

———. 1979. *Metro's Suburbs in Transition. Part I: Evolution and Overview.* Toronto: Social Planning Council.

———. 1980. *Metro's Suburbs in Transition. Part II. The Planning Agenda for the Eighties.* Toronto: Social Planning Council.

Studenski, Paul. 1930. *The Government of Metropolitan Areas in the United States.* New York: National Municipal League. Reprinted by Arno Press, 1974.

Tator, C., and F. Henry. 1991. *Multicultural Education: Translating Policy into Practice.* Ottawa: Multiculturalism and Citizenship Canada.

Teaford, Jon C. 1979. *City and Suburb: The Political Fragmentation of Metropolitan America, 1850-1970.* Baltimore: Johns Hopkins.

Thoman, Richard S. 1971. *Design for Development in Ontario: The Initiation of a Regional Planning Program.* Toronto: Allister Typesetting and Graphics.

Tindal, C.R. 1977. *Structural Change in Local Government: Government for Urban Regions.* Toronto: The Institute of Public Administration of Canada.

Toronto and York Planning Board, 1949. *Report.* December 1. Toronto: Toronto and York Planning Board.

Toronto Bureau of Municipal Research. 1972. *Reorganizing Local Government—A Brief Look at Four Provinces. Civic Affairs.* Toronto: The Bureau.

Toronto City Council. *Minutes.* Various years.

Toronto Civic Advisory Council, The Committee on Metropolitan Problems. 1949. *First Report.* Toronto: The Committee.

———. 1951. *Final Report.* Toronto: The Committee.

Toronto Committee to Enquire into Housing Conditions in the Several Areas of the City of Toronto. 1934. *Report.* Toronto: Press of the Hunter-Rose Co. Ltd.

Toronto Urban Development Services 2002. *Toronto Official Plan.* Toronto: Toronto City Planning Division.

United Way of Greater Toronto and Canadian Council on Social Development. 2004. *Poverty by Postal Code: The Geography of Neighbourhood Poverty City of Toronto, 1981–2001.* Toronto: United Way of Greater Toronto.

U.S. Department of Commerce, Bureau of the Census. 1948. *The Growth of Metropolitan Districts in the United States, 1900–1940.* Washington, D.C.: U.S. Government Printing Office.

Voith, R. 1992. "City and Suburban Growth: Substitutes or Complements." *Business Review,* (September/October), 21–33.

Wakstein, Allen M. 1972. "Boston's Search for a Metropolitan Solution." *Journal of the American Institute of Planners,* 38 (September), 285–296.

Walkom, Thomas. 1994. *Rae Days.* Toronto: Key Porter Books.

Wallace, Marcia, and Frances Frisken. 2000. *City-Suburban Differences in Government Responses to Immigration in the Greater Toronto Area.* Research Paper No. 197. Toronto: Centre for Urban and Community Studies, University of Toronto.

Warner, Sam Bass. 1968. *The Private City; Philadelphia in Three Periods of its Growth.* Philadelphia: University of Pennsylvania Press.

Weaver, John C. 1979. "The Modern City Realized: Toronto Civic Affairs, 1880–1915." In *The Usable Urban Past: Planning and Politics in the Modern Canadian City,* 39–72. Edited by Alan F.J. Artibise and Gilbert A. Stelter. Toronto: Macmillan and the Institute of Canadian Studies, Carleton University.

White, Richard. 2003. *Urban Infrastructure and Urban Growth in the Toronto Region, 1950s to the 1990s.* Toronto: Neptis Foundation.

Williams, Oliver P., Harold Herman, Charles S. Liebman and Thomas R. Dye. 1965. *Suburban Differences and Metropolitan Policies: A Philadelphia Story.* Philadelphia: University of Pennsylvania Press.

Williams, T.R. 1976. "Some Facts and Fantasies Concerning Local Autonomy in the Metropolitan Toronto School System." In *Politics and Government of Urban Canada*, 296–309. 3rd ed. Edited by L.D. Feldman and Michael Goldrick. Toronto: Methuen.

Wilson, Jennifer. 1990. *Group Homes: Their Historical Development and Legislative Framework*. Current Issue Paper No. 96. Toronto: Government of Ontario Legislative Research Services.

Wolfson, Joanne, and Frances Frisken. 2000. "Local Response to the Global Challenge: Comparing Local Economic Development Policies in a Regional Context." *Journal of Urban Affairs*, 22 (4), 361–384.

Working Group on Education Finance Reform. 1996. "Report to Minister [of Education]." Toronto: The Working Group.

Wood, Robert C. 1958. *Suburbia: Its People and Their Politics*. Boston: Houghton-Mifflin.

———. 1964. *1400 Governments*. New York: Anchor.

Woolstencroft, Peter. 1990. "Education." In *Urban Policy Issues: Canadian Perspectives*, 145–169. Edited by Richard A. Loreto and Trevor Price. Toronto: McClelland & Stewart.

Zamparo, Edward R. 1984. *The Influence of Fiscal Land Use Planning on Local Municipal Decision-Making: The Case of Metropolitan Toronto*. MA thesis, University of Waterloo.

Copyright Acknowledgements

Tables

Table 2.1: H. Carl Goldenberg, Commissioner, "Changes in per capita assessment, Metropolitan Toronto and area municipalities, 1954–1964," from *Royal Commission on Metropolitan Toronto 1965*. Copyright © Queen's Printer for Ontario, 1965. Reprinted by permission of Queen's Printer for Ontario.

Table 4.2: "Distribution of assisted household within Metropolitan Toronto, 1976," from *The Assisted Housing Study, Final Report, City of Toronto Archives, Series 1143, Item 1099 (Figure 4)*. Copyright © City of Toronto Archives, 1976. Reprinted by permission of City of Toronto.

Index

Note: The following abbreviations have been used in the sub-headings: M.T. (Metropolitan Toronto), GTA (Greater Toronto Area), U.S. (United States)

The Neptis Foundation

The research, writing, and publication of this book has been supported by the Neptis Foundation. The Neptis Foundation conducts and publishes non-partisan research on the past, present, and future of urban regions. An independent, privately capitalized, charitable foundation, Neptis contributes timely, reliable knowledge and analysis on regional urban development to support informed public decisions and foster understanding of regional issues.

The Neptis Foundation wishes to express its gratitude to Frances Frisken for her invaluable contribution in helping the Foundation determine its focus and objectives in its early days, as well as for her continuing wisdom and advice.

Neptis Foundation
50 Park Rd.
Toronto, ON
Canada
M4W 2N5

www.neptis.org